In a Sea of Bitterness

In a Sea of Bitterness

REFUGEES DURING THE SINO-JAPANESE WAR

➤⭠

R. Keith Schoppa

HARVARD UNIVERSITY PRESS

Cambridge, Massachusetts

London, England

2011

Library of Congress Cataloging-in-Publication Data

Schoppa, R. Keith, 1943–
In a sea of bitterness : refugees during the Sino-Japanese War /
R. Keith Schoppa.
p. cm.
Includes bibliographical references and index.
ISBN 978-0-674-05988-7 (alk. paper)
1. Sino-Japanese War, 1937–1945—Refugees.   I. Title.
DS777.533.R45S36 2011
951.04'2—dc23   2011022421

For Kevin Landdeck,

Student and scholar par excellence,

Friend, adviser, and supporter,

A true intellectual "son."

Contents

Dark suffocates the world; but such
Ubiquity of shadow is unequal.

From "An Autumn Park"
David Gascoyne
October 1939

➤⬩

The Thousand–Person Pit

THE LUNAR NEW YEAR fell on January 31, 1938. It was the most important holiday of the year. Family members returned to their native places—where their ancestors had lived and died, where they themselves had been born and probably had grown up, where relatives in their lineage still lived. If not quite sacred, the native place anchored Chinese onto and into a particular space, giving them personal identity and lifelong connections to others who shared that native place. Families feasted and celebrated; they paid respects to family elders and participated in rituals to those departed. Donned in brightly colored clothes, families made visits to other relatives, to neighbors, and to friends. They gave gifts. For good luck they placed on their houses and businesses "spring couplets" written on red paper and calling for prosperity. Chinese burned incense in their rituals, and, probably most indicative of the celebration, they shot off string after string of firecrackers. In his story "The New Year's Sacrifice," Lu Xun noted the cacophony of early New Year's mornings: "I was woken up by firecrackers exploding noisily close at hand.... Wrapped in this medley of sound, ... I felt only that the saints in heaven and earth ... were all reeling with intoxication in the sky, preparing to give the people ... boundless good fortune."[1]

The New Year's celebrations ended formally on the fifteenth day of the first lunar month on the Lantern Festival, in 1938 on February 14. Candles burning in brightly multicolored paper lanterns were hung in homes and businesses, bringing swatches of brilliant colors to enliven the usually drab midwinter. Depicting birds, butterflies, dragons, and historical figures, the lanterns were often adorned with riddles for families to contemplate while enjoying traditional dumplings filled with bean paste, vegetables, sesame paste, or meat. Family-centered, the holiday focused especially on women and children.

There was nothing to suggest that the 1938 celebration of the New Year and the Lantern Festival in the town of Qiaosi, located less than five miles from the outskirts of Hangzhou, the provincial capital, was different from that of other years. Historically, Qiaosi had been a center of the salt industry and trade, as its territory was located on Hangzhou Bay; from the Song dynasty on, Qiaosi had been Hangzhou's main supplier of salt. In 1938, it was a bustling midsized market town with a population pushing ten thousand. The highway between Hangzhou and Shanghai passed through it; the Shanghai–Hangzhou Railroad ran just to its north.

We can expect that family members came home to their native place during the holiday season; that families enjoyed banquetlike meals and performed age-old rituals for family elders; and that there were most certainly firecrackers, the sounds of which would have filled the streets with staccato blasts. There was, however, one thing different from preceding years: the presence of Japanese soldiers. The Japanese had seized Hangzhou on December 24, 1937. Sometime after that, an unspecified but growing number of soldiers had occupied the town.

Then, four days after the Lantern Festival, everything changed. Qiaosi experienced a tragedy that shocked all who heard of it. It is not that the town had not known tragedy before: in 1413, it had been completely destroyed by a tidal wave.[2] But this time, death came by fire instead of water. Whether the townspeople had heard about the infamous Nanjing Massacre of December 1937 and January 1938, some two hundred miles away, is not known. The date of Qiaosi's holocaust, February 18, was ironically the date that the famous Nanjing International Safety Zone ceased to function as protector of Nanjing civilians.

An eyewitness account of events in Qiaosi comes from Feng Xinfa, then a sixteen-year-old adolescent. Though the Japanese attacked the town in the middle of the night, Feng's story began the next morning.

On the early morning of February 18, a large Japanese force from nearby surrounded our town. They began what became an inhuman massacre. They stationed sentries at spots along the main street. After that, they set fires and began to kill people north of the main street. My family peeked out the door and saw that houses not very far away were burning. Our ears were deafened by the sounds of intense gunfire. At that time, we were a family of five: maternal grandparents (my grandmother was blind), father, mother, and I. My father, in a panic, told me to go wait at the Yongren Temple, a mile north of town. Carrying two quilts of cotton wadding, I ran as fast as I could.

As I ran past the Baoqing Bridge, I could see that behind the Chongshan Temple to the east, there were many Japanese soldiers setting fires. Whenever the Japanese saw Chinese, they would open fire. I raced to the Yongren Temple and hid behind it. From that vantage point, Qiaosi looked like a sea of fire, red flames shooting high into the air; gunfire was incessant. In a few minutes my father and grandfather arrived with some neighbors—but my mother and grandmother did not come. Father said that Mother needed more time to arrange the house for my grandmother, who was staying put because of her blindness. We three family members waited behind the temple for a long time, but still my mother did not show up.

At this time the fire was spreading and growing bigger and fiercer. The gunfire seemed to get even more intense (if that was possible). We had no choice but to leave. We fled to the northwest to spend the night with an old friend of my grandfather. That night we were anxious and worried since Mother had not yet arrived. We couldn't sleep and often got up to look outside to see if she might be approaching. We could only see the west side of town, where flames still reddened the dark sky.

After getting little sleep, we woke before daybreak and discussed going to look for Mother. Because of his age, my grandfather decided not to go. So my father and I set out. We had walked less than half a mile when we ran into a female acquaintance, Wang Fengzhen. Father asked if she had seen Mother. Wang blurted out in tears that she had seen her yesterday when Wang was hidden in a boat under the Baoqing Bridge to escape the bloodbath. As Mother passed by the bridge, she was shot by Japanese soldiers standing there. I remember that I was so shocked and horrified that I almost fainted. Father told me to return quickly to the temple. He said that to go into Qiaosi was very dangerous; since I was an only child, my father did not want to risk something happening to me. But I persisted, arguing, "Mother has already been killed by the devils; I want to go see her for the last time." Father did not have much time to ponder this request; but he solemnly agreed that I could go with him.

When Wang Fengzhen told us the terrible news, she had briefly described her own brush with death. Yesterday after the Japanese had set the fires, she had gotten into a boat with six other women and one young girl to escape down the river; but Japanese soldiers were already guarding the bridge when the boat approached it. The Japanese immediately opened fire. The other women and the girl all fell dead in the bottom of the boat. Wang feigned death by hiding under the corpses, daring not to move. The soldiers assumed that all were dead and did not inspect the boat.

At daybreak on February 19, we heard from people fleeing Qiaosi that the Japanese soldiers had left the bridge area. When we arrived at the bridge, the whole area was littered with corpses—along the road, on small lanes, beside the bridge, along the river and in ponds. There was the body of the proprietor of the Huangyuanxing Tavern, sliced open by a Japanese bayonet, his intestines flowing out of the wound.

The bus station near the bridge had become an execution holding center. Zhang Yufu, who had escaped the Japanese encirclement, told us what had happened. Yesterday before noon, when we were still hiding behind Yongren Temple, the Japanese killed any Chinese they saw, initially several hundred. After that, they went to search house by house and business by business, grabbing people and pulling out those who were hiding. They then dragged them to the large bus station, which they filled with several hundred people—men, women, and children—and locked them in. Over the next several hours, the Japanese brought the imprisoned Chinese out one at a time and executed them in the street. The bodies of the first several dozen executed were dumped in the pond near the station and bridge. People inside the station were terror-struck, for they knew that sooner or later it would be their turn. They wanted desperately to escape, but the physical presence of the encircling Japanese soldiers prevented that. In the end, only two people held in the bus station (one, obviously, Zhang Yufu) survived. Altogether several hundred were slain. Most of them lay where they had fallen scattered over the ground; rivulets of blood were everywhere. This was truly cruel barbarism.

Going past Baoqing Bridge, we discovered my mother's body. I felt my hands shaking; my legs were so unsteady that I couldn't walk. I wept silently. I could only see the bullet wound in her neck. Her cotton-padded jacket was dyed red with her blood. Father said that before taking care of the body, we should go home to see what the situation was there with my grandmother. When we got there, we found her alive; the house had also survived the firestorm. (Alas, three days later, the Japanese did burn it down.)

We did not dare stay at home long. We hurried quickly to the bridge to move Mother's body to the countryside for a peaceful burial. But by that time the Japanese soldiers had already returned, entering Qiaosi on buses. As soon as they got off the buses, they opened fire on Chinese with rifles and machine guns. We had no alternative but to flee the area as quickly as possible. That morning several hundred more were killed. The Japanese attack drenched Qiaosi in blood—with execution-like murders, sniping attacks, and blazing fires—for many days. In a circumference of about three miles, over 1,300 were killed. The town itself lost 80 percent of its houses. The thriving, bustling town lay in ruins. For a huge majority of the population, there were no homes to return to: Japanese barbarism had created homeless refugees.

Not until the autumn did the Japanese pull out of the town. Only then did we return. On our return we looked for my mother's corpse, but never found it. We learned that it had been buried in a public cemetery. However, several days before our return, a traditional Chinese doctor, Fang Shouceng, had proposed that the bodies of those who had been killed in the area of the bridge and bus station be exhumed, collected, and buried in a public mass tomb with the tombstone reading "Wu Yin [the lunar year name] Cemetery," commonly known as "the thousand-person pit." It's a witness to the wartime atrocity. It tells us: Never forget the sea of blood and the deep hatred engendered by this militaristic Japanese attack. And declare that it will never happen again.[3]

Modern warfare is total war: as Derek Summerfield puts it, "the targeting of ordinary people, politicized or not, is not incidental but central to the modus operandi" of this type of war. Moreover, it is not only the killing of human beings but the "crushing of ways of life—the economic, social, and cultural institutions and activities which connect a particular people to their history, identity and lived values."[4] War is the ultimate uprooter, displacer, and world shatterer. To its chief by-products, refugees—individuals, families, governments, schools, businesses and industries, and all those displaced in various ways—war brings cataclysmic change in the way people, in David Turton's words, "collectively imagine the world and their place in it."[5]

The Sino-Japanese War (1937–1945) was a total war. The Chinese masses and Chinese institutions were the targets in what Japanese historian Fujiwara Akira called a war "waged without just cause or cogent reason."[6] In this book I focus on the spatial, social, and psychological displacement of tens of millions of Chinese refugees who chose to flee Japanese-occupied areas of the province of Zhejiang for the rear areas free of Japanese control, and on those institutions whose leaders opted to leave occupied areas for presumably safer and freer sites. These are stories of heroes and scoundrels; of the moral, amoral, and immoral; of gallant risk taking amid an almost palpable quaking fear; of startling experiences and mistaken choices amid the mind-numbing violence of war at or near the battlefront; and of the maddening uncertainty and psychic turmoil in the great rear-areas.

Despite the disruptions of any refugee flight, the degree of shock in the experience was determined in large part first by whom refugees fled with (individuals and families as opposed to institutions) and then by the conditions under which they took flight (before the enemy reached the area, while the enemy was bombing the area, or after the Japanese army had already invaded and occupied the escapees' native place). In addition to spatial displacement and searches for wartime "home" places, Peter Loizos notes, "Forced migration introduce[d] a different kind of time, disjunctive in the sense of dividing experience into Before and After periods. It is as disjunctive as a revolution, but often more unexpected. This is often accompanied by a period ... [of] months [or] years ... of radical cognitive and affective uncertainty about where and how life is to be lived, with the possibility of a return to [the] earlier home ... in tension with the need to make life more sustainable in the here-and-now."[7]

Key existential issues for refugees were "questions of time, space, continuity, and identity."[8] In Zhejiang disjunctiveness brought by war was kaleidoscopic for different places, times, and people. Some counties were controlled by Japan for eight years; many were never invaded or occupied by the enemy; some were held for four or five years, others for several months, others for several weeks; and still others were invaded and occupied for months at several separate intervals during the war. A move to County A at a particular time presented a different existential pattern than a move to County A or B three months later, much as an ever-so-small turn of a cylindrical kaleidoscope creates completely new patterns, shades, colors, and arrangements. Provincial residents, therefore, just by the nature of the war, experienced myriads of patterns.

This book analyzes the official policies and institutions dealing with various forms of displacement and examines how these policies affected refugees and others whose lives were wrenchingly displaced. We see the approach of the state at a time of total war, as its official policies tried early on to shape successfully wartime society and support the lives and experiences of its citizens. But even more important, from my perspective, this study gets beyond the state and its policies to the stories of individual and institutional refugees. I focus on how Chinese elites and nonelites strategized about their wartime choices, what choices they made, what expected and unexpected difficulties Chinese faced, and what buoyed them in time of suffering to make it possible for them to survive. My concern is the physical and psychological displacement Chinese experienced and what it shows about Chinese society and the state, and about larger issues like the role (or lack) of nationalism. Finally, I am interested in questions of identity: What realities faced the refugees? How did those telling their stories see themselves and their plights? How did their identities shift through war experiences? How did they frame and articulate their experiences?

I rely on Chinese, elites and nonelites, to tell their stories. Though some were written down in the 1960s (twenty years or so after the events), most were written or given in oral interviews in the 1980s. Taking memoirs as history is notoriously risky. In his magisterial book *Realms of Memory,* Pierre Nora notes, "Memory, being a phenomenon of emotion and magic, accommodates only those facts that suit it. It thrives on vague telescoping references, on hazy general impressions of specific symbolic details."[9] Memory also includes forgetting. Indeed, any journals or autobiographical writings are, as another scholar notes, "corrective intervention[s] into the past, not merely a chronicle of elapsed events."[10] There are discernible errors in many of the Chinese accounts; I will comment on them at appropriate times. One would expect most accounts to be closest to what actually happened in the broad picture of the events or in those details that loom in the narrators' experiences as being especially frightening, challenging, or disastrous.

We need to hear the Chinese voices. What kinds of things do those who lived these experiences tell us? What might this testimony say about questions of identity? What tropes do these survivors use in telling their stories? Above all, what commonalities appear in the accounts of both elites and nonelites? What do these narratives reveal about the situation of family, state, and nation from 1937 to 1945?

Feng Xinfa's memories highlight the core Japanese military strategy: to terrorize the Chinese population so thoroughly that surrender might seem the best alternative to continuing the fighting. The arrival of Japanese forces on both February 18 and 19 was marked by arson and the indiscriminate killings of civilians. Feng repeatedly mentioned the raging fires and the intense sounds of firing guns. Using the bus station as a holding area for executions performed one by one was a sadistic terrorist tactic—excruciatingly torturous for those awaiting their turn. For those townspeople able to escape, landscapes filled with dead and bleeding family and neighbors made the refugees so fearful that, in the case of the Feng family survivors, they did not return to Qiaosi until the Japanese left that autumn, some seven to nine months later.

This flight, at least on February 18 and 19, was not distant from the town, a response probably most typical of refugees who could not afford or tolerate the idea of long-distance travel. Not all could flee: Feng's blind grandmother is a case in point; her fate is not described. In this initial escape, the importance of the family is apparent throughout. Feng's first reactions to hearing of his mother's death and then finding her body were understandably ones of horror, if somewhat understated. His father's concern for the safety of Feng—as an only child—underscored the cultural importance of sons.

Finally, Feng's memories point to some realities of war and Chinese reactions to it: the unpredictabilities of Japanese actions—when soldiers would appear and what they would do; the separation of family members and the anxiety created by that separation and the situation in general; and the Chinese view of the Japanese as "devil," a term much more graphic and malevolent than simply "the enemy." The Japanese attacked in the middle of the night; for many Chinese writing about their war experiences, "night" itself generally seemed infused with forebodings of danger and threat.

ONE

A World Where Ghosts Wailed

WHEN THE UNITED STATES began its war in Iraq in March 2003, the phrase "shock and awe" shot out from Washington and ricocheted through the media; the arrogant-sounding words indicated the desire to intimidate, indeed to terrorize, the perceived enemies in that country. Every aggressive nation hopes to win its military campaigns in part by psychologically crushing the opposition and by destroying its morale and any hopes that it can compete with a stronger, more violent outside invader. The events in Qiaosi in February 1938 cannot but have helped spread terror and dread among Chinese, who heard what must have been anxiety-driven rumors of the killing and the burning. The Japanese had launched the invasion of Zhejiang Province in November, after an earlier bombing raid on Hangzhou that had coincided with Japan's attack on Shanghai on August 13. That bombing raid, with Taiwan-based planes, had targeted the capital city's train station and, more importantly, the province's main air base nearby. The raid precipitated a massive exodus of city residents to the presumably safer countryside—and was a harbinger of future flights to escape either Japanese bombing or Japanese troops themselves.

To flee from one's home was not a decision any Chinese would take lightly. Choosing to become a refugee was difficult and emotional: the Chinese were rooted in their localities for their very identities. For many, if they chose to take flight and become refugees, they were leaving the place where their ancestors had lived, had died, and were buried, a place that gave them considerable part of their personal identity. Usually when Chinese met someone for the first time, the initial question was "Where are you from?" In traditional gazetteer biographies, locality was the first information following the name of a person. In a culture that depended on personal connections and networks that had been built up over many years in one's native place, leaving that source of security and sustenance was daunting. Beyond that native place was a world of strangers, where there were no connections, only threats and dangers. As one editorial in the *Southeast Daily (Dongnan ribao)* described the plight of refugees, "They have lost what their lives relied on and have added the fetters of hunger and cold, groping for ways to live on amid the desolation and sorrow of life as a 'guest.'"[1] "Guest," a word with pleasant, hospitable overtones—but, nonetheless, in the Chinese context, an outsider with whom one must keep one's distance however politely, a role producing, in the end, a life of "desolation and sorrow."

In Zhejiang, the smallest Chinese province, population records during the war show that there were 5,185,210 long-distance refugees; those in Zhejiang ranked behind only the numbers of refugees in Jiangsu, Hubei, Hunan, Hebei, Henan, and Shandong.[2] Not included in this number were countless more, like the Fengs of Qiaosi, who became short-term refugees, that is, those who fled their homes for a day or two to neighboring villages or nearby mountains, hoping to return home after the Japanese had retreated. Whether in the short term or over long distance, becoming a refugee, in the words of artist and writer Feng Zikai, was to live "in a sea of bitterness."[3]

The Shanghai Prelude

The first terror to hit the Chinese was the Japanese attack on Shanghai that began on August 13, 1937. On the next day, in three separate accidents, Chinese bombers missed their targets and instead hit Hongkou, the northeastern sector of the International Settlement; a traffic circle filled with refugees in front of the six-story Great World amusement palace; and the Bund end of Nanjing Road, near the Peace and Cathay hotels. Almost twelve hundred were killed, mostly Chinese. Zhao Zhangtai, from Lishui County in Zhejiang, witnessed the Great World bombing and its aftermath: "It was a ghastly scene. Bodies and heads littered the ground. Bloody wounds looked like mush. Of a modern young woman who now sat atop a yellow car, all that remained were her legs with long stockings and high-heeled shoes: her head and torso were nowhere to be seen. Sounds of wailing vibrated throughout the heavens."[4] The Great World bombing was especially tragic because refugees had lined up for relief in front of a building at the intersection.[5]

A tsunami of refugees flooded the International Settlement, which, together with the French Settlement, quickly became known as Solitary Island and remained free of Japanese control until December 8, 1941. By November 1937, there were 142 refugee reception centers and camps located in parks and on college campuses in the International Settlement, with almost 92,000 refugees (and over 3,600 more surviving on streets and in alleys); in the French Concession there were 40 such camps, accommodating about 26,000—this in a thirteen-square-mile area. In addition, native place organizations and commercial guilds housed many more refugees, the numbers of which were not recorded.[6] The problems of providing basic care—food, clothing (as autumn turned to winter), protection against disease—and problems of preventing crime and civil unrest created an immense crisis for settlement authorities.

Many refugees decided it was unsafe to remain in the city, with the Japanese ensconced on all sides. Some Chinese fled to the west; indeed an estimated 30 million trekked west from the war front, with many headed ultimately to Chongqing, where Jiang Jieshi's Nationalist government eventually wound up.[7] What were their lives like? A reporter from the *Southeast Daily* gave an extended description of a refugee reception center in Wuxi, near the northern shore of Lake Tai and on the Shanghai–Nanjing Railroad, about seventy-five miles west-northwest of Shanghai. For us to understand the refugee plight, it is worth quoting at length.

> Yesterday afternoon, we went to the XX Refugee Center to express sympathy and solicitude for refugees from the Japanese bombings. The reception center rooms were not large, but there were over a hundred poor refugees inside on the floor, placed close together. The air was thick and marked by a foul smell. The refugees had an unusual paranoid look in their eyes.
>
> We went into the reception center's office to talk to the director, Mr. Sun, who said, "Those refugees who've come to this center have homes to which they can return; they're simply waiting until that day. We don't have long-term refugees here. They get two servings of rice gruel each day plus a quilt, but there are often outright fights over food—and the place is often noisy with frequent scuffles."

We interviewed a woman about 50, from Wusong on the Yangzi River north of Shanghai. She, her husband, and two children fled their home for Pudong in July, but Japanese bombing forced them to move to the French Concession, where they changed locations several times. A refugee reception center gave her money to go back to Yuanyang Township, where she had relatives. But the relatives were so poor, they did not have enough to eat themselves. This situation forced her and her family to move once again. But here there is not enough food: the woman eats only the evening gruel and lets her ten-year-old daughter eat the mother's lunch serving. The mother is consequently losing strength so that often others steal her gruel—and she can do nothing to stop them. She is thinking of simply going home and giving up her life as a refugee.[8]

The Wuxi reception center was crowded and unpleasant, suffused with the smell of unwashed bodies and dirty clothing. The paranoid looks in the eyes of refugees came obviously from their being crowded into a room full of strangers, from not knowing how long displaced people would be confined there, and from fearing that others might seize and eat up their gruel. It became a case of the survival of the fittest or, more accurately, of the strongest and most aggressive. The multiple moves by this refugee family seem par for the refugee course. The goal of most refugee centers was to send refugees on their way quickly; if they had relatives nearby, money might be provided to get them bus, boat, or train tickets.

The woman from Wusong contemplated returning home and ending her family's life as refugees. In that regard, Mr. Sun may have been a little unrealistic: many homes were destroyed in the Japanese bombing, making returning home for some an impossibility.

There were many thousands of Zhejiangese residents in Shanghai who, when the Japanese attacks began, decided to return to their native places, which were in theory at least bastions of stable support and peace. Zhao Zhangtai, who had described the Great World bombing, said the boats bound for Zhejiang "were packed like sardines."[9] When the Japanese seized the International and French settlements on December 8, 1941, Lou Shiyi decided to return home to Yuyao County to be with his old, ill mother. He described the scene at the Pudong Wharves on the Huangpu River: "Along the river bank a band of black, pressed down, ten thousand heads pushed together and moving. All were refugees in a difficult position. There was a family carrying heavy luggage and bundles, also physically supporting their old mother. Japanese military police, like fierce gods and evil goblins, formed a gauntlet through which everyone had to pass, but only after they paid a bribe in puppet currency. Frightened young children cried. The old mother walked haltingly and looked as if she had been overcome by paralysis. This was a world where ghosts wailed."[10]

In the crush of escaping Chinese, near the end of October 1937, so many people filled the train cars that frantic refugees crowded aboard the tops of the cars. In one episode, before a train was to take off, there had come the loud sound of approaching planes. The apparently startled train engineer, fearful of being bombed, took off suddenly; many people on the tops of the cars slid off. Some fell on the train tracks, in front of the wheels, which sliced off their arms, legs, and heads.[11]

The Seizure of Northern Zhejiang

Most of the Zhejiangese refugees in the province took flight in the midst of three Japanese military campaigns. The first was the Hangzhou Bay landings and the Japanese seizure of the three northernmost former prefectures—Hangzhou, Jiaxing, and Huzhou—from November to the end of December 1937 (for these counties, see Map 4). Part of the goal of the Hangzhou Bay landings was to end the hard-fought battle for Shanghai, which had been launched in August. As one scholar has noted, that "battle was of horrific proportions, second at the time only to Verdun in terms of overall numbers killed."[12] Japanese soldiers were said to be stunned and angry at the fighting ability and perseverance of the Chinese in this bloodletting. In late October, three and a half divisions were joined, under the command of General Yanagawa Heisuke, as the Tenth Army: its mission—to obliterate the Chinese armies and protect Japanese in Shanghai and its vicinity. It was the Tenth Army that landed on the north coast of Hangzhou Bay; these divisions would go on, joining with the Japanese Shanghai Expeditionary Force, to seize the capital of Nanjing in December and to be a main participant in the Nanjing atrocity.

The Japanese had undertaken surveillance of the area soon after the Battle of Shanghai began. Reports from Jiashan noted that Japanese planes flew over the county numerous times from late August, even drop-ping bombs—most of which did not detonate.[13] Cruisers off Pinghu County's port of Zhapu had been noted several times. The Japanese land-ing on the fog-obscured morning of November 5 was timed to catch the Chinese forces off guard.[14] The Sixty-second Division, the main Nation-alist forces defending the county of Pinghu, had been ordered to move to Pudong on the east bank of the Huangpu River in Shanghai; the divi-sion had begun that shift on November 3. Thus, when the Japanese landed, there were only relatively small contingents of Chinese forces at three locations in the county and to the east over the provincial border with Jiangsu. They were no match for the more than one hundred thou-sand Japanese soldiers who came ashore on board 155 transport cruisers. The Japanese forces took two routes, one due east, to finally end the battle for Shanghai, and the other to the northeast through towns in Pinghu County, to seize the city of Songjiang. Both Shanghai and Songjiang fell on November 12. The relatively small number of Chinese troops at Pinghu locations put up valiant fights—some lasting seven or eight hours—but almost all Chinese soldiers were killed. Japanese casual-ties were also high, with bodies littering some of the landing beaches.

Japanese strategy and tactics for the whole campaign were apparent from the start. The Japanese began with a focus on sizable market towns and bombed them with what seemed massive airpower to terrorize the population—action that inevitably led to panicked evacuations. After several more days of bombing, Japanese troops marched into the towns and pursued their strategy of using fire as their major weapon of terror, burning down, in many cases, most homes and businesses. The Japanese customarily bombed county seats and towns at the same time, but the county seat was the foremost prize. The Pinghu county seat was bombed on November 6, 8, 13, and 14; Japanese troops seized it on November 19; Japanese forces then occupied it for over seven years and nine months. During that time 1,548 civilians were killed—apart from bombing deaths—and 3,520 homes were burned to the ground.

Chinese patterns of reacting to Japanese warfare were also evident from the start. The bombing, burning, and killing of civilians gave rise to great fear and panic—an overwhelming drive to get out of the area as rapidly as possible to avoid death, injury, and rape. Not only did indi-viduals and families flee, but also the county government (and later pro-vincial government) withdrew to more peaceful areas: the Pinghu county government retreated on November 15. Within little over a month, as Chinese troops retreated west, the Japanese war machine seemed unstoppable, occupying county after county—Jiashan, Jiaxing, Haiyan, Haining, Tongxiang, Wuxing, Changxing, Wukang, Deqing, and Yuhang (see Maps 2 and 4)—and points farther west, in Anhui and Jiangxi. Individual refugees and county governments were joined in flight by a number of schools. In Jiaxing, one of the major provincial cities, over a thousand were killed in two months, and 20 percent of all homes were destroyed by arson. To get away from such a dreadful situation, on November 11 the Jiaxing Provincial Middle School students and teachers, led by Principal Zhang Yintong, fled first to Xindeng County, about 75 miles southwest of Hangzhou. En route, the group linked up with refugees from the Jiaxing County Women's Middle School; together they decided to trek all the way to Lishui County, about 180 miles southeast of Hangzhou.

The largest prize in the campaign after Nanjing was Hangzhou, which the Japanese seized on December 24, closing in on the city from three routes. The provincial government had made contingency plans to relocate to Jinhua in central Zhejiang. Estimates suggest that Hangzhou's prewar population had been about 500,000 and that when it fell to the Japanese, the exodus left only about 100,000 in the city. Other counties seized during this campaign experienced similar statistical losses: the Pinghu county seat and four of its main market towns lost over 47 percent of their population, while Jiaxing City's population loss was more on the order of Hangzhou's—just about 83 percent of prewar residents.[15] In 1938, about 31,000 refugees from Hangzhou returned; by 1940, the city's population was back up to 320,000. The same trend applied to other urban centers in northern Zhejiang.

Such movement clearly suggests that most people preferred a settled life under an occupying enemy to an unsettled, often precarious life as a refugee; that reality gives us some pause in considering the depth of nationalism among many Chinese. But, perhaps, only pause. Settledness, not fervent feelings for the nation, was key: native place, local connections, and a "known" life at this time of crisis, even if it meant living under foreign occupation, trumped nationalism, even though national commitment and local loyalty may have coexisted and may have remained as elements in the attitudes of many. Did Chinese refugees who returned to live under Japanese rule think in terms of nation and national fate? I think not: their perspective was much more local at this time of threat, uncertainty, and danger. When we see war at "ground zero" and tout Chinese resistance as evidence of nationalistic fervor, are we looking back through our own cultural lenses and seeing things that did not exist, at least at the same level of priority?

Refugee strategy at the beginning of the war was generally to get out of the cities and towns as quickly as possible—but not to travel very far. Traveling several hours or at most a day to relatives or friends in the country seemed to offer the ideal safety opportunity. Short trips meant not having to carry, usually by hand, many items needed for daily life; such trips also meant being able to return to check on the status of homes or to get items that refugees had left—if indeed the Japanese army had not destroyed their homes. Short trips were advantages to poorer families or those of more modest means; longer trips were simply not a possibility for them. In addition, short trips, though upsetting, did not pose the same psychosocial trauma raised by longer trips, which separated refugees from native place and comfortable community by many miles. If a family had no connections in the countryside, temporary lodging in caves or other natural sites in nearby mountains or forests might be possibilities. Four short-term refugees from Japanese-occupied territory in northern Zhejiang reveal some of the problems and concerns that they faced.

Sun Zuoliang of the town of Tanghui, just northeast of the Jiaxing county seat, described short-term flight and the reason most people felt compelled to flee (see Map 4). He said that when the Japanese first entered the town, almost all residents fled to surrounding villages and depended on relatives and friends. A small number of people stayed in their homes: the old, those who had no place to go, and those who decided to stay and try to protect their homes—most of them were killed by the Japanese. Refugees started returning in about five days to see what had happened. Many homes had been destroyed by aerial bombardment or Japanese arson, and rebuilding was made almost impossible by a shortage of wood.[16]

Li Yuchang's family were shop owners in the town of Shimenwan, where the Grand Canal makes a forty-five-degree turn toward the northeast and Jiaxing (see Map 4). When the Japanese came to Shimenwan, the Lis had already fled about three miles away to a rural township southeast of their town. When they returned several days later, their home and shop had been burned to the ground. They then returned to their refugee site, but Li went back to Shimenwan every day to make a living, peddling his wares among his fellow townsmen, from baskets on a shoulder pole. His every trip to Shimenwan was an adventure; since the area changed hands many times, he never knew what situation might greet him.[17]

Longer accounts by Li Genpan of Jiashan County and Feng Chenhua of Tongxiang County underscore not only the realities and problems faced by short-term refugees but also life in a war zone generally. The flight of reconnaissance airplanes over Jiashan beginning in late August rattled the county seat's residents. Fearful of being bombed, some people dug air-raid shelters beneath their homes. Causing some casualties, the first bombs dropped by Japanese planes, fell on Autumn Harvest Festival (that year on September 19); after that, the planes with their bombs came frequently. The people were terrified; Li noted that all over the city, in streets and lanes, he could see people in twos and threes discussing where it was best to go if they decided to flee. The tense situation was not helped by the flood of refugees coming through the city from Shanghai on the rail line to Hangzhou. Li corroborated that the tops of train cars were covered with frantic people. Then rumors spread like wildfire that the Japanese had landed and that they were killing at random and burning houses without compunction. Always the rumors! In time of war, before there were modern means of rapid communication, news came through rumors, which seemed to fly and soar on their own, often fictitious wings. The problem, of course, was that they could never be confirmed, and there were assuredly as many that were false as there were those that were true.

Li Genpan's parents wisely treated this one as true. His mother took Li's sister and younger brother to stay temporarily with relatives in Yaozhuang Township, only a few miles west of the city. Li stayed with his father in the county seat. Two or three days later, the Japanese engaged in a more general bombing, destroying the Temple of the City God and wide swaths of houses. People who had not fled to this point were conflicted as to what to do; some argued that it was more dangerous to flee than it was to stay put. Day-to-day choices were indeed issues of life or death, but since people could not know where the Japanese would strike or when, these choices simply immobilized many. But not father and son Li, who quickly left for their Yaozhuang relatives.[18]

There they might have stayed for a long time had they not been frightened by events on the evenings of November 9 and 10, when they heard intensive gunfire from the county seat and saw sky and earth lit up by flares. Li noted that the farmers in the area were "frightened out their wits" (*jinghuang shicuo*).[19] On this canal-laced plain, the fastest way to travel was by boat. Li's family used a boat of one of their relatives, but they were not alone: Li noted that there were so many boats on the canals that the prow of each boat was almost touching the stern of the boat in front of it. Many farmers and others in the boats had no idea where to head to be relatively safe, and whenever they passed any boat, the adults in both crafts would talk about where it was best to go. The Lis traveled about twelve miles to the north and west, ending up at Nanhui Town just inside the Jiaxing County border, far removed from either Jiashan's or Jiaxing's county seat. They decided to stay there temporarily.

Shortly thereafter, rumors spread that Jiashan had fallen and that everywhere the Japanese soldiers were raping, killing, and burning. The Lis heard no word on how many Chinese had been killed. Once they heard that the Peace Maintenance Committee (PMC) had been set up in Jiashan, they knew that relative peace had been restored. The PMC was the first collaborative body that the Japanese established in all communities as Japan moved to take full control of the locality. The Lis hired a boat and returned to Jiashan after the middle of March—about four months after they had fled.[20] Their house was still standing, but it had been pillaged: all that remained were two very heavy pieces of furniture that even the Japanese had given up on lifting and moving.

When the Japanese came to Chongfu Town in November (see Map 4), Feng Zhenhua's father, who ran a tavern, was bedridden and dying of a undisclosed communicable disease at age thirty-four.[21] Therefore, the family could not flee as most of the town's residents had done. Because of the Japanese arrival, his wife could get her husband neither a doctor nor medication. Few people remained in the town, and all businesses and offices were shut. Feng's mother, following old wives' tales and hallowed folklore, cut flesh from her own arm to cook it for her husband to eat. Whether this indeed happened, it did not do any good: her husband died. The Japanese presence and disruption of the flow of daily life killed people other than with bombs and fires, in this case making it impossible for Feng's father to get medical care.

Feng's inclusion of this bizarre cannibalistic detail alerts us to that fact that what Feng recounts in this memoir is most likely what he remembers his mother told him about the events in the war; he was six years old at the time. While he might personally remember certain traumatic events or ongoing trials, he would have been dependent on what he was told. Certainly, his mother would have wanted to use this story to convey to her son and family what a virtuous wife she had been.

After her husband's death, Feng's mother fled with her three children: Feng Zhenhua and his two sisters (ages fourteen and four) to her husband's family's home, only a few miles from Chongfu. Though her father-in-law had died, the house was maintained by his widow and two aunts by marriage. Feng Zhenhua's father had been the eldest of three brothers. The second brother had worked in a Shanghai silk factory until the war; when war broke out, he—interestingly and perhaps initially puzzlingly—decided to flee with some factory coworkers to Anhui Province rather than to come be with his wife. This choice, however, likely underscores what sociologist Fei Xiaotong, writing in the 1940s, said about Chinese marriages: he noted the lack of closeness between husband and wife (especially emotional closeness) and the preferred same-sex companionship among men who had connections of friendship.[22] The youngest Feng brother worked at a Jiaxing soy sauce shop, some thirty miles away from his ancestral home—too far for any regular commute. With the outbreak of war, however, he did return to be with his wife and two small children. Wartime choices threw together or (more elegantly) led to the creation of a new household, consisting, then, of one man, the grandmother, three women, and five children (ages two to fourteen). War and crisis brought new social combinations, reshaping old social structures and relationships, providing new opportunities, but especially new challenges.

While Feng's grandmother and two aunts had been alone with Feng's two cousins, these women had obviously ruled the roost. The return of the youngest brother changed all that. As the male of the house, he argued that the ancestral home was too close to the Shanghai–Hangzhou Railroad and that it was too dangerous to remain there. He insisted (and, of course, he got his way) that they move about fourteen miles west of the home, to Yongxiu Township. We are told neither why he chose that location nor what sorts of connections he had to that place. But it was ultimately not a wise move. The village and others on the plain were beset by a large and aggressive gang of bandits. The coming of the Japanese in aggressive war was like a typhoon that spun off bandit groups like tornadoes. Groups of local ne'er-do-wells and toughs ("local sticks," in Chinese parlance) took advantage of the turmoil to steal and loot. In Hangzhou Bay's Haining County, as another example, in the aftermath of a massive refugee exodus from county seat and towns to rural villages and the mountainous regions to the west, a band of pirate-bandits sailed into the port of Xiashi to loot. They were driven off by local militia.[23]

The bandits in Yongxiu Township were especially violent. It is said that once night came, the sounds of gunfire mingled with cries and shouts. The family could not eat or sleep in peace. The grandmother blamed her daughter-in-law, Feng's mother, for the decision to move to this arena of banditry—a non sequitur, but a response congruent with traditional family dynamics. Feng reported that his mother, in turn, cried constantly. Finding refuge in a robbers' den had obviously not been the objective of traveling this distance (which Feng's mother thought was much too far to go).

At that time, Japanese boats daily plied the nearby Grand Canal. The family discussed where it might be easy to get a boat if they wanted to move. Feng's mother went to the river everyday to watch for fishing boats. She was able to make contact with a man whose main business was transporting refugees; his boat was equipped with fishing nets to give it the appearance of a fishing boat. After paying for the boat to take them back to her husband's ancestral home, the Fengs started out the next night. While they were passing through Chongfu Town, Chinese soldiers stopped the boat at a bridge; initially the family thought it was an effort to commandeer the boat for military use. For civilians traveling by boat, this was a common and completely realistic fear. But the Chinese soldiers had a crasser motive. They rummaged through the family's luggage simply looking for money. Aware that such daylight robbery was a possibility in the more lawless atmosphere of impending war, the adults had their money on their persons—a strategy that could have been foiled by body searches. The two aunts had hidden some money in clothes in their luggage; and the soldiers took those private savings. But the family did make it back to their home.

In light of the death of Feng's father, the decision to bring the youngest brother to manage the tavern, assisted by the former assistant of Feng's father, seemed to make sense. But early in 1938, the brother returned to the soy sauce shop in Jiaxing. Feng's mother tried to run the tavern herself. But with the occupation in force, there was considerable social instability: Chinese collaborators with the Japanese and a new power structure in which high-handed bullies ran amok meant new connections needed to be made for a successful running of the tavern. Sometimes there were fights in the tavern, which Feng's mother obviously could not handle. Finally, because there was insufficient profit on which to survive, the mother closed the tavern. In an act that is not explained, nor, on its face, explainable, she moved her children to Hangzhou and worked as a street peddler.

Feng's story points to the power of contingency in refugee lives. First, the father's illness and death (the latter perhaps partially caused by the Japanese invasion) kept the family from fleeing in the beginning. The return of only one brother to the ancestral home changed the household dynamics, making him the only male and thus the decision maker in the move to a township besieged by bandits. Feng's mother's concern about the move being too far suggests the power of the hold of native place over her mental universe. The existence of boats that were outfitted with fishing gear but whose main role was ferrying refugees points not only to the ingenuity of the boat owner but also to the need for the protection of refugees from Japanese soldiers. The robbery by Chinese soldiers shows not only that the predators were not exclusively Japanese troops and local bandits but also that China at war was an open invitation to take advantage of others with greater impunity than at peacetime—a scenario, however, likely in any war.

The Shaoxing and Ningpo Campaigns

After the conquest of the north, Japan seemed generally willing to let Zhejiang south of Hangzhou Bay remain in Chinese hands. But Japanese forces did enough toying around in the area known as Zhedong ("eastern Zhejiang") to indicate that this seemingly disinterested stance was probably not in reality that disinterested: in July 1940, Japan occupied Zhenhai County (in former Ningbo prefecture) for four days; and in October 1940, Japanese briefly occupied Shaoxing and Zhuji counties. It seemed all nibble and tease.

But presaging the brief occupation of Zhenhai, Shaoxing, and Zhuji was the January 1940 seizure of Xiaoshan County, directly across the Qiantang River from Hangzhou, an indication that Japan would eventually probably pursue a more aggressive strategy (for these counties, see Maps 3 and 12).

Strategically, Japan's taking Xiaoshan would make an invasion of Zhedong much easier, obviating the difficult crossing of the wide Qiantang River at the launch of a campaign. The bombing of Xiaoshan began on November 30, 1937, little more than three weeks after the Zhejiang campaign had begun: thirty Japanese planes attacked the county seat, killing two hundred and wounding many.[24] From then until mid-June 1938, Japanese bombers struck the county sixty-eight times, killing 604, wounding more than 2,200, and destroying about 4,500 homes. Major institutions began to move into the interior: county offices moved into the southern part of the county; the famous Xiang Lake Normal School relocated to Songyang County in the far southwest of the province.

On the evening of January 21, 1940, amid a heavy snowstorm, Japanese troops, reportedly donning white outerwear as camouflage, crossed the Qiantang River and secured a base, and the next day they took the county seat. They proceeded to burn whatever they could: all the facilities of the Xiang Lake Normal School, an agricultural experimental farm and office, trees on the mountains, crops in the field, even grass on the roadside. As an indication that Japanese acts could stimulate or serve as a catalyst or a cover for unlawful acts, local people set fire to and destroyed their own school facilities, likely out of resentment for taxes for the school. During the war, Xiaoshan County experienced the most catastrophic destruction in all of eastern Zhejiang; almost forty thousand homes were destroyed (replaced, if they were, by thatched huts), and there was a 15 percent drop in the population. All the county's commercial prosperity of the early twentieth century was gutted.

After taking Xiaoshan County in January 1940, the Japanese Special Services unit in Hangzhou sent spies into the Ning-Shao (Ningbo-Shaoxing) region. The Japanese withdrawal from Shaoxing after a raid in October 1940, however, had led many city residents to conclude wrongly that the Japanese did not intend to occupy the city for the long term. By this time, the Japanese had pushed well into Hunan and Hubei, and the thinking was that Japan's occupying the few small- and middle-sized cities along the Zhejiang coast in an area already ultimately "behind the lines" would have no direct military value. Thus, despite the presence of Japanese spies, there was little expectation of an attack. Just as in the case of the troop redeployment into Pudong and the military forces' unreadiness in the northern Zhejiang campaign, here a naive false sense of security led to a lack of readiness that created greater chaos when the attack came.

Rumors of an impending Japanese advance began to sweep over the city on April 14, 1941, impelling some residents to pack up and move to rural areas. The Japanese goal in this campaign was to blockade Zhejiang's coastline, to seize stored commodities from ports on the seacoast and bay shore, to destroy the main Chinese forces in this region, and to solidify Japanese hold on the Nanjing-Shanghai-Hangzhou triangle of occupied territory. One Japanese army, moving south from Wusong, landed at Ningbo in the east to move toward the west; the other Japanese army moved from Xiaoshan and Fuyang counties eastward toward Zhuji County.

On the afternoon of April 16, on hearing news that Japanese forces were within some ten miles of the city, managers of three of the city's modern-style banks met with Xing Chennan, the recently appointed administrative inspector and public security commander of Zhejiang's Third Military Region, to get his permission to leave the city with cash reserves and precious metals. Xing, supported by the county magistrate, Deng Ren dissuaded such action, saying, "Reports show that there are relatively few Japanese soldiers involved; we've sent a division to halt their advance; the situation is tense, but it has stabilized. We need to wait until the 3 A.M. tides to know if they will reinforce the troops that have already landed. If you pull out now, the masses will panic. Don't do anything now; wait until tomorrow."[25]

Commentators have noted that the city that evening was schizophrenic: while economic elites frantically made arrangements to leave with cash reserves and portable property, government and military elites seemed amazingly nonchalant about any possible attack. Almost all were attending a production of Cao Yu's play *Thunderstorm,* performed by the drama troupe of the Eighty-sixth Army. Japanese troops entered the city about midnight, cutting communications between the city and the countryside. Before dawn they had secured and occupied the city's key points; only one regiment within the city put up any resistance. The early morning scene was chaotic: masses of people were in the streets as city residents tried to flee from Japanese troops, who, in some areas, had begun indiscriminate killings. In the vanguard of the flight in all directions were government and military leaders. The top leader Xing donned peasant clothes and hid in the hold of a boat fleeing west of the city. Magistrate

Deng disguised himself, but to no avail: he was shot and killed as he left the city. Some leaders fled because they feared they were on the Japanese list to head collaborative organizations.

The city fell on April 19. The government leaders' refusal to acknowledge the imminent danger and to allow bankers to leave the city meant that every modern bank's reserve notes (5 million to 6 million yuan) were lost to the Japanese. The Chinese lack of military preparedness in the face of certain attack was unconscionable. The early flight of military-political leader Xing outraged city residents; after banking leaders put pressure on the national government, Xing was imprisoned and in 1944 executed for desertion.[26]

The other major city targeted in this campaign was Ningbo, a very important seaport on the East China Sea. In 1842, it had become a treaty port with rules and political patterns imposed by imperialist powers. In the late nineteenth century, its merchant elites developed close ties to Shanghai, about a hundred miles to the north. The Ningbo connection to Shanghai became famous: indeed, an organization of Ningbo natives grew to dominate Shanghai's economy. Ningbo's political elites during the prewar years thus understandably had close ties to Shanghai. As Ningbo was about fifteen miles inland on the Yong River, its port was actually the city of Zhenhai on the coast.

Ningbo had felt the presence of the Japanese in the area well before April 1941; the leaders at Ningbo should have been totally on guard. Less than ten miles off the coast from Zhenhai lay the Zhoushan Archipelago, China's largest, with over four hundred islands (see Map 6). Well before the war, in spring 1931, the Japanese had shown an interest in participating in the region's lucrative fishing industry when over two hundred Japanese fishing boats appeared (in Chinese words, "intruded on Zhoushan's fishing grounds").[27] In March 1933, in a more ominous move—especially in light of what Japan was doing in Manchuria, Inner Mongolia, and northern China at the time—Japan's Third Naval Fleet sailed into Zhoushan's waters; Chinese sources say that Chinese gunboats drove them away. In the opening days of the war, on August 18, 1937, Japanese on two ships seized Sijiao Island, the northernmost of the chain, roughly sixty miles from Shanghai; again Chinese sources reported that Chinese gunboats drove them away.[28] If Japan could gain control of the islands, it would be an important step in instituting a blockade of the China coast. In addition, the Zhoushan Islands were at the entrance to Hangzhou Bay and were located in the crucial shipping lanes between Hong Kong and Shanghai.

To keep up their campaign of intimidation, in April 1938 a Japanese naval ship entered the harbor of Dinghai, the administrative county seat. In May 1939 over 120 soldiers landed on two of the small islands and killed over forty people. Then on June 23, 1939, over 1,400 Japanese soldiers landed at three places in the island chain, the most important being the port of Shenjiamen on the main island. The Dinghai government moved to the island closest to the mainland; most notably, Zhoushan was occupied by the Japanese from that day until the end of the war.

The Japanese were thus a constant presence in Zhenhai's and Ningbo's waters from that time. On April 15, 1941, more than ten Japanese warships floated outside Zhenhai's river mouth; indeed, sporadic Japanese artillery attacks had begun on sites in the city where defending Chinese soldiers were based. Two divisions, the 34th and the 194th, were the mainstays of Ningbo's defense. However, when word reached Ningbo that Shaoxing had fallen on April 17, all but one regiment of China's 34th Division was ordered to retreat to the Shaoxing region to protect the Cao-e River there. As in the Hangzhou Bay landings and the Shaoxing debacle, the Ningbo defense was weakened at a critical time. Preparedness and strategic perspicuity were not Chinese watchwords in any of the Japanese campaigns in Zhejiang.

The Japanese attack began in the middle of the night at 1 A.M. on April 19. The landings were given cover by an artillery barrage and air support. The Japanese soldiers were on the beach in two columns before dawn. Reportedly, the Chinese soldiers put up a valiant fight, but all the officers and soldiers in the regiment were killed. The city fell at 9:40 A.M. The Zhenhai county government retreated to western Yin County.[29] The Japanese conquered the other counties in the two former prefectures as well as coastal counties all the way south to the Fujian border: Ruian, Wenzhou, Linhai, and Xiangshan. They also captured the ports of Haimen and Shipu.

During the period of the Shao-Ning campaign, most refugees from the counties affected by war fled to the countryside, with large numbers also going into the Guiji Mountains, near Shaoxing, and the Siming Mountains, close to Ningbo. The people who had fled the northern prefectures in the Hangzhou Bay campaign for Shaoxing and Ningbo now fled farther south, to Jinhua, Quzhou, Taizhou, Chuzhou, and

Wenzhou.[30] Refugee accounts in this phase of the war mirror those from northern Zhejiang over three years earlier: reports reflect the impact of rumors, the indecision about where to go, and second thoughts when choices were at last made. But, on the whole, in these stories of refugee experiences there is a greater sense of fear expressed about the Japanese than there had been earlier and a willingness to believe that the enemy had almost superhuman powers. These reactions most certainly came because of the news and rumors of Japanese brutality and heartlessness—which spread like wildfire along the road and from village to village. The Japanese were linked to fire in the popular imagination, from their aerial bombing to the deliberate arson of homes and businesses.

One trope that occurs in these accounts and those throughout the rest of the war is a description of night and darkness that is thoroughly malevolent. The simplest explanation would be that many refugees had their worst or most horrific experiences at night. Alternatively, for some, the most challenging, reshaping episodes of their lives as refugees may have occurred at night. It is interesting that Japan's attacks on Hangzhou Bay's northern shore, on Shaoxing, and on Ningbo all occurred in the middle of the night; that was well known because the timing and nature of the attacks were reported in newspapers.[31] As news for the majority of people traveled through the air in exchanges between people, it would have been improbable for people not to have developed a subconscious connection between the Japanese and night.

Compelling refugee stories for this campaign of the war stem from the Japanese bombing of Xinchang County (see Map 8). The first, written under the pseudonym of Zi Xi, is the account of a student whose short course at the Xinchang County school was cut even shorter by the Japanese bombing of the county seat. The teacher immediately and frantically dismissed the students, telling them to return to their homes. Zi and a fellow student, Ye, had to travel through the market town of Caozhou. They had planned to walk along the main highway, a straight road over a plain; but the two became panicky over the possibility of running into Japanese soldiers—a situation appearing even eerier because they seemed to be about the only ones on the highway. Ye suggested taking a small winding mountain road, where any Japanese danger seemed lessened. Zi reported, "It was dark, so dark that if you stretched out your hand, you could not even see your fingers. Groping along, our hands became bloody, and we felt our way until midnight."[32] They presumed a dim light ahead was in Caozhou: it was not—they had, in fact, walked in the wrong direction. A woman they passed on the road warned ominously, "The Japanese devils are coming quickly; you'd best get out of here now." [33]They ran as fast as they could in the dark and reached Ye's home just before dawn.

Zi then had to walk until dusk of that day before he reached his home, only to be greeted by more dire predictions and choices. His mother was crying: the issue—whether to stay or flee. His older sister announced the minute he arrived, "The Japanese devils are already at Xikou [in Fenghua, an adjacent county]. They'll certainly be here tonight. If we don't leave, we'll be captured and killed."[34] (For Fenghua, see Map 8.) Zi's brothers agreed that they should flee quickly. Zi's grandmother was obstinate: "I'm old; I will die in any event. This is my home. If I die, I will die here."[35] But the family would not hear of it. All of them left, traveling again at night deep into the mountains. They lived for four weeks in an abandoned broken-down charcoal kiln.

In contrast to Zi, Lu Zuoyang was the son of a wealthy businessman who, before the Japanese bombing, had owned a native bank, a cotton-goods store, a fried-goods and candle store, and an oil mill. He lost everything but the oil mill in the bombing. As the fires raced through the town, the people fled. The omnipresent question: where would Lu and his family go? Leaving for the Tiantai Mountains in Tiantai County to the south was a possibility. But Lu pointed out that one could never be sure of what one would find; going "far away," he and his family might end up "in an area of bandits" (as the Feng family of Tongxiang did indeed.)[36] They decided to stay near the county seat so that Lu, once things were more peaceful, could check on his oil mill. When the Japanese occupied the town a year later, however, Lu fled with his family because he heard that the Japanese were going to force him to become one of their chief collaborators. The Japanese often tried to coerce leading businessmen and Chamber of Commerce leaders to become their Chinese agents. To avoid that possibility, Lu and his family moved to Taoyuan, a market town southeast of the county seat. There he lived incognito, concealing his name out of fear.

The Zhe-Gan Campaign

In histories of the Pacific War, the Doolittle Raid is little more than a footnote. Since sustained bombing of Japan did not begin until 1944, the raid seemed to be little more than a strike to exact a small amount of vengeance for the Pearl Harbor attack. Yet the aftermath of the raid had a large impact on the war in Zhejiang: it was the context of Japan's Zhe-Gan (Zhejiang-Jiangxi) campaign. On April 18, 1942, sixteen B-25s with seventy-nine crew members commanded by James Doolittle took off from the aircraft carrier *Hornet* to drop incendiary and demolition bombs on Tokyo, Yokohama, Nagoya, and the Kobe-Osaka area. The planes were scheduled to land at the air base at Quzhou in the southwest part of Zhejiang, refuel, and fly on to Chongqing. Jiang Jieshi was very apprehensive about the plans for the Doolittle raiders to land in China, for fear of severe Japanese retaliation.

The end of the mission itself was an unhappy one. Met by stronger headwinds than expected, the flight from Japan to Zhejiang took longer and consequently consumed more fuel than expected. The weather was misty and rainy; night closed in as the planes neared the coast. Radio homing beacons had been requested for Quzhou. Despite Chongqing's assurances that they would be installed, they were not. Consequently, the pilots could not locate the airfields. U.S. Army historian S. L. A. Marshall noted, "Not only was the field totally without homing arrangements, but when the planes were heard overhead, an air-raid alarm was sounded, and all lights were turned off."[37] All the planes crashed, either with their crews inside or after they had parachuted out.

The Japanese were outraged. Not only were the bombs destructive and the surprise attack a loss of face, but the landings in China and the existence of air bases from which the Japanese islands could be bombed were intolerable. The Japanese had been aware since reconnaissance flights in late March that base runways at Quzhou, Lishui, and Yushan (Jiangxi) were being extended. Indeed, two days before the raid, the Imperial General Headquarters had set forth the operational plan for what would be the deadliest campaign of the war in Zhejiang Province. The mission: defeat enemy forces and destroy the air bases from which aerial raids on Japan could be carried out. Marshalling forty infantry battalions and fifteen or sixteen artillery battalions—over a hundred thousand men—the Japanese began the campaign on May 15. There were three fronts: from the Hangzhou area southwest along the Fuchun River; along the Zhe–Gan Railroad, including the key cities of Jinhua, Lanxi, and Qu; and from just south of Ningbo into the province's center. In a spectacular battle in the Jinhua-Lanxi area, the Chinese for the first time in the war inflicted heavy losses on the Japanese forces, killing over a thousand Japanese; but in the end, the Chinese retreated. Both Jinhua and Lanxi fell on May 29 (see Map 2).

In many ways the climactic battle of the campaign was in Qu, the tragic city whose air base, only a few miles out of town, really triggered the Japanese actions (see Map 9). From June 3 to June 8, the battle raged day and night; the Japanese army seemed a juggernaut. As the Chinese armies retreated repeatedly, the enemy proceeded, meeting up with Japanese forces from Jiangxi and succeeding in Japanese campaign goals.

In the case of Quzhou's residents, Chinese authorities presented almost as much of a threat as the Japanese forces. On May 20, the leaders of the Eighty-sixth Chinese Corps, one of the key military units in the city, ordered the evacuation of the forty thousand residents of the city within three days; that is, by May 23, all residents had to leave with their possessions. The county Nationalist government also ordered the people to move at least forty *li* (13.3 miles) from the city in order "to make the fighting more convenient."[38] There were no special measures taken to assist in the evacuation, which, in effect, forced all residents to become refugees. Many of the wealthy had already left. But laborers, shopkeepers, and others simply had to comply with the orders on their own. Those who were ill, incapacitated, or elderly and could not leave on their own were expelled by the military police.

The tragedy of the situation was compounded by the fact that the evacuation coincided with the worst flood the area had seen in sixty years. The main bridge crossing the Qu River, on which most evacuees had to leave, was under water, so the only way residents could evacuate was by boat— but there were far too few for the population. To make the tragic situation worse for some, the Eighty-sixth Corps, on the pretext of "fortifying the defenses in order to protect Qu City," ordered all residents whose homes were built alongside the city wall to destroy their homes. Reportedly eight or nine of every ten homeowners could not bear to carry out the order, so the military torched the dwellings. Taking a page from the Japanese army's tactics, the Chinese military also burned all houses outside the city wall and in the vicinity of the central railroad station.[39]

The Japanese softened up the city with heavy bombing as rain continued to gush from the sky. Constant fires started by the bombing over-
came the rain and turned the city into rubble. On June 5, Japan attacked
Qu by using poison gas and launched a blistering artillery attack on the
train station. On June 7, Chinese commanders ordered Chinese soldiers
to move out of the city and to retreat; that same day began Japan's twelve-
week occupation of Qu. In the first days of the occupation, the Japanese
executed over 200 soldiers and civilians; and in the surrounding countryside, the Japanese summer was remembered for its rapes, arson, pillage,
and murders. The commercial sectors of the city suffered heavy destruction. There were still no markets open on September 23, almost a month
after the Japanese withdrew. Most areas inside the city wall saw up to 90
percent of the houses (8,228) destroyed. In Qu County 19,112 were killed
or wounded; 28,800 houses were burned to the ground; 6,600 water buf-
falo were killed, as were 119,000 hogs; and 97,000 catties of grain were
stolen. Total economic losses were estimated at 142 million yuan.[40]

Numbers and Destinations

For those non-Zhejiangese refugees traveling through the region and for
those residents of Zhejiang whose refugee flight took them out of the
province, the most important destinations were northern Fujian, southern
Jiangxi, and southern Anhui. These areas were alluring, for they never saw
any military action; the Fujian sites also provided work for refugees in land
reclamation. These regions were especially popular as a destination at the
beginning of the war and even more so during the Zhe-Gan campaign.
Before December 1941, some Zhejiang residents fled to Shanghai's International Settlement, most from northern Zhejiang (Hangzhou-Jiaxing-
Huzhou) and businessmen from Ning-Shao.[41] For Zhejiang refugees
fleeing to the southwest provinces of Sichuan and Yunnan, two routes
were used: the route of the Yangzi upstream or the Zhe–Gan Railroad
into Jiangxi and then west. In 1937 there were 3,150 Zhejiangese in
Chongqing (Jiang Jieshi's capital after late 1938); in 1945 there were
48,799.[42] The majority of those Zhejiangese leaving the province for
Chongqing came from Hangzhou, Shaoxing, Ningbo, and Jinhua—towns
and counties that were most directly impacted early by the war and areas
that were more modernized, whose residents tended to be less dependent

on staying in their localities—though the attraction to native place remained strong.

Inside the province, refugees tended to head to Guomindang-controlled
rear areas, though sometimes refugees chose rural or mountainous sites in
occupied territory. According to reports from seventy-two counties, there
were 56,289 refugees in Zhejiang from other provinces in early 1945—
most (36. 2 percent) in Hangzhou.[43] Until northern Zhejiang fell in late fall
1937, most refugees coming into or through Zhejiang used the Qiantang
River to enter southern and eastern Zhejiang, aiming for either the Zhe–
Gan Railroad in Xiaoshan County or Shaoxing and points southeast. From
counties west of Hangzhou, a favorite route was to go up the Tong River
and then perhaps south. Fewer refugees came from Shanghai by boat for
Ningbo and Wenzhou. A July 1938 study of relief for refugees moving to
the rear areas noted that, up until then, the number totaled 1,310,801. Of
those, 30 percent (390,623) went to Jinhua; 21 percent (273,407) to Shaoxing; and 15.2 percent (199,450) to Ningbo.[44] The other key prefectural
cities had significantly fewer. The figures for these three are staggering in
their implications for localities having to deal with this flood of people.
Jinhua's policy was to dispatch arriving refugees as quickly as possible to
towns and villages in surrounding counties.[45]

The ages of 284,020 refugees who registered at Zhejiang reception
centers from January to August 1938 underscore who was more likely to
choose to become refugees. *Sui* signifies the Chinese way of keeping age
that makes infants one year old when they are born; thus, in terms of
Western age-counting, 36 to 50 *sui* would be 35 to 49 years old.

Table 1.1 Ages of Refugees at Zhejiang Reception Centers, Jan.–Aug. 1938

Ages	Number	Percentage
Birth to 8 *sui*	47,204	16.62
9 to 17 *sui*	46,364	16.32
18 to 35 *sui*	92,848	32.69
36 to 50 *sui*	67,732	23.85
Above 50 *sui*	28,872	10.52

Source: Zhang Genfu, *Kangzhan shiqi Zhejiang sheng renkou qianyi yu shehui yingxiang*
[Population movement and its social impact in Zhejiang Province during the Resistance
War] (Shanghai: Sanlian shudian, 2001), pp. 72–74.

These figures are consistent with national figures of refugee ages. When figures are broken down in half decades above 50 *sui*, the lack of willingness of the elderly to become refugees is even clearer. Of this refugee total, 5.97 percent were 46 to 50 *sui*; 1.26 percent were 56 to 60 *sui*; and 0.55 percent were 66 to 70 *sui*.[46] Reasons for older people not to join the refugee exodus were weak or ill bodies, a desire not to be a burden on children and grandchildren, a reluctance to give up a productive life and the accumulations of a long life, and a disbelief in the rumors the Chinese had heard about the Japanese atrocities.

A one-time snapshot of the proportion of male and female refugees suggests that almost half of the refugees were women. In August 1939 at thirteen Zhejiang reception centers, 53.6 percent (984) were men and 46.4 percent (851) were women. In terms of the professions and employment background of refugees, we return to the 284,020 refugees from January through August 1938. This table does not include short-term refugees.

Table 1.2 Employment Background of Refugees at Zhejiang Reception Centers, Jan.–Aug. 1938

Profession, employment	Number	Percentage
Farmers	98,178	34.57
Those unable to work	49,572	17.45
Domestic workers	49,518	17.43
Merchants	41,899	14.75
Industrial workers	24,036	8.46
Handicrafters	11,099	3.91
Unemployed	2,911	1.02
Educational and cultural workers	2,880	1.01
Government workers	1,212	0.43
The professions, especially lawyers and professors	1,155	0.41
Military members and police	732	0.26
Monks and priests	444	0.16
Doctors	384	0.14

Source: Zhang Genfu, *Kangzhan shiqi Zhejiang sheng renkou qianyi yu shehui yingxiang* [Population movement and its social impact in Zhejiang Province during the Resistance War] (Shanghai: Sanlian shudian, 2001), p 78.

Perhaps most surprising is the huge proportion of farmers who fled homes and farms for safety; for when they left their farms, they obviously were cut off from their source of livelihood. Many farmers were likely "intermediate-distanced" refugees, going beyond neighboring villages or mountains but not so far that returning to farms when local situations had settled down was impossible or very difficult. It was said of Pinghu county County farmers that "90 percent . . . left the war zone temporarily, seeking a time to return stealthily."[47] When the number of farmers is broken down, 20.22 percent were owner-farmers, 13.85 percent were tenants, and 0.5 percent were pasture owners.

Rather large numbers of refugees were also in business and industry (27.12 percent) in the categories of merchants, industrial workers, and handicraft. Whether they were industrial labor or large-scale capitalists, many had blood, marriage, or business ties to turn to for support in rural towns and villages. Many city workers were from rural areas, to which they could simply return. When war came to cities, often industries ceased operating; with no way to work, many individuals returned to their native places.

Men and women in education, cultural work, and the professions tended to have higher income than commoners; these professionals could bear the expense of traveling long distances. It is perhaps people in this group who likely became refugees because of national feeling: they could not bear to live under Japanese control. Sociologist Sun Benwen estimated that 90 percent of upper-level intellectuals (definition not specified) moved west, 50 percent of the middle level did so, and 30 percent of the lower level. Zhejiang intellectuals tended, however, not to go west: their destination was more likely Guilin in Guangxi Province. A crucial question is how the refugees were received when they entered new localities as "guests."

※

TWO

Confronting the Refugee Crisis

THE NATIONAL GOVERNMENT LINE on refugee relief and assistance could not have been clearer. Reports from an Executive Yuan meeting on January 4, 1938, under the heading "Relief for Refugees, Solace for the Exiled," noted, "The government expresses its great solicitude over the [losses] and tears of the refugees. To sooth and relieve them is its responsibility, which it cannot shoulder aside." In an even stronger statement of commitment, the Executive Yuan about a month later asserted, "To provide relief for refugees is our administration's key goal" (*yiduan,* literally, "one end").[1]

In its early actions, the central government took strong initiatives. In September 1937, two months after the Marco Polo Bridge incident, the government established the Refugee Relief Council for Extraordinary Times, or *(feichang shiqi nanmin jiuji weiyuanhui)* [(hereafter, the Relief Council),] with a branch office in each province. The Relief Council oversaw the establishment of refugee reception centers on important thoroughfares. As an indication of the council's mobilizing the province to handle refugees, in mid-November, about the time that northern Zhejiang counties began to fall under Japan's control, the provincial council sent a delegation to visit five counties in central Zhejiang to see what provisions they had taken.[2] This area was key in any refugee emergency because of its location on crucial transportation routes: the counties straddled the Qiantang River, which carried boat traffic upstream from Hangzhou Bay, and the Zhejiang–Jiangxi (Zhe–Gan) Railroad passed through them.

If all the counties approximated the arrangements and preparation in Lanxi County in central Zhejiang, this area seemed well primed to deal with the refugee surge. On November 18, the Lanxi County subbranch of the Relief Council met to decide on procedures in receiving refugees: setting the location of separate reception centers for women and children and for men; detailing with clearly specified functions the reception centers' governance, which was a committee headed by one or two assigned local government officials; handling bedding and clothing ("Make announcements in newspapers soliciting cotton-padded bedding, clothes, trousers, shoes, and hats and collect them in three locations—the administrative office for the five city wards, the Chamber of Commerce, and the county orphanage"); specifying items—including iron cooking pots, a water bucket, chamber pots, and a wash basin—required for each reception station; handling refugee meals by providing two daily servings of food, with a per-person cost limited to seven *fen,* the equivalent of seventy cents, per day; and setting the reception centers' daily schedule so that refugees rose at 6 A.M., had meals at 10 A.M. and 4 P.M., and went to bed at 7 P.M. As events would prove, this was decision making in the calm before the storm; it was relatively dispassionate—before the flood of flesh-and-blood human beings brought the immense scope of the relief emergency before policy makers' eyes.

Obstacles to Coping with Refugees

Huang Shaohong (1895–1966), a military figure of the Guangxi clique and an official in various posts under Jiang Jieshi, served as governor of Zhejiang Province in 1934 and 1935 and from December 1937 to 1946. Thus, throughout the Resistance War, he was chief provincial executive, in the provincial capitals in exile, first in Yongkang County (1938–1942) and then in Yunhe County (1942–1945). His memoir reveals a man who wrote frankly about the issues as he saw them and about problems faced during the war.[3]

In their approach to refugee relief, the attitudes of most Chinese to public charity were shaped by the social importance of connections (or, here specifically, the lack of connections to refugees en masse). Referring to general attitudes, Huang wrote, "The Chinese people have negative attitudes about charity to relieve crises: they only want to distribute from funds which have already been collected. Even if they show their compassionate heart to the fullest, they do it one time for the favorable reputation they incur when others see them contributing.... Chinese negativity about charity certainly does nothing to bring success to a program for refugee relief."[4] In a pithier summation, an editor of the *Southeast Daily* noted, "Experience tells us that people who put down their chopsticks and pay 10,000 cash [at a restaurant] are not willing to offer refugees even one copper coin."[5] Some wealthy individuals and community leaders did make contributions, but these were generally small; if these citizens set up reception centers, for example, they were usually limited to receiving and processing a dozen or two dozen refugees.[6]

Statistics reveal the hard, cold reality and underscore Huang's evaluation of the situation. In the years from 1942 through 1944, for relief monies Zhejiang received 18,890,000 yuan from the central government; used 22,080,000 yuan of provincial funds; utilized 4,546,000 yuan from provincial loans; but collected only the paltry sum of 120,000 yuan in charitable contributions (0.2 percent of the total).[7] Thus, the general individual reluctance to make charitable donations meant that refugee assistance and relief had to come mainly from cash-strapped governments and from various public organizations.

In addition to having an aversion to relief charity, Chinese who received refugees in their home areas saw them as the Other. In the words of artist and author Feng Zikai, himself a refugee, "refugees [were] like an invading army," streaming in upon locals, who were besieged by the refugee presence and their requests and demands.[8] In many cases locals were inhospitable to what they clearly considered "undesirables," described by one official as being covered with lice and smelling of dirt and filth.[9] Local residents generally met refugees with mistrust, fear, and hostility and saw their presence as a source of potential social unrest. In the spring of 1938, for example, political leaders in the vicinity of Moganshan (see Map 4), a resort area north of Hangzhou, wired the capital, then located at Fangyan in Yongkang County, that there were some three to four thousand refugees in the area; although they had been peaceable to that point, the local fear was that their continued presence might lead to a disastrous shortage of food that would bring on social unrest and perhaps violence. Locals wanted the provincial government to assist in moving the refugees to Jinhua.[10] When Pinghu resident Feng Zongmeng wanted to flee by boat to Shimen, west of his native place, the boatman he had hired dissuaded him because the town had already received far too many refugees and fear of social unrest was intense.[11]

A large part of the hostility of locals was caused by what refugees took from the localities. The central government mandated the issuance of daily relief payments and some travel monies for refugee resettlement; localities often had to come up with the money through contributions or taxes. An even greater irritation and fear among local residents was the drain on available local resources for residents and refugees alike. The need for firewood for cooking, for example, in many areas exhausted the availability of this resource. Most crucial was the availability of sufficient food. Typical was the fear of Moganshan leaders about hundreds, even thousands, of extra mouths to feed from a food supply limited by shortages and a disrupted and often nonfunctioning transport system. Rice was especially in short supply. Before the war, Zhejiang farmers produced about 38 million piculs of rice, but the province's consumption needs were about 52 million piculs: thus the province was customarily about 14 million piculs short.[12] This shortfall had traditionally been purchased and transported from Jiangxi and Anhui. To make the situation even worse for unoccupied Zhejiang, the "rice basket" of the province—northern Zhejiang—was now almost completely in Japanese hands. The situation gave rise to episodes like the Fuyang County "incident" in late summer 1938. A large sandbank in the Fuchun River provided about thirty households with land that was quite productive. North of the river was Japanese-occupied territory, where the food shortage was severe and where people near the river looked with envy at the farmers on the sandbank and hatched a plan to raid those households. The county's Japanese collaborationist Peace Maintenance Committee gave their go-ahead for the raid. Reports indicated that raiders dressed as refugees for the successful nighttime raid (we are not told what would have been distinctive about refugee clothing). In addition to showing that the rice dearth fostered thievery, the episode suggested the thievish reputation that at least some locals attributed to refugees.[13]

Another local response to the refugees was to scheme and connive to bilk their money. A *Southeast Daily* editor noted, "Shopkeepers and those renting out houses and rooms not only do not have pity on these people from another place and with a strange dialect, but they cheat them."[14]

Price gouging and all manners of fraud were common practices, as refugee accounts in following chapters will illustrate. At this time of struggle for the nation, the war seemed to produce not national fervor but self-serving and self-centered outlooks.

Finally, concern about corruption in the refugee relief system hampered the dispensing of aid to refugees. The concern with registration at reception centers—requiring name, native place, and, later in the war, prewar occupation—reflected a fear that down-and-out locals might feign refugee status to gain some relief assistance of their own. Regulations made clear that a person receiving support at a reception center could not leave while receiving aid.[15] At most reception centers, policies called for getting refugees out to work as soon as possible to preclude the "lazy freeloader" syndrome.

Governor Huang, however, did not simply speak of corruption among refugees but among government agents of relief aid. The government representative who handled the money and released relief funds could be appointed, according to Huang, only if he did not have a past record of corrupt practices; Huang warned that telltale signs of corruption were officials who went about their work all very secretively. It was up to the government functionary to investigate or request an investigation of the applicant's legitimate refugee status, to register the applicant, sign names and affix the official seal, and perhaps even resort to the formality of taking fingerprints. If an investigation was called for, the probity of the investigator was crucial, for example, to avoid solicitation of bribes. Only if all checked out was the government official able to disperse relief monies, but then in amounts of only five to fifty yuan. Huang admitted that the system could be manipulated in every phase of the process. With this in mind, he argued that relief funds should only be released slowly. At a time of social normality, such a deliberate approach might seem reasonable; but as the streams of refugees became torrents in early 1938, and then a flood, this slow approach affected refugees in the most negative way. Huang revealed his own overall attitude to refugees and that of the government, as it sided increasingly with the views of many locals: refugees were downright untrustworthy. With that deliberate screening procedure in place, he went on to say, "You don't want there to be several months before you can get money into the hands of those who need it.... of course, there is the time and distance [necessary for actualizing relief]—

the hungry could starve to death; the cold could freeze to death—and the dead don't really need relief. I say: Chinese relief really is the 'idea of relief,' not relief itself. . . . China must reform its relief system."[16]

Jinhua: A Case Study of Refugee Besiegement

From beginning to end, the provincial policy for refugee relief was based on four principles, as identified by Zhang Genfu:[17] (1) "The front lines are more important than the rear areas." This principle can be read in two ways: That is, the refugees in the front lines need to be evacuated as quickly as possible; their plight is a greater crisis than those already in rear areas—or, fighting the war in the front lines is more important than handling refugees in the rear areas. (2) "Action is more important than passivity." Once again, this principle may be read in more than one way: For relief givers, taking action to deal with refugee problems is more important than "letting things ride." Or, the passage may be saying that it is more important to have refugees active at work than lazing around reception centers. (3) "Staying on the spot is better than moving." Registering refugees and knowing their whereabouts is better than having them continuing to move and adding to possible social instability or unrest. (4) This principle seems to contradict the third: "Dispersal is better than collection." The key is not letting too many refugees accumulate in one location, where the problems they could cause might exhaust local resources or pose problems for the military. Case in point: At the opening of the war, so many refugees from Jiangsu and the Zhejiang counties north of Hangzhou Bay crowded into Fuyang and Xiaoshan counties at the mouth of the Qiantang River that they hindered the deployment of troops. Under such circumstances, the transcendent need was to disperse the refugees.

The central problem always was too little money and too many refugees. The city of Jinhua, the former prefectural capital located on the Zhejiang–Jiangxi Railroad and on the Wu River, a major tributary of the Qiantang River—and thus a site easily reached by refugees—provides a case in point. Between November 1937 and March 1938, some twenty-five thousand refugees passed through the city; and as of early March, four thousand still remained. At that time the city had seven reception centers, mostly at temples and shrines; but there were also centers opened in six nearby villages. The problem from Day One was money. The local Relief Council branch began strong public appeals for contributions from businesses and individuals. It received only fifteen hundred yuan from the provincial Relief Council, an insignificant amount, given the scope of the problem: that might have been enough for four hundred refugees, but there were ten times that number in the city.

To deal with the refugee crisis, the head of the provincial Relief Council came to Jinhua for discussions with local government leaders and city elites. When he arrived on March 3, the city had only enough resources to support the refugees for three days—the rice supply was already exhausted—and another three thousand refugees were arriving. Because of the harsh reality of the situation and the unwillingness of the wealthy to "shell out," the talks were nonproductive; the only alternative seemed to be additional local taxes. Reports of the meeting disclosed paltry contributions from private individuals, ranging from ten to twenty yuan. As a last-ditch effort, the county government telegraphed an urgent plea for emergency assistance from the national government, then headquartered in Wuhan; pleaded again with local businesses and individuals for contributions; and placed a surtax on hotel bills, earmarking this revenue for refugee relief. The other crucial decision, made in order to lessen the crisis of numbers, was the county government's immediate dispatching of roughly three thousand new refugees to the counties of Longquan and Yongkang and to northern Fujian. Those at reception centers who were judged to be not legitimate refugees were sent away.[18]

But by mid-April, hundreds more poured into the city at the same time as the provincial Relief Council announced that all refugee food supplies in the province had been exhausted and pleaded desperately for contributions.[19] Refugees were reported to be at the point of subsisting on tree bark and grass roots. The only answer—and an increasingly common pattern of dealing with refugees—seemed to be to get them out of Jinhua as quickly as possible. That meant the local Relief Council's contacting other county Relief Councils in the rear areas and establishing procedures for these other centers to receive the Jinhua refugees. The hope among Jinhua relief officials—and at this critical time it was only a hope—was that those reception centers would have the food and clothes that the refugees needed.[20] Another nine hundred refugees who arrived in the city from May 15 to 17 were sent to Yongkang County and counties along the Zhe–Gan Railroad.[21] Coincidentally, the demands of Moganshan elites that Jinhua take two thousand to three thousand of the Moganshan refugee population came precisely at the time of the May crisis.

In June 1938, Jinhua experimented with placing refugees in work units, a strategy that had begun earlier in the year elsewhere. Early in the month two units were formed, one a sanitation unit, which was to sweep and clean up public institutions, and the other a public laundry unit, which would charge low fees.[22] The work program for refugees expanded later in the month, when the provincial Relief Council collaborated with the Jinhua council to form five work units: sanitation, including laundry; sewing; service, providing a wide range of work, including school and road construction and jobs for coolies, maids, and nurses; production, the manufacturing of textiles, bamboo items, ramie; and a unit for children, a program that stressed character training, learning anti-Japanese songs, and telling stories.[23] We are unfortunately not told of the efficacy of this more elaborate plan.

As the influx of refugees continued in the subsequent months, emergency meetings were the order of the day. Emergency measures included deducting sums from official salaries, levying an additional 10 percent on hotel bills, paying nothing for transport in the annual winter-clothing drive, and holding a charity benefit for refugees and wounded soldiers.[24] July 1938 brought the first overseas contributions for refugee relief from Britain and the United States.[25] In 1939 overseas Chinese in southeast Asia also became active in sending contributions for the cause.[26]

But with the Ning-Shao (Ningbo-Shaoxing) campaign in 1941 and the Zhe-Gan (Zhejiang-Jiangxi) campaign in 1942, Jinhua's number of refugees soared. In the summer of 1941, Jinhua reported over twenty thousand refugees in its environs. For the first time, the Jinhua authorities received substantial amounts of money from overseas Chinese whose native place was Jinhua.[27] A *Southeast Daily* reporter described the situation as follows:

The enemy actions in Ning-Shao caused much destruction and created many homeless refugees. The central government, responding to the province, has already sent funds for relief, but it's a pity that the funds are completely inadequate and quite useless. Refugees are coming slowly to the rear areas seeking help, most to Jinhua, where they want to stop fleeing and want to work. The county relief society has set up extensive measures [three new reception centers] for receiving people. If adult male refugees are strong and have abilities, then the authorities will devise a way for them to work. Refugee children will be sent to a children's education office that recently received 50,000 yuan from a county fund designated to provide relief after military catastrophe.[28]

The use of this fund, not directly targeted toward long-distance refugees, suggests that under certain circumstances other government monies might have been used more pragmatically during the refugee crises in 1938.

Several weeks later, the provincial Guomindang provided grants of rice to three counties, Jinhua, Qu, and Lishui, to help in feeding Ning-Shao refugees. Newspaper reports indicate that more money began to flow into Jinhua from overseas Chinese, specifically from Chinese who did not hail from Jinhua.[29] Despite the changing face of the sources of relief monies over time, in the end, the money problem—and with it, the refugee problem—was never solved. The *Southeast Daily* noted in January 1939 that considering only food and lodging, there was only one county in the province where refugees' needs were being met—Yongkang County, the site of the provincial capital in exile.[30]

Work Relief

In addition to the kinds of ad hoc work that Jinhua authorities administered in 1938 and after, there were several other notable work-relief efforts. A small one was a project to make refugees themselves relief administrators. Initially, the military was charged with managing refugee centers, but some argued that eventually refugees themselves could fulfill these functions.[31] The Zhejiang branch of the Relief Council organized an examination system to select refugee men and women of high scholastic and moral standing for a refugee service unit to administer refugee relief work. The initial goal was to select thirty-four people between the ages of twenty-two and forty, an extremely modest goal for such an immense problem. Subjects for the examination were Mandarin and current events; a physical exam was also required. After the examination (the first held April 17, 1938, in the Yongkang County middle school) came a two-week training period. In early May the new administrators were commissioned and sent to neighboring counties. I have found no record of their impact on the refugee situation in those counties. But the effort points out the official desire to regularize management of refugees in the localities where they had settled at least temporarily.[32]

In Yongkang County, the site of the provincial government in exile from 1938 to 1942, the government sponsored its most important project in refugee work relief, the Refugee Dyeing and Weaving Mill at the town of Zhiying (see Map 5). Because relief expense had no offsetting income, the government hit upon the idea of setting up a mill to make cloth and clothes for provincial public workers, provincial and county police, and military units. The Relief Council began efforts to establish the mill but was stymied by various complications involving regulations and procedures. Governor Huang then asked Lu Gongwang (1879–1954), who had served as Zhejiang's military and civil governor in 1916–1917 and whose native place was Yongkang, to direct the project. There was no auspicious beginning. Lu reported, "From the start, matters were very thorny; we lacked experience, qualified personnel, and material resources. We were dogged with the thought that the whole thing might be impractical. We didn't have even 1 percent of the necessary funds."[33] With a loan of a hundred thousand yuan arranged by the Farmers Bank of China and with the help of local elites in Zhiying, Lu established the mill in April 1938, when over thirty-eight hundred refugees were sent to become workers there. The first task was having the refugees, many of whom were covered with nits and were very dirty, bathe in batches of a hundred. To house both the refugees and the mill, Lu commandeered temples in the town.[34]

From 1938 to 1942, which Lu called "the peaceful period," the mill and twenty-one other work sites in the county seat and at seven towns and villages throughout the county provided work, relief, and education for between three thousand and four thousand persons each year.[35] A public nursery, kindergarten, and elementary school were established for refugee infants and children under thirteen *sui* in order to free their parents for work. Night classes were held for illiterate youths; a modicum of military training was included in these classes. The elderly who could not do mill work performed alternative tasks. In addition to the room and board the work sites provided for the refugees, each finished bolt of cloth brought a monetary bonus for workers to use for daily expenses. Men and women lived in separate dormitories. Lu took a strongly paternalistic stance vis-à-vis the refugees, distributing printed directions and restrictions and offering instructions in military preparedness.[36]

The success of the refugee mill venture lay in Lu's ability to mobilize local resources to help in the organization, funding, and management; there were reportedly over 140 men involved in the management of the mill in its seven-year existence. Zhiying, a market town since the Ming dynasty, was home to the Ying lineage, one of the most powerful and economically and politically successful in the county. When the county Chamber of Commerce was established in the early Republic, three of its seven-member board were from the Ying lineage. The chairman of the county assembly elected in 1922 was Ying Huaisen. When Lu received the mill assignment, he contacted Ying Wenlong (1881–1950), who had served previously as mayor of Zhiying and head of the tax office in the district *(qu)* where Zhiying was located. The administrator of the Ying lineage temple, Wenlong led the way in responding to Lu's request and made large and small temples available for the mill. He appealed to his fellow elites for subscriptions to be used for managing the enterprise and for the purchase of machines and materials. Originally the elites purchased one thousand wooden looms, but as work expanded, the number rose to twelve hundred. Local elites also became integrally involved in mill management roles and several years later in branch workshops of the Zhiying mill that were established in four other market towns. On the whole, local leaders here were willing and even eager allies of the government in dealing with the refugee crisis.

Although some refugees allegedly resisted having to work for their food and shelter, the benefits of mill work and the feeling of security in a settled place produced a growing sense of identity with the mill and its system. Lu contended that the mill refugees came to identify the mill as their wartime household *(jiating),* to which their loyalty was bound; he claimed that much of the bitterness of their being refugees came to be forgotten. This sense of belonging, in an atmosphere of chaos and uncertainty, was most certainly more important for these refugees than any textiles they produced.

The second phase of the chronological life of the refugee mill Lu called "the move." It might better be called "the dispersal." Whereas the original mill, though headquartered in Zhiying, was located at sites around the county, "the move," stimulated by Japanese military activity, led to the relocation of mill sites around the province. In the summer of 1941, during the Ning-Shao campaign, the Japanese took Dongyang County, contiguous to Yongkang, and bombed Yongkang from the air. Lu and the mill's leaders decided to move five hundred looms to Jiangshan County in far western Zhejiang on the Jiangxi border, a distance of about 125 miles. The big problem by late 1941 was that ready sources of cotton yarn had been cut off. Shanghai and Hong Kong were closed by the enemy, and the textile mills in Xiaoshan County and Ningbo had been either taken by the Japanese or destroyed. Mill leaders decided to establish seven branch mills in Yongkang County; each mill would be responsible for purchasing its own yarn from whatever source it could find, and each mill would be responsible for its own profits or losses. The main mill, now moved to Jiangshan, would be in charge of sales, taking 1 percent of the value of the finished cloth from each branch mill for administrative expenses. The Military Provisioning Office set the quota for the amount of finished cloth it needed. The main mill and the seven branch mills were charged with deciding among themselves the amount of cloth that each mill would produce and therefore the funds that each needed. The turmoil of the time of "the move" was apparent in the total production. In 1938, the mill workers had produced 27,903 bolts of cloth; in 1939, 72,268; in 1940, 100,206; and in 1941, 56,361, a drop of 56 percent from the previous year.

Shortly before Yongkang fell to the Japanese in 1942, Lu mobilized a thousand workers to dismantle, pack up, and transport the branch mills' machines along three preestablished routes and also to carry the not-yet-distributed finished clothes and the cloth and yarn reserves. The institution set up to provide relief work for refugees itself became a refugee. Pursued through the mountains by Japanese soldiers and ambushed by straggling soldiers and thugs, many refugees were killed on the road. The eight thousand finished bolts of cloth (not yet delivered to the military when the evacuation occurred) and yarn were seized by bandits along the way. After a six-month trek, the surviving mill-worker refugees reached the town of Chishi in remote Yunhe County, which also became the new provincial capital. Lu's office was in the Chishi Christian church, and the mill itself was about two miles outside the village. In this out-of-the-way location, purchasing cotton yarn became harder than ever. Discussion about alternatives led to a plan to barter tong oil, produced in the area from the seeds of tong trees, for cotton yarn from Shanghai's Southeast Company: this meant trading with the enemy, or a company that had ties to the enemy. Though it was illegal, the government, taking into account the dire circumstances and considering the mill to have made a great contribution to the war effort, gave the go-ahead. The agreement was to send twenty-two hundred piculs of tong oil for seven hundred packages of cotton yarn.

But bureaucratic snafus and bad luck created headaches, even disasters. The first oil shipment of five thousand piculs was held up because the bureaucrat who filled out the special trading certificate wrote fifty instead of the correct amount. Arrangements for the exchanges to correct the mistake were unbelievably lengthy, according to Lu. Moreover, once that shipment was transported to Wenzhou, from where it was to be sent to Shanghai, it was detained by customs officers and military units for four to five months. Given the problems in Wenzhou, the second shipment was sent up the Fuchun and Qiantang rivers toward Hangzhou Bay. But the ship transporting this shipment was sunk in a typhoon, and only about 50 percent of the cargo was salvaged.

Despite new refugees moving in to work in the mill, there were long delays in getting the yarn, the price of which had also risen in the general inflation, which became more and more serious. In the meantime, Lu was involved in other industrial efforts in the region: a kerosene refinery, an iron foundry, a soy sauce brewery, a soap factory, a match factory, and a *doufu* [in Japanese, *tofu*] factory. While the textile mill was staffed mainly by women, refugee men participated in some of the other efforts.[37]

When the Japanese took nearby Lishui County in August 1944, Lu and other mill leaders warned that the factory could not continue: in its last year workers produced only thirty-five hundred bolts. Lu asked Governor Huang to agree to the dismantling of the mill and the dividing of its remaining assets among mill staff and a large group of refugees. The mill had been a winning venture in large part because of Lu's leadership. An interviewer in August 1943 called him a "problem solver and a forceful decision-maker" and said that he was "robust in spirit." Repeatedly, the interview referred to Lu as an "old young man" (at sixty-four years).[38]

Not surprisingly, the Zhiying mill became the theoretical model for effective refugee work-relief projects. Unfortunately, establishing similar mills was never actually tried. Though the provincial government mandated that refugee factories be established in every county, wartime realities precluded the setting up of factories on the order of the Zhiying mill. Other places did not have the happy confluence of circumstances—a government-arranged loan, a leader like Lu, and local elites who bought into the idea and contributed money to make it a success. Apart from expense, the other intimidating problems in undertaking such projects were locating and purchasing machines and materials and transporting them.[39] Other, much smaller factories—for sewing, sock weaving, and soap making—were set up in Fenghua, Tangxi, and Longquan counties.[40]

Much emphasized by the national government, the refugee work relief with the greatest long-term impact was land reclamation. In February 1938, 1,417 heads of households (with over 4,000 family members) moved from Zhejiang to Fujian (1,226 households) and Jiangxi (191 households) to reclaim land that these provinces had designated.[41] The government paid for refugee travel to reclamation sites; specifically, in Zhejiang the Relief Council negotiated with the Zhejiang–Jiangxi Railroad to take those refugees bound for Jiangxi.[42] The success in the land reclamation projects is attested to by a 1940 visit to Fujian by five men on the Zhejiang Relief Council to negotiate with the Fujian governor to open up more reclamation projects to relieve refugee pressure in Zhejiang. There were also reclamation projects, within at least nine Zhejiang counties, that turned barren land into productive farms growing tea and other crops.

In addition to the textile mill and reclamation, local governments found other tasks they could assign for refugee work relief.[43] During the refugee exodus and the war itself, finding sufficient conveyance vehicles for materials was difficult. In April 1938 the provincial government decided to set up refugee work relief in wheelbarrow brigades. The initial investment: a purchase of twenty-three hundred wheelbarrows in Shanghai with money from Highway Bureau funds. Over twenty-two hundred men (with family members totaling over five thousand) joined the wheelbarrow brigades. The provincial government designated a wheelbarrow commander and drafted refugee men "in the prime of life"—selected by county branches of the Relief Council. Wheelbarrow brigades proliferated on routes between Jinhua and Lishui, Jinhua and Jiande, and Yongkang and Zhuji, and into Anhui and Jiangxi. By December 1938, there were seven thousand refugees pushing wheelbarrows—a significant contribution to the refugee relief effort.[44]

Several hundred refugees were put to work constructing or repairing public roads and deconstructing the Jinhua city wall.[45] Beginning in April 1938, between three and four hundred refugee women and children were hired in Jinhua, Xiaoshan, and Yongkang counties to make straw sandals for the military. Earning two to three *jiao* (twenty to thirty cents) per person each day, the refugees reportedly produced over sixty thousand pairs per month to be sent to the front. Governor Huang traveled to Chongqing in January 1939 to plead for additional relief monies for repair and reconstruction of sea dikes on Hangzhou Bay and at Taizhou on the East China Sea and for expanding local industrial production using the Zhiying mill as the prototype.[46] We do not know the extent of Chongqing's response, but some money was apparently received for refugee work that began on the Hangzhou Bay dikes in Haining County.

Other Forms of Government Relief

In February 1939, the Relief Council was replaced by the Central Relief Council [*zhongyang zhenji weiyuanhui*] [(hereafter, Central Council)], whose Zhejiang branch was headed by Governor Huang.[47] Administrative structures were changed, as the Relief Councils were retained to do the actual administering of relief as opposed to making policy decisions. The Central Council, like its predecessor, also had subbranches in each county. Huang noted that provincial governments repeatedly had to beg Chongqing for relief and then, in turn, were hounded by constant pleas from its own counties.[48] At various times during the war, Chongqing sent several million yuan for refugee relief, sums made worth less and less by soaring inflation.[49] Furthermore, despite what seemed meaningful lump sums of assistance, the amounts of relief money for families were paltry. National, provincial, and local governments contributed for daily expenses at reception centers and for refugee travel allocations—though localities varied greatly in their ability to pay.[50] In general, if refugees registered with their names and native places at reception centers and if these refugees retained documentation, they did not have to pay train fares. Between July and December 1939, the number of refugees receiving travel assistance from centers at the key cities of Jinhua and Wenzhou totaled 19,103 people.[51] Refugees had to apply for subsidies to local relief committees to purchase provisions, but there was precious little to give out: Yongkang County, the site of the capital from 1938 until May 1942, budgeted a maximum of fifty yuan per month for all subsidies.[52] In 1939 in Wukang County, northwest of Hangzhou, households of one or two people received one yuan, and households of three or more, two yuan, for the year.[53] To put that into perspective, renting a bare-bones house cost three or four yuan per month.

Price control attempts and the doling out of rice gruel were relatively common during the war. With the Zhejiang–Jiangxi Railroad being out of commission during much of the war and havoc being wrought by Japanese campaigns in Ningbo-Shaoxing in 1941 and central-southwestern Zhejiang in 1942, the shortage of rice was critical; and its price naturally rose higher and higher. In April 1938, the cost of rice in the Ningbo-Shaoxing area was over eleven yuan per picul, while in Jinhua it was only five yuan and four *jiao*.[54] Prices could be lowered through the purchase of additional rice, which could be put on the market by the government to bring down the price. The provincial government loaned counties money to buy rice and distribute it. In 1943 forty-seven counties (of seventy-six) received such loans.

One of the major relief efforts was the annual winter-clothing drive and distribution, essential to refugees and the poor. Each county had its own office to manage the drive, in which money and in-kind contributions were encouraged. Town and township *baojia* heads took the lead in the drive, which was directed by party and government officials and representatives of local institutions and schools.[55] The central and provincial governments provided assistance. From December 1938 to January 1942, approximately 2.45 million yuan was allotted for winter clothing—various kinds of cotton-padded adult and children's apparel as well as outfits for infants.[56] The annual period of assistance was from December to the end of March, with temples in city, town, and township to serve as collection points. In the cases of refugees and the local poor, Jinhua city regulations noted that applicants for subsidies or rice gruel were to be questioned. If they could not support school-age children, they had to be questioned about household registration, age, and recent financial situation. After submitting their household registration, applicants had to report on any major difficulties recently suffered in their financial situation.[57] As indicated at least by coverage in the *Southeast Daily,* winter-clothing drives were major undertakings, with local organizational meetings beginning in mid-September.[58] In clothing campaigns in 1942 to 1944, the government specified certain groups as recipients for different sums of money doled out: "refugees," "bitterly poor refugees," "students in war zones," "students and youths," and "the poor."[59] We are not told how relief givers differentiated among "refugees," "bitterly poor refugees," and "the poor": in name, they seem largely indistinguishable.

For all the details of the winter-clothing drives—the meetings, regulations, the sending out details of what was needed (going as far as specifying clothes only in blues and grays), and the hundreds of thousands of yuan from the government for the drive amid a spiraling inflation—it is hard to tell exactly how much was accomplished. The 2.45 million yuan that the government spent for winter clothing from December 1938 to December 1942 bought only 1,609 cotton-padded waistcoats, 3,050 cotton-padded suits, 70 oversized padded suits, 12 lined suits, 136 blue and white cloths (whose purpose was not noted), and 363 padded clothes for infants. In January 1942, the provincial government requisitioned the Zhiying mill to make 1,900 padded suits to be sent to nine counties in western Zhejiang and sent the mill 20,000 yuan to do the job, only about 10.5 yuan per suit.[60] On its face, the almost 2.5 million from the government bought far less. If one combines all the items purchased (mixing different types of clothing together—an unsatisfactory approach, since obviously the infant clothes did not cost the same to make as did adult clothes, yet the combined sum is perhaps instructive nevertheless), 5,240 items were produced. That would have meant they were produced for an average 467.6 yuan apiece, clearly outrageously higher than products of the Zhiying mill. There is no immediate explanation other than perhaps corruption: in the fifth meeting of the Jinhua relief committee, a decision was pointedly made that if any corruption was discovered, the guilty person on the committee would be fined and punished.[61] Even with the legitimacy of the government resting in part on such relief activities, it apparently could not control corruption that undercut the relief refugees had to depend on.

One other area of relief—public health services—was a drop in the bucket in relieving physical suffering. Refugees spent long hours on the road, often with little food to sustain them, and thus rendered themselves less resistant to diseases. Epidemics took staggering tolls: a cholera epidemic in Shaoxing in 1940 sickened 5,674 people, of whom 1,321 died, a mortality rate of almost 25 percent.[62] Epidemics spread wherever refugees traveled and resettled: dysentery, encephalitis, typhoid fever, and malaria. Bubonic plague was spread by bacteriological warfare, when Japanese bombers dropped plague-infected fleas on a half dozen Zhejiang cities from 1940 on. Refugees from cities the Japanese "bombed" in this way carried the deadly disease to locals in surrounding areas. In addition, plague was endemic in parts of northern Fujian and was easily spread by infected Fujianese refugees traveling into southern Zhejiang, where, from May 1942 to the end of the war, provincial government offices were scattered in different sites throughout these counties. At the root of epidemics in most remote counties to which many refugees fled was the lack of knowledge of the importance of sanitation. Public health staffs, if they existed at all (and they can be documented only in Yongkang and Yunhe counties, which served as sites for the provincial government in exile), had not been trained sufficiently to manage crisis situations that developed.[63]

Nongovernmental Refugee Relief Agencies

When a refugee registered at a reception center, a crucial question was his or her native place; in a powerful sense, in the refugee experience basic identity came to be territorialized. It should not then be surprising that native place organizations *(tongxianghui)* were generally an important reality for refugees. This is especially clear in relation to Zhejiang native place associations in Shanghai. After the beginning of the Japanese campaign in the Lower Yangzi region, the Ningbo native place association in Shanghai organized a disaster relief committee to manage first aid, refugee reception, and (most relevant for surveying Zhejiang localities) repatriation.[64] It took three months to rent twenty ambulances, to establish fourteen reception centers, and to rent four boats to repatriate 200,000 people of Ningbo. In addition, the native place association subsidized more than 82,000 Ningbo natives who lacked money to flee as refugees, and the association contributed to emergency medical aid for 2,500 Ningbo natives. After Shanghai fell, the Ningbo native place association continued its repatriation efforts, returning 3,535 to Ningbo from August 1942 to September 1944. The seven-county Shaoxing native place association in Shanghai was less successful in its repatriation efforts. It originally set out to return Shaoxing natives back in batches of two hundred in boats that it rented. But military crises and expenses delayed the plan and only 54 were sent back through this organization in the first year.

In February 1938, all Zhejiang native place organizations in Shanghai joined to form the Zhejiang Refugee Relief Society, headed by Qu Yingguang, who had served as governor of the province from 1912 to 1916. It ultimately became an arm of the International Red Cross. As such, the society sent representatives to each Red Cross organization in Zhejiang, to provide for emergency relief and to help in establishing reception centers. The society distributed thirty thousand quinine tablets to twenty-six provincial orphanages in October 1943. It also was active in matters of provisioning—purchasing, for example, three thousand piculs of rice to carry to and distribute in the counties of Fenghua and Shangyu in the Ningbo-Shaoxing area. As another example of the relief work of native place associations, in April 1938 the Jiaxing Native Place Association Service Society, which had been organized in Jinhua, established a free elementary school for refugee children from the Jiaxing area.[65]

Religious bodies—Buddhist, Daoist, and Christian—all helped in refugee resettlement and relief. Beginning in mid-August 1937, several thousand refugees streamed into Hangzhou every day from Shanghai and its environs. All Buddhist bodies in the city organized reception centers at several schools and hotels, offering individuals a bed and two meals each day; the centers also provided expenses for those refugees wanting to return home.[66] In and around Hangzhou, Christian pastors set up reception centers at thirteen sites that functioned as well as protection-from-the-cold centers and soup kitchens. In a little over two months, these centers served over seventeen thousand refugees; but they then had to close because they had exhausted their money.[67] Branches of the Red Cross provided some relief in both occupied and nonoccupied areas.[68]

In June 1940 in the central Zhejiang county seat of Tangxi, the branch of a Christian relief agency opened a textile mill for refugees on the grounds of an old temple. The work space was a large thatched-roof house, where the air and light were good for workers as they spun and weaved. Eventually, the complex supported fifty-two refugees from several counties in Jiangsu and from Hangzhou and Shaoxing. Refugee ages at the mill ran the gamut from infancy to sixty-eight. During an eight-hour workday, there was a resting time after lunch, during which workers listened to Christian proselytizers, who also taught the refugees Chinese characters and songs. The greatest problem for the mill was providing food for refugees. The goal in early 1941 was to provide three meals per day, to serve pork once a week, and to allocate to each person half a kilogram of rice per day. The reporter notably asserted in his account, "This is mostly idle talk." He continued, "But the refugees see the intent and share the weal and woe. The promise helps them forget their past difficulties."[69] Such nongovernmental refugee assistance was the exception, as we have seen; it is easy to understand why this project received enthusiastic support from the county party and government and from leaders of all public organizations.

Modeled on the Red Cross was the Red Swastika Society. Founded in the 1920s as a voluntary benevolent association, it chose as its insignia the Buddhist swastika, a symbol of moral duty. Prasenjit Duara has denoted the organization a "redemptive society": its ideological underpinning divided civilization into East and West, with the cultural hallmarks of the West being science and material culture and that of East Asian civilization being "hope for the spiritual and moral regeneration of the world."[70] The society appealed to elites, especially to "tradition-oriented intellectuals [who] felt burdened in the wake of May Fourth."[71] In terms of relief, the Red Swastika Society began to prepare in 1936 for getting in place structures for relief in southeastern China. When the Japanese took Nanjing, the Red Swastika Society was the network by which they recruited collaborators; its head, Tao Xisan, led the six-man collaborationist Self-Government Committee, two members of which were also Red Swastika members, as were three (of five) on an advisory panel.[72] Early on in the war, the organization became particularly known for its burial of unclaimed corpses, a task, unfortunately, that was a crisis situation on the streets of Nanjing.

As war broke out, the organization's headquarters in Shanghai sent a relief team *(jiujidui)* to Zhejiang to handle organizing local branches. This team moved west with the fighting, establishing branches in many counties. In February 1938, the Red Swastika Society joined the Zhejiang Refugee Relief Society. In the city of Jiaxing in mid-August 1937, the Red Swastika Society established ten reception centers in and around the city and a temporary hospital as well.[73] From August 12 through December 24, the Jiaxing reception centers received and dispatched some sixty thousand, each day hiring boats to return refugees to their homes in Suzhou and Wujiang. The goal of most localities was to serve only as a temporary site for refugees and then to get them out, either to flee further or to be returned home if it was not in a war zone or occupied territory.

In Wuxing, west of Jiaxing, the main refugee reception center was located in a city temple. It was run by the Peace Maintenance Committee, the collaborationist forerunner of the Self-Government Committee; it was supported by the Red Swastika Society, in a duplication of the pattern that was followed in Nanjing.[74] Thus, at least at Wuxing, refugee relief was bound up with collaboration with the Japanese. Though this link is not specifically made in sources pertaining to the other cities of northern Zhejiang, the fact that the society's relief team was the main organizer of relief in these sites would tend to suggest that the Red Swastika Society believed their goal of relief could best be achieved by working with the Japanese. If the working relationship between the society and the Japanese was as visibly close and open as in Nanjing and Wuxing, one wonders if refugees, who were fleeing from the Japanese, had any reactions to the cozy relations between the enemy, who had caused them to need relief, and their relief givers.

The Red Swastika Society's refugee relief role in Hangzhou was imposing. It had over twenty thousand yuan for the development of its reception centers, relief itself, medical aid, and repatriation, and it had over ten thousand piculs of rice on hand. The society provided relief assistance to those without money, who "ate in the wind and slept in the dew" (that is, endured the hardships of an arduous journey). Up to Hangzhou's fall on December 24, the society's reception centers received over 70,000 refugees; in addition, travel allocations were given out to 309,256 people, and the society oversaw 1,679 burials. The society's temporary hospital examined an average of over 100 per day. For about six weeks after Hangzhou fell, the number of refugees passing through the city totaled roughly 2,700 per day, mostly women, children, and the elderly and weak.

Once Hangzhou was occupied and the flood of refugees crossed the Qiantang River, "all roads led to Shaoxing," which quickly filled with over two hundred thousand people.[75] Shaoxing shared with Hangzhou, Jiaxing, and Wuxing the Red Swastika Society's scope of relief for refugees. Refugees in Shaoxing reception centers reportedly had the luxury of three meals per day and received free clothes if they were in dire need. The ill could be treated at an American hospital, the Fukang; and a clinic for refugee medical examination was headed by a Western doctor. In Shaoxing the Red Swastika Society established an elementary school for refugee children, whose flight had naturally forced them to leave their former schools; teachers at the refugee elementary were members of the society. The society also paid refugee women to sew cloth trousers. Even relatively out-of-the-way counties like Shangyu (a part of former Shaoxing prefecture) received tens of thousands of refugees, with the Red Swastika Society providing the bulk of relief.

Heavy Japanese bombing in central Zhejiang in the counties of Jiande, Tonglu, Lanxi, Yongkang, and Jinhua created additional refugees, who joined those coming from the war zones. The Red Swastika Society sent three men to administer relief in the area. In Tonglu over five hundred homes had been destroyed, forcing out into refugee status at least 1,000 people, who were joined by some 400 refugees from the Lower Yangzi region, all begging for food along the road. With the advice of the society's representatives, the county received almost twenty-five hundred yuan as emergency assistance. The success that the Tonglu society had in lobbying the local government for more relief aid is noteworthy; the government was certainly aware that without the Red Swastika Society its own load would have been much heavier. Jinhua and Yongkang counties each received more than 2,000 refugees; in each county the Red Swastika Society established a kindergarten for refugee children, provided rations and medical care, and offered extra cash for assistance. On the whole, the contributions of the Red Swastika Society were extremely important. Refugees who were received and spent some time at society-sponsored centers totaled 249,550, and the society gave travel money to

772,444 refugees.[76] The following table reveals more details about the assistance provided by the Red Swastika Society to refugees at various sites in Zhejiang.

At least as refugee relief is described by William Rowe in nineteenth-century Hankou, the repertoire of refugee help remained much the same during the Sino-Japanese war in Zhejiang: "dispensations of cash or grain, dumping of grain reserves on the market or their sale at below-market prices, activation of gruel kitchens, [and] intensification of the normal range of services provided by benevolent halls."[77] In Zhejiang the Red Swastika Society and the native place associations took the place of benevolent halls. In one more way, attitudes during the war toward refugees seem to reflect attitudes of nineteenth-century Hankou: the desire of, even an obsession with, "getting those unwelcome visitors back out of the city as quickly as possible."[78]

One striking difference between twentieth-century and earlier reaction to refugees is the apparent decline of the private philanthropic spirit that Rowe noted had emerged among the scholar-gentry since the Ming dynasty. Rowe, however, did see cycles of different approaches: "the pattern . . . of a upsurge in private social initiative during the seventeenth

Table 2.1 Refugee Assistance Provided by the Red Swastika Society Per County

County	Refugees received at centers	Refugees receiving money to return home	Refugees receiving medical treatment	Disbursements in yuan
Jiaxing	19,897	98,514	4,571	15,852.0
Wuxing	4,188	16,719	5,641	8,451.4
Hangzhou	108,911	309,256	9,973	63,245.3
Shaoxing	7,459	7,038	3,385	17,361.8
Shangyu	8,136	26,322	4,518	9,554.7
Siming	3,859	217,595	5,515	19,891.3
Xiaoshan	Those received and those receiving money to return home totaled over 60,000			
Zhenhai	Those received and those receiving money to return home totaled over 60,000			
Total	249,550	772,444	33,603	134,356.5

Source: Zhang Genfu, *Kangzhan shiqi Zhejiang sheng renkou qianyi yu shehui yingxiang* [Population movement and its social impact in Zhejiang Province during the Resistance War] (Shanghai: Sanlian shudian, 2001), pp. 110.

century, followed by a more effective state assumption of these duties, and a corresponding decline of local societal self-help during the 'high [Qing],' followed again by a resurgence of social initiative in the nine-teenth century."[79] Though elites in the war years participated in organi-zations like the Red Swastika Society, Governor Huang Shaohong's observations that Chinese were negative about individual private charity and that "Chinese relief really [was] the idea of relief, not relief itself" seem to reflect more accurately individual attitudes toward refugees. These attitudes bring to mind Fei Xiaotong's depiction of "selfishness" in Chinese society.[80] Perhaps, since Huang and Fei both wrote in the 1940s, a new cycle of attitudes toward relief had been produced by a decline in the values of Confucian morality, the chaotic context of war and (into the 1930s in places) warlords, and the financial crisis wrought by the Great Depression and by the malignant inflation of the period.

Though it can be said that refugee relief programs helped a large group of hungry, cold, poor refugees, that it protected them and un-doubtedly reduced wartime deaths, in the end relief was limited. Out of 5 million long-distance refugees in the province during the war, gov-ernment programs reached about 1.5 million, while native place asso-ciations and the Red Swastika Society and other religious groups helped about 1 million; thus about 50 percent of the refugees received relief in some fashion. The greatest number of refugees moved from place to place, finding a means of livelihood on their own. Assistance organiza-tions did not work together; they operated on their own with few lateral ties—overall, there seemed little coordination in the effort. The greatest amount of coordination in relief efforts and local governments came, perhaps ironically, in the collaborationist efforts of the Red Swastika Society in northern Zhejiang.

As we have seen, the flight of refugees came generally in three waves: with Japan's seizure of northern Zhejiang (Zhexi) in late 1937 to early 1938, with the fall of Ningbo and Shaoxing in spring 1941, and with Japan's Zhe-Gan campaign in spring and summer 1942. Most relief assistance came during the first wave of refugees. After that flurry of relief aid, the level of refugee assistance declined for three reasons. First, and most impor-tant, after the first wave, relief givers' money and materials were almost completely exhausted. The Red Swastika Society and other nongovern-mental organizations as well as the government experienced great financial difficulties—some nongovernmental organizations indeed ceased to exist. Second, before the Ning-Shao campaign, the area south of Hangzhou Bay had been quite stable. During that stable period, a number of relief organs in that area had simply stopped functioning and were not restored later. Finally, as the early defense phase of the war turned into a protracted war, people who had not fled before sometimes chose to flee when their area was experiencing renewed fighting. In other words, they became refugees at a time other than during the three waves, when organizations were no longer mobilized to dispense relief. It was such existential realities, coupled with the psychological and cultural issues faced by refugees and their host communities, that created much refugee suffering.

THREE

→←

Veering into the Ravine

A RENOWNED GRAPHIC ARTIST, cartoonist, and essayist, Feng Zikai (1898–1975) hailed from the town of Shimenwan in Zhejiang's Tongxiang County on the north shore of Hangzhou Bay. In his ancestral past, there were many men who had held civil service examination degrees. His father, Feng Huang, had passed the provincial civil service examination in 1902, but when the examination was permanently abolished in 1905 in favor of a modern school system, Zikai's father's hope of taking the highest-level examination was dashed. Huang tutored Zikai. During those days Zikai slowly became obsessed with painting, much to his father's chagrin. In 1914, he went to Hangzhou to attend the Zhejiang Provincial First Normal College, where he studied with Li Shutong, an artist, a musician, and a Buddhist monk. After graduation in 1919, Feng Zikai married Xu Limin, the daughter of a prominent family in Chongde County, very near Shimenwan. In 1920 he joined others in opening in Shanghai a school that dealt with Western art, and in 1921 he spent ten months studying oil painting in Japan.

When he returned to China, Feng taught at several schools in Zhejiang and Jiangsu provinces, moving in 1924 to Shanghai, a city whose coldness and social verticality made him claustrophobic. He was drawn back to Shimenwan, his ancestral family home for some three hundred years (see Map 4); there he felt social relationships were more open and friendlier than in Shanghai. In 1933, he designed and had constructed in Shimenwan a spacious two-story home, Yuanyuan Hall; it became his and his family's haven for almost the next five years—becoming idealized in memory and epitomizing his rootedness in native place: "In the summer, the bright cherries and the green banana leaves created a brilliant contrast, while hinting to all of the ultimate truth of impermanence. The delicate shade of the lush grapevine curling over the trellis reflected into the house and tinged everything and everyone with a pale green light, adding a painterly sheen to our lives. Through the slats of the bamboo screens over the windows the movement of people cast fleeting shadows, while the sound of laughter and chatter from the swing reached us inside. . . . I will never forget those joy-filled times."[1] What seems striking in this passage of domestic happiness and contentment is the rather jarring mention of "the ultimate truth of impermanence" and the ambivalent meaning of "people cast fleeting shadows." The note of melancholy is understandable, however, when we see that Feng wrote this essay while he and his family were refugees in Guangxi Province in August 1939, at a time when his world had been turned upside down and Yuanyuan Hall had been destroyed by Japanese bombs.

The Coming of War

For Feng, the nightmare began on August 13, 1937, with the Japanese air raid on the provincial capital of Hangzhou, some thirty miles from Yuanyuan Hall, where Feng was at the time with his family.[2] For several years Feng had rented a home in Hangzhou, which he called his "temporary palace" (xinglu), to be near his children at boarding school and to be refreshed by the beauty of West Lake. In the wake of the bombing attack, Feng sent someone to cancel the rental of the temporary palace and to bring his books and other items back to Shimenwan.

The possibility of flight away from native place for Feng and his family was first raised in the early days of the military campaign. He received letters from friends in the central city of Hankou and in Sichuan Province, who said that Zhejiang was too close to the action, that war was sure to spread, and that Feng and his family should move into the interior. Feng thought that such a decision seemed far too premature. The weeks that followed saw a flood of refugees traveling on trains, boats, and feet into northern Zhejiang from Shanghai, Songjiang, and other Jiangnan cities. The residents of Shimenwan did not see that many, since it was close to neither the main Shanghai–Hangzhou rail line nor the major highway.

That distance had led to some sense of immunity against a Japanese attack on the town. In conversations on street corners and in alleyways, townspeople rationalized why they were safe and did not have to concern themselves with any defensive, protective measures. One townsman opined that the relatively insignificant quality of the place would leave it out of Japan's plans: "Bombs are expensive. Even if the town asked the Japanese to come bomb, they wouldn't be willing to come." Another based his rationalization on some prior military experience: "After they attack Songjiang and Jiaxing, they'll surely go north to use the Shanghai–Nanjing highway to attack Nanjing. They won't attack south of Jiaxing. Hangzhou is only a tourist site and is of no military importance. Therefore, we don't need to worry in this place." That being said, he did not offer an explanation for the August 13 bombing attack on Hangzhou. Nor did another resident who also linked Hangzhou to Shimenwan and who found solace in Hangzhou's status as a Buddhist pilgrimage site: "Every year Hangzhou has unlimited capacity for incense burned and candles lit. West Lake is at base completely ashes of incense. This Buddhist area absolutely cannot meet with disaster. And so long as Hangzhou has no trouble, we won't either." And on and on the conversations went, some offering plausible likelihoods, others, rather flimsy possibilities— but all self-assuring and ultimately self-deluding. In times of approaching war, the easiest way out, it seemed, was talk.

When the possibility of flight crossed his mind, Feng framed the option in notably Chinese social-cultural terms and clearly spelled out, in "Bearing the Tumult," the crucial obstacle to flight in the Chinese context. "Our family," he said, "has lived in Shimenwan for many generations. We have very many relatives, friends, and acquaintances." If war came, he suggested, the family could take refuge in nearby settings and then return, the key being that there would continue to be close contact with relatives and social connections. That contact among members of the same social group would be crucial for keeping one another informed about the latest situations, news, and rumors and for consoling one another. A longer flight completely out of the area would mean that Feng and his family would go into totally new localities, where the residents there would console each other, but the Fengs, essentially alone, would have only themselves. He ended these thoughts with "Alas!" Becoming a refugee, in Feng's words, was to live "in a sea of bitterness."[3] It was leaving the all-important social world that gave the individual and the family groundedness—in a word, identity.

On October 29, Feng became forty *sui*, thirty-nine in the Western counting of age. Despite the likely imminence of war and the increasingly likely defeat of Chinese forces in Shanghai and Songjiang—the latter a mere thirty-five miles from Shimenwan—family, relatives, and friends flocked to Yuanyuan Hall to celebrate with Feng; the house was filled. Guests feasted on, among other things, birthday noodles, cake, and peaches. The bad news of the day came from guests who traveled from Shanghai. One had been aboard the train where refugees atop the cars had slid off and were killed. Another, fearful of taking the train because of the much-talked-about crush, came by water transport; he reported that Shanghai's Chinese city had become a sea of fire in the wake of the Japanese attacks, and he noted that for too many refugees there would be no home to return to.

This was the last large gathering of family and friends at Yuanyuan Hall. One week after the birthday celebration, on November 6, the event that the town's residents had argued was impossible occurred: Japanese planes bombed Shimenwan. The first bombs hit near an elementary school where two of Feng's children were studying; neither was injured, but on that day over thirty townspeople were killed. Feng's younger sister and her husband, Jiang Maoqun, lived in a village little more than a mile from Shimenwan. Having heard the bomb explosions, Jiang rowed into town to pick up Feng and his family—at that time they had six children and were caring for a young niece. They took clothes and other necessities to the village, arriving after dark in a heavy rain. The Feng entourage included Feng's mother-in-law, who was visiting at the time and who, through force of circumstance, joined the family in their efforts to seek a safe refuge.

Feng did not believe at this point that anything beyond this short flight would be necessary. In his own mind, he had decided on a trigger event that would put them into flight more or less automatically. If the city of Jiaxing, twenty miles away, fell, then the Fengs would flee; if it did not, they would stay put. Most of the Shimenwan residents had joined the Fengs in fleeing to neighboring villages, where people were close enough to their homes to return for other items and to check on their homes' status. The Fengs stayed in the village fifteen days, traveling back to Yuanyuan Hall several times at night to retrieve other items. Walking along the deserted streets of the town deep into the night, Feng wrote that he was overwhelmed by memories of the happy times there. The stress of making conditional plans to flee farther was great. He had to continually remind himself that the family had to wield great restraint in what they could take with them. But in his planning, perhaps evidence of his being an absent-minded intellectual, he overlooked thinking about financial support along the way. Apart from several banknotes, unusable on the road, he had only several dozen yuan. When he spoke to the family about the situation, one son said that the children had some. Unbeknownst to Feng, over the years the children had saved the birthday money that he had given them in red packets—now totaling over four hundred yuan, with several dozen more in coins. They fortunately then had enough money to leave.

On November 21, a clerk at a town shop told Feng that the county seat of Tongxiang, about seven miles away, had been bombed by the Japanese and was burning. And then it hit Feng. His precondition for leaving had been the fall of Jiaxing. But the Japanese had not attacked Jiaxing directly: they had come from the north and were circling around, taking a string of towns, Puyuan, Tongxiang, and Shimenwan, with the goal of surrounding Jiaxing. In his thinking about the trigger for the flight, Feng mused, who would have known that Shimenwan would fall before Jiaxing? His was the classic human problem of ascribing to the Other actions that seemed rational to himself but which did not consider the possibility that the worldview and strategies of the Other might be completely different from his own.

Before noon the Fengs bade good-bye to the villagers and to his sister and brother-in-law, with whom they had lived for half a month, and to other relatives who got the word that the Fengs were leaving. They ate a quick lunch and got on the boat, which arrived right at noon. Feng later wrote that at the time he felt like his heart was being stabbed, but for the children's sake he had to put on a strong face. Urging his relatives to dig a bomb shelter, the Fengs left Shimenwan: he wrote plaintively that he did not know when they would return.

Where to Go?

For all the raw angst and reality of leaving security and social connections, Feng as an artist and intellectual apparently felt compelled to place the flight in a larger cultural perspective: "The home of Jiangnan culture ... was [now] choked by sulphurous gunpowder fumes and became suffused with the stench of violence and murder. The fragrant atmosphere of books and art had long been dispelled, and without this air to nourish us we could no longer survive there. We now set out, a family of ten, accompanied by four friends from our town."[4] This seems frankly an elitist rationalization and cover for the fear that inspired flight and perhaps for the desire not to be under Japan's control. The Fengs got out just in time: Japanese troops entered Shimenwan two days later.

Memory and history are strange bedfellows. How one remembers the past—or forgets the past—is shaped by numerous psychosocial forces. The essays in which Feng discusses his experience as a refugee were written roughly two years after the events, a relatively short time, to be sure, compared with the twenty to forty years of some of the memories in other survivors' writings. A notable thing about Feng's essays focusing on his flight is what appears to be remarkable precision: the completion of essays is dated, and Feng provides the days and often the times of day when certain things occurred. Yet there are contradictions and flat-out errors in these matters. Both "Leaving Yuanyuan Hall" and "Bearing the Tumult of War in Tonglu County" state precisely that the Fengs left the village on their flight at 1 P.M. on November 21. But just one page earlier, in "Bearing the Tumult," Feng asserted that they set out "one day at dawn." Could this have been metaphorical, suggesting the flight as the dawn of a new kind of day? The numbers in the entourage were also quite variable. At the beginning of "Bearing the Tumult," Feng claimed that the travelers numbered fourteen, but a page later the number shrinks to twelve—ten family members; a Feng lineage member, Pingyu; and a store friend, Zhang Gui. They would add a three-year-old boy relative in a stop at Yuehong Village. Perhaps Feng's "fourteen" reflected the number of travelers on the majority of the trip.[5]

Even in dating the "Leaving Yuanyuan Hall" piece, there was an apparent error. Feng records the essay's completion in Si'en, Guangxi, on August 6, 1939; but the editor noted that Feng did not get to Si'en until

August 18 and questions whether Feng meant September instead. These specific details can be seen as relatively unimportant, but we must be aware that the pliability of memory was always a major factor in Feng's (or anyone else's) depiction of what had actually transpired. Memory of events that passed in the midst of the continual existential challenges that Feng faced on the flight was, certainly as more time passed, increasingly murky. That is why when reading Feng's narratives, and all the refugee accounts, we take them with more than a grain (perhaps a pound or even a ton) of salt; that is why what is key in these memoirs is likely the descriptions of those most dramatic developments, which would have been etched most deeply into memory.

Deeply rooted in Shimenwan, Feng had long before the Japanese invasions planned a destination in case the situation propelled him to leave. Feng's family had come to Shimenwan at the end of the Ming dynasty from his lineage home in Feng Village in Tangxi County, about 125 miles southwest of Shimenwan. Feng rhetorically asked, "How could we forget our own origin and development?" When he was in Tokyo in the early 1920s, he had met Feng Hui'en from his Tangxi lineage; they had worked out their ancestral roots and ties. Although Feng had never been to Tangxi, he had idealized what he imagined as its bucolic prosperity and peace: if forced to flee, Tangxi would be the place to go, even if Hui'en was the only person he knew there. As Geremie Barmé has noted, Feng "thought of this proffered homeland as if it were a Peach Blossom Valley, the mythical rural utopia described by the fourth-poet Tao Yuanming": "It would certainly have," in Feng's words, "rich fields and pleasing ponds, luxurious with mulberry and bamboo. There, too, surely the elderly and children would wear their hair loose, and live content and peaceful lives."[6]

But, now when the time came, Zikai remembered that he had seen Hui-en in Shanghai a few months earlier and thought it unlikely that he would currently be in Tangxi: "Now we don't likely have anyone to introduce us to Feng Village: do we rashly go there for shelter anyway?" Like his reason for not wanting the life of a refugee at all, his biggest concern about possible life in Tangxi was social, a fear that he and his family "couldn't participate in the life of the village." Despite his being a member of the lineage, he would really be an outsider in a culture that functioned smoothly only for insiders: that was again the crux of the tragedy of becoming a refugee. So he gave up the plan to travel to his old lineage home.

Shortly before he and his family left Shimenwan, Feng received a letter from an old teacher, Ma Yifu, a reclusive philosopher, inviting them to Tonglu County, where he was residing. Tonglu, on the Fuchun River, was only seventy-five miles from Shimenwan (see Tonglu on Map 2); its relative proximity and the warmth of Ma's letter made Tonglu their destination. The size and makeup of the refugee group made traveling unwieldy—twelve to fourteen or even sixteen people, including small children, a seventy-two-year-old, and Feng's pregnant wife. They traveled on a boat that was not a traditional passenger boat, most of which had been already commandeered by the Chinese military. Feng faced the continual fear of being stopped by the military and having their boat commandeered on the spot, leaving the Feng travelers without any means to proceed.

From Shimenwan to Hangzhou

In a small town Feng saw from the boat two acquaintances at a small tea shop on the riverbank, one who had been his fellow student *(tongxue),* an important connection in the Chinese social world. The other, from Shimenwan, had fled to this town after Shimenwan's first bombing. Feng was faced with a decision of whether to call out to them; his description of that moment captures much of the "now what do I do?" in this totally new world of flight into the unknown: "I very much thought of calling to them. However, if it was possible to speak with them, I would have had to get off the boat and then part with them in this sea of bitterness. In the end I didn't call them. Because they both had parents, wives, and children, their lives were rooted here—and that would require stopping our boat to pick up their families. Therefore, I didn't call them and avoided a situation where there would have been useless melancholy."[7] Feng thought that most of the residents of Shimenwan were like those two—so rooted in their locality that they would not consider fleeing. He noted that those who were brave or desperate enough "to eke out their existence anywhere" were relatively few; most people did not choose to flee. Those who braced themselves to stay continually warned against fleeing: "You should resign yourselves to fate" and "If you flee, you will also starve and die."

The Feng family reached their first-day destination at dusk, Yuehong Village, from which their boat had originated. They were to have dinner and rest at the home of the younger sister of Feng's youngest uncle's wife; it was the sister's husband who had arranged for the sending of the boat. Though the life of these hosts was fairly comfortable, Feng could detect changes that the proximity of war had brought: The village had heard, he asserted, "the sound of the wind and the cry of cranes" (that is, the fleeing army's suspicion of danger at the slightest sound). People they passed on the stone wharf, slick with moisture from the heavy mist, looked extremely worried, their eyes carrying the look of a thief, stealthily coming and going. Even family members in whose home the Fengs stayed spoke little, their eyes glancing furtively amid worried looks. This host family insisted that Feng take their three-year-old grandson along as a refugee. "There is no other choice," they said. "Being a refugee will only be temporary . . . [but] there are three unfilial things and to have no descendants is the worst."[8] To protect the lineage, Feng's relatives were not afraid of staying in their dangerous place, but they wanted their grandson to be taken to a more peaceful area. One wonders how realistically the grandparents saw the hazards and uncertainties of being a refugee. The immediate danger seemed to have obscured their recognition of the possibility of deadly situations down the road. This turn of events made Feng somber, even sorrowful. The three-year-old's father stitched money in the boy's cotton-padded coat at his neck, shoulder, and sleeves.

The Fengs rose in the middle of the night, had a meal, and walked to the boat—fifteen people with seventeen or eighteen pieces of luggage. Knowing that the journey ahead would be onerous, they had tried to keep baggage light. Each person took only one change of winter clothes, bedclothes, and daily use items: toothbrush, comb, and hot-water container. All the children (rather difficult to believe under the circumstances) brought books to study English and math. Feng brought only a few selected books, but did bring a pocket watch, a cigarette case and pack, a money pouch, a compass, a stone chop, and a miniature copy of a Buddhist sutra carved on ivory.

Next morning they had already gotten to Xinshi (about eight miles from Shimenwan). The weather was clear. In the distance they could hear rumbling sounds—not thunder, but big guns. Using the compass, Feng could tell that the sounds were coming from the north. Feng and the other adults were suspicious that Tongxiang and Puyuan had come under attack and were afraid that the sounds would frighten the young and old; so they said nothing, keeping this fear in their hearts. But their silence did not matter, for everyone on board was frightened. Suddenly a squadron of enemy planes came into view, dropping bombs. If the planes continued in their direction, the Feng boat could clearly have become a target. Rumors had spread and were later corroborated that during the initial evacuation from Shimenwan, enemy planes had bombed two refugee boats on the Grand Canal, killing two boat trackers and injuring many aboard. Feng did not want to be caught like that on this cloudless day on the Grand Canal.

It was between eight and nine in the morning when their boat pulled up under a big tree on the bank and stopped. Nearby was a dilapidated nunnery, White Cloud Convent. The refugees walked there. Piled on a table was raw taro and *nai* (a kind of root vegetable). They asked a woman there to cook it for them and gave her money for the cooking fire and the food. She agreed and moved some stools for them onto the veranda, where she indicated they could eat. The room faced south and the rays of the sun were warm: Feng wrote that they felt temporarily happy and almost forgot they were homeless refugees. They ate their fill. After the women and children changed clothes and put on mufflers, they walked out under the trees next to the canal to relax. It was, Feng suggested, almost like walking along West Lake. Indeed, it seemed a respite from the unnerving reality of traveling in a war zone.

And yet, during this relaxing moment of relief, Feng had a premonition that something bad was about to happen. Feng told the women to return to the boat to put away the clothes that they had changed from: they had two rather new suitcases hidden in the boat's cabin. Suddenly there appeared four middle-aged men dressed in black. They went into the nunnery, sat down and riveted their eyes on the Feng entourage, occasionally whispering among themselves. The sun was high. The rumble from the north kept up. Now a steady stream of Chinese soldiers was entering the nunnery. Suddenly there sounded what seemed like an approaching plane; everyone was frightened and looked for places to hide. But the sound turned out to have been a steamboat and not a plane. At this point Feng didn't dare get on the boat as the four men in black stood about a dozen steps from the nunnery beside a tree and were continuing to stare. He wrote that he really could not explain his apprehension; but that because of his almost palpable fear, he even hesitated to look at them. Like most refugees, Feng suffered continual paranoia: in a world away from one's social connections, everyone was a potential threat. It followed that one could not relax one's guard—that's what made the nunnery meal such a respite. Once the men dressed in black appeared, Feng endowed them in his mind with some sort of devious malevolence. In that jittery context, the sound of the steamboat automatically was translated into that of an enemy plane. In Feng's text from which these passages are taken, he uses the word "suddenly" twice in five sentences, a word ("happening or coming unexpectedly") that again reveals the state of mind of the refugee, as the potential victim of forces that he could not control and which might in an instant change the trajectory of his life.

At about 2:30 P.M. the boatman called everyone to get on the boat. There is no indication why the stop had lasted five to six hours or more when haste should have obviously been a crucial goal. Feng had made the boatman aware of his suspicion of the men in black, who watched the Feng party board the boat; Feng's relative, Pingyu, standing nearest the men, shouted, "On to Xinshi Town!" to throw the men off the trail, if they were indeed up to something. The Feng boat had just come from Xinshi and was actually headed toward Hangzhou. At this point Feng's paranoic thoughts continued:

> I thought, as the men continued to watch us, that they could certainly see through Pingyu's ruse. I was deeply afraid that Pingyu was going to outsmart himself. After I boarded the boat, my apprehensions only increased. If they took a small boat to chase after us, they wouldn't even have to have handguns to board our boat and take our money. We all had the fear of veering into a ravine. To make things even worse, there were still a number of hours of daylight on this very sunny day—where enemy planes could still bomb us: yet another kind of fear.[9]

The prosperous town of Tangxi was dead ahead. During the war it would be sacked by the Japanese, who burned over a hundred houses and the same number of shops; all its rich merchants would flee as refugees, leaving the masses to the hands of the Japanese.[10] As the boat neared Tangxi, the Feng party had a different kind—and perhaps more realistic—scare: a boat filled with uniformed Chinese soldiers heading toward it. As the two boats passed, a soldier on board shouted to Zhang Gui, who had been sitting near Feng, "Where are the Japanese devils?" Zhang did not hear him. So the soldier repeated the question. Zhang still did not hear him but answered, "I don't know." As the two boats drew farther away from each other, there was no more to the encounter. It seems apparent that Feng included this rather prosaic incident as an indicator of his fear and as a harbinger of a more dangerous encounter.

After recounting the episode, Feng put up a stiff upper lip regarding the Japanese. He suggested that although the continual roaring of the bombing likely meant that the Japanese had already taken Tongxiang and Puyuan, he would not let himself accept it. He felt personally that he would never come face to face with the Japanese, and he did not prepare anyone in his party for doing so. Yet he did tell Zhang Gui that it was likely that the Japanese devils were already nearing them; Feng felt certain that the boat of soldiers who had passed was headed to the battle-front. Feng again shed light on the mind and emotions of a surviving refugee: in the midst of paranoia and fear, he was unwilling to fathom the idea he would ever have to deal with flesh-and-blood Japanese soldiers. Such a "yes, this might happen, but no, it cannot" denial revealed a strong element of escapism but also was some psychological protection against despair about the future. Feng gazed out over the waters of the Grand Canal, and he thought, "The Japanese devils use steamboats to travel up and down the canal; so our people-powered boat will likely be chased by the Japanese. Until that time, I have to maintain a cool head. The wrong action might leave the whole family at the bottom of the Grand Canal for a long sleep in the bed of the river."[11] Becoming more nervous, Feng urged the boatmen to row more quickly.

Suddenly (that word again) from the other side of the boat came a shout for them to stop the boat. It was yet another boat of soldiers, who were approaching Feng's boat much too rapidly. One of the soldiers shouted, "Seize their boat." The Feng boat proceeded as if those on board had not heard the command; in retrospect Feng thought that perhaps they had risked death by continuing. The soldiers' shouting became more vociferous. When Feng looked at them again, he saw that the soldiers had aimed their guns at his boat. The boatmen stopped rowing, but a strong wind and choppy water continued to carry the boat along. The soldiers' boat circled Feng's boat and came up alongside it. Two soldiers grabbed the awning of Feng's boat: the two boats were together in the middle of the Grand Canal. Feng assumed that the soldiers were commandeering the boat and that he and his party would be taken to the canal bank. But that was not the case. The soldiers wanted only to "borrow" a boatman. They explained that the situation at the front was critical, that they had to transport equipment and supplies as quickly as possible, saying, "Give us one man; we will have him row thirty *li* (ten miles) and then release him." They pulled a male rower (over the age of thirty) into their boat. He struggled and shouted; a soldier began beating him with a rifle butt. Feng urged the rower not to struggle, that they would wait for him at Tangxi. "Who knew," Feng wrote, "that we would never see him again?"

For, when they approached Tangxi, the stores and houses on both sides of the canal had been requisitioned by the Chinese military and turned into army barracks. Soldiers on both sides stared at the Feng boat, frightening him into believing that they would seize his boat if they had the chance; the consensus on board was that the boat could not afford to stop at Tangxi to wait for the man the soldiers had taken and that for their own safety the party had to proceed. There was a flurry of self-criticisms followed by rationalizations about leaving the man. One reasoned, "For them to say he'd row thirty *li* and then be released was just talk. Waiting for him at Tangxi would have been useless." Another suggested, "Under the circumstances, we're willing but simply unable to help the man—there's nothing we can do." Yet another, apparently a boatman, noted that if the rower went to Tangxi and did not find them, he would simply go home. But that person noted that if the soldiers did not pay him before they released him, he would go hungry on the road. Feng for his part deeply regretted not being able to wait for the man and wanted to find a way to thank the rower. After they reached Hangzhou, he urged the boatman to return to Tangxi and to pay the man double what he ordinarily received.

In the middle of the night, the boat reached the Imperial Arch Bridge on the north side of Hangzhou's city wall. This suburb was the headquarters for many of the transport companies whose boats plied the canals and creeks that crisscrossed northern Zhejiang. It was a bustling town, a port of entry for a large number of travelers and now refugees, and was known, among other things, for its large population of prostitutes. Feng's boat anchored outside the bridge. Everyone on board was hungry.

After they had eaten rice and black beans aboard the boat, another boat anchored beside them. Zhang Gui, Pingyu, Feng, and a servant went to talk to a boatman whom they recognized as Mr. Zhang, who had been a lower public functionary in Shimenwan. Feng was especially eager to hear any news from his hometown. Zhang's boat was very small, without an awning; there was nothing to block the wind and keep out the cold, and Feng reported that it was a bitterly cold night. Zhang and his passengers had to seek lodging on shore. He punctuated his words with curses and sighs; he was one who, Feng said, could not control his anger. Zhang and his passengers went onshore, and the four from Feng's party joined them to continue hearing Zhang's news. Zhang had come from Tongxiang, where his wife and children lived and where the killing and the burning now centered. Fortunately, with his small boat, he had a way of escaping. Feng described the scene as Zhang spoke: "The cold wind at midnight made the lingering sounds of his voice blow into trembles and shivers, almost like the sound of mourning."[12] They walked, mainly silently and entered an inn. The Feng party asked Zhang again about what he saw in Tongxiang. Speaking disjointedly, he said, "People killed! Fires blazing! Rapes!" The four men from the Feng boat were frightened by Zhang's report. They found the inn's old hunchbacked manager, to ask him whether there were buses running from Hangzhou to Tonglu. The manager looked at Feng with disdain, laughed, and said, "You're thinking of road vehicles? There aren't even any boats. Until the last several days now, those who hired a boat headed for Tonglu had to put down 160 yuan. Now it's 1,600 yuan!" They went back to the boat; on the way Feng warned the others not to mention to those on board what Zhang had said about the killing and the fires.

After Feng returned to the boat, he was very tense. He knew that a single boat would be hard to come by, but he feared that they could not go on if they went on foot—the young and the old in the group posed huge problems in this regard, as did their fifteen to eighteen suitcases. He encouraged all to choose the smallest pieces of luggage and to cut down on what they were carrying. What they couldn't take, they could let the boat take back to Yuehong Village, from which the Feng party could pick them up on their return. Feng's wife and another woman only reluctantly went through their things and reselected what they wanted to continue the journey with. Feng took out three books to send back on the boat: Robert Louis Stevenson's *New Arabian Nights,* an English dictionary, and an English-Japanese dictionary. That left him with only a few volumes.

Since it was already considerably past midnight, most people on the boat were asleep. But Feng could not sleep. He thought about two other books in his bundle, *A History of the Japanese Imperialistic Invasion of China* and a book of his sketches done the month before at Yuanyuan Hall, titled "Pictures of the Japanese Invasion History." He realized that having these two books along was dangerous. He thought that if by any chance the Japanese seized him tomorrow morning, searched his things, and found these books, all the people on the boat might die. At the very least, he would be shot and then the other refugee-travelers would have to go on without him: how could they cope? Suddenly, Feng was terrified. In the dark he stretched out his hand to grope for the bundle; he pulled out the book and the draft collection of his sketches, used a flashlight to verify these were what he had, and threw them overboard. Feng recorded his thoughts.

The sound of the splash was like a blow that hit me in the heart: the pain was unceasing—I had never thrown away any of my sketches. With these, I had already finished the textual criticism, the composition of the sketches, and deliberated over each one. I don't know how much of my heart's blood was amassed in the collection, but now it's completely flowing to the east. I hope it follows the current to the east and will take root at the bridge at Yuanyuan Hall, and that, on the one hand, it will keep away bombs, and, on the other, that it will banish evil spirits.[13]

The memory of Yuanyuan Hall and the thought of living there again after the refugee trauma sustained him. Sitting in the pale moonlight, at last he fell asleep. But it was fitful sleep. On the boat, cries from some of the children because of a headache or stomachache or discomfort woke him as well as other children.

From Hangzhou to Tonglu

At 5 A.M. with the sky still dark, everyone was awake. The Feng party
took the children off the boat first and then their more carefully selected
luggage onto land. Even though the group had selected them, in the
end, the cotton quilts used for making bundles still weighed two to
three catties (2.2 to 3.3 pounds). It was a huge problem, for there were
no porters around. Several soldiers were on sentry duty: they looked
ugly and ferocious, in Feng's words, "seething with murderous looks."[14]
One came up to search them, using a flashlight to check out this apparent group of refugees. His suspicious expression relaxed and disappeared
as he searched.

The group eventually found two porters. But the luggage still weighed
two piculs (about 270 pounds)—Feng thought it much too heavy. All
agreed they had to make it lighter, and they took out enough for two
more bundles that the boatmen could take back. As refugees in all areas
found, a relatively small thing like handling luggage when going by foot
was physically onerous and took far too much time, something Feng saw
as a "regret." Because the two sent-back bundles had all the silk wadding,
the refugees had none on the long trek ahead. Feng noted, "Every winter day everyone inevitably thought back to those bundles and all complained about my impulsiveness."[15] After lightening their load, the group
thought they had found a third porter, apparently someone another porter knew, but in the end, he got lost and never showed up.

The whole luggage story had a particularly unfortunate ending. When
the Japanese seized the village where the head boatman lived, they pillaged all the houses. The goods of the Fengs that had been sent for safe-
keeping were plundered. Therefore, as Feng expressed it, what they had
given to the boatman to carry back was equivalent to throwing it along
the roadside: "If we had known this earlier, when we were on the bank
at Imperial Arch Bridge, no matter what we would have put on the porters' backs, they would have had to carry them." Feng noted that the
family was still complaining about this loss two years later.

The porters of Feng and his party were carrying their luggage to the
Six Harmonies Pagoda, south of Hangzhou overlooking the Qiantang
River (see Map 3). But there were difficulties with walking the thirty-six
li (twelve miles) from Imperial Arch Bridge to the pagoda. Of the fifteen

currently in the group, all could walk except the three-year-old boy and Feng's seventy-two-year-old mother-in-law. The little boy could obviously be carried, but not the old woman. One of Feng's servants engaged Afang, a tall, robust fellow who thought he could handle the old woman. There were thus sixteen people with luggage totaling two piculs. With the first rays of the sun, they began down the winding road to the pagoda. Feng saw Hangzhou as his second native place; he had lived there a number of years, most recently two months before. The family thus knew Hangzhou well, but they almost did not recognize it. The streets, usually busy and flourishing even at this early hour of the morning, were deserted; shops along the main streets were closed. The fear and trepidation of people passed on the road was noticeable on their faces.

The Feng group walked little more than three miles when Feng's mother-in-law protested. Afang was carrying her on his back: her chest was against his backbone, and with each step the pressure on her chest was increasingly painful; for his part, the strain of her weight was making him so out of breath that he could not even speak. He said that he could not go any farther. They asked Afang just to support her with his arms as the old woman walked; but her steps were no longer than five inches each, and she could go only about ten steps in a minute. At this rate they would not reach the pagoda until the next day. Fortunately, Pingyu suggested hiring a sedan chair. We are not told how long finding one and hiring it took, but as with repacking the luggage and hiring Afang, these details took valuable time. It was, however, the solution to the problem.

After walking a bit further, they came to West Lake. Feng noted that Baochu Pagoda, north of the lake, still looked exquisite, elegant and graceful on the top of Green Mountain, and was reflected in the waters of the lake. In the past he had been moved to tears by the beauty of the lake, but this day when he saw it, he cried tears of grief. He wrote, "I see West Lake as an innocent and lovely child. It ignores the changes in its surroundings; it does not recognize the vicissitudes of life. Toward the people around it, it always has a smiling countenance, promoting the recognition of its loveliness. In this current situation, where great calamity has come, its demeanor is lovelier than ever. Its very being compels people to get past this heartbreak. That's why I cried—for the first time since we left Yuanyuan Hall." Like Yuanyuan Hall, West Lake sustained people and "[compelled] people to get past this heartbreak."

As they walked south on South Mountain Road, the air-raid warning sounded. Because some in the group walked faster than others, the group had become spread out along the road. Rather surprisingly, given the fact that many in the group were children, Feng took the attitude that "it was best for each person to protect his own life." He ran into a grove of trees, where he waited. Planes roared above and bombs exploded farther to the south; Chinese soldiers along the route said it was the bombing of the Qiantang River Bridge. They were mistaken: the bridge, an engineering marvel, was completed only in September 1937; and it was destroyed by Chinese bombs as part of a scorched-earth campaign against the Japanese, not by Japanese bombers. Fortunately none of the Feng group had been injured—since the bombing, whatever the target, took place farther on.

At about 2 P.M., roughly eight hours after they had set off to walk the twelve miles from the Imperial Arch Bridge, they came—tired and hungry—to a small teahouse at the Six Harmonies Pagoda. All the stores along the road were closed except for this teahouse. Outside it was a vendor selling *zongzi,* dumplings that are made of glutinous rice and perhaps meats or beans and wrapped in the leaves of bamboo or reeds. They ordered several bowls of tea and bought some deep-fried dumplings. Like the White Cloud Convent near Xinshi, this place was to Feng a respite, a welcomed haven on the refugee road. At the convent, he had experienced a surging suspicion of the men in black. At this teahouse, Feng wrote later, he was overwhelmed with waves of negative emotions: "fear such as [he] had never known in [his] entire life," "worry to the point of being scorched by it," and "the taste of humiliation." The process of being uprooted plus the continual challenges and dangers along the way (some of which he created in his own mind, to be sure) gave rise to emotions that could make the refugees' trek even more challenging and exhausting.

Now Feng and his group had to find a boat to continue on to Tonglu. First they tried the teahouse proprietor. Right from the start, the proprietor laughed in their faces when he heard they planned to go by boat. He told them about all the difficulties refugees had had in recent days when taking boats. He said that now there was no way to rent a boat. He said that the pedestrian bridge on the Qiantang River Bridge had been destroyed with explosive charges. (Here it seems certain that Feng's memory was mistaken, that he had telescoped events. If we can take Feng's description of the timing of what had happened since the refugees left Shimenwan, they would have reached the teahouse on the afternoon of November 23. The Qiantang River Bridge was not actually destroyed until December 22. It seems safe to say that in Feng's narrative the most certainly believable aspects are the major shape of the experiences and probably Feng's descriptions of accompanying emotions.)

The proprietor continued, saying that there was another way to proceed: "Continue walking along the road and spend the night in the wayside pavilion up ahead." But then he gestured to Feng's mother-in-law and pointed to the drizzle and mist falling outside and the increasingly muddy roads, as if to say, "You're going to have to go by boat if at all." Feng quickly perceived that this man was only trying to take advantage of their misfortune and make some fast money; to Feng's mind, the proprietor wanted to make them victims. The paranoia Feng experienced at White Cloud Convent was not in the least dissipating but rather becoming rawer.

At about 3 P.M., Feng sent Pingyu and Zhang Gui out to look for a boat. An hour later a woman appeared in the teahouse, announcing that there was a boat going to Tonglu and that it would cost seventy to eighty yuan. Feng was suspicious of this outrageously high price; and when he said no, the woman huffily withdrew into the inner rooms of the teahouse. His suspicions about the proprietor were thus confirmed: the "boatwoman," it turned out, was none other than the proprietor's daughter. Feng became increasingly angry, though he simply sat, continuing to sip tea. Then the proprietor angrily approached, to attempt to expel them from the teahouse. "What are you people going to do? You've sat here half the day and are still not going. You've occupied all these seats." Feng replied, "We have no other choice; we just have to sit here a spell. Brew some more tea for us. I'll pay for it." The proprietor laughed coldly: "We want to close the shop. There was a boat you didn't want! What do you think sitting in my shop is going to accomplish? We want to close—get out and sit outside by the road." The group was being evicted when Pingyu and Zhang Gui returned with news that they had found a boat; the boatman wanted Feng to go to the boat to negotiate. Feng sat a little longer, obviously trying to irritate the proprietor. As he left the teahouse, the proprietor, in a rumbling voice, yelled something out at Feng, who ignored him.

When he met the boatman, Feng thought he looked like a policeman but did not say why. The boatman named the price as twenty-five yuan; Feng paid him fifteen yuan, with the remainder to be paid when they reached Tonglu; Feng then went back to get the others. Some were on the road halfway between the teahouse and the boat, saying they refused to stay inside the teahouse because of the proprietor's anger and would rather walk along the road even in the falling rain. Feng went to get the members of the group who had remained in the teahouse and to pay the teahouse bill. On his return, his earlier temper had waned. He said that the proprietor's face had also lost its anger and that probably after the man had failed in his attempt to cheat Feng's group, he felt a bit of regret for his heartless *(bu ren)* actions. Probably, Feng conjectured, his heartlessness was forced by poverty, which then created in him the drive to oppress others. Feng concluded, "This world is a sea of bitterness. I didn't see evil here; I saw only hardship and bitterness."[16]

It was already after 5 P.M. Feng was anxious to begin the trip to escape what had become a frightful Hangzhou. But suddenly (that word, again, signaling another complication), an incident occurred that delayed the departure of Feng and his party. Afang was just getting into the boat when a soldier pulled toward himself Afang's carrying pole. Feng and the others tried to intercede. The soldier said, "In a bit, I will release him to return to you." They walked away. The day before they had lost their rower on the boat coming from Shimenwan; Feng deeply regretted that. Feng felt all the losses of the last few days: his home and native place community, the horrible changes in Hangzhou, the watery destruction of his sketch book, the conscripted boat rower, and, now, Afang. The situation of the group constantly remained tense. They were determined to wait for Afang in order to flee together, so they stopped the boat along the water's edge.

The policemanlike boatmen came to them to say, "You have to go quickly. The soldiers have seen you. They'll certainly order you to go ashore, and they'll commandeer the boat." They tried to tell him about the refugee situation and the Afang matter. But suddenly (again!), a soldier leaped on the boat and ran up to the front saying, "Let me borrow it." He began pulling in the mooring rope and grabbed the punting pole. Everyone was shocked. Shortly, they learned that the soldier was residing on a large steamboat that could not reach shore, so he had anchored it in the middle of the river. He wanted to use Feng's boat to ferry out in order to get some things he had left on the steamboat. Everybody relaxed somewhat. He proceeded to tell them the latest news from the front. For refugees, news was picked up from whomever they met or had time to speak with along the road; the news oriented them in the context of their flight. Most of the time "the news" was simply a rumor that was passed down the road via passersby, and there was no way to authenticate or verify anything refugees heard. Refugees, for all practical purposes, groped, as if in the dark (as Zi and Ye did on the mountain road in Xinchang), for any hints about where they should go or avoid going and how they should proceed there. The soldier told Feng and his party that the Chinese army had won a big victory at Pingwang near Huzhou— not that far from Shimenwan: "Many of the enemy were killed or wounded. No matter what, they will not be able to take Hangzhou." Everyone clapped. Feng thought that if the Chinese armies could prevail, then maybe his family's home would not fall into Japanese hands.[17] But the soldier was wrong. Pingwang had instead fallen into Japanese hands on November 13 as the Japanese onslaught continued.[18] Whereas most rumors frightened, this one filled listeners with false hope. For the refugee, reality was malleable.

After the soldier completed his mission, the Feng party took the boat back to the shore so that they could start out. They were relieved to see Afang waiting for them. They set out. Feng went to sleep. He dreamed that he heard children laughing: he thought he was back at Yuanyuan Hall. But he was then roused from his sleep to hear Pingyu talking to the boatman. The boat had stopped. The boatman was asking Pingyu, "How much money are you giving me to take you to Tonglu?" Pingyu answered, "Isn't it 25 yuan, 15 that we already gave you and 10 when we get to Tonglu?" The boatman responded, "You gave the 15 yuan to the man who looked like a policeman; you didn't give me anything. And I'm not going any farther." Then he headed for shore.[19]

From the boat Feng gazed at the pitch-black darkness on the shore; he could barely see a stretch of wasteland. Along the shore were several villages; there was a very large boat nearby casting frightening black shadows. The malevolence of black night and eerie black shadows loom ominously in Feng's prose. He wrote that at that point his heart was filled with resentment and that he had to give vent to his feelings. He said in a loud voice to the boatman, "Hey, we understand what's going on. Where is your trustworthiness? You extort us with bamboo oars and cheat us fleeing refugees. You, this . . ." Pingyu stopped Feng and in a more politically savvy, lower voice said to the boatman, "Hey, old boatman, you've made good progress. The current situation is really not like peaceful times. You want more—that we can negotiate. At least our family has escaped destruction at the devils' hands. Now we can only depend on fate. Whatever you want when we come to Tonglu, we can meet with relatives and friends and borrow it to pay you. At least now that you are carrying us, we ask you to get us there and save our lives." Feng admitted that his own words had had the potential for disaster and that Pingyu had been right to intervene. Feng, following suit, changed tones from tough and angry to tactful and sorrowful. The boatman, however, responded that he was not going to continue punting the boat and that the group could eat there.

Pingyu and the boatman got out of the boat. Feng noticed that Pingyu picked up a large branch from a tree and spoke in a low voice, negotiating with the boatman for awhile. The boatman agreed on being paid forty-five yuan at Tonglu, with the fifteen yuan paid at Six Harmonies Pagoda to the policemanlike man not counting as pay for the boatman. They got back on the boat; though everyone was awake, they did not speak. Pingyu let Feng know that he was planning on punishing the boatman once they reached Tonglu. Feng disagreed, saying he would be happy to carry out the agreement.

It was a clear morning when the boat arrived at Fuyang. Everyone was starving: they had eaten nothing warm in about two days. Everyone went to find something. Feng took two children and found a small shop with plain fare. They shared a bowl of hot, pungent food (nothing more specific is said about the meal) which, under the circumstances, Feng found incomparable to other food he had ever eaten. Then a local figure came up to Feng and urged him to get everyone back on the boat, as a soldier was planning on commandeering it. Feng bought several sticks of sugar cane and got on board. Some of the others bought *mantou* (steamed buns); inside each *mantou* was a big piece of meat, so big that half protruded from the bread. Feng wrote that he hadn't yet left Fuyang, but whenever he thought again about arriving there, he remembered only two things: the bowl of hot, pungent food and the spectacular nature of the *mantou*—and that's it. The would-be commandeerer-soldier who was supposed to attempt taking over the boat never appeared.

It was a fine sunny day, late autumn at its best. The refugees sat under the awning in the front of the boat, looking at the scenery, counting it as enjoyment in the midst of misery. On the river the group often met or passed other refugee boats. They frequently spoke briefly to the other refugees, mutually sharing past routes and destinations. One refugee in another boat asked if, once Feng and his party reached Tonglu, they would continue on their way walking or take a boat. The Fengs said it was not certain yet. From the boat, the Fengs could see things that suggested, even so relatively close to their home and to Hangzhou, different cultures and customs. Feng saw on shore a kind of simple sedan chair: hanging from bamboo poles were two planks, the taller one for sitting and the lower one for the sitter's feet. In the beginning the Fengs assumed a special refugee had built a sedan chair, but afterward they found out that this was a simple sedan chair used by country people in the area for long-distance traveling. The first assumption, that it was a mode of refugee travel, betrayed the family's vantage point as refugees, the Fengs assuming that practically anyone traveling at the time must have been refugees.

The boat arrived at Tonglu at 10:30 P.M. The group watched the lights of the town when they were still quite far away. Everyone was happy to think that this was at last a place where the group could rest—and not be continually in transit. After they had anchored, Feng went with Pingyu and another servant to find a hotel. They asked at several places, but there were no empty rooms. Occupying all of them were soldiers, who were even sleeping in the hallways. Only one hotel had a large meeting room, but it was half-filled with sleeping soldiers. The hotel offered to rent the Feng party the other side. They were sixteen people, but only five of them were adult males—all the rest were women and children, who would not be willing to mix with the soldiers in the room. Feng himself was not willing to do so either. The only alternative was to seek out his teacher Ma Yifu, who had extended the invitation to Tonglu; Feng hesitated, as it was already past 11 P.M. and Ma was most certainly asleep. With profuse apologies for his rudeness and countless pleas for forgiveness, Feng and the others woke Ma, who was staying in a suite on the upper floor of the hotel, and told him about the situation. Ma invited all sixteen refugees to stay at his place; Feng did not decline the offer—there being no other apparent alternative. He sent Pingyu and the other servant back to the boat to bring the others to the hotel.

Pingyu had nursed his grievances against the boatman all day. Feng called Pingyu "not-Pingyu," since he had dispensed with his usual good-naturedness in favor of an angry countenance. Pingyu said, "I have a method to express my views when we arrive at Tonglu." People in the group started calling him "Tonglu Method to Express." After all had gotten their luggage ashore, the boatman waited in the front of the Ma lineage temple for his payment. Pingyu, sputtering and grabbing the boatman's chest, thundered a boatman's curse: "You're a son of a bitch—half the night you extorted from these good people. I'm dragging you to the Security Bureau office." Feng and others, including Ma, came forward to mediate. Under Pingyu's torrent of words, which Feng compared to a "bolt of lightening," and physical intimidation, the boatman was soon kneeling on the ground, crying, confessing, and—addressing Ma, who obviously possessed considerable gravitas—seeking to vindicate his actions. In the end, Pingyu gave up the idea of turning the boatman in to the Security Bureau, agreed to restore the twenty-five yuan of the Six Harmonies Pagoda agreement, but did not carry out the forty-five yuan deal negotiated in the dark of night.

The realities of being a refugee seemed to weigh heavier on Feng as their trek continued. He wrote, "That night in bed at Mr. Ma's, my body was comfortable, but my mind was not. In human relationships, to drift about, disheveled and without structure, with no fixed place is difficult. I was taking with me a big group of my lineage; together we were in this drifting and uncertain situation. We gradually came to feel that that situation was comparable to the overturned nest of a bird. This evening we were fortunately perched on a high branch; however, this was no long-term solution. In the end, we had to plan a new nest."[20] Zhang Limin, an acquaintance in Tonglu, advised Feng and his group to go farther; Zhang offered, given the inconvenience and rigor of road travel, to have Feng's mother-in-law stay with him, as he was already caring for his two elderly parents. Feng, who really wanted to find a "nest," did not immediately take Zhang's advice and offer.

Instead, it seemed as though Feng found that nest in the rental of a house in Hetoushang, about twenty *li* (six to seven miles) from Tonglu. On November 28, they said good-bye to Ma and used his boat to go to Hetoushang. The rented house was in a beautiful setting surrounded by mountains and bamboo forests. They would stay there, however, only twenty-three days, many of them spent in discussions and arguments about what to do. During this time the national troops were contending with the Japanese at Shimenwan; the enemy would soon carry the battle to Hangzhou. Feng wrote that he hoped New Year's Day would never come, for he would have to take on the "burden" of happiness when happiness was not easy to come by.

One day well before New Year's, when Feng and the others were talking about bearing the burden of war and refugees, they heard a distant thunder, which they knew—from the rumbling sound typical of their first days as refugees—was bombs and gunfire. They planned to go, but the question was always whether to choose "long-distance travel" or "up into the mountain fastnesses." Feng proposed that they choose the long-distance strategy and also that Mr. Ma accompany them. But even though he was alone, Ma was unwilling to brave the rigors of becoming a refugee. The group decided for Feng's mother-in-law to stay—not with Zhang Limin, however, but with another friend who also had elderly relatives. Afang and Pingyu, whom Feng called "the center of [their] refugee troop in terms of leadership and experience," left to return to Hangzhou and points north. Pingyu had a friend in Tonglu named Che, who began to do servant-type work for Feng. When the Feng group reembarked on their trek, they were joined by Che, his father, and his son, making a total of sixteen.

Che arranged for a boat from Hetoushang to Tonglu, and they found a larger boat to Lanxi for twenty-eight yuan. They left in the early afternoon of December 21, exactly one month after their odyssey had begun. Faces were long on board the boat. The children were unhappy that their grandmother was not with them; Feng's wife was also downcast. At Tonglu, Feng had seen a bus schedule. Given the situation, he stopped the boat, sent a servant to take a return boat to Hetoushang to accompany Feng's mother-in-law to Tonglu, from where she would take a bus to Lanxi. Feng's one major concern was whether the bus service had been disrupted by the current situation or was overwhelmed by huge numbers of refugees.

He was also disconcerted by an incident during the trip to Lanxi. When the boat stopped at a small town, Sanhe (Three Rivers), near the county seat of Jiande, Feng met a female refugee from Shanghai. With knitted brow, she related that she had relatives in Jiangxi, and she was fleeing to them for safety. But people had told her that the Jiangshan and Yushan roads into Jiangxi were not open and that travelers could not get into Jiangxi—which is where the Fengs were headed. She had lost hope and was living destitute in Sanhe. Feng was depressed by this conversation, but he decided that, as the die had been cast to continue the trek, they must press ahead. He made a resolution: to carry the entire troop to Hunan Province.

The good news on the group's reaching Lanxi on the morning of December 23 was that Feng's mother-in-law was waiting for them; the buses ran, even on time. They stayed that night at the Jianjiang Hotel. There Feng unexpectedly ran into his old classmate, Cao Juren, now serving as a war correspondent for the *Southeast Daily,* the major newspaper for Zhejiang and Fujian provinces. The meeting was also one that depressed Feng, who saw Cao as one who would be knowledgeable about the travel situation. Cao categorically stated, "You want to go to Changsha? To Hankou? You cannot! I make contacts with the military and can use cars, and still it's not easy to travel—let alone with your traveling with over ten people, old and young. You've only gone halfway; you can turn around. I'll make some suggestions. Either go to Yongkang or Xianju County [both in central Zhejiang]; they're nearby. The level of daily life there is low, but they have police. I can let people there know that you're coming."[21]

Cao initially convinced Feng that they should not continue into central China. But, in the end, he decided to chance it. He was not willing to remain in Zhejiang. It might have been easier to go to Xianju County, but he wanted to go to Changsha in Hunan Province. The route was an all-water route and took them through Quzhou and Changshan in Zhejiang Province; Shangrao, Nanchang, and Pingxiang in Jiangxi Province; Changsha in Hunan Province; and Hankou in Hubei Province. As it turned out, along the way there were no obstacles whatsoever; it is likely that the difficulties that they had experienced in their home province were due to the proximity and approach of war. In their post-Zhejiang travels, they found the military very helpful.

Yuanyuan Hall

On their trek, the Fengs stayed over three weeks in Pingxiang. They lived in an abandoned lineage hall of the Xiaos', which was surrounded by rice paddies with mountains in the distance. There were very few intimations of assertive human presence; Feng found it to be quiet but lonely, an atmosphere not helped, to be sure, by the weather—cloudy and rainy the whole time the Fengs stayed there. The rooms were empty, and the walls bare. The overwhelming sense was of desolation.

Thoughts probably inevitably went to their warmer and happier Yuanyuan Hall in Shimenwan. Several days before they had left Tonglu, Feng had spoken with a military officer who had come from the north. The officer said that he had been involved in the fighting around Shimenwan. He said that the whole town was burned to the ground, that it lay in ruins. Feng's thinking in Pingxiang on February 9, 1938, was overcome by deep sadness. Every person, Feng thought, has only one real home: "How evil are the Japanese devils!" That night his wife slept in a bed across from Feng. She laughed in her sleep and then woke up. Feng asked her why she had laughed. She said that in her dream she was returning to Yuanyuan Hall and saw that it was just as they had left it. She asked Feng to write a poem to express their sadness.

> Our family home was near the old Qiantang / Its deep red balustrades reflected on the white-washed walls. On fine nights we would gather happily / And under the beautiful sun in spring and fall, we were busy with play and with travels. It was a peaceful and orderly world when we did not yet know of the bitterness of wandering destitutely, . . . last night as a visitor, she had a good spring dream—Not knowing that her body was in watery Pingxiang.[22]

In the fall of 1946, Feng and his family returned to Shimenwan. The return was devastating. The military officer at Tonglu had been right. Feng described the scene.

> After our little boat moored at the wharf next to Nan'gao Bridge, I looked around and wondered whether we had somehow come to the wrong place. This was not the Shimenwan I knew; surely it was another town entirely. Although the bend in the Grand Canal was the same as before, absolutely

nothing else was familiar. But this was indeed the place where I was born and raised. Strangely, I felt no more at home here than I did when I first went to Shanghai. For the past decade my memories of the old Shimenwan had sustained my wanderer's dreams but the town I now encountered had nothing to do with the homeland I once held so dear.[23]

The Fengs had much difficulty even locating the exact site of Yuanyuan Hall.

Memories of the past had allowed Feng to go on during the refugee and war years; he still had those memories, though the reality that had shaped them was gone forever. Unfortunately, the other sustaining memory for Feng, Hangzhou's West Lake, was now equally upsetting: "It was as though everything had been inundated by a great flood; only a hundredth of what had once stood now remained. I hastened to quit this place, for although I had come in search of West Lake, what I saw made me realize that it is far better to savor the dreams of what once was."[24]

FOUR

✦

Days of Suffering

WHILE FENG ZIKAI'S INTROSPECTIVE and thoughtful detailing of his life as a refugee in Zhejiang was written about two years after the experience, some refugees, soldiers, and Chinese caught in war penned their thoughts and descriptions of daily occurrences in diaries and journals. While these sources have their own problems—a lack of perspective and perhaps a tendency to overdramatize and therefore distort events that were perceived as personally traumatic—they avoid some of the major problems of memory: its forgettings, reshapings, and distortions. In his preface to "Ten Days of Being Confronted by Danger in My Native Place," Jin Xihui frankly described his experience writing as a diarist.

> I am not a good writer and generally write very little. But what I write I [can] cut; what I write can be [seen as] generous or can cause one to frown. A writer naturally expects this. However, in writing a diary, one can give his own viewpoint and therefore, cannot be demeaned and dismissed automatically as shallow. I ignore whatever I want, write casually, and call to mind whatever I want. I write it down immediately. When I finish what I have to say, I simply stop writing. This is exactly the tack of Lu Xun, who spoke of an "immediate diary" [*mashang riji*].[1]

Diarists provided a day-by-day account; in essence, they were at work ordering the facts in order to present an intelligible and meaningful narrative of their experiences and their perceptions, to work out their immediate places in society and in the war.

This chapter looks at three diaries that confront issues of spatial and psychosocial displacement brought on by war. First is the diary of Feng Zongmeng of Pinghu County, the first county on Hangzhou Bay to be invaded by Japanese forces in November 1937; little is known about him apart from his having nominal, yet unspecific ties to the scholarly world. The second is the diary of Wang Mengsong, a sojourning merchant from Anhui Province who was resident of a small town near the tragic city of Qu in southwestern Zhejiang. The third is the story of Jin Xihui, who was enrolled in a training course for leaders of the Zhejiang Boy Scouts. But he was trapped in his hometown during a short-lived Japanese invasion in 1941. Analysis and explication of these excerpts appear in italics.

Community and Family: The Account of Feng Zongmeng

[*Feng Zongmeng's story, which is quoted at length below, is somewhat unusual.[2] With his family, he was a refugee from November 6, the day of the Japanese attack on Pinghu County, until his return to the county seat on December 13, just over five weeks later. Though Feng's home was in the same general area as Feng Zikai's native place, the two men, despite a common surname, were unrelated. Zongmeng's diary is not as psychologically introspective as Zikai's account. Zongmeng's entries focus on his acquaintances in the Pinghu county seat, that is, in the larger community, and depict far more graphically the brutality of the war.*]

November 6, 1937—Japanese planes have flown over Pinghu every single day as the summer passed to autumn. Though these repeated fly-overs should have pointed to imminent danger, most people did not prepare contingency plans in case bombs began dropping from the planes and war erupted here. No matter! At 1 P.M. today [*on the same day that Zikai's Shimenwan was first bombed*] Japanese planes appeared and dropped ten bombs. [*Zongmeng then describes the sites bombed and the substantial numbers of homes destroyed.*]

Some time before, the daughter-in-law of one Shen Jixiu hired a small boat to carry several chests outside the city at South Watergate. Suddenly, in the middle of doing so, she turned around and went back home—just in the knick of time. Boats that were in canals at the time of the raid were bombarded and sunk. Most of Zhang Houben's family was crushed when bombs flattened their house's walls. But freakishly the bombs catapulted the 14-year-old daughter high up into a tall tree. Her clothes were torn

in horizontal strips—like she had been doing a ribbon dance; they flut-
tered in the breeze at the top of the tree. With the deaths of her entire
family and the mass exodus of citizenry, her body remained impaled up
there for a whole month. Even more grotesque, fragments of the head of
Lu Zhenchu had been found beside a small cloth chest; her body had
been eaten by wild dogs and there were no other remains. When Zhang
Houben's second son returned from Shanghai, he used the chest for the
few remains of his lineage members.

Our house was also hit by a bomb; but, though it fell through the
roof, it did not explode, because it fortunately landed on mosquito netting and thick bedding. The raid ended about 5 P.M. That night people
fled from the city in all directions, an endless stream that continued until dawn. They supported the old and carried the young [*a stock phrase in
refugee stories*], carrying heavy loads of goods and supplies on their shoulders and backs. Those who had no temporary place to lodge huddled up
in a nearby waterwheel shed. After dusk there was wind and rain, punctuated by constant sounds of weeping and wailing. That night I took my
family west of the county seat, to stay with our son-in-law, who was a
tenant farmer for the Xia lineage and who lived near a Catholic church.
During the night there was drizzle, which had the effect of further ob-
scuring people's vision in what was an increasingly ominous situation.
The next night we moved to the home of a member of the Shen lineage. [*Zongmeng does not tell us why they made this move.*]

November 7, 1937—In yesterday's raid, neighbor Zhang Liansheng suffered a head wound. But we heard today that, tragically, his wife and son
were killed by the falling rubble. This morning saw more wind and rain,
with the wind even stronger than yesterday. Though there was one flyover
by enemy planes, the bad weather not only prevented more bombing runs
but also provided cover for people to move. [*The fate of refugees was inti-
mately caught up in the world of weather: bad weather could both help and hinder
the refugees and their antagonists—enemies or collaborators. Here mist, drizzle,
and wind played havoc with plans and strategies. In Wang Mengsong's accounts, as
we will see, the weather demons were tragic floods.*]

November 8, 1937—Clear weather today: consequently, Japanese
planes dropped more bombs, setting off serious fires in the eastern part
of the county seat. Each day between 6 and 8 P.M. refugees warily come
back to the city to survey the ruins of the day and to pick up things that

they had left in their homes. When my family and I fled on the evening of November 6, we had carried only our bedding. I came back in the rain yesterday to get some necessities for staying longer with the Shens; their place was only about three *li* [*a complete English mile*] from the city. Each evening when I left the house, I locked the door as usual.

When he took over as chief county official, it was said that Magistrate Qiu [a graduate of a military academy] had thorough knowledge of military affairs. But in office, he did not do a single thing to prepare us for war or to protect us; his only tack was an ostentatious show, consisting of assessing a "national salvation" tax on the county in order to provide military supplies. Then, the night before the Japanese attack, he simply absconded with his family—no one knows where. The scoundrel carried with him all his official perks, and now he's totally gone and out of sight. [*Magistrates, as the government bureaucrats in closest contact with the people, often bore the brunt of the people's ire: it was obviously the magistrate's function to protect and see after the people's needs. Zongmeng's perception is that Qiu took advantage of the people and then, when the crisis came, simply "cut and run," leaving his people to their own devices.*]

November 11, 1937—When I returned home today, I found that the little gate on the east side of the house had been broken into, with a gaping hole also torn in the main gate. Surveying things hurriedly, without taking the time for a thorough evaluation, I did notice that the chests and trunks, along with the mosquito nets, were missing.

The wife of my neighbor to the west, Pan Xianqing, had been in ill health when she fled west of the city to stay with a farm family. Her condition had been worsened by the stress of the Japanese invasion and the flight itself. Because she was on the edge of death, the farm family, housing her temporarily, thought her presence was inauspicious; so they forced her out. Having no choice, she returned home last night where she died. When I met her sister-in-law on the street, she told me what had happened. Today [*the*] body [*of Pan Xianqing's wife*] was placed into a coffin; but only about an hour later the Pan house was hit by a Japanese aerial bomb and the coffin blown completely apart. Before noon, in another ghastly tragedy, another bomb fell in front of the Guanyin Temple; inside, a chanter of sutras was killed when an iron strip, blown off the roof, decapitated him.

November 15, 1937—We were still staying with the Shen lineage. At night, my nephew Damei came, warning that we had best not stay in this area so near to the county seat—that we should flee and do so quickly. I rented two boats from the Shens and loaded them with family members, including my 90-year-old mother, my grandson of several months, and the family of my daughter and son-in-law. In the middle of the night we headed toward Gaojiadai, where the Tangs (the family of my father's sister) lived. From the boat we saw flames lighting the sky: were we heading straight to the enemy? [*As the passage indicates, refugee movement at night was especially terror producing, since there was no way to know where the enemy was or was headed.*]

November 16, 1937—Soldiers passed three times in front of the Tang house in Gaojiadai; we did not dare open the door.

November 17, 1937—In the evening, we rented three boats, planning to go to Shimenwan. [*At this time, Feng Zikai was still at a village outside of Shimenwan and would not leave until November 21.*]

The boatman asked, "Do you have relatives in Shimenwan or not?"

I said, "No."

"Yesterday," the boatman replied, "I carried refugees [*literally, 'guests'*] to Shimenwan. There are already way too many refugees that the people of Shimenwan have to deal with. I'm afraid it will not be a retreat that will give rise to either peace or happiness."

I asked, "Where would you recommend?"

He responded, "Xinshi."

That night there were cloudbursts and thunder crashes. Thinking it safer to travel in dark, early morning hours, we got onto the boats at midnight; there were many children. We had to take care that we didn't turn the boats over.

November 18, 1937—At dusk we arrived in Xinshi. Today we had huddled on the boat. We didn't stop for food or drink. Fortunately, the rain, which had already lightened, finally stopped. We quickly went ashore and straight to a small restaurant, where we ate our fill. We received preferential treatment from the restaurant manager, who allowed us to spend the night.

[*Feng notes that the Japanese armed forces entered the Pinghu county seat on November 19 and that Japanese arson on November 20 and 23 destroyed most of the city. He reports that on November 27, the Peace Maintenance Committee, the earliest collaborationist organization, was established, a day when "the central county seat was all burned and lying in ruins, bandits were controlling the public, dogs were eating the flesh of the dead—all scenes on which people cannot bear to look closely."*]

December 13, 1937—I bought a boat and returned from Xinshi. I did not dare to enter the town hastily; I went instead back to the Shen lineage, with whom we had stayed the initial days of our flight.

December 14, 1937—I went home to begin to put the place in order.

December 17, 1937—My family returned to Pinghu. Both large and small streets in the town were filled with the rubble of destruction; everywhere the streets were blocked by huge piles of rubble: there were no "through" streets.

Late February, 1938—Though we have been back for the past two months, there have been no settled, "normal" feelings about living in Pinghu.

[*Feng never tells us why he and the family made the decision to return home and live under the Japanese occupation. Although Zongmeng does not describe his native place as euphorically as Feng Zikai did, its meaning was obviously highly emotionally and psychologically important to him and his family.*]

Wang Mengsong's Diary of a Local Calamity

[*Wang Mengsong (1882–1954), a native of She County in Anhui Province, was a sojourning merchant—manager of a southern-goods store—in the small town of Lianhua, about thirteen miles northeast of Quzhou (see Map 9). He lived, however, at Gaojia Town, very near to the Qu River on the upper reaches of the Qiantang River. Gaojia was only a few miles downstream from Quzhou, a proximity that enabled Wang to travel to the county seat and return home frequently. During the War of Resistance, his diary entries are studded with frequent mention of the roar of Japanese planes on bombing runs over Quzhou, some two hundred kilometers from Hangzhou. Indeed, from May 1938 to September 1944, the Japanese bombed Quzhou 647 times, an average of once every 3.5 days. Excerpted at length below, Wang's diary entries are for the most part short and to the point, written by a man generally of few words. Often instead of offering the specific names of his subjects, Wang protected their privacy by using "X" or "XX" instead.*[3]

His first entry on September 26, 1937, the day of the first bombing of Quzhou, came almost six weeks before the Japanese landed at Hangzhou Bay and is untypical in its length. On this day, Wang had business in Huayuangang, between Gaojia Town and Quzhou, so his description is mostly of the planes and sounds.]

September 26, 1937—About 11 A.M. today, I saw three planes flying very high. They flew to the river and then returned. I heard some firecracker-like sounds; I still didn't know it was machine-gun fire. After that I heard two explosions; I assumed they were shells fired by antiaircraft guns. Black smoke billowed up. The planes flew far away, but then returned; I then knew they were enemy planes. There were three consecutive blasts. Moreover, local people claimed they could see the bombs falling from the planes. It was abundantly clear that these were indeed bombs. Fifteen minutes later, I met a woman carrying a small child, followed by a man. He said to me, "We'd just fixed lunch and then the bombs fell. We picked up our child and left; we didn't carry a single thing with us. Who knows what's going to happen?" In the afternoon there was an endless stream of refugees with their family dependents.

[*The calamitous day in Quzhou that Wang alludes to unfolded like this. About 11 A.M. three planes coming from the direction of Jinhua (to the northeast) entered the skies over Qu. The Guomindang air command did not sound the air-raid siren. The people in the city did not know the planes belonged to the enemy. A combined passenger-freight train from Hangzhou had just pulled into the station. The platforms were crowded with travelers and hawkers. About fifteen train carts with fifty to sixty draftees from Changshan County to the west were hooked to the train. The planes passed over several times without firing; then they suddenly swooped down and bombed the station, and then returned for two more bombing runs. On the platforms, in the carts and cars, blood spurted and pieces of flesh flew. All the draftees burned to death; their remains later filled only thirty-two coffins. In terms of the total number killed and injured, the chronicler of these specific events noted that there was no way to know. The impact of the bombings could only have trumpeted total terror, an effect the Japanese, wanting to maneuver a short war, almost certainly desired.*]

September 27, 1937—In the afternoon I was in Quzhou. The people in the streets were in a state of panicky anxiety. When someone said the enemy planes were coming again, all the people shrieked about, fleeing. Later there was a false alarm; but the fear was palpable.

September 30, 1937—Before noon I went to the Little West Gate [*in the Quzhou city wall*] to board a boat. The people on the riverbank were rushing along. Some said that planes were arriving. People could not bear the constant tension. They shut their houses in the city and fled.

December 2, 1937—Today I heard the police warning-siren five times in central Quzhou City; people's nerves have stayed continually jangled for over two months.

December 10, 1937—In the afternoon, I heard the sound of plane engines growing louder—then the sounds of bombs. I counted ten explosions. Later I ran into X, who was on the court; he told me there had been no fewer than thirty-four bombs. A corner of the middle school had been blown away and the Sanguan Temple was destroyed. The rest of the bombs were dropped on the air base outside the city.

December 13, 1937—Before noon, the police sirens sounded again. Still my friend and I went out Western Peace Gate, where there was a vegetable market, which remained crowded. Then the enemy planes arrived. People said there were nine planes; I saw only three. People later said that there were thirty-five explosions; I don't think anyone can adequately judge the actual number. [*Wang's continual concerns and those whose reports he was noting seem almost fixated on the number of planes involved in each attack and the numbers of explosions. It is almost as though people felt that if they could settle on a solid number, that solidity might provide some macabre consolation in the midst of so much fear, confusion, and uncertainty.*] My friend invited me to dinner; however, the police sirens sounded again. Fortunately it was almost dark, so there wasn't another attack.

December 16, 1937—Last night I went to bed early but couldn't sleep. I thought about all the warnings and bombings and of the road filled with terrified people. Everybody has heard all sorts of rumors. At dusk, I hear panicked voices on the road: people leave the city early and late, at any time they feel threatened. At night I talked to two friends about the current situation. People don't agree on where they should go to be safest. You hear arguments about this on the road all the time.

[*Wang Mengsong made several diary entries detailing planes, bombing, and refugees: in 1938—on January 8, 10, 22, 24, 26; on February 1, 21, 27, 28; on May 30; on September 28; on November 26; on December 1; in 1939—on April 5; on December 7, 21; in 1940—on February 8, on April 7, on July 27, on December 12; and in 1941—on April 2 and 15, on November 14. These last two bombings caused many deaths.*]

March 27, 1942—A bomb hit the Catholic Church, where there was a nursery; between ten and twenty small children were killed.

[*Planes and bombs are mentioned several times in Wang's diaries: in 1942—on April 1, 24, 30; and on May 3, 4, 12, 13, 20, 21. Many of the bombs were dropped on the airbase.*]

May 22 and 23, 1942—On the streets of Gaojia were endless streams of refugees from around the cities of Jinhua and Lanxi to the northeast. Many, coming into the area by boat, wanted to buy food in the town. On the second day a great crush of our soldiers merged with the continuing flood of refugees, fleeing the advancing Japanese army.

May 27, 1942—Heavy rain brought flooding. Rumors flew that the Japanese were in Longyu, contiguous to Quzhou on the east. People who had not already fled had to do so, but the flooding made leaving and traveling at all almost impossible. In Lianhua, after lunch, a company of Chinese soldiers stopped at the residence of a town shopkeeper. Then another group of soldiers showed up. Both groups wanted to spend the night. Near evening some wounded soldiers came, demanding that the people supply porters to carry them. There was no way at this time for the town office [*zhen gongzuo*] to respond. The wounded soldiers started talking about simply grabbing townsmen and conscripting them; they [*the wounded*] were joined by the nonwounded soldiers. When this talk began, townspeople fled quickly. General fear was the constant reality.

May 28, 1942—Even though these soldiers' threats of conscripting civilians were not carried out, the people of Lianhua were fearful in the extreme. But then the Japanese stormed in. Townsmen fled, most going only four or five *li* [*that is, less than two miles away*]. But then we heard that the Japanese were taking a different route and perhaps might not even come to Lianhua. People breathed a little easier.

June 2, 1942—But no, it had been only a rumor. The Japanese did come to Lianhua. The soldiers went to every house, rich or poor. Without exception, they literally tore up the town. In every house, they turned over every chest and basket and cleaned everything out. They trashed the stores and shops.

June 10, 1942—I heard that Gaojia (where my residence was) was totally destroyed. That meant my chest of books (my chief pride and value) must also have been destroyed.

June 12, 1942—Planes flew all day, coming and going. Some claimed that the Japanese had entered Quzhou, that planes going north and east were carrying wheat and rice to Hangzhou and Shaoxing, and that planes going south and west were carrying ammunition for the destruction of Quzhou. But certainly these simply had to be rumors, didn't they? How could we possibly believe that such things were happening? After lunch I decided to go with a friend to the Li household in Lianhua. We met a platoon of our own guerrilla soldiers, who stubbornly blocked our path and would not permit us to go any farther. They said that after noon today they had met several people carrying backpacks. Searches found Japanese military scrip and a Japanese uniform. Our soldiers clearly assumed they were collaborators, and they [the soldiers] refused to give [the people] their belongings. Our soldiers confined them. Now, distrusting all, they were stopping everyone, the soldiers said; no one could proceed. I think this really made no sense and could only lead to violence.

June 15, 1942—In Lianhua, Japanese soldiers killed a woman who resisted their attempts to rape her.

July 5, 1942—In the morning, I left with two friends to scope out the situation in Gaojia. We had heard that the enemy had returned to Gaojia no fewer than seven times after the initial trashing of the town. And now Chinese bandits aggressively crawled through the area's ruins and rubble. My house had not been completely destroyed so that night I climbed the stairs to go to bed. But outside there was great commotion with dogs barking and people talking excitedly. Even at night you got swallowed up in rumors. They were reporting that the Japanese were returning yet again. All who heard this panicked and fled their homes even in the pitch-black darkness to take to the road as refugees.

July 10, 1942—I once saw a newspaper with photographs showing the enemy bandits burning, killing, and raping. The photos established the story as fact to me. But, I thought and hoped, perhaps the enemy bandits could not really go that far. Today they returned to Quzhou, and the horrible news is that they're even worse. They have completely lost all human empathy and compassion. They taunt us. We must move more quickly to wipe them out.

July 17, 1942—Yesterday, of five who tried to escape from Quzhou City, only one, a Buddhist monk, succeeded; the other four were killed. The enemy had already looted electric generators, telephone lines, and precious porcelains, all carted off in their trucks. The air base was two-thirds destroyed. Inside the much-damaged walls of the county seat there are not more than one thousand people remaining. The city was destroyed first by the Japanese and then by the floods. People have met the robbers but have no idea how many there are. Alas! Bayonet, soldier, flood, and fire merged together!

August 25, 1942—The enemy forces passed through Lianhua yet again, this time demanding porters. When no one volunteered, the devils abducted only the strong, robust men.

[*In his diary Wang appended an untitled poem. He wrote of the heavy rain that poured from the skies from late May until early July. His poem captures well the late-spring despair as death from floods accompanied death at the hands of the enemy. The despair and melancholy of the poem is softened at the end by his gesture toward the rustic mountain dwellers spatially separated from the firestorms of both war and modernity.*]

> Every day the pouring rain continues;
> Refugees are filled with pains of homelessness.
>
> The cruel barbarism of the Japanese weighs our people down,
> All the more so because the deserted and desolate fields cannot be
>   planted.
>
> The continuous rain is vexing, making life melancholy.
> When will the skies clear and relieve our hundred worries?
>
> Mountain roads are slippery with mud—
> And perhaps in part from the tears pouring from everyone's eyes.
>
> At dawn there's emptiness and fear; in the evening, terror,
> And the increasing, incessant rain gives rise to undesirable weeds.
>
> How can we deal with the aggressive enemy running roughshod
>   over us?
> Crowds of refugees hurry to consume a cooked dog—food, at least!
>
> Fleeing calamity, the far-removed mountain dwellers at least feel no
>   terror.
> Our hearts are drawn to their experience of peace and prosperity.

The Diary of Jin Xihui

[*Jin Xihui, training to be a leader in the Zhejiang Boy Scouts, noted that the weather on all ten days that he detailed was clear, in sharp contrast to the bleakness of the period's terror or the floods of 1942. The immediate context for the Japanese attack of Dongyang County was the Japanese seizure of Shaoxing and Ningbo in April. At the time, the Japanese attacked and held other counties that had been a part of Shaoxing and Ningbo prefectures. Though Dongyang was not, it was contiguous to Sheng and Zhuji counties. The Japanese invading force numbered only about four hundred and was in Dongyang from May 14 to May 17.*[4] *Jin's preface follows.*]

The devils came. Everyone was in danger—whether of becoming a refugee or being killed. It was certain that the confusion of the situation, experienced over and over again, was what's been seen in wars from the beginning of time.

Ultimately, our luck wasn't bad. The devils, flouting law and morality, invaded our native place, plundering Dongyang County for several days [*see Map 5*]. We were at home so that our eyes saw and our ears heard the actual violent deeds of the devils. We gnashed our teeth in hatred. The devils brutally occupied our native place for no more than three or four days. But this record is of ten days, because there were things on subsequent days that should be included. I felt that these ten days bled together, and I bitterly recall the aftertaste of the experience.

The devils did leave. The pain they caused was psychological; and after the pain, they left us stewing in hatred. To begin writing this now necessarily reignites my anger and sadness and fills me again with a sense of emptiness and tragedy. Again, I am not very good at choosing the right words to describe the tragic situation. It does not matter whether one has personally experienced it or not; [*reading about the events can*] show one afterward how thoroughly thought patterns from that time persist and color our thinking in the present.

Wednesday, May 14, 1941

The weather ignores the clouds and sun; it's half cloudy and half sunny.
One can ignore *one* plane coming and going; the problem is that they're coming and going over and over again.

Before the Japanese invaded, I had planned several times to return to Lishui, where I was taking training classes under the director of education for the Zhejiang Boy Scouts. But financial difficulties (no money!) made it impossible for me to return. When the class had been postponed because of the military threat, I left Lishui to come home to the village of Xianlang. That was twenty days ago. Last month on the 22nd, the military situation was already dicey. I heard rumors that the enemy had left Wenzhou, so it was possible that the class might have actually already begun. When I thought about this turn of events, I was filled with anger and hatred; but I could voice this only to my wife. She's been of late continually befuddled—as if she'd had a morphine injection. But my being able to talk to her allowed me to pull back on my anger and replace it with indignation. I just didn't know what I was going to do about getting the necessary travel money.

My elder brother's wife had plans to join him, who was already in Shaanxi [*with the Communists in Yan'an*]. Because of the difficulty of coming up with travel money, plans had been set for her to go with one Wang Cunguang, who planned to leave tomorrow from the county seat. I agreed to accompany her; going to the county seat would also allow me to discuss arranging a loan from my friend Sun Jiantang, to be able to get back to my class in Lishui.

Last night I quarreled with my wife. In the end, neither of us could settle down. It was late into the night when we finally fell asleep; so I rose later than I'd intended. Sister-in-law came in to hurry me up. We got her luggage and left. I carried several pieces for her. Her fat body wriggled down the road; I followed behind. Despite her being overweight, she did not need to rest; but I did, likely from my poor night of sleep. When we started, the road was quiet and mostly empty.

Yet very quickly, it became more crowded, confused, and disorderly. From the passersby came all sorts of conflicting rumors. One was that the Japanese had taken the large market town of Huaxi, about ten kilometers west of here in Yiwu County. Now we met a crush of soldiers, who (rumor had it) were retreating after being routed by the Japanese at Maofeng. The next moment we heard the rumor that the enemy was pushing to the market town of Shanghu, just a few kilometers north of the county seat. However, we walked our own road. We didn't give any of these rumors credence: they belonged to the realm of stupid people who, with these rumors, delude others. Furthermore, yesterday people came from the county seat and did not mention any situation so tense and dangerous. Without a doubt, we could proceed to the county seat. [*Seemingly like many Chinese in the immediate threat of war, Jin seemed to accept at face value word that suggested the best-case scenario; here, after just saying that he gave no rumors credence, he chooses a rumor that apparently best suited his existential frame of mind.*]

When we neared the small town of Hucang, the situation suddenly changed. We heard gunshots in the distance. My first thought was that it was simply some hunters. Not in the least concerned, I went on. But Sister-in-law, walking behind me, was more hesitant and stopped. Then there were more gunshots in succession. The closer they were together, the tenser we got. It now indeed sounded like a battle.

Panic-stricken people were streaming out of Huadian, saying that the enemy army had gotten to Shanghu. Because Shanghu is a periodic market and was open today, many people had been killed in the crowded marketplace, only about three kilometers away. We passed six or seven students and their teacher from Dongyang County Middle School; they were carrying chests and baskets and walking quickly. The teacher, Chen Shaofan, stopped me and said, "Believe what I'm telling you. Turn around and go home. There is a rushing flood of refugees headed this way; on their heels are the Japanese devils. The situation is very tense." We followed his advice and hurried back home as quickly as we could.

Some of our soldiers were billeted at the local temple, and also at sites in neighboring Shima and Louquantou. An officer told me that the enemy was rumored to be about a hundred *li* away [*thirty miles or so*]. He continued, "In a few days, you'll see things in chaos. Stock up on food and drink. A great calamity will be facing you." Most people were not that scared; but there was no way to maintain any state of equanimity. We ate lunch about 12:15. Everyone was talking angrily about how our soldiers seemed to be barging at will into people's homes to cook their meals. In talking about our possible courses of action, Mother was adamant about remaining at home rather than leaving and becoming a refugee.

As the soldiers were finishing their lunch, we heard sounds of battle from the direction of Shima, as well as the ominous rumble of planes. I had not yet begun to make preparations to flee. Sister-in-law and I had only been home half an hour, and now it seemed like the horrifying beginning of a ferocious battle. And from the direction of Xianmu, there was more gunfire. We seemed to have become engulfed in a continuous volley of cannon fire and gunshots.

As we left, we were almost instantly thrown in with a crowd. We had to hurry. In a panic, I had to support my mother and take the children. I called Sister-in-law and shouted to my wife. Panicky, we picked up many cloth-wrapped bundles and bamboo baskets. We headed south in a desperate hurry to escape. The faces of people on the road were ashen; many were crying and shaking. My wife was crying hysterically, saying that she had not had time to bring along anything important. The sounds of guns and cannon came ever nearer and more ferociously. Villages in both plains and mountains echoed with gunfire. I had tears in my eyes, looking at my own native place, about which I knew so much and felt so ardent. Alas! My native place, *my home* [emphasis added] is being buried in the flames of war.

At this time, my wife, with almost the speed of an airplane, turned and ran back to get some things from our home. It was as if she was in some sort of an entranced stupor. She made her way amid continual fire. I shouted at her, but she did not respond. Clutching our daughter Ming'er, I did not—I could not—stop her. Bullets shot past in the open air; as she raced back, the bullets must have had eyes because none hit her. Her impulsively reckless behavior fortunately did not bring calamity.

We stopped at Twisted Pine Mountain. Unfortunately Sister-in-law and her son had become separated from us; they had no idea of where to head. [*Like the brief separation of Feng Zikai's mother-in-law from the rest of the family, this separation was the very stuff of grief, panic, and terror.*] At sunset they hid themselves in Yunduan Village, afraid even to stick their faces out of their hiding place.

With nightfall, this first spasm of war ended; gradually peace and quiet was restored. With heavy hearts, we plodded home. . . . The elderly, who did not flee, claimed to have seen twelve devils with their own eyes. . . . Sister-in-law and her child fortunately returned later. When I think back on this one-day battle, it seemed two years and dreamlike—as if ultimately I hadn't really experienced it, but it was framed in great shock and studded with terrifying palpitations that were all too real.

Thursday, May 15, 1941

Last evening after I returned home, I was uneasy and fidgety—as if all my vigor and spirit were lost. Our villagers had long maintained a blind faith in the god Caigang, and, in these dire straits, they prayed to him to send spirits to tell their fortunes. They said the result of their prayers was the appearance of a beacon fire in the night. [*This reference is a clear warning about impending danger: beginning in the late Warring States period (700–800 BCE), the Chinese early warning defense system against invaders was to light beacon fires on promontories.*] Notably they did not say "Don't worry." Even if they had said this, I would still have been afraid. I then decided to act defensively, not knowing what was going to happen. I led my whole family to sleep in the woods behind the cemetery at the foot of Tomb Mountain. The cawing of birds and the crying of small children filled me with fear.

It was late in the night when villagers came to tell me that the enemy was in the center of the village, going from door to door and knocking—a very shocking situation. My usually quiet temperament became tense. I thought, we have no alternative but to flee to a point farther south. But, then, if we left now, we would be fumbling and groping in the dark in order to move on. If we went to the south side of Stone Support Mountain, there would be a thick forest. We would have to be silent, not communicating, but holding our breaths in case soldiers were waiting in ambush. But the courage of my wife and sister-in-law was almost non-existent. Deep in the forest, they would only be bundles of nerves.

There was, of course, no alternative but for us to leave together. Ordinarily, in both day and night travel, people feared ghosts. Now, given the frightening aspects of war, ghosts were no longer the threat. We went to the house of my father-in-law in Zhang Village; they were sleeping soundly so they were frightened and confused when we woke them up. Well they might be, since, at that very time, Japanese soldiers were also entering their village. The battlefield was ubiquitous. There was simply no place where we could feel at ease.

We took advantage of the night, since it was not yet daybreak. The moonlight was dim. We looked for a small, narrow, winding footpath to Auspicious Lake, a basin surrounded on four sides by mountains. There we might be able to take temporary shelter. But then I had second thoughts! In the Auspicious Lake vicinity were Wuliang and Liushi, both large villages. We had heard that the enemy was already occupying Liushi and oppressing its people. So, I thought, staying at Auspicious Lake is really like making ourselves fish in an urn—isn't staying there then especially dangerous? Shouldn't we leave it? Wuliang was where the Chinese army was blocking the road, not permitting any travelers to pass through. Furthermore, everywhere the Chinese army were grabbing victims to serve as coolies for forced labor. People were really like mice trying to escape a cat: they would hide and then try to escape so that there would be no trace of their existence.

Throughout the day, rumors wafted through the air from other refugees: the Gu Yuan township head, a Mr. Li, had been killed. A *baojia* head had almost died of fright in a lengthy aerial bombardment. Were these things true? Zhang Village, we know, had already been trampled by enemy brigands. And we had heard after noon that several hundred enemy troops were passing through the area and that at a nearby site they had killed seventeen of our troops. In the middle of a big refugee trek, hunger became a huge problem; but a refugee couldn't dare think of hunger. If he thought of food, he couldn't possibly allow himself to imagine that it would taste good. The body certainly got a lot thinner when placed into the refugee mold.

The wan sunlight was fading rapidly in the west. In the skirmishes I had heard last night between our troops and the Japanese, both sides had looted before pulling back. [*Traditional Chinese armies were infamous for looting whether they won or lost any particular battle.*] We decided we would be safer if we once again returned home. But we had to do that warily, step by step, constantly aware of any changes in our surroundings that might portend danger. We could see from the road over four hundred enemy troops occupying the mountain behind Gaotaimen Village. Even at dusk, the cannons and the machine guns, no more than half a li [*about 900 feet*] away, dazzled the eyes. The villagers imitated neighboring villages in trying to ingratiate themselves with the enemy: two village elders took a picul of wine [*about 133 pounds*] and three hundred eggs to the troops on the mountain. Then, at night, the villagers stealthily killed all their chickens and cooked the meat so that their families might eat what they owned before the Japanese stole it [*a none-too subtle culinary scorched-earth approach*].

At nightfall after we were home, about fifty or sixty enemy soldiers entered our village, probably to serve as sentries. I hid in the garden; leaning against a wall, I could peek out. I could see that they wore leather boots and helmets. [*Refugees and nonrefugees alike often noted that Japanese soldiers wore leather boots; most Chinese donned straw sandals.*] When they walked past, they certainly seemed spirited. I hated myself for not having a weapon in my hands with which I could have killed them. I brought my wife and son out of the house to hide behind the garden wall. My wife did not understand that we were not leaving, and she stubbornly wanted to drag along heavy bags. I scolded her with my expression.

After the soldiers had passed by, I hurried her up to pack up household goods for a possible night flight from home. Moving quietly, we packed up and moved my books in several square-bottomed bamboo baskets to the pigsty. We stuffed Western-style clothes into a large crock. My wife was paranoid about everything so she burned quite a few things, including an old newspaper; that made me angry because it had some things in it that I wanted to save. We put legal papers in a hole that we dug. We covered it with a lid slathered with mud, and on top we placed the wooden pail we used for urine.

For dinner, we didn't dare turn on a lamp. So we fumbled around, using our hands to tear the chicken meat. We wolfed it down amid panicky fear, so strong, in fact, that the chicken didn't have any taste to me. That night we slept at the foot of the stove, to make a rapid escape, if necessary, from the gate behind the vegetable garden.

Friday, May 16, 1941

It was not yet dawn; there was only a hazy moonlight. I was in the midst of a dream when something startled me awake. I shot out of bed. The night was rent by continuous gunfire, and the nearby enemy camp was ablaze. It seemed like an impossible situation. Experience had taught me that to attempt to flee when both sides were firing was dangerous. It was better to stay put, even though that meant waiting for possible death. My cousin in the room across the hall, Wang Duanzhi, got up to tell Sister-in-law not to be afraid and not to follow her impulses to flee; he said this was just the enemy's empty show of strength.

As dawn broke, the firing stopped. Not knowing what was about to happen, we had to decide whether to flee or not. We went back and forth all morning on the decision. After lunch we heard the good news that the enemy that had been based on Gaotaimen Mountain had retreated; and the enemy in our fire-ravaged village was also pulling back toward Shima. The area around Shima was littered with seventy or eighty corpses. Alas! Our own poverty-stricken civilians went out among the corpses like vultures, taking money, rice stained in blood, cloth wrappers soaked in water, baskets, and leather trunks. Many of our people participated in this looting. Generally Shima residents had all fled and not yet returned. The walls and buildings there were full of bullets—the scars of war. Hand grenades, bullets, and rifles had been scattered among mountains, paddies, and fallow land. The Japanese military had temporarily retreated, but, without a doubt, they would return. At that time the people who had suffered now would have an even worse time. That is why my cousin and a dozen more decided to dig caves to serve as temporary refugee protection.

I buried seven to eight hundred copper coins and some jewelry. We put my wife's leather suitcase in the barn. I also moved my books from the pigsty and buried them in the garden near the wall. We even went to the trouble of planting vegetables above them.

That night we stayed in the Yan Cave; perhaps because of that, the night was peaceful.

Saturday, May 17, 1942

The night at the Yan Cave was like staying at Peach Blossom Spring [*the utopia described by Tao Yuanming in the fourth century and called upon by Feng Zikai in as he looked for a respite from war*]. It frankly seemed quite out of this world. We left after noon. The enemy had gone, without a trace; *our soldiers* [emphasis added] had also disappeared. People seemed to return to their daily routines quite calmly.

Tuesday, May 20, 1941

But Chinese robbers took advantage of the raw fear in people's minds and in the middle of the night fired guns. People panicked and fled; the robbers then went into their homes and hauled away their loot.

After the military invasion of the Japanese, Dongyang County went through a dark time. The government did not know where to relocate;

bandits sprang up everywhere, extorting and blackmailing. There were masses of the impoverished, especially in South Township, a place where straggling troops caused many disturbances.

Wednesday, May 21, 1941

Now the villagers have become as afraid of the bandits as they had been of the Japanese.

The Refugee Experience

In their descriptions of their own refugee experiences, Jin and Wang highlight the almost unbearable palpable fear, the psychic pain, the engendered hatred of the enemy, and even psychogenic heart palpitations as at the core of the experience. In striking contrast, Feng is quite matter-of-fact and clinical in his descriptions, only once—in his reaction to seeing the flames in the sky from his boat—giving evidence of any sort of fear or uncertainty. Yet his depictions of the grotesqueries of deaths around him—the dead girl catapulted into the tree; the woman, eaten by wild dogs except for her head; and the woman hounded from her refuge by hosts fearful of her impending death and the bomb's bursting open her coffin after the body was inside it only an hour—all conjure up the horrors of everyday life in war that gave rise to the sorts of fears Jin and Wang describe.

All three diarists speak of the centrality of night for fleeing as a refugee. Wang notes that people "fled their homes even in the pitch-black darkness to take to the road as refugees." For Jin and his family, "nightfall" was a time for danger as "enemy soldiers entered [his] village." Feng and his family set off several times on portions of their trek in the middle of the night. Night travel could be fearsomely unnerving, especially in unknown areas. Wang and Feng emphasized the heavy rains and floods, the inhospitable, even hostile face of nature. The destructiveness of floods simply compounded the destructiveness of war. Wang comments, "Alas! Bayonet, soldier, flood and fire altogether." His description of the baleful effects of the floods on refugees recalls Feng Zikai's analogy regarding the West Lake area after the war: "It was though everything had been inundated by a great flood."[5]

As we have seen in almost every account, rumors were the lingua franca of the war. Everyone who Jin met on the road had a different story of where the Japanese army actually was. Wang reports, "Everybody has heard all sorts of rumors." He also writes, "Even at night, we were swallowed up in rumors." Some rumors filled people with hope—the speculation that the Japanese might not even come to Lianhua Village was dashed five days later—but most rumors ignited a sense of panic. Paul Fussell muses over the significance of war rumors, and what he says about soldiers must also be said about refugees.

> In the prevailing atmosphere of uncertainty for all and mortal danger for some, rumor sustains hopes and suggests magical outcomes. Like any kind of narrative, it compensates for the insignificance of actuality. It is easy to understand why soldiers require constant good news. It is harder to understand why they require false bad news as well. The answer is that even that is better than the absence of narrative. Even a pessimistic, terrifying story is preferable to unmediated actuality.[6]

A potential rumor-rich context is typically a crisis situation in which there is marked personal anxiety, overall uncertainty about what is happening, a general shortage of information, and people so panicky that they are ready to believe almost anything. Jin, at least, gave no credence to rumors, arguing that rumors only delude; but he seems in the distinct minority in this regard, if indeed he truly believed what he was saying.

Feng Zikai's metaphor of refugee life was living in a "sea of bitterness" (pointedly, another image of great quantities of water that echoes images of floods in refugee accounts). What were the most important elements of that life according to the diarists? First, there were the threats of violence from both Japanese and Chinese soldiers. The Japanese trashed, looted, and burned; Wang notes that they were even worse than the rumors that preceded them. There is little wonder that people, hearing the rumors, felt the necessity to ingratiate themselves with the Japanese by taking them wine and eggs, in Jin's account. Chinese soldiers, billeted in village temples, thought nothing of barging into people's homes to cook their meals; and in Wang's account Chinese soldiers seemed eager to prey upon, snatch up, and conscript porters from among the civilian population. The rule of thumb for refugees was to avoid both armies. Chinese refugees had to be ready to leave anytime, even, as Wang points out about the young couple he sees on the road, during a meal. But Chinese civilians, thrust into the brutality of war, could turn into vultures themselves, looting dead refugees. The rules of war on both sides seemed to be steal, rape, and kill.

One reality of the road was the rapidity of change that might sweep over an area. When Jin and his sister-in-law traveled to the county seat, they continually met changing situations so that there was nothing of which they could be certain. From being unconcerned about the gunfire in the distance, Jin came to believe that "the battlefield is ubiquitous." The Chinese people in his metaphor were animals—mice, seeing the cat: "they would hide and then try to escape so that there would be no trace of their existence." As Jin and Wang point out, commenting on "endless streams of refugees," it was rather easy as situations unfolded for family members to become separated in flight, a reality that produced even greater panic when the separated person had been an integral part of the group. Jin's sister-in-law and child became separated from Jin and the others and spent a night of terror in a neighboring village. Feng recounted the story of a woman who had been separated from her traveling companions and then killed and eaten by dogs. Once refugees were on the road, the conversation continually turned (as it had with the Feng Zikai group) to where should they be headed for greatest safety.

All the accounts point to one attitude that may have hampered some refugees in flight: a naivete about might be ahead and what might be done to ameliorate certain situations. Feng noted that Japanese planes had flown over the city for weeks before the first bombing attack, and yet people were not prepared when the attack came. Feng lambastes the magistrate, who, though he had military training, did nothing to prepare a defense or even defense readiness. Jin claims that most people were not scared; and he himself almost blundered into a dangerous situation, unconcerned as he was with the sounds of gunfire. Feng Zikai had had a strong sense that he would never actually have to face the Japanese. When presented with the possibility that Japanese planes flying south and west were bringing bombs and that those flying east and north to Hangzhou and Shaoxing were carrying wheat and rice, Wang concluded: "But certainly these simply had to be rumors, didn't they? How could we possibly believe that that such things were happening?"

Jin's diary gives evidence about how the wartime situation and refugee status affected his relationship with his wife. Admittedly, we don't know about the quality of their relationship before the war; but the wartime situations created misunderstanding and conflict. Jin noted that since the war neared their locality, his wife "had been continually befuddled—as if she had had a morphine injection." He used her as a sounding board, so that he could control his anger to a degree. They quarreled and were not able to reconcile before they slept. On their first refugee trek, his wife cried about not having taken important things along, and then rushed back, risking death. His wife and sister-in-law's lack of "courage," in his estimation, prevented him from choosing the alternative of spending the night in a forest. Finally, the husband and wife misunderstood each other, or, more likely, he did not explain to her all that was happening; he reproved her when she tried to drag heavy bags out of the house when they were not really leaving. Domestic relationships, indeed all interpersonal relationships, were stressfully challenged by the crises and hasty decisions that war compelled them to make.

Peach Blossom Spring

The fourth-century poet Tao Yuanming described a rural utopian escape from the political unrest of his period.[7] One day a certain fisherman following the course of a stream came upon a grove of blossoming peach trees. He walked on. At the end of the grove was a spring and a hill, and in the hill a small opening, which he was barely able to enter. But on the other side, he entered a rich and pleasant land of farms with abundant crops, impressive homes, and a happy and contented people, knit together by networks of paths that connected all. They reacted with surprise to the fisherman, but they showed great hospitality by inviting him into their homes for lavish feasts of chicken and wine.

Their story revealed to the fisherman how their world came into being. Their ancestors, in an effort to escape the troubles of their lives, fled to this isolated place—which they never left. They had been cut off from the outside world and lived in this secret world of peace and plenty. Having been feted by them all, the fisherman left, repeatedly marking his route so that he could return. But when he tried to do so, he could not find the marks and never found his way back. And the utopia was never found again.

It is not very difficult to understand the appeal of Tao Yuanming's account of Peach Blossom Spring to a people inundated by a sea of troubles in a war of aggression and terror. A utopian escape from fear and chaos was alluring. Both Feng Zikai and Jin Xihui use the image. Zikai supposes that his lineage's ancestral native place in Tangxi County will be "a pastoral haven, an arcadian retreat," his Peach Blossom Spring.[8] Jin's mention of the historic idyll came on the night of May 16, when he and his family spent the night in the Yan Cave: it was, he said, "like staying at Peach Blossom Spring." He added, "It frankly seemed quite out of this world." For Jin and his family, their time spent in the magical world of Peach Blossom Spring seemed indeed to have transformed the outside world as well. Jin notes, "We left [the cave] after noon. The enemy had left without a trace; our soldiers were also gone. People seemed to return to their daily routines." The reality for the Chinese at this time was tragically not so simple.

><

FIVE

The Kidnapping of Chinese Civilians

ONE OF THE CRUELEST individual dislocations of the war for Chinese civilians was to be kidnapped and conscripted for work by Japanese forces (though, it must be said, Chinese forces often did the same thing—and that was not a less dislocating experience). In a sense these individuals were double victims: general victims of the war, but specifically targeted personal victims of, in Chinese thinking, the Japanese devils. Here the striking experiences of Zhang Dayan and Wu Yingcai, two civilians—a journalist-turned-businessman and a middle school student—reveal the sudden and immediate dangers of civilians in a war zone. These experiences also tell us more about the nature of the war, since both victims were forced to travel with Japanese combatants; refugees, in contrast, were evading the Japanese if they were in a frontline area or were generally far from them in the rear areas.

The lengthier account, by Zhang Dayan, is most detailed about having to live under the abusive hand of Japanese soldiers.[1] The essays that tell his story were written in May and September 1988, forty-six years after his kidnapping occurred. We are not told whether there were earlier drafts of his accounts or whether he had compiled, closer in time to his kidnapping, some basic accounts or outlines of events. As we saw with Feng Zikai, who wrote about experiences two years or less after the facts, memory plays tricks and can significantly alter perspectives. Zhang's account must, therefore, be approached warily, but it is a strikingly revealing narrative of the experiences of men requisitioned for labor.

Dislocations of War

In late fall and winter 1937–1938, Zhang Dayan, a first lieutenant from Hangzhou, served as secretary at the 107th army hospital in Dehua, Fujian Province.[2] A bubonic plague epidemic swept over the area, threatening, he felt, his health and life. He wrote Xu Qinfu, president of the newspaper *Zhejiang Commercial News,* or *Zhejiang shangbao* (hereafter, *Commercial News*), and an important secretary in the Zhejiang Reconstruction Ministry, to ask for a job. Zhang had two connections to Xu: Zhang had worked at the *Commercial News* previously, and he had personal links to the manager of the *Commercial News,* who was none other than Xu Qinfu's younger brother. Xu quickly responded, telling Zhang to come to Lishui, where the Reconstruction Ministry had relocated even before the Japanese took Hangzhou. Lishui (see Maps 2, 7, and 10) was the former capital of Chu-zhou prefecture, located on the Ou River some 45 miles northwest of Wenzhou and 130 miles south of Hangzhou as the crow flies. Zhang went to Lishui in the spring of 1938. How he could so easily have left his military post at a time of war we are not told; most likely it was through the con-nections of Xu Qinfu to high-ranking individuals.

Once Zhang reached Lishui, he became involved in a business venture stimulated by dislocations wrought by war. One of his close friends, Zhang Tianfang, had joined with Xu Qinfu and a wealthy Lishui resident, Que Kongsun, who thoroughly knew the ins and outs of navigating on the Ou River, to form a boat company. Because of a paucity of roads and high-ways, moving goods and commodities to and from Lishui was totally de-pendent on the Ou River. The group also invited in one Wang Zhihao, who had worked for Yongjia County in an office dealing with transport and thus knew the details, connections, and existential realities of trans-port on one end of the boat line. They decided on a particular type of boat, made in Wencheng County, that could serve to transport both pas-sengers and cargo. Wang Zhihao worked to enlist boat captains and work out the details. Soon the Li-Qing-Wen (Lishui-Qingtian-Wenzhou) Boat Transport Company was in operation. While Wang Zhihao served as man-ager at the Wenzhou terminal, Zhang Dayan was hired on in the same post at the Lishui terminal.

During the Zhe-Gan campaign in the first ten days of the fifth lunar month (June 14 to 23) of 1942, Zhang Dayan suddenly heard that Japanese soldiers stationed in Jinhua were moving along the Jin–Wen (Jinhua–Wenzhou) road to seize Lishui. As the Japanese attack on Lishui became more imminent, Zhang's mood darkened; he began to feel, he wrote, very great pressure. Rumors proliferated about objectives of the Japanese , their whereabouts, and their treatment of those they had already conquered. When the Japanese struck, everyone in the city fled in all directions. Company boats took cover in out-of-the-way sites.

Zhang urged his fellow workers to take the next boat to Wenzhou (see Map 7). Once they landed in Wenzhou, he and his family frantically joined the company's Wenzhou business manager, Wang Zhihao, and his family. They all fled north from the city, across the Ou River, to the household of a relatively nearby farmer named Wang, perhaps a relative of Zhihao. After they stayed there several days, Wang Zhihao urged Zhang and his family to go with the Wangs deeper into the mountainous interior for greater safety. The plight of refugees was that they were never certain they had gone far enough or gone in the right direction; they were naturally always on edge. Zhang found himself in a similar situation to that of Feng Zikai and many others: among Zhang's family there was an old woman and at least one young girl. The women simply did not want to flee further. Zhang also thought that if he stayed where they were, he would still have the possibility of some boat work, being relatively close to the Ou River—an opportunity that would evaporate if they were holed up in the mountains. Further, the living arrangements at Farmer Wang's were good: it was a newly built two-story house with five rooms. Zhang and his family had one of the rooms. They could continue to reside there and have at least relative peace of mind. Therefore, Wang Zhihao and his family left on their own for the mountains.

Rumors that the Japanese were nearing Wenzhou were upsetting, but several days passed and no Japanese had appeared. The news of what had happened at Lishui was murky. And then one day near evening in the last weeks of the fifth lunar month (early July), a unit of Japanese soldiers from Lishui came into the area north of the Ou River and set up camp there. Zhang realized with great chagrin that the haven to which he and his family had fled for safety now fronted a growing Japanese military camp. Zhang felt an aching regret that he had not heeded Wang Zhihao's warnings and urgings. He wrote, "When we thought about moving at this time, it was already too late. It was best now to harden our courage and resign ourselves to our fate."

The day after the Japanese first encamped, a traitor *(hanjian*—that is, a Chinese collaborator with the Japanese) named Jia came to their door. Speaking with a Shandong accent, he encouraged them not to be alarmed. He told them that the Japanese would not cause them trouble. Zhang and his family half-believed Jia and at the same time were deeply suspicious of him. When several more days passed and the enemy did not approach, they felt better. Several days later the traitor Jia returned to their house and chatted. This visit also relieved the Zhangs, encouraging them to relax their sharp vigiliance.

But then it happened. Early in the morning of the first day of the seventh lunar month (August 12), Jia suddenly appeared, accompanied by two enemy soldiers. They had come to take (actually, to kidnap) Zhang as a requisitioned laborer. They also seized his younger brother, Zhang Tao; a younger relative from the Zhang lineage, Zhang Daquan; and the two brothers of Zhang's younger brother's wife—Meng Donglin and Meng Yaoting. They were seized to become coolies for the Japanese. That day the Japanese kidnapped over thirty men in the village. The captors tied their hands with rope and then tied the men to each other. In Zhang's words, they were led away "like lake crabs."

The Japanese took the men first to the military base camp but later that day marched them into Wenzhou and put them on the top floor of a large hotel on New River Street. Traitor Jia, who accompanied them, told them that this army unit was a mopping up guerrilla detachment that would return to Wenzhou in three to five days. He told them that they should not be afraid and that by no means should they try to escape: "If you do, you will be killed." For Zhang and the others, there was no possibility to escape at that point; it was best to bide their time and wait for a better opportunity. The Japanese untied the men (obviously for them to be able to sleep) and gave each man a large square handkerchief to protect himself from the sun and two food containers with instructions to save the food for the next day.

At midnight the enemies started out with captives in tow, backpacks slung over their shoulders; many more men from Wenzhou City itself had also been commandeered. Able-bodied and strong men were needed to carry the litters packed with supplies and weapons. The Japanese and their captives split onto three routes: the first group crossed the Ou River and walked along the highway; the second went down a small road heading northwest from the city; and the third traveled on the Ou River aboard light boats. The five Zhangs and Mengs were assigned to the small-road contingent. The Japanese marched in front; the coolies followed. They headed northwest in the direction of the town of Teng Bridge. Just after daybreak the temperature had already become oppressive; the coolies' only protection from the blazing August sun was the flimsy handkerchiefs that Traitor Jia had distributed.

They did not go far or long; they trekked over a small mountain and then two steeper ones. But when they came to a valley, machine-gun and cannon fire suddenly erupted from a small mountain opposite them. It was an ambush by a Chinese guerrilla unit. The sounds of ammunition blasts were deafening. The Japanese soldiers were caught completely by surprise and were none too quick to mount a defense. Within several minutes, however, they were able to marshal a counterattack; during the next few minutes, continuous gunfire from both sides cut through the air. Then, just as suddenly as the attack had begun, the Chinese guerrilla unit melted away. Over ten Japanese soldiers had been killed or wounded. Zhang could not tell whether there were any casualties among the coolies.

The Japanese took the wounded soldiers to nearby boats for evacuation. The surviving soldiers took the dead, placed them in white cloth, raised them up, and carried them into a small grove of trees, where they cremated them. The surviving enemy soldiers were all concealed in the grove, standing in silent tribute to the dead. Though Zhang referred to the Japanese continually as "enemies," the picture of the Japanese that emerges in his piece is generally not one of brutish devils. Here he suggested a certain nobility, if only in the ritual care of the bodies and their treatment.

The coolies, in the meantime, were standing or sitting under the broiling sun; Zhang remarked on the complete unpleasantness of this experience. It had been a long time since the area's last rain. "Who knew," Zhang later wrote, "that in this lonely place there would suddenly come a downpour from the heavens?" The Japanese soldiers had raincoats, but the coolies had to cut pine boughs to cover their heads. They were thoroughly soaked in the rain, from head to foot; the deluge kept up for almost two hours. After the extreme heat, now they were shivering from the cold. Zhang remembered, "This was the first time in my life when I had to eat this kind of bitterness." The rainstorm gradually lessened to a steady light rain, and then the skies finally cleared.

The cremation of the Japanese dead had been completed before the storm. Now the coolies watched as the Japanese soldiers picked up the bones and ashes in their hands and wrapped them in white cloth. They tied each cloth together, and each soldier hung one around his neck. At the same time, the enemy soldiers ordered the Chinese to eat their meal and to prepare to hit the road. The coolies took out the soaked food containers. Zhang had choked down only a few bites of tripe when suddenly the Japanese barked orders to begin walking. They walked on a muddy road around the foot of a mountain. They passed civilians and horses. Zhang detested slogging through the sloppy mire. When he took a step, his feet sank inches into the mud, and then it took a huge surge of strength to pull them out. It was a heavy burden just to walk down the road. Add that to the sodden clothes, and the coolies were miserable.

Dusk turned into night, but they still kept walking. The farther they walked, the colder they got. With the black darkness, they couldn't even see the road. The coolies bent their bodies forward as they walked, fearful of falling. If they fell, they could expect the Japanese to beat them savagely. The Japanese were well aware that the darkness and deep mud were making walking difficult and took steps to help. The first attempt helped almost not at all: they lit three candles. They were not very bright, and the wind snuffed them out almost immediately. The second strategy was generally more effective, but it revealed the complete disdain of the Japanese military for things Chinese. Whenever the marchers passed a building by the side of the road or slightly off it, they set it afire to illuminate the surroundings. The marchers walked until midnight with the assistance of arson-created light.

When they arrived at Teng Bridge, they made camp. The coolies were gathered on the upper floor of a distillery. They took off their still-soaked trousers and curled up on the floor to sleep. The enemy placed two soldiers on either side of the stairway as guards to prevent the coolies from escaping. Before the captives slept, they got out their food containers. The rice was for all intents and purposes inedible, mixed with sand and mud. The enemy told them that they could find no fresh water and thus had to cook the rice using water from a nearby stream that was yellow from its mud. Zhang does not mention the cooking process, but in the end, though he was very hungry, he couldn't force it down. On that first day, then, they had marched into a guerrilla ambush on the road and had almost nothing to eat. The routine of this military unit was to travel by night and to rest during the day. Therefore, they remained at Teng Bridge all through the next day and at night moved on.

They groped their way on the dark night, with only the dim starlight to illuminate things. Up a step, down a step: it was difficult to proceed, so they walked very slowly. In order to deal with fatigue, they generally walked an hour and then were given orders to rest for about half an hour. With this kind of walk-walk, stop-stop effort, they arrived at a village at daybreak. The villagers had already fled. It was obvious that they had fled just before the Japanese soldiers arrived: in some rice pots the rice was still giving off heat; in addition, some vegetable dishes, set out on tables, were still warm. The enemy scoured the village, searching for food. After they had eaten their fill, they gave the coolies a small serving of rice with bits of vegetables. The soldiers then herded their captives into a house to sleep; outside the Japanese kept constant guard, making it impossible for the coolies to escape.

They marched again on the third night, arriving in the vicinity of the Qingtian county seat in the morning. In front of the marchers was a shallow stream. The Japanese passed through it quickly with the coolies following; apparently aware of present danger, the Japanese urged them to hurry. Sure enough, from the nearby mountain machine-gun fire ripped the morning stillness; however, there were only a few gunshots. The Japanese were not apparently prepared or ready to attack. They all continued walking. Ahead was a small grove. The Japanese ordered the coolies to rest. Zhang noted that where he was about to sit, there was a small garden plot of tomatoes; he was just getting ready to lay down his backpack and sit down when suddenly, from the top of the small mountain just opposite the marchers, came a massive barrage of machine-gun fire. As what he called "fire-red bullets" rained from the mountaintop, Zhang crouched down in a ditch. He later said that this was the first time he saw war clearly. He had to keep telling himself "Don't. Don't"—so that he wouldn't jump up and try to run away. Only a brief moment passed before the vanguard of Japanese soldiers began returning fire; their response was much faster than in the first ambush.

Beside Zhang was a wounded Japanese soldier, who spoke to Zhang in awkward Chinese. "This is Mr.[he gave his last name]. We are striking back."The sound of gunshots was intense; the Chinese guerrilla attackers had used light machine guns, but the Japanese responded with heavier artillery. And then suddenly, all was quiet. One Japanese was killed in the attack. The ritual that Zhang and the others had seen after that first ambush was followed again: cremation, a time of silence, and the placing of the remaining bones and ashes into a container, which was wrapped in white cloth and tied around the neck of another soldier.

This was the last attack Zhang experienced while in Japanese custody. But the Japanese began to take out their frustration on coolies, whose lives were obviously considered as negligible as the buildings the enemy burned to light their way. Along the forced march, Zhang saw Japanese soldiers bayonet a number of coolies to death. When the Japanese had done this several times, the bayonet became a powerful tool of intimidation. To get coolies to obey and cooperate, they simply threatened their captives with being bayoneted. In the beginning the Japanese were fearful of walking on the main roads, afraid that the coolies would call out to passersby for assistance; they therefore forbade coolies from speaking with each other. There were several coolies who became ill with colds and high fevers (Zhang attributed these illnesses to the hot sun or the rain). To combat the fevers, Japanese soldiers poured cold water over the heads of the feverish. Zhang said that this action only caused the illness to worsen. Soldiers forced ahead those who were sick until they fell. When captives could no longer stand, the enemies considered that these men had already lost their value and got rid of them by killing them with the dreaded bayonet.

Zhang was ordered to carry the backpack of a wounded enemy soldier with a slightly lame foot. It was the soldier who had spoken to him earlier. What followed was a most remarkable episode, given the stereotypical Chinese view of the Japanese as "devils."The Japanese soldier's facial expressions showed that he was responding in friendly fashion to Zhang. His Chinese was halting and awkward, but his actions and words were positive. Right after Zhang was assigned to him, the marchers had sat down to eat. The Japanese soldier gave Zhang some food, saying, "This is yours." Zhang said that he was thirsty; the Japanese soldier handed him his water canteen for a drink. He then said to Zhang, "I am a slightly wounded soldier. According to regulations, I had to be given a coolie who could carry my backpack. We can walk at the back of the group of Japanese soldiers so that other soldiers do not mess with you. Do you understand? We can walk at the back."

At the next rest period, the soldier again struck up a conversation with Zhang. Though Zhang later said that he lied about the truth, the Japanese soldier opened up about his own life. He told Zhang that he had been studying at the university when he was drafted into the army. His household consisted of his parents and one sister. He expressed mild antiwar sentiment, and he insisted that he was adamantly against, indeed detested, violent behavior. The soldier seemed obviously sympathetic to Zhang's plight.

He said, "Be sure to keep in mind not to run away. You could become a corpse by the side of the road. This is what happens to those coolies who attempt it. We are going to Suxi in Yiwu county. There we have an automobile; I'll teach you to drive." Zhang responded to him very positively. Because of the warm relations between them and the protective attitude of the Japanese soldier, every time the group camped, the soldier sent Zhang back into the area where the coolies rested. Moreover, the soldier made it clear that he would look after Zhang: "I can come to call you. You don't have to run about looking for me." It was an extraordinary situation: an enemy soldier, one of the "devils," being warmly and paternalistically solicitous for Zhang.

They had finished the evening meal. The sky was darkening, and Zhang assumed they would start out soon. Suddenly, an enemy soldier whom Zhang had seen being especially cruel and brutal saw Zhang resting and shouted, "You! Come!" Zhang responded that he was carrying the other soldier's backpack. "Oh, no, you're not," the soldier growled. He yanked Zhang up roughly and dragged him to the litter loaded with supplies and weapons. One of the coolies who had been charged with carrying the litter was apparently given a different assignment; and the soldier, looking for a replacement, had seen Zhang in the area and at rest. Zhang really had no choice but to comply, but he had no idea that the litter would be so heavy and difficult to lift. There were four carriers and only one was able to bear the weight rather easily:

Zhang could not. He later wrote that he had never lifted anything so heavy. To make things worse, the road was not level or flat, and it was getting darker and darker. It was altogether possible that one of the four carriers might stumble or crumple under the weight. That, Zhang thought, could bring the stabs of a bayonet. The more he thought of it, the more frightened he got. In the rest period, he sat, short of breath, and sweated profusely.

Suddenly, directly in front of him was his wounded "patron" soldier. When the soldier saw him, he said, "Come with me." But what looked like Zhang's salvation was not. The cruel soldier would not permit Zhang to change jobs; seeing and hearing the lame soldier did nothing but annoy the cruel one. Zhang was silent, suffering intensely. At this critical moment, Zhang saw a high-ranking Japanese officer riding upon a large roan. The officer sat there, as if paying respects. The lame soldier made gestures of respect; talking in a low voice and muttering, he spoke in Japanese, using his hand to gesture toward Zhang. The officer listened to the lame soldier; then, he turned to the cruel soldier and asked him about the unpleasantness. They talked at length; and after, the officer told Zhang he could go with the lame soldier. The officer dismounted angrily, went up to the cruel soldier, and, using both hands, slapped him several times with his palms. It seemed, Zhang said, that the Japanese had an unwritten rule that whenever a lightly wounded soldier was assigned a coolie, then it was not permitted to change that decision casually *(suibian)*. Zhang thought to himself that that rule was a good barrier from danger.

When Zhang was taken captive, he had been wearing a thin silk shirt, long silk pants, and cloth shoes; inside his trouser pockets were a small towel and the handkerchief that Traitor Jia had given the coolies. These clothes Zhang had worn since he was taken captive; they had been daily drenched in sweat, and Zhang was conscious of his stench. His clothes had also been torn and were very dirty. Holes had been rubbed in the bottom of his shoes; he had tried to do various things to get by, for he obviously could not go barefoot. He decided the only possibility would be to find some replacements in one of the homes in the villages where they had been sequestered during their daytime rest. He first found a pair of old, worn cotton shoes, but they had no holes. At another place he found a tight short shirt and some trousers made for a woman, with a pattern of delicate willow branches. Although they did not fit well, they were, he wrote, much better than what he had had.

One night the group had walked well past midnight when they arrived at a small village. The moonlight was very bright (one wonders, if this was the case, why the Japanese soldiers did not continue until dawn). The dew was extraordinarily heavy. The Japanese ordered all to encamp; the commanding officer took one house. Some soldiers and the coolies were to sleep out of doors. The evening cool and the dew made it seem like they were lying in water. Zhang felt that he needed something to put over him. Fortunately, here Zhang had a first chance encounter with his brothers. How and when they became separated we are not told; we were not even told they had gone elsewhere until this moment. It seems very strange that Zhang had not mentioned this, given the bonds of brothers and family members in general. Perhaps they were separated when Zhang was called out by the wounded soldier to carry his backpack. In any event, his two brothers and the two other relatives had found some coarse, blue sheeting. The five of them chose a piece of relatively level cleared ground on a mountain slope to sleep on, protected from the dew by the sheet. As they were preparing for sleep, they suddenly saw a Japanese soldier approach. In an instant, he grabbed the sheeting, pulled it off Zhang and the others, and walked away.

They did not dare speak, only cursed him under their breath. Coolies were not permitted to have exchanges with Japanese. Zhang asked his relatives if this would be a good time to run away. They replied that soon they should try to make it to Lishui, but they were not familiar with the terrain in this area, and they should wait until they were in more familiar territory. When they saw an opportunity, they would make a run for it.

The Japanese across the way set fire to a house. Zhang wrote, "It's like a cigarette addiction. They order us around and we march. If they don't light fires, it's as if they wouldn't know how to continue. Therefore, whenever enemies choose a village to camp in, the houses chosen are especially unlucky. The people who have fled, our fellow refugees, had left a very good house; when they return, it will have been destroyed."[3]

When the group came to the village of Shifan in the vicinity of Lishui, the food supply was completely exhausted. Searching the houses in the village turned up nothing. The soldiers ordered the coolies to dig *fanru*, a type of root. It was very difficult work; they found too few, and their time was limited. So for this meal, while the soldiers got more, the coolies each got a portion of a root that was three-quarters the size of an index finger. They had to count that as eating their fill.

The walk-walk, stop-stop regimen kept up for twelve days. They arrived in Lishui on the twelfth day of the seventh lunar month, that is, on August 23, 1942 (see Map 10). The coolies were sequestered in the courtyard of the home of a rich merchant. The number of coolies had increased greatly when those with Zhang met up with the third-route troops and their coolies. However, even with all the hubbub of the additional new troops, when Zhang and the others arrived in Lishui, there was no opportunity to escape. Then a rumor spread that Lishui had already established a Peace Maintenance Committee (PMC), the local ruling body of collaborators with the Japanese. Setting up this organization was Japan's first step toward asserting control after it had occupied an area. The rumor also named the head of the PMC, one Zhang Xuanyang. Meng Donglin looked stunned. Was it possible that Zhang Xuanyang was someone he knew, a man who had been in charge of the finances of the cooperative on Fuqian Street there in Lishui? Meng said, "Let me go and meet him to see if he can help us find a way out of our captivity." He went on this mission, but he never returned. The remaining four did not know what to believe: Surely he did not escape alone, leaving them in their desperate situation? Did something happen so that he might be dead or wounded?

After awhile, Meng Yaoting was called by the translation officer to go for translation work; Zhang thought it strange that Yaoting took his backpack with him. He also never returned; and the conjectures about what had happened went on for some time. Zhang talked with his brothers, Tao and Daquan, about escaping. How could they find an opportunity to flee? The courtyard where they were being held seemed an impregnable fortress. Zhang thought that it would have been impossible to escape even if they had been given wings. He felt very tense. The captives were kept there for two days. Then on August 25, they ate their evening meal and were suddenly ordered to move out—on another night march. After they had passed out of the city wall's Liyong Gate, they turned their heads to look back to the city. It was a sea of fire. Zhang realized that the enemy was retreating and would not return to Lishui. He and his brothers became separated on the march, but at the first resting stop he found them. Certainly they all wanted to escape—but separately: any disappear-ance of all three at the same time would be much more easily noticed by the enemy. Later, his brothers disappeared—and for good. Did they es-cape? Zhang turned this possibility over and over in his mind. In the dark, his thoughts were equally dark and troubled.

That night the area into which they were moving became killing fields. On their way to Jinyun County, they had to pass over Peach Blos-som Peak. It assuredly was not the utopian escape that its name tantaliz-ingly suggested and to which both Feng Zikai and Jin Xihui alluded. The peak was really only a small mountain. The trail on which they had to proceed was not steep, but it was very narrow. The problem was the heavy litters loaded with supplies and weapons that many men were forced to carry. Zhang was at the very back of the marchers, walking alongside the slightly lame soldier. Suddenly, up ahead, whether a litter bearer stumbled or strayed off the path or simply collapsed from fatigue, the litter bearers dropped the litter. At first the Japanese around it tried to help the captives pick it up and continue; but then the reality that Chi-nese coolies had the temerity to drop the litter enraged the Japanese, who began to attack coolies with their bayonets. In a matter of minutes there were corpses scattered everywhere. When Zhang passed the place, blood was still oozing from wounds; that stretch of the pathway was now dyed a deep red. Zhang counted forty-three corpses. He thought, "What an unendurable tragedy! Today's Japanese retreat is the day of our area's victory. And now this!" The darkness of his thoughts continued as he pledged in his mind to repay this blood debt.

The night passed, and the marchers hid again during the day. They met no gunfire as they headed toward Suxi in Yiwu County. At the crossroads where Route 4 headed to the Dongyang county seat, Zhang met a teacher named Fang, whom Zhang knew well and who had been taken captive for work in another group. In light of the massacre and of Zhang's relatives' escape, the two exchanged views about fleeing. Because there was considerable disorder at the moment, Zhang and Fang stealthily fell behind and ran away. The two men from Wenzhou thus became refugees together. This happened during the last ten days of the seventh lunar month (August 30–September 8).

They walked under a star-studded sky with a waning crescent moon. Paranoid, they were constantly looking all around; they knew they would be killed if Japanese soldiers discovered them. Fang said, "This area is comparatively bright. It's possible that there are enemy soldiers or our own soldiers camped nearby. We can use the moonlight, but we must leave the area of the enemy encampment and walk along the highway." Thereafter, Fang took the lead, climbed up a small hill, waded through a narrow stream, and groped about until the dawn of a misty day.

They then got up to a highway that had been destroyed. Fang said he was certain that they had left the danger zone. Both men heaved a sigh of relief. They walked as quickly as they could. Although they felt famished, they dared not stop until they reached Fang's house at dusk. Zhang marveled that they could, for the first time in weeks, eat their evening meal at a dining table. That night he slept in a bed and slept the whole night through. When he awoke, he ached from head to toe; but he was beginning the recovery from his ordeal. He talked and laughed and had friendly exchanges with Fang's family; and though he was in physical pain, he was quite optimistic and cheerful. On the second day at Fang's, Zhang washed his hair and clothes—and rested the whole day. He said that he felt he was a new person. On the third day, he ate breakfast early and bade good-bye to Fang and his family. He set out with two young men who were going to Wenzhou via Lishui. The two young Wenzhou men forged ahead of him and occasionally glanced back. Zhang, whose stint as a laborer for the Japanese had aged him markedly, thought that his body was tired and weak; his two legs felt very heavy, and he thought it best to go neither too fast nor too slow. He wrote, "Who knew that walking more than two hours, I would pass through a village where there were Chinese [Guomindang] troops encamped? I walked right into it."

Suddenly a sentry stopped him; Zhang had prepared for a moment like this and had his story down pat. He said he was a war reporter for the *Southeast Daily (Dongnan ribao)*. During the enemy's bombing of Lishui, he had lost his briefcase with his press credentials and thus had lost contact with the newspaper office. He said he was now on his way to Lishui to report. The sentry apparently did not buy Zhang's story; he marched Zhang into a building where there were several dozen new soldiers with shaved heads and worried looks, sitting on bamboo mats all over the room—the two young men from Wenzhou who had gotten ahead of him on the road were among them. All of a sudden, Zhang understood. These were coolies for the Japanese who had escaped from the enemy only to run into the tiger's mouth: they were now to be drafted not for labor but for military service at the front as soldiers in the national army. He wrote, "Alas! This world that eats its masses constantly flaunts its authority over people!"

Zhang knew that he had to plan how to survive this situation without being forced to become a soldier. The building now became a mess hall; food was served to the new soldiers. Zhang ate as well—two bowls of rice soup; he estimated that a bowl had between fifty and sixty grains of rice, mostly water, served with a smelly vegetable dish. Chinese soldiers were notoriously maltreated, fed poorly, with many dying before they could even reach the front.

After he finished eating, Zhang asked the sentry, "Who is your chief?" The sentry said, "The company commander." "Is he here? I want to talk to him," Zhang responded. "He's been out and has just returned," the sentry answered. While he was speaking, the commander came in.

Zhang asked, "Are you the company commander?" He said, "What business do you have with me?" Zhang responded, "I am a *Southeast Daily* war correspondent. In the previous enemy bombing attack I lost my briefcase with my credentials in the chaos; I also lost contact with the newspaper bureau. Today I really want to return to Lishui to report. But, as I was passing by, the sentry detained me. What's going on?" The commander asked, "What's your name?"

"Zhang Dayan." "What's the name of your boss?" Zhang was prepared for this and answered very quickly: "The bureau chief is Hu Jianzhong; vice-chief is Liu Xiangnu. The editor in chief is Wang Yuanhan, and the chairman of the board is Xu Shaodi." The commander waved his hand to stop Zhang from rattling off names. The officer called for the sentry and said to him, "Who gave orders for you to stop this man with a Hangzhou accent?"

Then Zhang understood. They were pulling in Wenzhou-dialect-speaking coolies. Zhang did not divulge why he was speaking in Hangzhou dialect nor how he knew the makeup of the *Southeast Daily* leaders. Since the *Southeast Daily*'s base before the war had been Hangzhou, Zhang's strategy in this personal crisis—adopting the Hangzhou dialect—revealed his quickness of mind and ability to adapt to changing situations: something that was apparent throughout his refugee and captive experience.

The commander ordered the sentry to send Zhang on his way. As Zhang turned to leave, he requested that the commander give him a safe-conduct travel pass in order to prevent another incident with the military along the way. The commander complied, and Zhang continued on his way back home. After he left the military company, he was intently on guard about what was happening around him. He entered Lishui through the Tiger Roar (Huxiao) Gate and went directly to the Huayuan Restaurant and Inn, which had been established by his boat company. After the bombing in Lishui, the company had already reopened for business. The restaurant manager, Huang Zixin, was very sympathetic once he heard Zhang's account of what had happened to him; Huang provided Zhang free food and wine to welcome him. Zhang raised his wine glass in a toast; later he wrote, "I had not smelled the fragrance of wine for many weeks. I was silent as tears rolled down my cheeks."

After spending the night at the inn, he took a boat early the next morning back to Wenzhou and Farmer Wang's residence north of the Ou River. Zhang's reunion with his family brought tears of joy mixed with tears of bitterness and grief. Of the five family members who were kidnapped, Zhang Dayan was the last one to return home; he said what had happened to him was a bad dream. He wrote, "I had been at forced labor basically just a month, a month where I received humiliation and hardship. I will never forget it. But now I've returned to my own business."

In 1988, when Zhang wrote this account, he reported that of the five men kidnapped by the Japanese, three had died, his younger brother and other relatives, Tao and Daquan, and Meng Donglin. Zhang recorded, "I wrote this in order to warn people who come later and also to take the opportunity for self-admonition." The latter goal is a cryptic comment, the exact meaning of which will never be known.

Zhang Dayan's experience is noteworthy and memorable for a number of reasons. We have in his account the first description of the work and activities of an active Japanese collaborator or *hanjian;* Mr. Jia consoled Zhang's family even as he carried out the bidding of the Japanese to facilitate the kidnapping of Zhang and others. The picture of the Japanese that emerges in Zhang's story is striking. The stereotypical understanding of the Japanese role in Chinese society ("there is no evil that they did not do") is evident in the case of the brutal Japanese soldier trying to take Zhang away from the task to which he had been assigned and in the murder of forty-three litter bearers on the dark Peach Blossom Peak—only because they dropped the litter. But the slightly wounded Japanese soldier who befriended Zhang, telling him of his own family background and his negative attitude toward war, endows at least this Japanese soldier with a humanity of which, as a group, they are usually deprived in Chinese narratives. The description of the Japanese funeral rituals also bestow on the Japanese soldiers a civility that stories of the Nanjing and other atrocities belie. The irony of Zhang's being detained by Chinese soldiers after his escape from the Japanese is great; only his quick wit allowed him to escape being forcibly taken to the front lines to fight. The Chinese forces were often seen as much of an enemy of Chinese civilians as the Japanese were, both in the capturing of men for forcible conscription and, in Zhang's story, the Chinese ambush attacks on Japanese and their civilian captives. Finally, the fact that the Japanese traveled at night and stayed hidden during the day emphasizes the importance of night, which in many refugee tales becomes a trope for the blackness, the groping, the stumbling, and the blindness of war. Significantly, once Zhang and Fang escape their dark nights of captivity, they walked under a star-studded sky with a waning crescent moon, Fang noting that this area [was] comparatively bright.

The Case of Wu Yingcai

Before the Japanese entered his home area (Gongshan Village in Yiwu County), Wu Yingcai was a middle school student.[4] On a morning in the middle ten days of the fourth lunar month (May 25–June 3) 1942, the principal unexpectedly announced, "We hear reliable rumors that the Japanese are only thirty *li* [ten miles] from here. We have to stop classes now; everyone should return home immediately." Wu was angry, at the Japanese and at the situation. He would be returning home just at the time of the grueling transplanting of rice seedlings, a task he would rather avoid. When he arrived home, he found, though, that the villagers were in a high state of anxiety, aware of the invasion of the "Japanese bandits" and of their harassment of the Chinese population. Though they were still busy in the fields, they villagers had also prepared food for a forced journey, packed some clothes, and were ready to flee at any time.

Two days after Wu's return, in the middle of his family's dinner, about 7 P.M., the sound of gunfire erupted from a small hill behind the village. A hail of bullets flew over their family's roof, making what Wu called a "hissing sound." Immediately, the whole village erupted in an uproar of shouts and wails. Everyone rushed toward the fields to hide. Wu's family, male and female, old and young, totaled ten. In a row, carrying what they could, they followed Wu's oldest brother and fled straight to a forested mountain alongside the village. Wu estimated that they ran only about two hundred meters, the maximum that some of his older family members could go. They lay down in a wheat field and rested. The skies darkened as night approached.

Because they were so close to the village, after a few minutes of rest, Wu's oldest brother quietly led the family farther away from the village for greater safety. Wu stayed crouched in the wheat field, wanting to see what would happen in the village. About 10 P.M., he could make out lamplight and rushing shadows; he heard the sounds of knocking on doors and the squeals of pigs: he knew troops had entered the village. "However," he wrote, "I didn't know whether they were Chinese or Japanese." That was a telltale admission: Chinese in Yiwu (at least Wu, at this point) seemed to expect that the actions of Chinese soldiers would not be very different from those of the Japanese. But, he asserted, he would not dare rush rashly into the village to find out who they were. Then he heard them speaking Japanese among themselves and speaking mangled Chinese with a villager who had stayed behind in bed with rheumatism. Wu took advantage of the Japanese interrogation to flee to the meeting point that his family had arranged. He walked through the night, noting that he undoubtedly passed unseen dangers and perils.

In sunlight the next morning, Wu found his mother and what first seemed the rest of the family on the top of a mountain. But his oldest brother was not there. They told him that his brother had gotten separated from the rest. (Since the brother was leading the group, this explanation of what happened seems odd, at the very least.) Wu assumed his brother must have returned to the village; Wu foolhardily left his mother and the others to return to the village to try to find his brother.

When Wu reached the edge of the village, he spoke with two other Chinese youths who were also standing and watching. Suddenly two Japanese soldiers strode toward them with guns drawn. Wu fled—straight into the arms of two plainclothes Japanese soldiers. Wu pivoted and ran about a hundred meters in another direction—when he ran into a group of Japanese soldiers coming from a neighboring village. They swarmed around him, hitting his head with their rifle butts, nicking him in the back with their bayonets, kicking him with leather shoes, and shoving him to the ground. They searched him, taking only his leather belt (Wu noted that it was unusual for Chinese to have leather belts). They accused him of being a Chinese soldier. They beat him with his belt; his back became a mass of welts and bruises; blood ran from a head wound. They continued to slap him, and finally they beat him with a whip. The troop leader then had Wu tied up, "like," Wu wrote, "a prisoner just before his execution."

In the neighboring village, the Japanese appeared just as people were eating breakfast, and some were preparing to go to the market at Shangxi; villagers fled in all directions. Those who did not run far enough were nabbed to be porters for Japanese supplies and gear. About noon Wu and his captors arrived at the town of Shangxi at a periodic market crowded with people. Standing on a slope overlooking the market, the Japanese strafed it. The gunfire came as a total shock to the crowd, which scattered, panic-stricken. Those who were caught were seized as coolies. When Wu tried to answer some of the new captives' questions about the identity of this particular Japanese troop, the soldiers for some reason became enraged. In retaliation, they burned him on the face and back with lit cigarettes. Shoved onto the ground, Wu writhed in severe pain. Afterward, the solders took him and the other prisoner-porters to a different village, where the Japanese ate their lunch.

They marched all afternoon: unlike the Japanese troops described by Zhang Dayan, who marched during the night and rested in the day, these troops generally marched during the day and slept at night. Zhang's troops were guerrilla units, who stayed in the same general area. The troops who captured Wu were from the regular army and ranged far and wide. The Japanese did not give Wu any food. Along the road there were several dozen relatively old men and women who handed out bowls of savory greens to welcome the Japanese. It was rumored that this kind of thing might possibly win some favor from the Japanese, who, in turn, then might refrain from killing and pillaging. Hiding their true feelings, Chinese arranged places for the Japanese to stay, cooked meals, and killed chickens and pigs to feed the enemy. However, when night came, the male hosts were locked up in the sleeping hall and the next day, no matter what their ages, taken to be conscript laborers. The women too were locked up; Wu alleged that it made the inevitable rapes that occurred much easier because women could not escape. Still tied up as he had been since his capture, Wu was locked in an upstairs room, outside of which a Japanese soldier stood guard. Wu could not sleep. The hunger pains from not having eaten all day were intense. He cried out, asking to have something to eat. Perhaps because his captors thought Wu would make a terrible row that would disturb their rest, they brought up a bowl of leftover rice.

The next day Wu remained bound. The soldiers headed for the larger city of Lanxi (see Map 2). The way took them over Taiyang Peak, a tall and steep mountain, not easy to climb and even harder now because the paths were muddy after heavy rain. The Japanese army's store of supplies and equipment was great, so movement was difficult for the packhorses and human porters. Horses were an important part of the Japanese war machine. Here, with the horses going up the slope, one Japanese had to go in front and pull; another had to be behind pushing and hitting the horse's buttocks. Great care had to be taken lest a horse fall and break its leg, because the Japanese would then have to shoot it—and thus lose a valuable military asset. A few weeks later, in an area to the west near the Qu county seat, the Japanese cavalry did lose many horses that died of bloating after eating soybeans in ripe fields and then drinking too much water.[5] Horses were one resource that the Japanese could not replenish.

The porters' burdens fell on shoulder and back. Younger ones could move ahead, yet with some difficulty, step by step. But the task resulted in tragedy for the older and weaker men, who had no alternative but to stop and rest frequently. When they stopped, the Japanese hit them with rifle butts and kicked them. The weaker captives faced constant Japanese retaliation and harassment along the march. Some of the old simply could not go farther. Wu saw two whom the Japanese nonchalantly bayoneted and kicked to the side of the road. During that day Wu counted five such corpses along the way.

Wu himself had only one soldier's supplies on his back, and they were not heavy. But he was barefoot and the soles of his feet were completely bloodied: blood and earth mixed together. He wrote, "It hurt so badly that I couldn't bear to speak." Although the mountain route was between ten and twenty *li* (about three to seven miles), the group took a whole day to traverse it. It was already dusk when they encamped at a small village. They entered a house, where there was still a feeble cooking fire going, a full bowl of white rice, and a bowl of salty greens sautéed with bamboo shoots. The Japanese did not want the food, giving it to the porters, who fought over it. Wu did get a bite to eat.

Late the next day, the marchers reached small villages fairly near Lanxi; to be able to launch an attack on the city the next day, the Japanese used nighttime for preparation and some further marching. Again, Wu had eaten nothing that day, and his thirst was unbearable. In the darkness he saw light reflecting on some water along the road. Not caring whether it was clean or polluted, Wu drank it. The morning light revealed that the water contained night soil. One wonders whether Wu was so exhausted that he could not taste the pollution. As the troops were about to ford a river about three miles from Lanxi, Chinese forces from the opposite bank opened fire. The Japanese and their porters panicked: some fell; others ran. Wu lay flat on his back on the ground. The soldier who had been guarding him fled. Wu used his head; they were near a cemetery. He was able to get to the cemetery in order to rub the rope tying his hands against a tombstone until the rope broke. He wrote that he had "liberated himself." He quickly rushed to join a group of porters so that he could be perceived a free porter once the chaos of battle ended.

The fight between Chinese forces and the Japanese lasted all day and night. On the next morning, as the Chinese withdrew, the Japanese entered the city, marching from the train station to the city center. All buildings had been leveled, and corpses of soldiers and civilians littered the streets. Some people had been burned to the point of looking like pieces of charcoal. It was, Wu noted, difficult to look at the horrific scene. Bodies had already started to decay, and the stench was overpowering. After the Japanese entered the city, they started to loot; anything was fair game: money, jewelry, ham, mushrooms, wood ears (a type of fungus used in cooking), ancient paintings, and objets d'art—anything that struck their fancy. Wu lamented, "And we porters had to carry all the stuff." The Japanese ordered the captives to carry the bodies of Japanese soldiers into a house. Firewood was piled around the house, doused with kerosene, and set on fire. Later, the Japanese combed through the burned rubble, picking out any remaining bones and wrapping them to be sent to Japan.

They stayed in Lanxi two days; then they started for Quzhou (see Maps 2 and 9). Wu was treated as a full-fledged coolie, but he only had to carry the bundle of one soldier. Because the Chinese had already destroyed the main road, the Japanese had to travel on mountain roads or on the small pathways between paddies. Understandably, there were not many people on these "roads"; occasionally they would pass the decomposing body of what was probably a farmer. Even given the fact that the marchers were not on roads or highways, they met continual harassment by withdrawing Chinese forces, who killed Japanese soldiers and porters alike. Once Wu and several porters were carrying supplies on bamboo poles. Chinese bullets hit one of the bamboo poles and it broke, dropping its contents into a rice paddy. If there had not been military action, Wu and the others would probably have paid with their lives.

Japanese soldiers attacked the Qu county seat for four days and nights, as the weather ranged from blistering sun to drenching rains. After the battle, soldiers and porters marched on westward. For many days they walked on the raised paths between flooded paddies. They passed through villages whose main occupation was raising ducks in sheds. Wu noted that, even in their simply passing through, their own bodies seemed to have absorbed the odors of duck shit; it was hard to stand themselves. Yet Wu suggested that the only way to get the smell off was to use paddy water (itself mixed with night soil) to wash it off. Chinese prisoners of war, Wu asserted, were like ducks driven helplessly across a field.

The Japanese summarily shot those who were too wounded to march. Wu remembered one day when the porters were locked in a barn guarded by a Japanese soldier. There were piles of wheat in the barn, and the porters decided to climb on the piles and rest. Beneath them they heard a low, moaning sound. They searched in the straw and slowly a man completely covered with bruises crawled out. One of the coolies cried out in horror at the way the man looked. The Japanese guard outside the door heard the sound, rushed in, and pulled the wounded man out. Then the guard beat the man to death with a wooden stake. Wu's judgment of the Japanese: "They were people without principles."

The marchers walked for six or seven days into Jiangxi Province, reaching the town of Guangfeng (about sixty miles southwest of

Quzhou). All the porters had contracted dysentery. Wu suffered through twenty bowel movements a day; his body became progressively weaker and weaker. The coolies were locked in a room with rice straw to sleep on. But Wu had a fever, his stomach hurt, and he had urgent loose bowels. On the second day, he couldn't move. The Japanese gave him four or five pills that halted the attacks, but he suffered from bloody stools for many days.

Then the Japanese offered a horrifying object lesson in the treatment of porters who tried to escape. All along the way, the Japanese had seized victims to serve as porters, yet when they reached Guangfeng, there were only about a dozen remaining. By then, since so many conscripted porters had fled, most current porters were Jiangxi men. In the middle ten days of the seventh lunar month (August 22–31), one day before noon, Japanese soldiers called Wu and three or four of the others to gather in the courtyard. In a minute several dozen soldiers carrying rifles with bayonets surrounded them. On the steps to the side were several machine guns. Wu and the others were panicked, not sure what was happening. Then a Japanese soldier led in four coolies, two in their forties or fifties and two in their twenties— all from Jiangxi. They were men who had escaped the night before but who had been captured and returned. "Today," a Japanese shouted, "we must 'Pineapple, pineapple, death basket, death basket—behead [*boluo, boluo, siluo, siluo—shatou*]!'" After that was said, a tall Japanese raised an officer's sword and from left to right made four swaths punctuated by snapping sounds; four heads left their bodies, blood spurting out; the bodies fell— their legs twitched repeatedly before they stopped moving.

Another time, late into the night, soldiers called Wu and five other porters. They took them out of the city wall and up onto a mountain slope. The soldiers ordered them to kneel. Because the night was very black, it was impossible for Wu to know how close the soldiers were to them. Suddenly a soldier yelled, "Pineapple, pineapple, death basket, death basket"; Wu and the others knew what this meant. There were then six gunshots. Wu wrote that it wasn't clear to him whether he was dead or alive until a soldier ordered him to march. Of the six porters taken out of the city, only four returned. It is not therefore surprising that Wu said that while at Guangfeng, he felt the continual danger of being killed. Jiangxi porters who tried to escape and were caught were killed and their bodies hung on the city wall.

Wu and an older porter from Shaoxing were at last able to escape once the Japanese had pulled back into Zhejiang Province and were one day short of reaching the city of Jinhua. At midnight, Wu and the porters were fixing food for the Japanese as usual; they could see that there was no special defense against their escaping. Wu and the porter from Shaoxing went out of the city on the pretext of getting water for making rice. To put the sentinel at the city gate at ease, they brought one bucket of water from the city pond about fifty meters from the gate and went back for a second. The night was very dark; the moon had sunk in the west. The sentinel could not see them clearly, so he walked toward the pond. When he saw them, he turned back to the gate. The Shaoxing man attacked him from behind and knocked him down. Wu then grabbed the sentry's rifle and hit him again and again in the head with the rifle butt. When the guard stopped moving, the two captives fled. Over the next days, they talked frequently with local villagers, who warned them about villages where there was a Japanese presence.

Wu's captivity lasted over three months. He said about his return, "My skin and bones were like firewood; my clothes were shabby and covered with grease stains. I didn't feel like a human being." He claimed that it took him over six months after living in the midst of brutality to return to a sense of the normal. At the end of his account, he included lines of a poem he wrote after the events.

> Bloodshed everywhere in our sacred land [*shenzhou*],
> The Japanese robbed me and brought many clouds—I am bitter.
> I swear to do whatever it takes [literally, "mow down mansions and
>   orchids"] to restore my native land [*gutu*],
> So that I may leave a good name to shine for a thousand autumns.[6]

The Japanese pictured in Wu's account are the more stereotypical brutal destroyers for whom Chinese life was of negligible value: once porters were wounded or disabled, they ceased to have any function for the Japanese. The porters' treatment—being kicked to the side of the road—was in marked contrast to the ritual for the Japanese dead. But for all the Japanese soldiers' brutal control, the troops were amazingly unable to control the porters and keep them from escaping. The Japanese locked the porters up every night and posted one or more guards to make sure the captives did not escape. One other labor conscript reported that the

Japanese would not even let a porter out at night for urination or defecation.[7] Yet another student labor-captive corroborated that restriction in his experience. He also reported, "In the middle of the night there was a commotion. One of the porters, who was well known, jumped from the second-floor window, planning to run away. But a guard saw him and shot him dead on the spot."[8] In Wu's account, the Japanese soldiers' brutal object lessons—the beheadings and the shooting of two other Chinese—seemingly stopped no one from trying to flee, from trying to become refugees, as it were, from captivity. We are left to wonder why Wu stayed for as long as he did; he was not the sort to be easily intimidated.

The accounts of men who were kidnapped to serve as laborers indicate that the men "served" as long as the Japanese wanted to hold them or until they could escape. For Zhang Dayan, it was about a month; Wu labored around three months. But for both, it was a time of suffering. The experiences—ambushes by their own countrymen, time spent in whatever houses the Japanese chanced to take, the difficult nighttime marches—had great and often deleterious impacts. Further, the families who did not know what had happened to their relatives—if they were dead or alive—suffered deep psychological pain.

One wonders why the Japanese with captives in tow came into so many villages where the food was still warm on kitchen tables, where cooking fires were still flaming. The villagers would almost have to have known that the Japanese troops were in the area. Why wait until the very last minute when danger was so imminent? I have found no accounts that offer explanations to such lack of preparedness. But the cause may be the same mind-set as that of Feng Zikai, who believed he would never come face to face with the Japanese, or of Jin Xihui, who said that most people were not scared and who presumed ingenuously that the gunshots he heard in the distance came from hunters. There seems to have been a naivete afoot; perhaps it was only the naivete that comes with not having experienced war before, but it is surprising and striking. And it contrasts greatly with the reactions of other Chinese who fled, terrorized, in many areas.

Finally, these accounts raise questions about how deeply nationalism had penetrated Chinese society. The closest thing to an expression of nationalism was Wu's poem, in which he speaks of doing all that he can to restore his native land. He wrote this after he had recuperated at home and had time to think about the nation and its trauma. Perhaps national-ism was the game played by those away from the front lines. For while these labor conscripts were Japanese captives, they were really on the front line, experiencing ambushes and battle, seeing death all around, and suffering physical and mental anguish "in the now." In none of their sto-ries nor in any that I have read is there noticeable evidence of national feeling. Both Zhang and Wu seemed to see Chinese soldiers as equally dangerous as the Japanese. Feng Zikai seemed to see all Chinese as a threat that could cheat and take advantage of him and his family. When Zhang's relative Meng Donglin heard that Zhang Xuanyang was the head of the collaborative Peace Maintenance Committee, Meng did not condemn the man as a traitor but as someone he could use to get himself and his family members out of labor captivity. Chinese villagers served the Japanese troops meals, killed precious farm animals to feed them—even invited the enemy to sleep in Chinese homes, assuming such cour-tesies would earn better treatment from the invaders. But on the face of it, the Chinese were not displaying much national feeling. The concern of refugee, labor conscript, and food-supplying villager alike was the im-mediate present and the safety and well-being of themselves and their families. During this time of crisis, at least for the time being for the vast masses, the nation was not the priority.

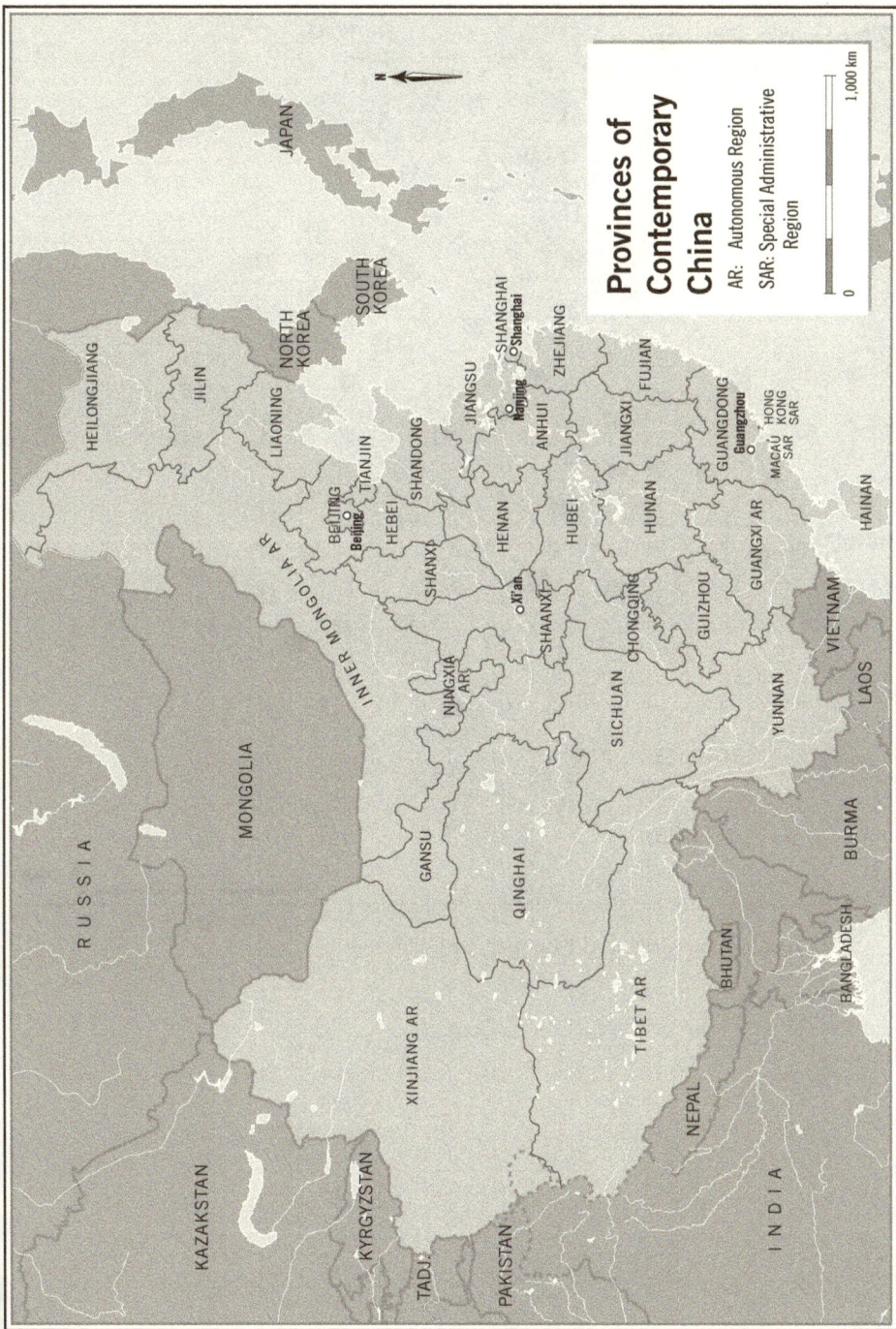

Provinces of Contemporary China

AR: Autonomous Region

SAR: Special Administrative Region

0   1,000 km

Map 1.

Map 2. Zhejiang provincial base map with counties

Key to County Map of Zhejiang

County	Map Number	County	Map Number
Anji	11	Songyang	70
Changhua	20	Suian	54
Changshan	56	Suichang	73
Changxing	8	Taishun	65
Chongde	6	Tangxi	48
Chun'an	51	Tiantai	29
Ciqi	23	Tonglu	49
Deqing	9	Tongxiang	5
Dinghai	21	Wenling	33
Dongyang	41	Wukang	10
Fenghua	25	Wuxing	7
Fenshui	50	Wuyi	44
Fuyang	16	Xianju	31
Haining	13	Xiangshan	26
Haiyan	4	Xiaofeng	12
Hang	14	Xiaoshan	40
Huangyan	32	Xinchang	34
Jiande	52	Xindeng	18
Jiangshan	59	Xuanping	69
Jiashan	1	Yin	24
Jiaxing	3	Yiwu	43
Jingning	72	Yongjia	62
Jinhua	45	Yongkang	42
Jinyun	66	Yueqing	61
Kaihua	55	Yuhang	15
Lanxi	47	Yuhuan	60
Lin'an	17	Yunhe	71
Linhai	30	Yuqian	19
Lishui	68	Yuyao	37
Longquan	74	Zhenhai	22
Longyu	58	Zhuji	36
Nantian	27		
Ninghai	28	**Prefecture**	**Map Numbers**
Pinghu	2	Jiaxing	1–6
Pingyang	64	Huzhou	7–12
Pujiang	46	Hangzhou	13–20
Qingtian	67	Ningbo	21–27
Qingyuan	75	Taizhou	28–33
Qu	57	Shaoxing	34–40
Ruian	63	Jinhua	41–48
Shangyu	38	Yanzhou	49–54
Shaoxing	39	Quzhou	55–59
Sheng	35	Wenzhou	60–65
Shouchang	53	Chuzhou	66–75

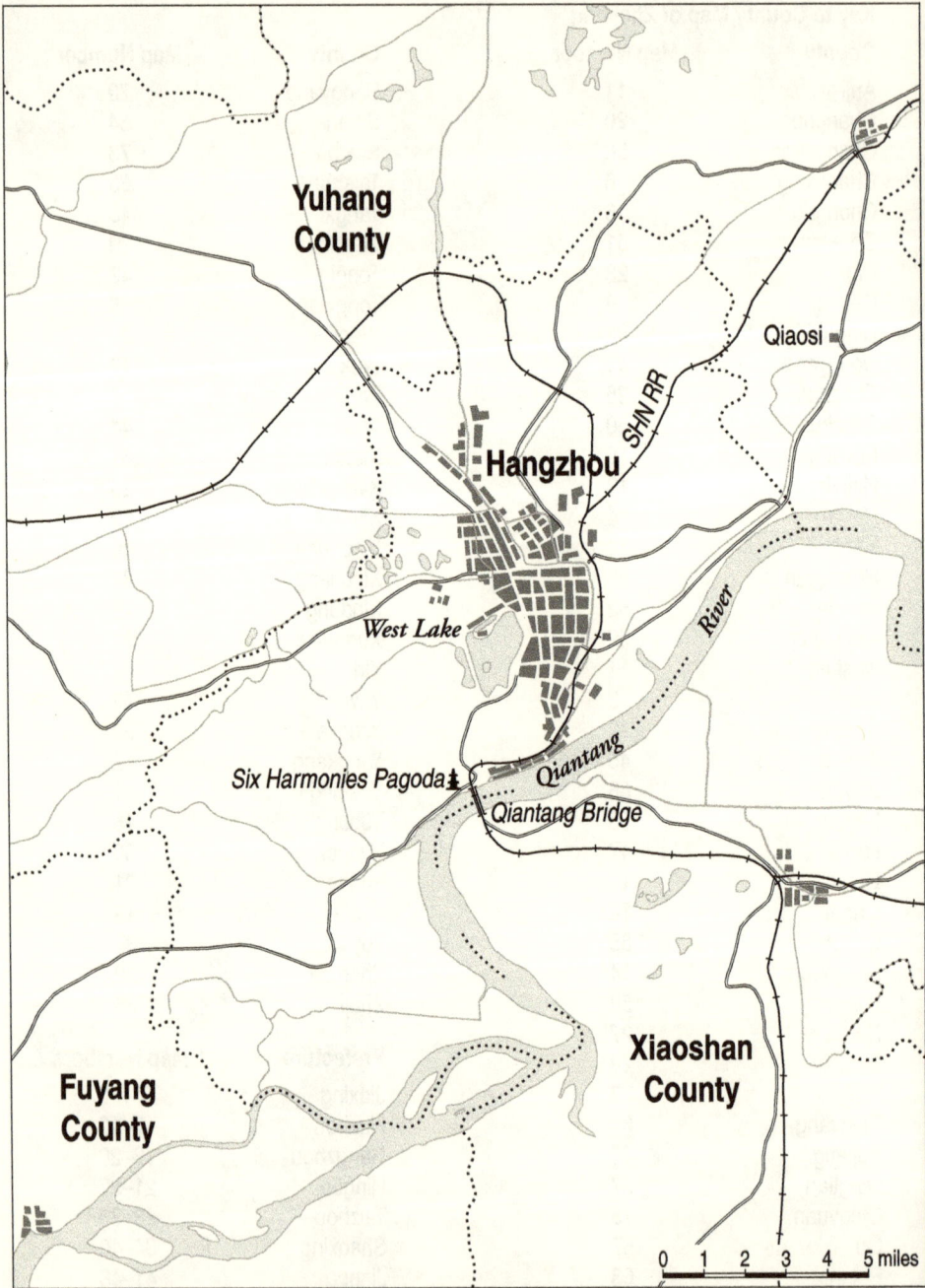

Map 3. Hangzhou and its environs

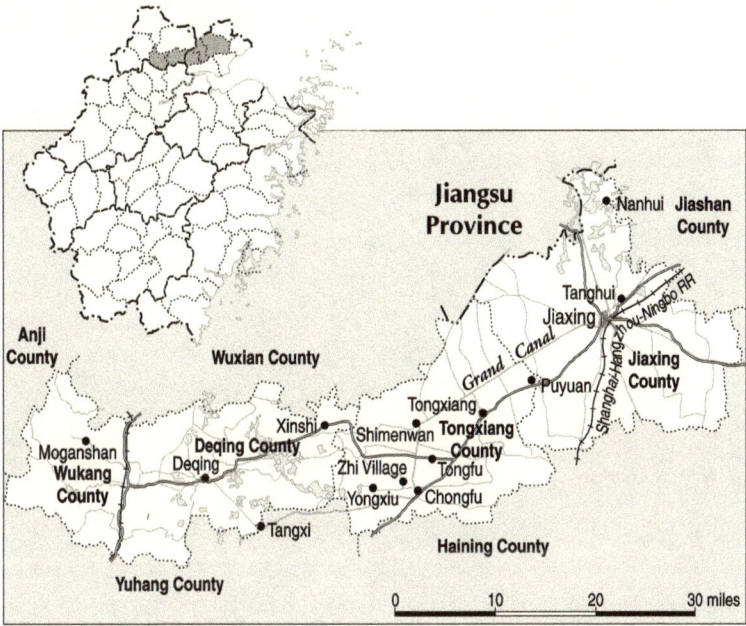

Map 4. Northern Zhejiang (Zhexi) counties from former Jiaxing and Huzhou prefectures

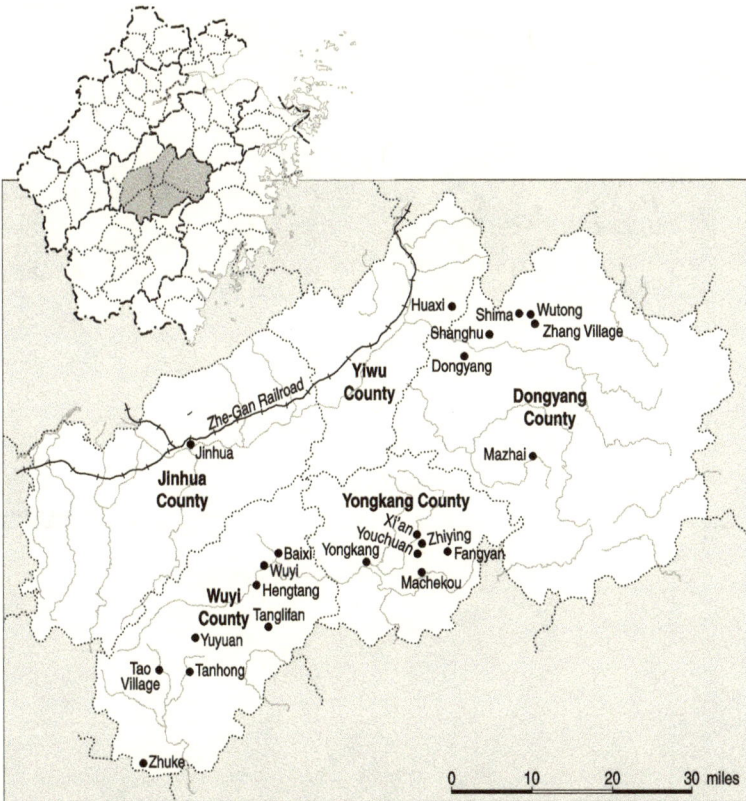

Map 5. Central Zhejiang

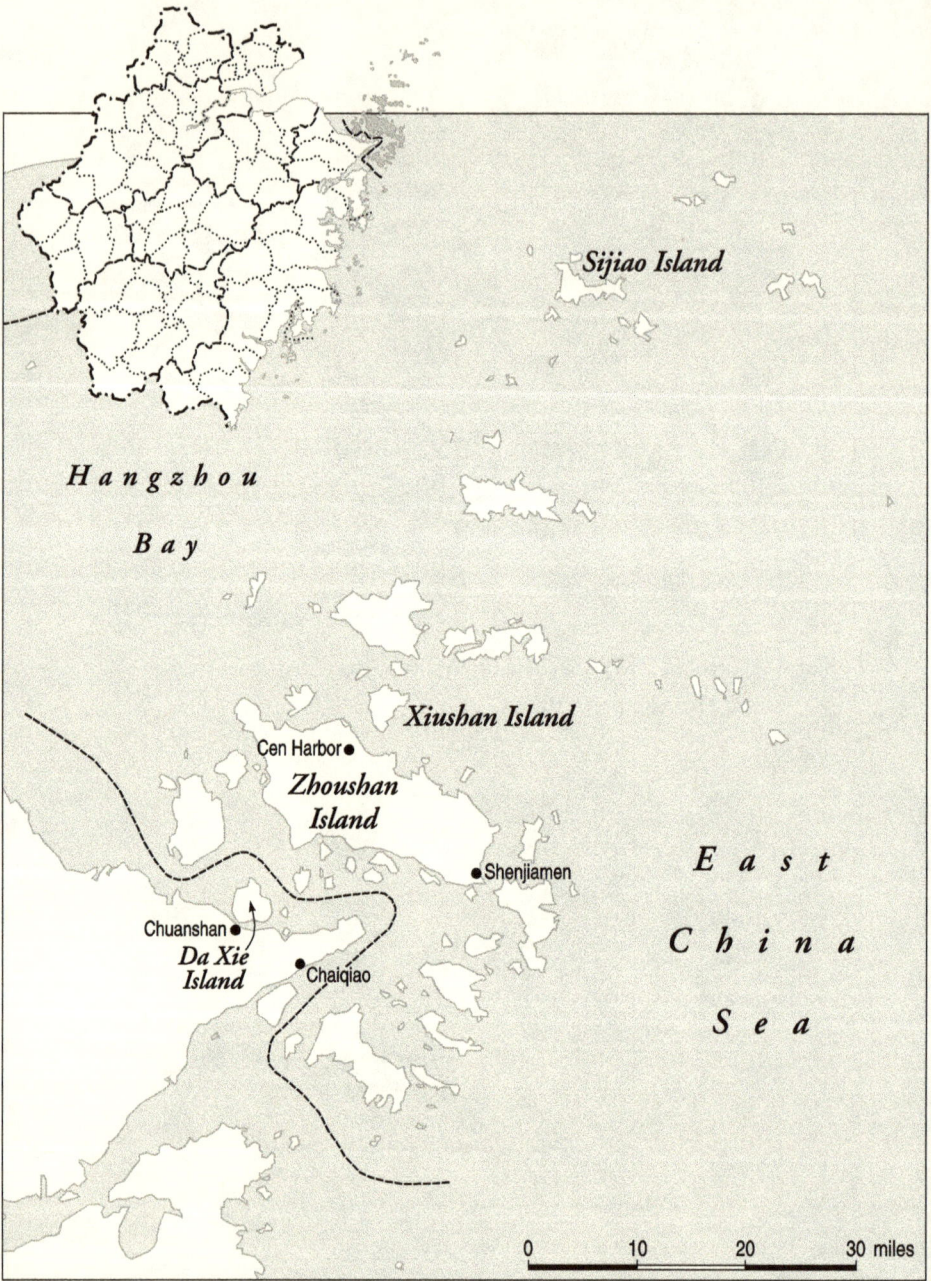

Map 6. The Zhoushan Archicapelago

Map 7. Coastal Zhejiang

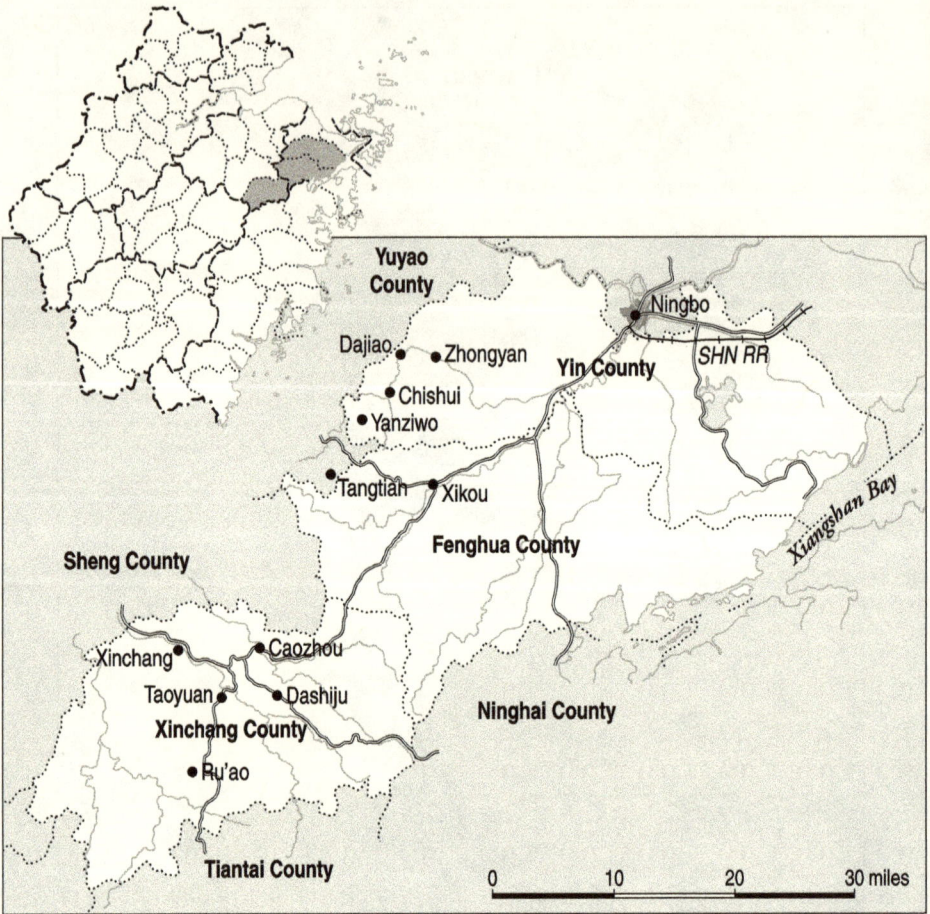

Map 8. Northeastern eastern Zhejiang (Zhedong)

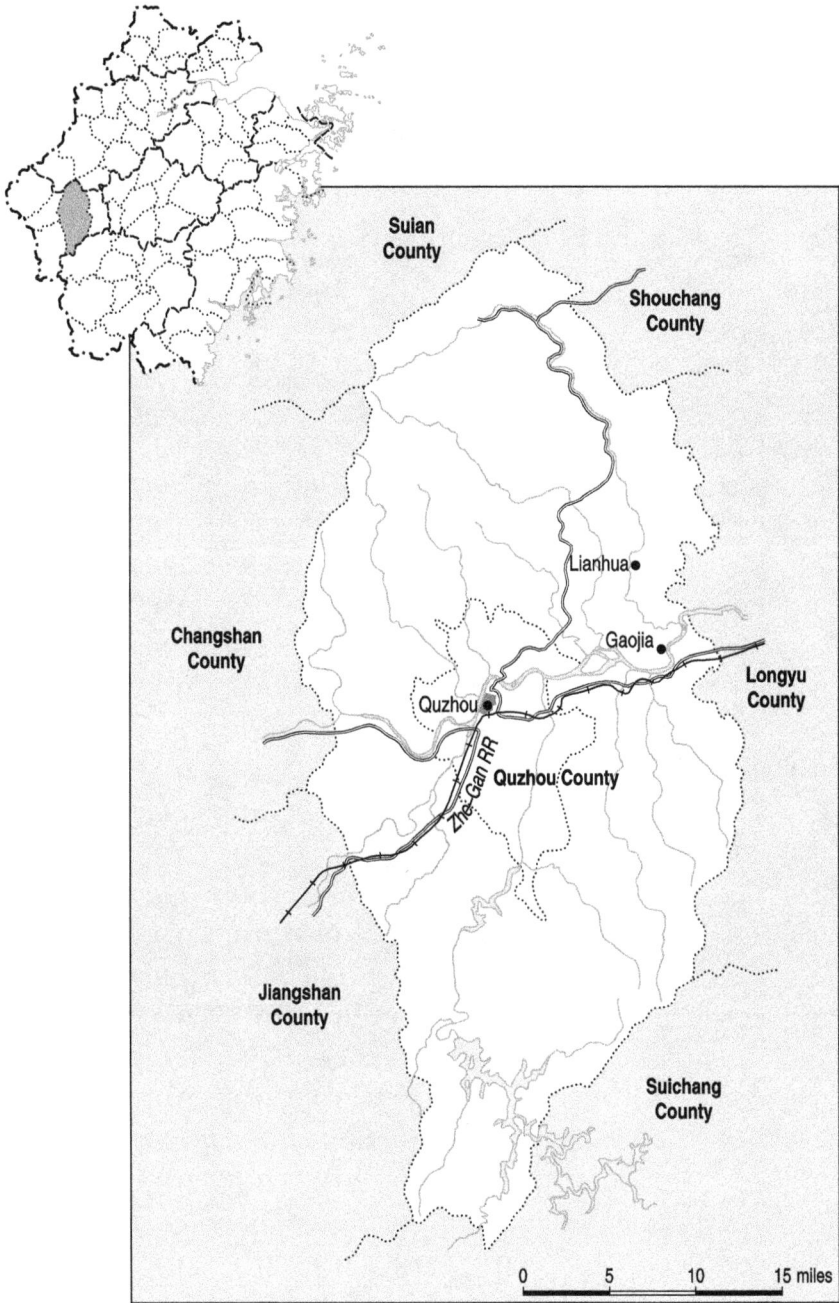

Suian
County

Shouchang
County

Lianhua

Gaojia

Changshan
County

Longyu
County

Quzhou

Zhe-Gan RR

Quzhou County

Jiangshan
County

Suichang
County

0   5   10   15 miles

Map 9. Quzhou County

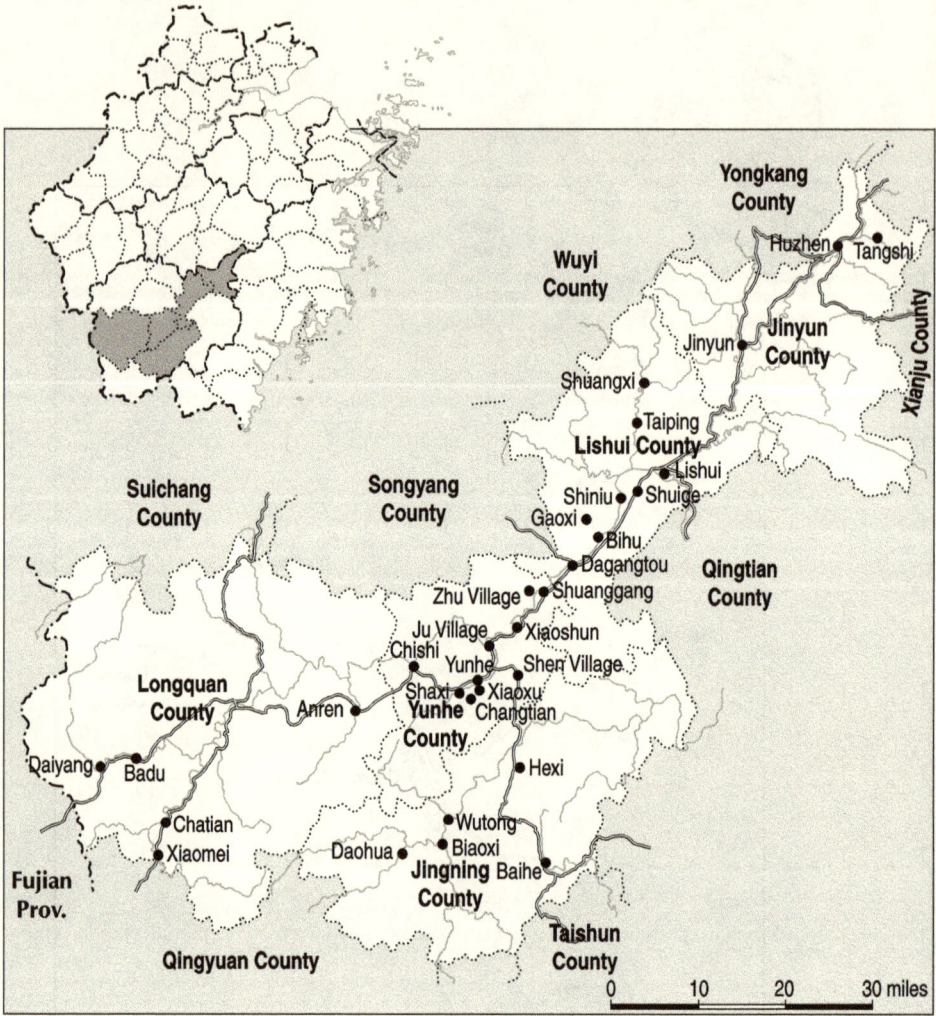

Map 10. Southwestern Zhejiang

Map 11. Lin'an County

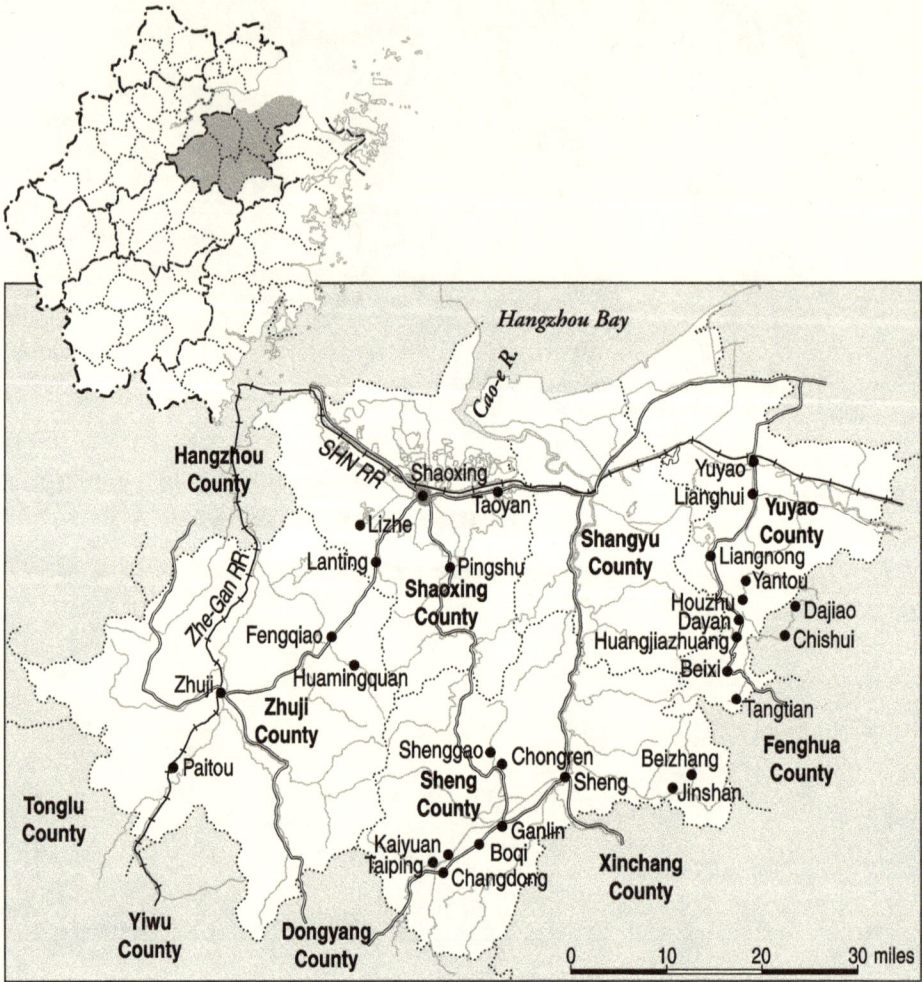

Map 12. Counties in former Shaoxing prefecture.

SIX

⇥⇤

Government on the Move

THE LEADERS OF CHINESE institutional refugees—government, schools, and businesses—all had to wrestle with some of the same questions as individuals and their families: Do we go? When do we go? Where do we go? How do we get there? These institutional decisions, made by provincial elites, were even more complicated and difficult than they were for families. The government with its many bureaucrats (often fleeing on their own to designated locales) had to move documents and other papers as well as office equipment; schools moved libraries and laboratory equipment; businesses had to move machines and other resources, including in some cases raw materials. And most institutions moved more than once during the war, a reality that raises questions about the wisdom of the moves and the viability of the transplanted institutions. This chapter explores the years when the provincial capital was located in the small town of Fangyan in Yongkang County and then in isolated and remote Yunhe County.

The Move to Yongkang

Hangzhou's capture on December 24, 1937, was the culmination of the Japanese autumn military offensive in northern Zhejiang. Chinese officials had decided earlier to move the provincial government to Jinhua because of its convenient transportation and communication—it was located on the Zhe–Gan Railroad and a tributary of the Fuchun and Qiantang rivers. Jinhua having earlier served as prefectural capital, there were sensible political, military, and economic rationales for choosing this location.[1] But the new provincial governor, Huang Shaohong, who had taken over the gubernatorial post only a few weeks before the fall of Hangzhou, found Jinhua chaotic once he reached it. Party, government, and military institutions from both Hangzhou and Shanghai had moved there. The city was teeming with refugees because of the relative ease of transportation to and from the city. We have already seen the crises in handling refugees that the city faced throughout the war. It is no exaggeration that fear roamed the city. Households kept their doors closed. Even finding food in the city was difficult. A reporter traveling to Jinhua in late 1937 described the reality of the situation: "It was already night when we arrived; a light rain was falling. The apparent emptiness of the town was like the gloom of a deathly silence. We could see no lamps or people; there were no open stores. I and my fellow travelers were covered in mud; and after awhile, we assumed we would not find a place to eat or sleep. Late into the night we did find a hotel, where we slept. But the next day, stores were still closed; and we couldn't find any restaurant. On the streets were uniformed soldiers but few others: a city of the dead."[2]

If the refugees found approaching Jinhua easy, the enemy also would have an easy time of it; thus a key advantage was, at one and the same time, a key disadvantage. Further, since Hangzhou was now a Japanese base, Jinhua was within close bombing range and became the base's number one target; the first bombs fell on December 26. Even more troublingly dangerous was that if the Japanese military seized the Zhe–Gan Railroad, enemy troops could simply ride right into the city.

If not Jinhua, then where? West? Huang suspected that the city of Quzhou, like Jinhua a former prefectural capital, might work. However, Quzhou was also on the Zhe–Gan Railroad line; so the Japanese had ready access to this city as well. Huang also found the distance from Jinhua a little daunting: as the crow flies, about eighty miles, but more by rail and water. South? Lishui, the old prefectural capital of Chuzhou, was not quite as far from Jinhua as Quzhou. Though Lishui was peaceful, its downside was that it was far removed from the rail line and too isolated; since the shipment of military weapons and equipment was crucial, it did not seem logical to be so far from the fastest way to move them. Lishui could remain a backup if another move was required later.

The decision was to go southeast a little more than forty miles to Yongkang County, in the center of the province. That county seat was connected to Jinhua by highway and was not distant from the rail line. A plan rather quickly developed to locate the party and main government ministries and offices in the pilgrimage site of Fangyan (see Map 5), in the village of Yanxiajie, about twelve miles from the county seat, where minor government organs could be situated. The pilgrimage destination was the temple of Song dynasty *jinshi*-degree-holder Hu Zizheng, a longtime, upright civil and military official. Pilgrims in the tens of thousands annually came to visit Fangyan from Zhejiang, Fujian, Jiangsu, and Shanghai. On-its-face advantages for locating the government and party headquarters in Fangyan included what seemed like sufficient hotels to house government bureaucrats and offices, and mountain caves that could logically function as natural air-raid shelters. Huang dispatched two trusted officials to scope out the site for its suitability to house the capital. They returned with glowing reports about the facilities and possibilities.

Fangyan also had a symbolic appeal. Ruan Yicheng, who became head of the Ministry of Civil Administration in August 1938, wrote, "Fangyan is in eastern Zhejiang's scenic district; if we are to talk about culture, Zhu Xi [the founder of Neo-Confucianism] studied at the Five Peaks Academy [at Fangyan]; if we are to talk about people's customary beliefs, there is the temple commemorating Hu to which pilgrims come every spring and fall."[3] Selecting Fangyan even seemed to lessen psychologically the displacement of the capital and government: a site of natural beauty, though obviously not replacing the temporarily lost beauty of Hangzhou, could help ameliorate the forced relocation. Even more, at Fangyan, the anti-Japanese resistance government would be linked to traditional Chinese culture embodied in men like Zhu Xi and Hu Zizheng. The goals of the Zhejiang provincial government—to resist Japan and reconstruct the country—could be clearly tied spatially to this symbol of traditional culture.[4]

The move to Fangyan from Jinhua, however, was not easy. The war brought a transport crisis. In central Zhejiang the only trains were the Zhe–Gan line and a branch line that ran from Jinhua to Lanxi. The only highways ran from Jinhua to Wenzhou on the coast via Jinyun and Lishui and from Jinhua west to Longyu. But the highway construction standards were low; transportation facilities were simple and crude. Further, the only vehicles the provincial government owned were twenty-four flat-bottomed trucks and five passenger cars. When Fang-yan became the capital, refugees flooded into Yongkang and Jinhua. Commodities—cotton piece goods, white sugar, groceries, household supplies, gasoline, and kerosene—were in critically short supply. Overnight transport costs soared. Oil that was priced at only 12 cents a catty (1.1 pounds) cost 1.10 yuan to move from Lishui to Yongkang. Over the long term, the government had to build a wartime transport network.

But the short-term goal was moving the capital. On January 12, 1938, the Transport Office in the Reconstruction Ministry dispatched a staff officer named Xu to Yongkang to accomplish the mission of organizing a wheelbarrow corps.[5] He met a very cold reception there from officials who were not interested in the least in additional monetary outlays. Only Lu Gongwang, the man who would establish the refugee mill several months later, was cooperative. In the end, with Lu's help Xu was able to form an initial transport corps of 156 wheelbarrow pushers, the number later reaching 300. Each wheelbarrow worker could theoretically carry up to 450 catties (about 495 pounds); on average they could travel roughly 50 *li* per day (roughly 16 to 17 miles). Thus, for example, the roughly 220-*li* round-trip from Yongkang to Lishui with wheelbarrow loaded on the way out and empty on the way back, or vice versa, would take four to five days. For this work the county government had to come up with 0.50 yuan per day for each worker. The payment system was changed on March 1 to add incentive pay for extra work. On the whole, the Yongkang wheelbarrow corps was lauded for its performance.

But after the move, the alleged advantages of Fangyan as provincial capital faded very quickly. Fangyan was actually a small rural village, with not even one hundred permanent households; its one street stretched only two-thirds of a mile. Apart from the spring and early fall pilgrimage seasons, the village was sleepy and inactive. During the pilgrimage season it was another story: tens of thousands of pilgrims attracted large numbers of outside merchants, who flocked to the village to hawk their goods. The several dozen hotels were completely filled by pilgrims. Indeed, when bureaucrats and party leaders came to Fangyan, they found that innkeepers were loath to rent out rooms for office space, since many inns had built up longtime connections to certain groups of pilgrims, whom the innkeepers even customarily met at Jinhua or Lanxi and accompanied to Fangyan. Many of the hotels had been built in the Ming and Qing dynasties; while most were three stories, each generally had only twenty to thirty cramped rooms.

The needs of the provincial government trumped the needs of pilgrims, of course; but innkeeper policy was to allot only the smallest rooms for government offices. Because of the lack of space, the government had to take over the Five Peaks Academy and the spacious temple to Hu Zizheng to have sufficient, though still limited, office space. The space problem meant that two government ministries, Education and Reconstruction, had to be sent to Lishui, about thirty-six miles to the southeast. In addition to the regular government units' need for space, while the capital was at Fangyan, it hosted two all-province administrative conferences, one all-province police administrative conference, and an all-province land administration conference—all well attended, according to Ruan Yicheng, the provincial minister of civil administration.[6]

Governing at Fangyan seemed like working light-years away from Hangzhou. At the hotels, tourist rooms and government offices were intermixed; officials talked disdainfully about pilgrims barging into their offices, disrupting work, and about the cacophony of pilgrim shouts and loud chatter at the crack of dawn. As there was no electricity in the village, any work at night necessitated the use of rapeseed-oil lamps. The whole situation made bureaucrats, according to one report, "gloomy and depressed."[7] Enervated by boredom brought on by insufficient work and nowhere or no way to travel, many officials and staffers drowned their ennui in drink or whiled away their time in gambling.[8]

Ruan Yicheng, like Feng Zikai, tried to imagine local sites as West Lake–like. Ruan even indulged in images of Peach Blossom utopias and held at least one evening party reminiscent of age-old Daoist groups like the Seven Sages of the Bamboo Grove. He set up an "administrative" library with gazetteer collections and public papers at the village of Shihou in 1941: "In front of Shihou was a stream, beside which there was a large Peach Blossom forest—several thousand trees. I placed a small boat in the stream; it resembled a skiff on West Lake. On the day of the spring equinox, the peach blossoms were opening—magnificent rosy clouds. Beside the stream, I held a sunset gathering of people from all walks of life, from students to family elders—to play games and act in a play."[9] More subtly, he noted afterward that he scheduled this respite-from-the-war gathering at sunset to hint that the "the day of the Japanese bandits might soon be dying."[10] In order to make the place more their own, Ruan and others built homes during the four-plus years at Fangyan; but they were faced by a paucity of building materials, including glass for windows. Other services that had been accepted as givens in Hangzhou, such as health care—specifically, the availability of hospitals, doctors, and nurses—simply did not exist.

With large numbers of government officials and staffers descending on Yanxiajie, even getting sufficient food was a problem: chicken and vegetables, for example, were especially in short supply. Not surprisingly, prices shot higher daily. When the first government officials arrived, they could buy seven catties (almost eight pounds) of pork for one yuan; only thirty-two days later, one yuan purchased only five catties (five and a half pounds). One upshot of the government's move was that the outside merchants, who had originally served the community only in pilgrimage season, moved to Fangyan permanently, building some new stores on the village street.[11] Publicly, officials greeted the overall situation stoically. Governor Huang, whose intelligence-gathering officials on the suitability of the Fangyan locale had proved so off the mark, wrote, "Even though I was disappointed, in the wartime situation it was best to embrace the idea 'since we're already here, let's make ourselves at home.' We could settle down, lessen our desires, and reduce expenses. This kind of life could train our general office workers in a simple life and a spirit of ending hardship."[12]

One report suggests that the people of Fangyan reacted to the wave of official newcomers with support, even allowing government bureaucrats to move into citizens' homes in order to provide additional office space and doing what they could to provide daily necessities.[13] Since the report came from a scion of the wealthiest and most famous lineage in the county, who would want to make the county seem politically correct and au courant, that judgment must be taken with a grain of salt. We have no written reactions from those who may have been required to give up rooms or who may have been requisitioned for those daily necessities.

Governor Huang criticized what he saw as the ignorance and superstition of the people in Fangyan. Particularly, he scoffed at locals who argued that Fangyan early on had escaped serious bombing because it had good *fengshui,* that is, it was sited auspiciously: "[Therefore it was said that] the spirit of Hu [Zizheng] came to protect it. When enemy planes flew above, Hu appeared powerful; he mounted the clouds and rode the mists; he clouded the eyes of the enemies, preventing them from bombing."[14]

The Government Dispersed

The most evident feature of Guomindang government in exile in the war years was that it was too big to locate as a unit in a single place; as a result, it became an increasingly decentralized government with little efficiency and cohesion. We've seen that two major ministries were located almost forty miles away from Fangyan in Lishui. Most major government and party units managed to stay in Fangyan, though many support units and all four major provincial banks were in the county seat, twelve miles away. Because of a lack of roads and vehicles, the only travel between the two communities for the most part was by foot or sedan chair. Under such circumstances the distance between Fangyan and the Yongkang county seat was a substantial obstacle for the government agencies and offices that were located in those sites. But these two county locations were not the only ones where government units were placed. A number were in villages scattered around Fangyan, up to four to five miles distant—and some of these units were not minor—the provincial wartime police bureau, for example.[15] Communication between these sites most of the time required runners. In addition, Ruan Yicheng noted the difficulty of effective and consistent provincial administration when parts of Guomindang-controlled territory kept falling into Japanese hands. The spatial situation raises significant questions: How did the separated government units, often working independently, affect existential thinking about China as a unitary nation? If fighting a national enemy gave at least a theoretical rise to a psychology of national feeling among some, how did the day-to-day practical realities of unpredictabilities and spatially broken government ultimately shape views and attitudes?

In his memoirs, Governor Huang admitted that administrative efficiency nose-dived during the protracted war; he focused on two things, delays in decision making and a flourishing corruption.[16] Huang traced the delays and inefficiency partly to an exhaustion of spirit caused by the meager salaries allotted even to ministry heads; to excessive wartime demands placed on the government; and to the lack of effective communication. He

talked about the government officials who set up street stalls to sell cigarettes and green tea in order to earn enough money to live on; government
parsimony, he alleged, fostered corruption. Minister of Civil Administration Ruan noted that in Fangyan his ministry received eight hundred
communications each day, an impossible load; indeed, in an effort to deal
somewhat more effectively with the workload, the staffers in this ministry,
who had numbered twenty-five when it left Hangzhou, were increased
over 100 percent, to fifty-five, in little more than six months.[17]

Huang's main complaint, in fact, was about the communications system. Huang noted that telephones were necessary for both rapid and secret communications, but telephones were initially available only to the
provincial government and military headquarters. At the county level and
below, there were generally few phones. Therefore, communication came
through telegrams or the mail. But the delivery of telegrams seemed to
get slower and slower; several hours, he asserted, used to be the norm, but
in the wartime situation telegrams often took ten days, even up to half a
month, to arrive. He said that a great many telegrams simply collected in
offices or were sent off to other offices through the mail, the senders not
caring in the least when the messages would reach the other office. Huang
had recently been in Chun'an County, northwest of Jinhua, and had sent
telegrams with dated material to several high-ranking military and political officials in the capital in exile, then at Yunhe County, about 150 miles
away. But he was back in Yunhe for four or five days before the telegrams
he had sent began to trickle in. Mail, he averred, was always slow but was
actually more reliable. If something untoward happened with a telegram,
there was no way to figure out when or even if it would arrive.

Finally, Huang found that the wartime governmental system itself fostered stagnation. He noted the reality of displacement and dispersion,
which had in effect decentralized the provincial government. But at that
very time, the central government in Chongqing, was demanding the con-
solidation of national unity and instituted measures to centralize governmental control over the provinces, demanding, in turn, that the provinces
also centralize control over their counties. The crunch, according to Huang,
came in budgeting, an area in which until 1942 the provinces had enjoyed
considerable freedom. In that year, however, the central government announced that it had to approve all budget lines. Faced with many detailed
regulations from the Chongqing, the province had to seek permission and

spell out the rationales for all expenditures. Huang complained that he routinely had to wait one or two months to get any permissions, which in effect tied his hands and made provincial government even more ineffective and ultimately exceedingly slow to act.

Other Governmental Difficulties

The West Zhejiang and East Zhejiang administrative offices, charged with keeping a toehold in counties occupied by Japanese troops, had the effect of further fracturing the provincial government.[18] Since the offices were located in areas controlled by the Guomindang provincial regime, they became, in a sense, alternative centers of government. They were established with the goal of insinuating Guomindang organs into counties of occupied Zhejiang. The West Zhejiang Administrative Office *(Zhexi xingshu)* in West Tianmushan (see Map 11) was established in February 1939 and operated for almost seven years before its official closing in December 1945. Its purview was the twenty-two counties that made up the former Hangzhou, Jiaxing, and Huzhou prefectures; four of these counties were never occupied by the Japanese and one was only half-occupied. Those latter five counties also remained under the theoretical control of Fangyan, so "dual control" government dispersal was yet another handicap to an effective unitary government system. Having the character of a field headquarters overseen by a civilian official, the office tried to play as much of a role as possible in the occupied areas, where the scope of operation depended on the power of the enemy in each county. General aims included appointing men to serve as magistrates and getting them approved by the provincial government; preparing appointees for assignments; organizing militia units for those counties and supporting them with guns and ammunition; and establishing effective means of ongoing communication with Chinese elites in the occupied counties.

Before a magistrate could be infiltrated into the county, a surveillance agent was sent to spend two or three months preparing the way; potentially, like the magistrate positions themselves, that was a dangerous assignment. Surveillance agents, like one Liu Min killed in 1941, were often targeted by Japanese soldiers or military groups collaborating with them. It was fairly easy to infiltrate counties near the West

Zhejiang Administrative Office but much more difficult in the counties northeast and east of Hangzhou. Magistrates sometimes tried to maintain residence in the occupied counties' peripheries but had to always be ready to move. Magistrate Li Pufu, for example, was able initially to infiltrate Jiashan County; but when he left briefly, he found he could not reenter it.

Since West Tianmushan was relatively close to the occupied areas (less than fifty miles west of Hangzhou), it saw even more bombing attacks than Fangyan did. The administrative offices were housed in a famous and spacious Buddhist temple (with over a thousand rooms), the Shanyuan Temple. Besides serving as Administrative Office headquarters, the temple also housed the wartime First Middle School, which had more than a thousand students. The staff of the Administrative Office numbered 150 men (no women) and was divided into twenty-one units organized under the rubrics of political, economic, education, public health, and military affairs. Some of the most important constituent units under these ministry-like units focused on propaganda: the National Culture Office, National Newspaper Bureau, National Drama Troupe, and National Communications Office. In contrast to the dispersed provincial government, until April 1941 all functions of the West Tianmushan Administrative Office were centralized in the temple. But on April 16, 1941, Japanese planes dropped over thirty bombs on the temple, turning it into an inferno; it was completely destroyed, along with all of the documents and equipment of the Administrative Office. After this disaster, units of the institution had to disperse. Though all remained in the same general area, they were scattered about, thereby losing not only the convenience of the Administrative Office but also its spirit.

The East Zhejiang Administrative Office existed from July 1943 until the end of the war. Like its counterpart in Tianmushan, it pursued the goal of keeping the Guomindang alive in occupied counties; however, unlike the West Zhejiang office, this one was primarily created to combat a Communist-led resistance in the Siming Mountains in occupied Yuyao County. The East Zhejiang Administrative Office was established at the town of Jietou, in a very remote area some twenty miles west of the Tiantai county seat, directly south of Xinchang County (see Maps 2 and 8). The purview of the office was eighteen counties in the former prefectures of Shaoxing, Ningbo, Taizhou, and Jinhua; three of those counties were never occupied by the Japanese. In part because the office was established so late in a protracted war that had revealed the incompetence and corruption of China's leaders, the East Zhejiang office bureaucrats suffered from low morale and lack of vigor; leaders of the east office were not so committed to success as was He Yangling, a close ally of Governor Huang, who chaired the west office. While Huang visited the west office twice, he never journeyed to Jietou to see the east office.[19]

Playing even more havoc with effective governance, factionalism riddled the Guomindang. One faction, the CC (Central Club) Clique— formed in 1927 by Chen Guofu, a close ally of Jiang Jieshi—dominated Zhejiang politics. If it had been unified, the CC Clique might have brought a measure of cohesion that would to some extent have ameliorated the dispersal of government power. But the group was itself split into four factions. Wartime only increased the factional infighting and power plays among provincial leaders. Most powerful was the Western Zhejiang (Zhexi) faction; it sponsored the provincial party bureau chief, Luo Xiatian, during much of the war. This group was challenged bitterly during the war by the Wenzhou faction (headquartered in both the cities of Wenzhou and Lishui). Although the Wenzhou leader, Zhang Qiang, was not seen as completely legitimate because he was not a graduate of the party's Central Political Affairs School, he had the personal support of the founders of the CC Clique, brothers Chen Guofu and Chen Lifu. Both the Western Zhejiang and Wenzhou factions vied with each other to appoint more provincial government bureaucrats, subbureaucrats, and county magistrates so as to expand each faction's power base. This open struggle was worsened by the government's spatial relocations, first to Songyang County very briefly in 1941 and then to Yunhe, Lishui, and Longquan counties from 1942 to the end of the war. One of the leaders of the East Zhejiang Administrative Office, Tu Wei, wrote later that the moves left the provincial government and party "badly battered" and that government and party could only be propped up in its new locations with difficulty.[20]

The weakest faction was the Eastern Zhejiang (Zhedong) faction, whose leaders were often frozen out of appointments and generally unable to extend their power by making appointments. The smallest faction was the Fudan faction, started by graduates of that Shanghai university. As did the Wenzhou faction, the Fudan faction had that ace in the hand of strong support from the founding Chen brothers. Indeed, the closeness of this faction to the brothers is shown by the fact that the Chens turned to this Fudan faction leaders to handle some of the Chens' personal family matters in Huzhou during the war.[21]

The provincial government's dispersion during the war was not helped by the fact that Governor Huang Shaohong was not a CC Clique member but belonged to the Guangxi Clique, as he hailed from that province, not Zhejiang. Huang had previously served as Zhejiang governor, from 1934 to 1935: the CC Clique did not like him. Jiang Jieshi, who did not trust Huang a great deal, knew the power of the CC Clique in Zhejiang and likely thought that that political reality would check any undue power expansion on Huang's part. Soon after the government moved to Fangyan, the Western Zhejiang faction, hearing of the Wenzhou faction's schemes for expanding its power, got Huang's ear and approval to begin immediately to fill posts with their own factional members. The Wenzhou group was infuriated and responded by attacking Huang; instead of having gratitude to Huang for his help, the Western Zhejiang faction joined in the attack on the governor. It rummaged through the province to find evidence of Huang's openness to Communists and to get that information to the Guomindang Central. For example, Western Zhejiang members accused the magistrate of Suichang County of assisting the New Fourth Army, composed at this time of Guomindang and Communist units; and the faction accused two Longquan country magistrates of having Communists in the county government.

For his part, Huang sowed disruption for the CC Clique by pulling the Fudan faction into his orbit, at least nominally—naming its head, Xu Shaodi, as education minister. In an attempt to begin to build his own base, in February 1938 Huang established two cadre-training units, the Wartime Political Work Training Unit *(zhanshi zhengzhi gongzuo renyuan shunlian tuan)* and the Wartime Youth Training Unit *(zhanshi qingnian shunlian tuan)*. The first was composed of five hundred men who were nominated by their counties, while the second, of fifteen hundred, was made up of young men who had fled the war in their occupied home areas for refuge in this rear area. Huang named Education Minister Xu to head both units, which were situated in the town of Bihu in Lishui County (see Map 10). Xu moved there with the Education Ministry, to take over what he probably instantly realized could become his power base. He threw himself into the position, often participating in morning exercises, clad in a gray cotton military uniform with boots. Realizing that he had sponsored an aggressive power seeker, Huang eventually removed Xu. And the two units were abolished when the central regime ordered the establishment of the Three People's Principles Youth Corps in mid-1938.[22]

The power-grasping struggles between Huang and the CC Clique were of the brass-knuckle type. In appointing magistrates, Huang had an obvious interest in keeping CC Clique partisans out of local posts. Control of such appointments was in the hands of the Ministry of Civil Administration, an organ headed after August 1938 by Ruan Yicheng, a strong CC Clique member. Huang himself was rarely in Fangyan, as he had a military role as well as that of civilian governor. For that military function, he lived in Jinhua—a situation that was yet another element in disconnected and dispersed government. Huang's man in Fangyan was Li Limin, the chief secretary of the Ministry of Civil Administration, an Anhui native, but someone firmly allied to Huang. Li, doubtless with Huang's encouragement, appointed on his own over ten men from Anhui to Zhejiang County magistracies. Ruan attacked Li, accusing him of making the appointments to fulfill his corrupt desires to profit from them. Ruan's accusations, sent to Huang and commander of the Third Wartime Region, Gu Zhutong, brought no responses. But the whispering campaign against Li reduced his standing, and as a result, Ruan was able to appoint many magistrates—since there was a wave of general reappointments at that time.[23]

One of the CC Clique's main weapons against Huang was the Provisional Provincial Senate (linshi canyihui), which the clique dominated. The clique's direct line to national CC officials allowed it to inform the national capital continually about Huang's failings and shortcomings; sometimes, following up, Wuhan and (later) Chongqing gave Huang dressings-down. In June 1938, Huang received an order from Wuhan, reproving him for some action; he traveled to Wuhan to resign, but his resignation was not accepted.[24]

As we have seen, a concerted Senate effort to dismantle the Huang governorship followed the Japanese seizure of Xiaoshan County, across the Qiantang River from Hangzhou, in January 1940 (see Map 3). Guarding the riverbank was one regiment of the Zhejiang Provincial Resist

Japan Self-Protection Corps—units that Huang had established, trained, and funded. Allegedly, when units of the National Defense Army were called by the Self-Protection Corps for assistance, they did not respond. Xiaoshan fell to Japan's assault. In May 1940, the Senate announced three days of hearings on the responsibility for this loss, in what became known as the Xiaoshan Incident. Huang was defensive. He gave factual information about the situation but refused to assess responsibility for gains or losses in battle. He argued, "If we start an argument, we will necessarily expose weaknesses that exist for the whole military. We would end up quibbling over every aspect of the situation and could not maintain harmony. In 'the Xiaoshan Incident,' what was lost was only a triangle of land. 'Incident'? You're making a military mole hill into a great mountain. Look, when Hangzhou was lost, did it get a special name?"[25]

Senators generally took this attitude: "You are governor of the province, yet you take no responsibility? It is you who are guilty and should resign."[26] Ruan Yicheng charged that Xiaoshan was not an isolated case. He said that it was obvious that the soldiers were not rabble, but they had outmoded weapons and insufficient training. The defeat of Huang's trained forces would, he asserted, have been predictable.[27] Though Huang did not resign, it is notable that later that year he reorganized the provincial military and in the process likely affirmed some of the charges brought against him.[28]

In sum, the political realities—the two administrative offices, the extreme factionalism, and the struggles between Huang and the provincial party regime—tended to exacerbate a dysfunctional system brought on by moving the provincial capital with its government ministries, bureaucrats, and official papers. The unfortunate reality was that Fangyan was not the last move.

Moving to Songyang County

In April 1941, both Shaoxing and Ningbo fell to the Japanese; with their loss, the most productive parts of Eastern Zhejiang were gone. Fear swept Fangyan and Yongkang that the Japanese drive might continue. The decision: move the provincial capital to Songyang County (see Map 10), about fifty-five miles southwest and relocate the Ministry of Civil Administration to Xuanping County (see Map 2), separating this key administrative organ from the provincial capital. When Minister Ruan Yicheng reached Xuanping, there were no roads; travel by foot was the only option. For an undisclosed reason, the Ministry of Civil Administration was set up at the Qingxiu Temple, three to four miles outside the county seat, in a village of several dozen households. Ruan reported that when the ministry staff reached the temple, they found it in ruins. The ministry also found itself in almost complete isolation. Their phone could reach only contiguous counties.

Ruan ordered two young staffers to cross the high mountains to Lishui to purchase a radio transmitter-receiver so that the ministry would be able to communicate. The trek was at least twenty miles over high mountains—a difficult undertaking. Once the staffers returned and the transceiver was set up, Ruan had contact with other government organs and military units. He established a regular communications time with the ministry's head secretary, Li Limin, who remained in Songyang, a situation that continued to make it difficult for the ministry to function. In August, two months after the trek from Fangyan, the provincial government moved back; the new concern was making contingency plans should the Japanese start another campaign.

Minister Ruan Yicheng and the Move South

The Japanese launched their Zhe-Gan campaign in May 1942, cutting a large swath down the center of the province and then to the southwest into Jiangxi.[29] The campaign posed an acute emergency for the provincial government in Yongkang County. On May 17, Governor Huang ordered the whole government to be moved. Each government unit would determine for itself where it would go—despite the fact that in planning since the preceding summer, they had decided to evacuate to Yuyuan in Xuanping County. Wartime realities and perhaps panic displaced earlier, more dispassionate decisions.

Civil Administration Minister Ruan Yicheng's account puts us on the ground as the flight took place; it shows the nature of decision making and the impossibility of planning ahead in a wartime situation. Ordinary life and judicious choices of action were displaced by emergencies and contingencies necessitating immediate decisions that might have to be changed in an instant. Ruan decided that his ministry would indeed head to Yuyuan; under his control were the Land Administration Bureau, the Provincial Police Battalion, the Provincial Police Training Institute, and the New Masses Upper Middle School—altogether almost a thousand people. As for vehicles, the ministry had only two small, quite dilapidated sedans and a large truck. Ruan decided that the ministry would not travel the Yongkang–Jinyun–Lishui route with the other government ministries but rather travel from Yongkang to Wuyi to Xuanping to avoid potential bottlenecks with refugee crowds on the highway through the mountains (for the placement of counties, see Map 2). The downside of this route was that ministry staff would have to walk from the Wuyi county seat to Yuyuan, about fifteen miles, burdened with public documents as well as personal luggage. Thus, they had to requisition porters.

When Ruan arrived in the Yongkang county seat from Fangyan, he went to the Chinese Local Bank guesthouse, where the heads of other ministries were waiting. The turmoil and chaos of war gave rise to rumors from every direction. One was that Governor Huang's home on the outskirts of Jinhua had been bombed twice the day before and that his secretary had been killed; altogether, rumors had it that more than a hundred had been killed in the city. Around dinnertime Huang and his wife arrived in Yongkang, their expressions revealing the grimness that destructive bombing attacks fostered. With an evident lingering fear, Huang described what had happened, announced that he would stay in Yongkang overnight, and asserted the imperative that the military had to stand fast in the Jinhua-Lanxi sector. He was interrupted by a long-distance telephone call from the magistrate of Tiantai County, who reported that Japanese forces had already passed through Sheng County and were entering Dongyang County, contiguous to Yongkang.

Huang quickly put on his military cap and walked to his car. Countermanding his decision minutes earlier to stay the night in Yongkang, he told Ruan he was going to Jinyun County because the Japanese were simply too close to Yongkang. From this time on for a whole month, Ruan had no communications at all with Governor Huang—certainly a situation that would suggest no effective governance. Ruan's project late in the day was convincing the heads of the four national banks that had been in the Yongkang county seat since early 1938 to move by the next day; bank officials were initially unconvinced of the urgency, unaware that the Japanese were already taking over the next county.

The next morning Ruan rode to the Wuyi county seat and then walked to Tao Village, where his pregnant wife and son, who had left Yongkang the day before, had gone (see Map 5). The looming unanswered question was where the Japanese were headed, the same question that bedeviled individual and family refugees about where they themselves should go. The Wuyi magistrate, Ye Wen, whom Ruan contacted by phone, told him that the Japanese had already taken Yongkang; Ye asked whether he should use military forces to defend the county if the Japanese attacked Wuyi or whether he should flee. Ruan told Ye to flee with the town's population, since the number of men he could command were too few and his weapons outmoded. Ruan tried to ease his concerns, noting that Wuyi was not Japan's objective; rather, Japanese were targeting the larger cities of Jinhua and Lanxi. He warned that if Ye did fight and lose, then there would be no buffer between the Japanese and Xuanping County, where the ministry documents, official chops, account books, and staffers were headed.

The next day Ruan heard from Ye that the Japanese had come into the county but had marched across it straight to Jinhua. For his part, Ruan found that Yuyuan, his flight objective, had already been filled with other government organs and bureaucrats. So he chose to head for the Qingxiu Temple, where he had worked for the two months in summer 1941, about eight miles from Yuyuan. He decided to make this out-of-the-way temple the ministry's site, at least temporarily. As Li Limin, his chief ministry secretary, had done in 1941, Li headed for Songyang County, in a very infelicitous arrangement for governance— other than for the reality that the two men detested each other. Ruan received the news that Jinhua and Lanxi fell to the Japanese on May 28; he was also warned that Japanese soldiers might be only a few miles away from his Ministry Office, since Jinhua was contiguous to Wuyi. Ruan mused, "I absolutely cannot defend the ministry effectively. If, by chance, they come here, I could not bear it."

The problems brought by the coming of government bureaucrats, refugees, and wounded soldiers into this rear area—marked, as it was, by poverty and the lack of modern development—were acute. The Songyang County magistrate, Chen Chunren (Ruan's former teacher at Hangzhou's First Normal School), relayed his concerns to Ruan about the tsunami of outsiders. He said they were demanding provisions, housing, government jobs, and the right to borrow money; coping with these demands where resources were few was impossible in the extreme. Under the pressures of the invading outsider population, social unrest and violence seemed all too likely. The flammable situation was made tenser by rancorous gambling disputes among wounded soldiers that threatened to explode in widespread violence. Ruan wanted to ban gambling to end the social volatility that had led to a number of severe social outbursts. With this goal, he planned to go to Songyang to see what he might do in the tense situation; but the very next day he received word that Magistrate Chen had suddenly died of a hemorrhage. Ruan left immediately to pay his respects to his former teacher.

While at Songyang Ruan heard from roving secretary Li Limin that Li was moving yet again, now to Yunhe County from Songyang to use the yamen in that county seat as his office. Li was his own man (and a close ally of Governor Huang), who treated Ruan almost as a lackey. Upon returning to Tao Village, Ruan learned that Wuyi had been seized briefly by the Japanese; but they had held only the northern portion of the county, the locale of the county seat—and that area for only eight days (June 18–26). That was more than enough time, however, for Ruan, who wanted to put more territory between the Japanese and himself, his family, and the ministry; he decided to go to Songyang with his family. The trip (a replay of what he had just made alone) was twenty miles through and over the mountains. Hiring porters to carry their six pieces of luggage, which included the ministry seal and important documents, was imperative. But like Feng Zikai early on the November 1937 morning he and his family left Hangzhou, Ruan and two ministry staffers had great difficulty in finding anyone to do the job. They found only one porter but decided, nevertheless, that they had to start out; though Ruan does not explicitly tell us, it is likely that the two ministry staffers were also in the traveling party.

In the middle of their trek, a heavy rain began to fall. Though the road was very narrow and was dangerously slippery, they walked until dusk. Along the road there were no homes or places to eat. Ruan did not tell us where they spent the night, likely along the road; but with a pregnant wife and small child, it must have been trying. The next day they trudged on until about 3 P.M., when they came to the house of a bamboo logger. We do not know exactly what transpired between the travelers and the resident, but Ruan records that the logger made them a meal of mountain taro and congee. Ruan's wife, obviously pushed to the limits of what she could endure, pleaded with the man to be able to sleep the night on a bed; he offered her one, while Ruan slept on a cabinet. Fortunately, the next day was clear, and they reached Songyang about noon. They stayed temporarily in a bank's reception hall just outside the city wall. But it was not a quiet time. Every day from dawn to sunset, the city was besieged by constant air-raid sirens and Japanese bombing attacks. In one, Ruan took cover in a small teashop. He thought that the bullets hitting the tile roof sounded like beans being dropped and scattered on the thick tiles.

Governor Huang then decided that the provincial capital in exile should be moved to Yunhe County. Even so, Ruan moved the ministry and the Land Administration Bureau to the town of Badu in Longquan County, where he set up his office for several months at the Wu lineage hall. It was not until after the Mid-Autumn autumn Festival (late September) that he and his family finally moved to Yunhe (see Maps 2 and 10).

Displaced and Dispersed

During the last three years of the war, the dispersed governance of the Yongkang period became even more pronounced as governing bodies were scattered in towns and villages over eight counties.[30] In Yunhe County, where many of the main governing institutions were set up, they were situated in twelve separate towns and villages. The war years mangled coordinated and consistent governance. One measure of the mangling is the number of moves of key government bodies. Each move entailed packing up papers, seals, supplies, and equipment; moving them and the officials and staff to the new site, along roads mostly destroyed, with few, if any, vehicles to facilitate the move; arriving at the new location, unpacking, and discovering new routines of living in a different site; and getting patterns of governing going once again. Depending upon the distance of the move, the numbers of people involved, and the amount of materials transported, the move from start to finish could take several months—during which time, governance was essentially on hold.

The moves of three important government bodies offer evidence of the reality of refugee government. Ruan Yicheng's Ministry of Civil Administration—located in Fangyan from early 1938 on with the exception

of a two-month relocation to Songyang County in late spring 1941—
moved in June 1942 to Yunhe (a journey of about seventy-five miles). In
August, the ministry split into three units, which moved to Badu (fifty-
one miles) and Chatian (fifty-three miles) in Longquan County and
Xinyao on the border with Fujian Province (fifty-eight miles). Then, in
October, the ministry moved back to Yunhe (for these sites, see Map 10).
It is hard to see how the ministry was able to accomplish anything from
May to November 1942. The Education Ministry and its more than two
hundred employees, which had been located in the Lishui county seat
since the initial flight from Hangzhou, fled to Songyang in 1941 (a journey of fifty-one miles). In July 1942, it fled forty-five and fifty-eight miles
to two new sites (thirteen miles apart) in Jingning County. In September
Education Ministry personnel moved nine miles to a small village outside the Yunhe county seat. The Public Security Bureau, one would have
supposed, would have been located in the provincial capital in exile, but
in these years the bureau was never located there. In June 1942, it moved
to a small village outside the town of Bihu in Lishui County (see Map 10).
In just a few weeks, the bureau relocated to the town of Chishi in Yunhe
County, ten miles from the county seat. But in early August 1942, it
moved with its 910 officials and staff some seventeen miles to the county
seat of Jingning County (Hexi). While the Public Security Bureau remained there for the duration of the war, its repair shop was moved fifteen miles away, to Anren Town in Longquan County.

The majority of government ministries, courts, offices, bureaus, and
committees—thirty-one—were located in Yunhe. Surprisingly, none of
the governmental units in Yunhe were military or military related; and
there was shockingly not a single post office branch in that county seat,
now the provincial capital. Of the thirty-one units, only fourteen were in
the county seat itself; the rest were scattered among eleven villages, eight
within a three-mile radius of the county seat, one five miles away, another ten miles away, and the last eighteen miles from the county seat.

There were substantial numbers of government units in seven other
counties. It was estimated that in traveling the one hundred miles between Pucheng (in Fujian) and Lishui on the best road remaining in the
region, a driver could average at most eight to nine miles per hour. Since
not all these county seats were on this road, these mileages suggest, then,

the difficulties that provincial officials outside Yunhe had in reaching the capital. There were eighteen government units in Longquan (seventy miles away from Yunhe); ten units in Lishui (thirty-six miles); six units in Songyang (forty-three miles); four units in Jingning (nine miles)—including the Provisional Provincial Senate and the Provincial Secretariat; four units in Qingtian (seventy miles); one unit, the Provincial Audit Office, in Pingyang (sixty-two miles); and one, the Provincial Agricultural Association, in Qingyuan (eighty-three miles) (for the location of these counties, see Map 2).

Making regional travel even more difficult was that the key road from Lishui and Songyang to Yunhe had been torn up: Ruan Yicheng noted that there were hardly any highways or passable roads left in the province. Travel was restricted to walking or taking small boats going down the Ou River. When Ruan finally reached Yunhe, the Committee of Government Deputies *(sheng fu weiyuanhui)* met for the first time in three months. Ruan wrote, "For a long time, colleagues did not meet. For everyone, the chaos on war's road brought the bitterness of wandering from place to place. It had really separated them from life."[31]

Life in Yunhe County

Of Yunhe County's land area, 95 percent is mountainous and only 2 percent is plains; the mountains range from three thousand to five thousand feet in altitude. Before the war many people, even in Zhejiang Province, had never even heard of this county. That travel was difficult there was an understatement. Ruan Yicheng had been sent to Lishui, the capital of Chuzhou Prefecture, on a government assignment in early 1937. At that time, he became aware of the lay of the land in Chuzhou. Three of the ten counties did not have roads connecting them to the outside; only one of the ten (Songyang) was self-sufficient in rice production; in all ten, population was sparse, and education was poorly developed.[32] Yunhe County made Fangyan and Yongkang seem bustling and modern by comparison; for the government refugees, the operable description of what they found in Yunhe was culture shock. Newspapers reported that thirteen- and fourteen-year-old girls could still be seen there with bound feet, a custom that had begun to die away elsewhere in the first decade of the century. As another mark of its isolation and wildness, during the war the county seat was menaced by a tiger.[33] Yunhe County, according to the *Southeast Daily,* was the "land of a thousand hardships and of ten thousand bitternesses."[34]

Even before the provincial government moved to Yunhe, commodities there were scarce. Ruan reported that county residents never ate their fill, because food was in short supply. He averred that the level of civilization was primitive: before the government outsiders moved in, the residents did not know about raising chickens or planting vegetables. From other sources, we know that Ruan's assertion was specious. Perhaps he was simply enunciating the condescension toward the locals that he shared with many of his government associates. Ruan also claimed (truly or not?) that Yunhe residents never bathed, because they did not have washed clothes to change into nor, more importantly, did they have fuel to heat the water.[35]

When Shen Songlin came to Yunhe as the new magistrate in 1937, he was astounded to go out early in the morning and find that all the stores and houses remained shut until midmorning (a reality corroborated by Ruan).[36] Songlin's first reaction was that Yunhe residents were simply too lazy to get an early start. But an old resident told the new magistrate, "Few of these mountain people rise early because there is miasma, so that everyone opens their doors rather late." Shen explained that in forested mountains in the tropics and subtropics a "warm, even hot atmosphere" produced pestilential vapors that, locals believed, caused illness. Thus, the late rising. That said, however, malaria was endemic to the county.

The coming of government officials, their staffs, and families to this remote and impoverished county overwhelmed the several thousand residents, taxing the food supply and causing great social strain. The county seat had only a few businesses before the population influx and had no electricity; it was said that before the government moved to Yunhe, the people there did not have any lights at all at night—that, according to one resident, it was pitch-black and difficult even to take a step. A Japanese general at the time gave his verdict: "All of Zhejiang's troops and people have been driven into the rotten mountains, to eat tree bark, grass, and roots, to get mosquito and snake bites, to grope one's way at night, satisfied to accept a troubled death in the mountains."[37] After the government came, its offices initially used oil lamps and instructed locals to ignite bamboo strips for illumination.

The rushing Fuyun River divided the county seat; the only ways to cross were to take two narrow, rickety footbridges, a vertiginous experience; in 1944 a more sturdy bridge for people and traffic was completed.[38] Called the South Gate Big Bridge, it was opened with much fanfare: an opening ceremony with the cutting of a ribbon, fireworks, and performances by a drama troupe. A permanent marker was built on the river's bank. Locals were abuzz, saying things like "The provincial government has done a great thing."[39] The refugee invaders into this isolated world slowly began to change it. Rushing water was harnessed to produce forty kilowatts of power from a small hydroelectric generator that Governor Huang supported financially and that provincial engineers constructed; it was in operation by April 1943. Though electricity was produced for only four hours daily, it was the first electricity for the county seat and three small villages in its immediate vicinity.[40] It was another life-changing development for the people of Yunhe.

Residents and outsiders in Yunhe County could live without bridges and electricity; but their lives were dependent on sustenance—and the problem of food and provisioning was the most intractable that locals and provincial government officials and staff had to face. With so little cultivable land in the county, everyone knew that Yunhe could never be self-sufficient. The two government offices that dealt specifically with provisioning sought out food from Wenzhou, Quzhou, and other cities; in addition, the Provincial Trade Office took responsibility for bringing in food or food-related items that could yield ongoing provisions: it put priority on raising hogs, on planting vegetable gardens, on building *doufu* and noodle factories, and on setting up a rice mill. This office was in charge also of buying cotton cloth in Ninghai County, to help in providing clothes. The Trade Office set up a factory to print ration coupons. To handle the numbers of people being supplied with food and in order to preclude fights and other problems, food was distributed by people's units *(danwei)* on a certain date and in a certain order. Details of food distribution were announced on a large sign in front of the Trade Office, where the crowd could be overseen, order retained, and the crowd satisfied.[41] The longest-lasting difficulties with provisioning were twofold: First, the highest priority in provisioning was the military troops. Second, there was little stability in what was available: it seemed almost always to be either feast or famine. Another difficulty was transporting the commodities if they were being brought in from the outside. A paucity of vehicles and damaged and destroyed highways made travel and transport frustratingly slow and difficult, if it was possible at all.

It is easy to see why reliance on gardens became a key strategy. Yunhe's mountain climate is warm, with plentiful rainfall; the region also has fertile soil. There was a history there of developing mountainsides to grow turnips, cabbage, and ginger. Government units began to rent small parcels of land in order to grow their own vegetables; newspapers reported that garden making became a sort of mania.[42] Mountains were searched for any uncultivated soil; boulders were removed to open up any potential arable land. People spoke of barren mountains with fairly steep slopes being transformed into jade-green gardens. Gardening was a deadly serious undertaking. Every government unit that had its own garden also had a management office for the garden. Slogans popularized the endeavor: "Vegetables, self-produced," "Change your life through your own strength," and "Make yourself self-sufficient."[43] Lu Gongwang, who had set up the Refugee Dyeing and Weaving Mill in Yongkang and moved it in 1942 to the small town of Chishi, about ten miles west of the Yunhe county seat, managed a vegetable farm as part of his work projects for refugees. He began by growing celery, spinach, and tomatoes and talked of renting more plots. In terms of provisioning, he raised hogs, keeping on a hog farm about fifty head to raise and slaughter and maintaining a "production team" of about a dozen sows and one boar to produce more litters for raising and eating.[44]

Surviving the War

When Civil Administration Minister Ruan Yicheng moved to Yunhe, he and his family settled in the tiny hamlet of Guixi (which contained only three other houses), a mile from the county seat. Mountains banked up behind the Ruans' house; in front was a stream; and in a small courtyard were several trees but no grass or flowers. The house of three rooms was often filled with talkative friends. During the six months when the family lived there, Ruan came down with a two-week attack of malaria. In the sixth month of their residence, bubonic plague broke out in the hamlet; five people in one of the three nearby houses died.[45] Ruan quickly moved his family several miles away, to the site of an abandoned temple beside a pear orchard. They built a house, spare and rustic—they called it their "thatched shack."[46]

There they joined the gardening movement. Ruan's wife planted the vegetables—turnips, tomatoes, eggplant, beans, and melons. When Ruan returned from work during the growing season, he joined his wife and children in picking the vegetables and melons and then enjoyed eating them. When they had guests, they served them the garden vegetables, which, Ruan avers, the guests applauded as fresh and good. In the midst of war and deprivation, Ruan says that the garden gave them a focus for assiduous work and helped them economize. In the face of loss, of wandering from place to place, of uncertainty and violence, their hope was not simply to survive but to live meaningfully.

The garden was simply one alternative focus for Ruan. Another was a journal, the *Upper Classes (Shengliu),* which he created and edited, with the objective of focusing on serious issues in Chinese society. In the December 16, 1947, issue of that journal, Ruan noted in "Wartime Wanderings" another focus—travel—that could put the ravages of wartime and refugeedom into a different perspective: "I simply like to travel. Moreover, to rein in the customary disorderliness of life, there are fresh opportunities to travel. On active service, I could use my public duties to join the scenic world, passing both the famous mountains and the big cities."[47] He wrote poems about significant places to which he traveled. It is said that once Ruan returned to Hangzhou after the war, he had kind feelings for the years at Yunhe, but they must have been bittersweet memories, for, in many ways his life and plans were placed on hold there. He had written that he turned forty years old in November 1944 and that the difficulties of life in the mountains would not lead to a long life. (He would live until July 28, 1988.) The poem he wrote on the Yunhe experience is filled with ambivalence.

> Autumn comes. Red trees mirror the village's flowers.
> The wine has just been opened; in the goblet the chrysanthemum is
>   perfect.
>
> A humble home . . .
> People walking past laugh, chuckling that this is an official's home.
> In front of the door, there is a garden facing the mountain scenery.
> Idly, I speak with my wife and son about the mulberry.

Radishes are beginning to appear, with the cabbage growing taller.
It is good for the family to speak of the sweet roots of vegetables.
It is not necessary to wield the tongs if there are no fish.
In the wild there are, however, small cattle and sheep; within the fences,
small pigs.

How many times will we be forced to move and change residences?
Eight years ago we left the enemy for the deep mountain recesses [but]
Mournful music that is heard frequently and at length loses its meaning.
How many people in this generation have already worn white [the color
of mourning]?

Alone here—marauding frost and snow have not yet mutually invaded.
The new light has a way of reminding me about my childhood—
Turning my eyes to my father and two former teachers in front of the
temple.
Forty years have brought so many different experiences:
Considering my dedication to serving my country, I know what my
feelings are.
But now it seems as if all the actions of my life are blurred.

Yet I do not feel that autumn sounds and fallen leaves fill the courtyard.
In the past many solid and positive things have come [into my life] and
have lasted.

If the pine and cypress endure the frigid winter, sooner or later spring
will come.[48]

Yu Shaosong (1883–1949) was an elder statesmen, having served in the
ministries of Foreign Affairs and Justice.[49] He came to Yunhe in May
1942 and was elected vice-chair of the Provisional Provincial Senate in
April 1943, taking over as chair six months later on the death of the
elected chair. Civil Administration Minister Ruan, Minister of Education
Xu Shaodi, and Governor Huang selected Yu to head a committee to
write a new provincial gazetteer. On first thought, such an endeavor at
this time and in this place seems completely incongruous. With the lack
of monetary resources because of wartime expenditures and deprivation,
and the absence of key documentary materials (still mostly controlled by

Japan in Hangzhou), this decision seems quixotic, at best questionable. The last provincial gazetteer had been compiled during the reign of the Yongzheng emperor (1722–1736); an attempt to compile one after 1912 had been stillborn: the 1940s' attempt also failed because of war and revolution. In the larger scheme of things, this effort may have been an attempt to bring some order to wartime disorder. Certainly planning the gazetteer was another survival strategy. It became the laserlike focus of Yu and others; in addition to Yu as chair, there was a vice-chair, a chief editor, four to six editors, and twelve to sixteen compilers. Yu encouraged counties to bring out new county gazetteers; indeed, he asked each county and town to help in the collecting of materials for and the editing of the provincial gazetteer. For the other officials, including Ruan, the project allowed them to look past the present and to learn from the provincial past as they entered a time yet unknown, the uncertain postwar world.

＞＜

SEVEN

Playing Hide-and-Seek with the Enemy

ON DECEMBER 29, 1941, a blizzard hit the Siming Mountains with the brittle frigidity of dry ice.[1] After midnight, Cai Zhuping, magistrate of Yuyao County in exile in Huajiazhuang, was tense and exhausted but not in the least tired. He telephoned Cixi magistrate Zhang Ju, "exiled" at the town of Beixi seven miles away, to let him know the news that Cai had received about the location and movement of Japanese troops; Cai also wanted to ask Zhang about how certain he was about the sources of his own intelligence gathering. Cai impatiently waited, seemingly for five minutes before the operator, obviously asleep or dozing, answered. When Cai asked to speak to Magistrate Zhang, the operator, clearly irritated, answered, "It's the middle of the night. He's asleep; I'm not going to wake him. Call back tomorrow." Then, click: he hung up. Cai immediately called back and in a very firm voice warned, "The enemy is nearly to you in Beixi. You have to take responsibility and act now." The operator was startled: "Are you serious? Just a minute."[2]

Zhang came to the phone after several minutes to say he had received no recent intelligence. Cai told him what he knew: there were over three hundred plainclothes enemy soldiers nearing Beixi (see Map 12). Cai advised Zhang to take immediate emergency preparations, adding that Cai's headquarters had already seen skirmishes. Zhang said that he would send spies out immediately though it was in the middle of the night.[3]

The circumstances and the exchange highlighted the precarious nature and unpredictabilities of county magistrates and their governments as refugees. For, as painful and difficult as refugee life was for provincial government officials, they were at the very least continuing to dwell in the province they were serving. The same cannot be said of the county magistrate, traditionally known as "the father-mother official," the government bureaucrat in closest contact with the masses. In the spring of 1941, the Japanese invaded Shaoxing and Ningbo prefectures; they occupied some whole counties, but in the majority the Japanese occupied the northern sections of each county while the southern sector remained free. However, later that spring and again in the winter of 1941–1942, the Japanese continued to make sporadic forays into the unoccupied sectors of the counties, in effect keeping the towns and villages of these areas under siege. It was in these localities where the kaleidoscope of war was most obvious, where Japanese thrusts and forays and Chinese responses produced innumerable varying patterns of violence, life, and death. In addition, small detachments of Japanese soldiers almost continuously roamed throughout the area, creating a particularly dangerous situation, in which local peace and safety could be shattered at any moment.

For county magistrates this wartime reality posed huge problems, many insoluble. How did one serve as the father-mother official for his county's people when many areas were, on again and off again, in Japanese-occupied areas? How did a county government function when Japanese military pressure forced it to move repeatedly, perhaps to a town or village in the unoccupied sector of the county but also perhaps to another county? The stories of magistrates Cai and Zhang for one year from April 1941 to April 1942 provide insights into the particular realities and difficulties county bureaucrats faced under Japanese occupation and military threat.

The Peripatetic Yuyao County Government

Cai, a native of Yin County, became magistrate of Yuyao in October 1940. From April 23, 1941, when the Japanese took the county seat, into early 1942, Cai and the county government became a refugee in the Siming Mountains, fleeing to one county after the other: Yin, Cixi, Shangyu, Xinchang, and Sheng (see Maps 2, 8, and 12). Altogether, the county government moved eight times: in four of those temporary sites, Cai attempted to set up government structures; in the others, he was at the site from only one day to half a month. Perhaps, on its face, the most evident impact of the Japanese invasion and occupation of part of Yuyao County was the psychic toll on Cai, his government staff, and the people in general.

In the week after the fall of Shaoxing on April 16, Cai had been inundated by orders from higher-ups, telegrams about military matters, anxious requests from subordinates, and phone calls exchanging information. He noted that during this time he heard nothing but ringing telephones and enemy planes. April 23 itself was eerily quiet; Cai himself noted an old proverb in this regard: "There is no sound amid ten thousand trees waiting for the rain to come." He had not unloosed his belt; and he slept with his clothes on. He wrote, "I had my heart in my mouth as I waited for my fate and that of the country."[4]

His other actions that day seem strangely out of step with the imminent danger; indeed, over and over again at place after place, the Chinese did not seem to be prepared physically or psychically for the Japanese onslaught. On that day a personal acquaintance from an outlying town came to the county yamen, bringing a gift of twenty catties (about twenty-six pounds) of fresh pork. Cai wrote, "Excitedly he said to me, 'Let's have a bit of a good time—a big feast—amid the bitterness.'" The idea appealed to Cai, not only because the diet of county government figures had deteriorated in the past week but also, ironically, because the county government had successfully completed the most crucial prewar activity—the frantic transport of necessary commodities; an unexpected feast might help to slacken tense nerves, at least temporarily. As the pork was being prepared and aromas began to waft throughout the room, a number of Cai's colleagues had begun serious wine drinking. It was after 4:30 P.M. Mouths were watering in anticipation; as Cai put it, "The grand ceremony of eating pork was about to begin." But suddenly the air was filled with the sounds of machine guns and small steel cannon; and everyone immediately forgot the pork: it was a feast never to be eaten.[5]

Realizing that the enemy was so close, Cai telephoned the Military Affairs Office so that it could blow up the electric power plant to prevent the Japanese from using it; however, he was too late: all the people with authority there had already fled. The person who answered the phone impertinently told Cai to come blow it up if he wanted it done. Suddenly, regiment commander Chen ran in with the news that the Japanese were already at the gate of the city, less than a third of a mile from the yamen. Outside was chaos: civilians, military, young, and old fled to get out of the city, a tide of people running toward South Mountain. As Cai and his associates joined them, Cai realized that the phone on which he depended to give orders was left on his desk; it didn't matter, he decided—the lines would soon be in enemy hands anyway.

By the time Cai and his group had run about two-thirds of a mile, the sounds of gunfire receded. From behind came citizens who reported that the enemy had already occupied the county seat and were sending scouts to the south. People began dropping parcels they were carrying because the bundles' weight and bulk were slowing them down. Cai wrote that he was carrying only a tiny bit in his suitcase and sardonically noted that he had already discarded the county seat that he had headed for his country.[6] Japan's seizure of the county seat came so easily because the city police were also not prepared. Even after hearing the approach of the enemy boats at the steam dock at the bend in the river, the police did not have time to deploy properly. Enemy boats had already gotten past the county seat's Qian Gate and moved to attack the police. The police released only one volley of rifle fire before they, recognizing they were in an untenable position, fled to the west.

Porters carried Cai in his sedan chair to a distance about three miles from Yuyao. The trip and what it meant for Cai as county magistrate was not a good one: "I felt emotional and confused about the current situation. My lips and tongue were dry and swollen; I could not swallow any food. I could only nod my head a little and wave my hands. I thought about the uneaten pork and laughed coldly."[7]

That night he and his party (presumably also his family, though he did not mention them at this point) went to Liangnong, an important town at the foot of the Dagang Mountains in southern Yuyao County (see Map 12). The town was tense, crowded, and disorderly, filled with rumors and cacophony—waiting anxiously for daybreak. As soon as it was morning, the gentry gathered at the town office to discuss how to handle the refugees. County government bureau heads met and announced that a temporary county government would be set up in Liangnong. The *baojia* head related that after Chinese troops had retreated to South Mountain, the people in the occupied area were being insulted and mistreated. For Cai, the father-mother official to his county residents, these words were in effect "incisive criticism that hit [him] in the chest as with an arrow." He wrote, "It was like having a thousand boils and a hundred pains, like having ten thousand arrows pierce my heart. I needed to drink boiling water, to wash away the cluttered thoughts filling my mind and the agitation within my heart."[8] But even more troubling, what would be the attitude of those who had fled toward the obviously unprepared government? Even before dawn, Cai's associates had sent him word that some people were beginning to blame him for what had happened and to talk about taking strong action against him. The magistrate did not seem strong enough to respond to the pressure and to offer real leadership. His response was to leave Liangnong immediately. As it turned out, it was probably none too soon: two hours later the streets were filled with people carrying guns and raising a hue and cry: "The magistrate has run away!"[9]

On April 26, at Yantou Village in the center of the Dagang Mountains, almost twenty-five miles from Yuyao and seven from Liangnong, Cai established the Yuyao county government in exile. County government offices were set up at the home of Chen Yi'ou, the township head. Inside were several large desks arranged almost as if in a conference room; one large desk was used for dispatching and receiving mail, for using the official chop, and for drafting documents. With county governments as refugees roaming back and forth across the countryside, maintaining the county chop became a key determinant of power. That day again made Cai face the question of what the physical displacement of the county seat meant for his governance. He saw an office worker with flagging spirits staggering with his family up the mountain, supporting the old and carrying the young, a large bundle of bedding on his back. This scene made Cai sick at heart. Middle- and lower-ranking colleagues had begun to ask him to dismiss them: the living conditions and the physical hardships in the mountains were daunting. Cai was not unsympathetic to their plight, and he agreed to let some leave. But in this trying situation, as the numbers of people were reduced, work became even more stressful for those who remained.

The most important work at that moment was dealing with sparse and scattered commodities on the mountain and setting up phone lines at the top of mountains in the range. Other crucial roles for the newly reestablished yamen included investigating Chinese traitors (hanjian), setting up sentries to examine travelers, making contacts with county people not in the mountains, and dispatching spies to Yuyao to return and report on what was happening there. Even with all the important work, everyone felt completely empty at heart, even mournful. Cai commented,

> Especially in the evening when the mountain breeze moaned and the light of the stars and moon flickered, we felt the deep loneliness and dreariness of our lost homes. The thoughts of my narrow escape continued to give me palpitations; it constantly impinged on my thoughts. Everyone had similar kinds of feelings. We had been forced to become exiles. Thanks to my handling things inappropriately at a key moment, the county has experienced great catastrophe. I had the great majority of troops stationed in towns and townships in northern Yuyao along the coast; therefore there were too few troops farther south. Then, when the Japanese invaded, the government went south: connections between the troops and the government were cut off. We heard rumors that half of the troops had run off in different directions. I'd ordered troops still remaining to march south as quickly as possible, but they should have been here by now. We urgently needed to have every road or pass in the South Mountain area blocked. Later a unit of nineteen men and thirty-five guns came to South Mountain. We reorganized them as the Dagang Mountain 'self-defense force of the masses'; its expenses, weapons, and uniforms were to be paid for by the government.[10]

On Dragon Boat Festival (May 30, 1941), Cai and his associates decided to have a feast on the mountain, obviously without dragon boats; refugees were seated around tables, talking and drinking—wondering where they would be on Dragon Boat Festival the next year. A year ahead? In actuality, they could not even know where they would be minutes ahead. Suddenly the phone rang; the message was startling: the enemy had now come within six or seven miles of the mountain. It was a déjà-vu of the abandoned pork feast of little more than a month earlier. Again, emergency action had to go into play. Township head Chen telephoned people on the other mountains about transporting government goods and materials, documents, and cash from the county-managed Farmers' Bank to another mountaintop village, called Hongyan.

Cai telephoned Siming Hospital and told refugee medical students that staff and patients should come south to hide. But the hospital did not act in time; when the Japanese came, they bayoneted to death sixteen wounded soldiers and seized the hospital's food, equipment, and weapons. The county government units at Yantou also had to evacuate; recently arrived refugees at Yantou were transformed into fleeing refugees once again. Cai also called the Siming Guerrilla Headquarters for some assistance and heard that its staff had headed for Chating Mountain, about three miles from the mountain Cai was evacuating. Township head Chen stayed behind temporarily to man the telephones and to direct people living on the mountain to find hiding places for their flour, kerosene, and other commodities and then to flee and hide. The "self-defense forces for the masses," charged with guarding the mountain, jettisoned their guns and fled. When Chen and his group got to Chating Mountain, they were met with the word that more Japanese forces were only three miles away. The group discarded their luggage to make better time, taking only a few clothes. Panic-stricken, they fled the area, crossing the county border into Yin County, heading for the town of Xiling.

In the various accounts of the Siming Mountain campaigns, as in other Chinese narratives of the war, night and darkness are common tropes. Certainly, fleeing or marching in darkness was a reality, yet its allegorical or metaphorical connotations cannot be dismissed. Cai's account of traveling in darkness is, notably, the first depiction of his family.

It was dark; my family (including my old mother and a sibling, my wife, and children) were with me. There was no moonlight or starlight, and we had only one weak flashlight. Step by step we groped and fumbled our way in the darkness. We walked in the middle of a small mountain road, tremblingly tense in heart and spirit. The children called out that they couldn't see and that they couldn't go any farther. I had to coax them at every step and urge them to hurry. My younger sister, Xuemei, slipped and fell into a hole beside the path. Fortunately, it was not deep, but her glasses fell and broke. Our intense fear tired us out; we cried bitterly. When we arrived at Xiling, the Yin county magistrate, now a refugee like us, was already there; I figured we could retreat together. He was already planning to leave, for the sounds of gunfire reached us from Dajiao, only five miles away. Friends encouraged me to first take my family to Zhougongzhai, about seven miles away. It was already 9 P.M., so we had another groping along on an inky-black mountain road. Dajiao Village fell to the Japanese at midnight; Chinese troops were utterly routed."

Literally, Cai said the Chinese troops were "like fallen flowers carried away by flowing water."[11]

The refugees arrived at Zhougongzhai about 3 A.M. and stayed at the home of the local *baojia* head in a small, square room that was wall-to-wall refugees. Their host invited Cai to sleep in the thatched-roof attic—which turned out to be a nest for fleas; Cai got them all over his body. Even with the resulting insatiable, wild itching and only an hour or two of sleep, he woke and felt compelled to move his family farther away from the fighting. They left before dawn. Cai wrote, "As we hurried along between day and night, we were indeed genuine refugees. I remembered the lines of Tang dynasty poet Du Fu:

> After weapons of war have been scattered in the countryside,
> Flesh and blood were fleeing on the roads."[12]

Cai and his group headed to Jianyan Village, but when they were only a third of a mile away—exhausted, hungry, and on edge—a man met them with the news that Japanese troops had seized Jianyan. They obviously could not proceed on this road. Fortunately, a policeman on his way to another nearby village occupied by Chinese troops came along and offered to show them the way. Chance, happenstance, and unpredictabilities marked the lives of refugees and nonrefugees alike in facing wartime realities.

The group met Li Fei, the principal of the coed Yin County Normal School, located at a larger village farther on. Surrounded by his refugee students, Li came forward to greet Cai and his party. To Cai's eyes, the students seemed generally courageous; they all had backpacks with food. In village stalls, rice porridge was cooking; people gave Cai and the others some to eat. The students also shared some of the food they carried with them. Cai's group walked on with the students between three and four miles to Beixi, on the border between Yuyao and Fenghua counties. It was an area of natural beauty: the Siming Mountains, veined by clear, sparkling streams, were strikingly scenic. In this period of active military pressure and aggression, the area was a gathering spot for fleeing officials, active and defeated soldiers, and refugees, young and old. The Beixi township head received Cai and his group warmly. Beixi was a respite from the turmoil and anxiety in which Cai and his family and associates had been mired. Refugees were here from many places; Cai heard many stories about what had happened in their native places when the Japanese came.

The downside of Beixi was that there were too many people without sufficient facilities to support them for a longer period of time. So Cai and the others stayed there for only half a month. Then they moved with Cixi magistrate Zhang Ju and the head of Yuyao's local court to Jinxi in Sheng County, far to the southwest. The time would likely have been early October 1941.

Activist in a Polarized World

Cai Zhuping can be seen as a reactor, responding to events on a case-by-case basis; he was also a man who shared his emotional reactions quite openly and whose writings seem to downplay politics and emphasize the human dimension. In contrast, Zhang Ju, with whom Cai traveled to Jinxi, was a daring activist in a world polarized into Chinese and Japanese and into Chinese collaborators and Chinese resisters. Many magistrates had followed government guidelines that—should their county or a portion of the county be occupied—they make efforts to keep an undercover government or at least government offices alive in the occupied zones. This would let occupied Chinese know that their legitimate Chinese county magistrate indeed remained the father-mother official, caring, as best he could in such trying circumstances, for people who were subjected to Japanese rule. At the same time, at least theoretically, the presence of the legitimate Chinese government would make it easier, when liberation from Japanese control was finally realized, to rebuild and reconstruct more quickly.

Cai Zhuping never made such an effort: it was a dangerous undertaking; if the Japanese caught such a Guomindang magistrate, he would most certainly be executed. For the most part, Cai consistently chose to make his county seat in exile in a town outside Yuyao—and not even in his county's unoccupied zone. Zhang Ju was of a different breed, though he and Cai apparently hit it off in terms of friendship from the beginning. Zhang (b. 1904), the son of a poor family in Tangxi in central Zhejiang, had become an elementary school teacher after graduating from the Seventh Provincial Middle School in Jinhua.[13] He later went on to graduate from the Central Political School in Nanjing and receive several official appointments: head of the Education Ministry of the

Lanxi county government; secretary to the Third District's administrative inspector; magistrate of Jinhua County; and then, in January 1938, magistrate of Cixi County.

As county leader for more than three years before the Japanese invasion (in contrast to Cai, who served in Yuyao only six months before the invasion), Zhang had greater time and opportunity to build a record and become more fully acquainted with the county, its structures, its problems, and its elites and their social connections. Zhang's reputation was that he was not a schmoozer; rather, he was upright, scrupulously careful to avoid any hint of corruption, and—a negative—rather unimaginative. A calligraphic scroll that he had written hung on the wall of his office: "To go to Beijing for five days is a desire of the heart; to stand up throughout one's life is the will of the nation."[14] Many gentry reportedly tried to butter him up and establish connections with him; but Zhang rebuffed their overtures. He was unafraid to go up against anyone, solidifying his reputation as a stubborn fighter but angering some powerful people in the process. A local tyrant named Zhao in the eastern part of the county did all in his power to intimidate Zhang; but Zhang never genuflected literally or figuratively to Zhao. And there was Lu Jinting, who had served in the high provincial court and the provincial assembly. His political goal in the county in the late 1930s was to become a hegemon for an entire region; Zhang refused to do Lu's bidding, for which Lu excoriated him and called him an "official of pestilence."[15] Zhang was a reformer, handling the difficult problem of provisioning and encouraging the establishment of industry (paper mills and tin-can factories). He was frugal, almost to a fault. The county yamen was in such physical disrepair that his government colleagues were embarrassed and urged him to undertake repairs. Zhang's response? "At the present time, our country's difficulties are very great; updating the yamen is something that can wait."[16]

This frugality put him in good stead when Zhang relocated the county seat after the Japanese seized it. In the Siming Mountains, to which the government fled, material and money resources dried up quickly; being frugal and setting priorities were thus critical. He had retreated by May to Beixi, which, as we just saw, was a considerable magnet for refugees of all sorts. While there, Zhang decided to go to the occupied zone to try to rebuild the county government slowly from within.[17] His first trip came in June and was not auspicious: in a mopping-up operation, the Japanese Fifth Army almost caught him and the few men who worked with him there. The mopping-up operation, perhaps ironically, made the county residents more willing to work with Zhang, for most were reportedly shocked by the Japanese troops' "bestial" methods. Zhang reported that when county residents began to work with him, "they had their brains, but their psychic scars gave them a 'detached' quality." Indeed, social and psychological displacement was as much a part of Chinese in occupied areas as of Chinese refugees. But Zhang, in a newspaper account he published in the fall, noted that even after this first foray into occupied Cixi, the district *(qu)*, township, and town government structures began to revive.

He made plans for his second trip in early August, but it was postponed when Governor Huang Shaohong called a provincial administrative meeting. Zhang did not then begin his second visit until the last ten days of August; he spent twenty-five days traveling throughout the occupied zone and holding secret meetings with upright gentry, town and township heads, young people, representatives from various work teams, and colleagues involved in resistance activities. These meetings had several functions: to keep these people in the occupied zone abreast of what their county government was doing in exile; to discuss strategies in thwarting the plans of the enemy and their puppets; and to bolster spirits. Zhang frankly stated that in the beginning the names "enemy district," "fallen district," and guerrilla warfare district" had been extraordinary producers of fear. The fall of the county seat had ushered in a period in which public and private had met with disaster and tragedy. Zhang said these pep talks were to "console and comfort" the people. He fed them lines that were not "true": for example, "The enemy is nearing the end of its resources."[18]

On this first trip to the occupied district, Zhang bought into his talk the line of a man at one of the meetings: "The enemy is like a stupid cow: lead him east, lead him west; it is we who have the power to dispose of him." In occupied areas, he admonished, the Chinese must rise up for the great principles of the country. The bêtes noires in Zhang's talks were the collaborators: "They are abominable." Indeed, Zhang argued that it was the collaborators who established the methods and approaches for the enemy, who had no inkling of Chinese language, customs, and sensibilities. He stated unequivocally that if it were not for Chinese collaborators, the enemy would fail and that if all Chinese had the proper fighting spirit, there would be no collaborators.[19]

On his second foray into the occupied sector of Cixi County, Zhang was aware that his first trip, over two months earlier, had likely been much discussed by the Japanese and their collaborators.[20] This time he disguised himself alternatively as a farmer and a merchant; he also did not tarry long in any one spot. But Zhang had been in the county for a good period of time as the father-mother official; many people could recognize him even in incongruous garb. News of meetings could easily slip out. He claimed in October 1941 that he had almost been captured three times by the Japanese during his August–September visit. In terms of the first two episodes, it seems very unlikely that the Japanese were really on to him. But the third was serious. In Zhang's words:

> I was in the eastern district to hold a meeting at the Dragon King Temple, about seven or eight *li* [between two and three miles] from the Quiet Garden Temple. When the meeting on the third night was over, I had intended to spend the night at either Dragon King or Quiet Garden. But when the time came, I decided to stay with the Lang family in a nearby small village. To everyone's surprise, at 2 A.M. on the next morning, over 120 Japanese troops went to the Quiet Garden Temple. Two hours later about a dozen came to the Lang household. I had been afraid that somehow my shift in plans might slip out; so I was sleeping at a neighboring house. Since the dozen soldiers remained on guard around the Lang house, when daylight came, I left by the back door of where I stayed, retreating into a nearby bamboo forest. By this time, my self-defense unit leader had ordered over thirty soldiers to be sent to me immediately. They set up an ambush on the roads to the Lang house and to the Dragon King Temple, waiting for the Japanese to pass and then attack them. The Japanese were not prepared: we killed one officer and five soldiers, while we lost one soldier.

It was, he said, "an inexpensive one-hour victory." But the obvious Japanese determination to capture and kill Zhang pointed to the anger they had for what Zhang was trying to do. He was, in the words of a newspaper byline—which indeed is the title of this chapter--"playing hide-and-seek with the enemy."[21]

Zhang left the occupied sector on September 16 with a conviction that each local situation in the occupied zone had its own specific questions that had to be answered, that there was not one overall solution. He argued that each community had to actively and continually discuss its attitudes, situations, and policies. Some problems in the end may have been insoluble. He asserted that the people in the occupied areas were like the wards of a children's nurse, that the county government must take responsibility for them, thinking of ways to come to save them.

Autumn Restoration

In early to mid August, Governor Huang Shaohong called the first meeting of an administrative conference, to give his opinions about what was happening in the former prefectures of Shaoxing and Ningbo, to offer sympathy and solicitude for each magistrate in the guerrilla warfare districts, and to discuss county government work that had been disrupted and lost. The meeting, in a scenic area of Sheng County was not far from the provincial capital in exile in Yongkang County (see Maps 10 and 12); the gathering was attended by provincial government specialists, over twenty county magistrates plus a small number of county subbureaucrats, and local gentry. Cai Zhuping noted that the meeting was physically uncomfortable: the weather was stiflingly hot. Still, the meeting had the same function as Zhang's local meeting in Cixi: instilling morale and positive thinking. Cai reported that each magistrate spoke frankly, voicing much discontent and many complaints: "At least we were able to unburden ourselves, and Huang's response was soothing—like a gentle breeze blowing the floating clouds after a big rainstorm. He said that losses in the Siming Mountains came from a lack of guerrilla experience, but that overall there were too many subbureaucrats and too many government personnel, goods, and materials concentrated in too few places. Such 'centralized' areas—as at Beixi—could rapidly become invasion targets for the Japanese. This was a powerful warning."[22] Each magistrate had to be in charge of and carefully measure and preserve his resources.

After the meeting, Cai discarded his pessimism and decided to return to the Siming Mountain region of Yuyao County, the original base for the county government in exile and an area once again occupied by Chinese troops. Those family members, government associates, and gentry who had comprised Cai's refugee retinue traveled to the village of Huangjiazhuang, in the south-central part of the mountain range, where they set up the temporary county seat. The village had no more than fifty households. County government was housed in the Chen-family tea store, with the Police Security Bureau located in a nearby temple; also close by, the county Guomindang headquarters was housed in a private residence. The Liangnong district government, closer to the occupied sector, was restored, along with the Northern Yuyao Administrative Office. Cai had a list compiled of materials the county government still had and set up telephone service to neighboring counties. Finally, after months of almost continuous, unsettling moves, the late fall of 1941 seemed to bring a measure of stability.

Magistrate Cai had to rely on his own devices for military support for county government; support from the Chinese national army was not possible. The goal of the county was to recruit soldiers from both inside and outside of the region. Recruiters were sent to counties to the south and southwest, Lishui, Wuyi, and Yongkang, where there was no active Japanese presence or immediate threat. The difficult problem was supporting the recruits financially, a role that fell completely to the county. Because of the paucity of money-raising opportunities in mountainous areas, Cai's available troops were limited to only one regiment of soldiers. Word spread about the county government's new site. The reactions of people to the reestablishment of government buoyed magistrates and county governments. When county officials were literally in the wilderness, depression overwhelmed. But such a rapid response from citizens to create some stability filled authorities with hope. In this case, students from the occupied northern part of the county began to troop to Huangjiazhuang. Two teachers set up a middle school at a temple at the foot of the mountains, and Yuyao students and some from neighboring Shangyu County came to attend it. An elementary school was opened nearby. Funds for education were extremely limited, but interest in education never waned.

Cai noted that the Chinese fight was not only against enemy troops, traitors, and bandits but also against the easy spread of diseases. Being a refugee ground down the body, making the immune system weaker. Malaria was a continuing problem, striking especially, it seemed, students and soldiers. Dysentery and inflammation of the bowels were extraordinarily widespread. Most repugnant to many people was highly contagious scabies, caused by parasitic mites and marked by severe itching, most often worse at night. Ningbo and Yuyao merchants in the area were aware of these illnesses and asked two doctors in Ningbo for prescriptions; the merchants dispatched two men to bring the essential medications to the area. The provincial Relief Office did pick up part of the cost of these medicines.

Intelligence and Death

In late December 1941, the Japanese began another military surge into areas that they had ravaged from April through June. The Yuyao county seat at Huangjiazhuang was about seven miles north of Beixi, the location of the Cixi county seat, on the Yuyao-Fenghua border (see Map 12). Magistrates who had moved out of the occupied portions of their counties kept in touch so that all would be prepared if danger threatened. That is why Cai had called Zhang in the early morning hours of December 30 to check with him on his intelligence gathering. With mostly small, roving bands of Japanese soldiers scattered throughout the area, a site could be perfectly safe for a day or part of a day but in extreme danger very quickly.

The day dawned clear and cold. Dozing off and on, suddenly Cai heard the sound of airplanes. He ran out into the courtyard and watched two low-flying Japanese planes passing overhead, but then they began to spiral back around. The planes, officials learned, were loaded with more soldiers. Although Cai and his associates had not yet eaten breakfast, he hurriedly called them altogether for immediate evacuation. While he carried a suitcase of documents, all associates carried shoulder bags and bamboo canes to help their walking single file in the snow on narrow, twisting mountain paths. They decided to split up. A group carrying non-essential papers headed for Jinxi in Sheng County, where both Cai and Zhang had spent considerable time in the fall. A few chose to stay in the area and would obviously hide if Japanese soldiers approached. The head of the security guards, Cai, and four or five others were the last to leave.

Cai reported,

In the early morning hours, I spoke several times with Magistrate Zhang. He had sent out seven spies in the middle of the night, but as of 9 A.M. none had returned. We were both rather worried. At 10 A.M. one of the spies, the

political director of the self-defense militia, returned, flustered and exasper-
ated, his whole body muddy, his face marked by sweat and tears: 'The enemy is already up on the mountain,' he exclaimed. He also let them know
about Japanese actions elsewhere; the news was bad: in at least three battles
in the region, the Japanese had defeated Chinese forces. I advised him
[Zhang] to evacuate immediately, and I asked him about the situation in
Xianglianggang, where the Ninth Guomindang Army was based. Zhang
replied that an intelligence officer who had just arrived said that there had
not yet been any contact with the enemy in Xianglianggang and that the
enemy was still fifteen miles from Beixi. Zhang said that he would flee
when the Japanese reached Beixi. I worried about this decision. So, after we
hung up, I decided to retreat to Beixi.

It was 10:20 A.M. I was accompanied by four plainclothes security guards
and two of my staff. I had calculated the distance from Huangjiazhuang to
Beixi and estimated that I could be there for lunch at 1 P.M. Just as we were
leaving, we heard the sounds of a plane in the distance. After several sec-
onds, we saw a single bomber coming directly toward us. The enemy pilot
had most certainly seen us; the plane went past but then spun around. I
headed for the two snow-covered mountains beside the road; almost immediately a bomb exploded little more than twenty meters up the mountain. We did not even see the flash—were bombarded only by pieces of
falling and flying rock and fountains of grassroots, snow, and mud blown up
into the air. I was covered in mud and there was blood on my face. After
the explosion, we discovered that a nearby residence was the home of a
baojia head, who invited us in and asked us to relax and stay out of sight
from the Japanese and enjoy a simple meal.

But, seemingly only momentarily, a security guard burst in to announce
that within the last hour, the Japanese had taken Beixi. Even more serious,
they were reportedly within three miles of where we were now. I asked
him questions about the Beixi takeover, but he did not know anything
about it other than that it had happened. He left in a panic after gulping
down some tea. I didn't know whether the security guard's report was dependable, but the troublesome question, given Zhang Ju's intelligence
sources, was how the Japanese soldiers had been able to travel the fifteen
miles from Xianglianggang to Beixi so quickly. Facing our own imminent
peril, we couldn't dare stay in this area, so we left for Jinxi, where the group
carrying nonessential papers had headed. I sent a security guard on ahead

to reconnoiter so that we wouldn't inadvertently walk directly into enemy hands. But fortunately we were safe in that area.

We learned that Beixi had fallen at 11 A.M., after which the Japanese showcased their signature act, the burning of the town; fire was still visible on the horizon, almost twelve hours after the Japanese torched the place. I kept going over it in my mind. How did Beixi collapse so suddenly? Magistrate Zhang had clearly told me on the phone that the enemy was fifteen miles away; but it was only forty-five minutes after we talked that Beixi was taken. Over two hundred Japanese soldiers participated in the Beixi attack. The Beixi garrison was undermanned at the time because, as in Yuyao, the Cixi self-defense force had been mostly dispatched to northern Cixi. The Japanese force consisted of both infantrymen and cavalrymen, who had ridden their warhorses through paddies, to avoid the slipperiness of snow and ice on mountain roads.[23]

Because he had been up in the middle of the night, in the early morning Zhang had rested on his bed in his military uniform: it was standard at this time for the magistrate and county bureaucrats to wear military uniforms to work. One of his aides burst in, shouting that the enemy was coming. Zhang was doubtful. He called the military line at the Xiangliangang base, where he was told once again that the Japanese had not been there and would have to cross a strategic pass before reaching that base. He said to the aide, "Certainly it can't be that the Japanese will flap their wings and fly here, can it?" (The Cixi government officials, including Magistrate Zhang, were not even aware of the danger until after Japanese had entered the town.) When Zhang got up, he saw through the window Japanese troops swarming forward. All the county government bureaucrats had already changed into civilian clothes in order to make it more possible that they could escape; Zhang kept his military uniform on. He tried to flee from the back of his office by going up the mountain, but the Japanese saw him and shot him, hitting both his legs; and, then, as he struggled forward, they killed him with a shot to his chest. Most government officials escaped. The Japanese discovered Beixi's extensive gasoline and kerosene storage tanks and blew them up, destruction that explained the intense and long-lasting fires.[24]

The story about Zhang Ju's fate eventually came to light. The intelligence that he had received had been completely wrong. His death almost certainly came from decisions he made not to evacuate earlier, based on his calls to Xianglianggang. Cai Zhuping had had word in the middle of the night that there had been a battle at Xianglianggang. In other words, both calls that Zhang made to that base were placed after the Japanese had already been there. Any Chinese military figure there would have been able to warn Zhang to evacuate.[25] It is not hard to conclude that Zhang had likely talked to a Chinese collaborator, one of the very group he had excoriated on his trips to the Cixi County occupied zone. It is indeed highly possible that the Japanese, who would clearly have known Zhang was at Beixi, had made killing him a goal—before he might cause them more serious problems in his efforts to establish a continuing county base within the occupied area. Zhang's death also clearly underscored the weakness of the Chinese surveillance and intelligence-gathering systems.

In a postmortem of sorts, Cai wrote, "To my mind, the events of the past few days pointed out how thorough Japanese preparations had been for this largest enemy raid in the region; its scope was exceptionally broad. They had taken advantage of attacking our broken military remnants. I thought about how carelessly we had retreated, hither and yon without any overall or long-range plan. Our slipshod intelligence and decision making made losing almost an inevitability. Even after that day, the period of our fleeing would stretch on for another two weeks."[26]

Whether as a result of Zhang Ju's fate or something else, in early 1942 Cai seemed recommitted to fostering the reestablishment of the Yuyao government and party more devotedly: "I must do all I can to protect the county's party bureau. The county offices and court have already moved to Changyue Town in Sheng County—I'm relieved about that. I think: the enemy is like a poison worm as it comes and twists around behind our lines. We fail if we don't block its advances and if we don't head back to our original area. Moreover, that area still has the remnants of our lost and dispersed troops that we must coordinate with: we must rejoin our scattered colleagues."[27] Indeed, those scattered and left-behind associates also suffered "displacement" (despite the fact that they were not physically moved), since the people remaining when others fled lost part of their world and themselves—since identity was found in relation to others.

On New Year's Day, 1942, Cai was personally without money and, in Sheng County, had no way to gain access to funds in the county treasury, still in the Siming Mountains. In order to get through this crisis, he traveled to Dashiju in Xinchang County to the south, to borrow provisions and funds from the magistrate of Yin County, Yu Qimin, who had emerged as something of a regional strongman (see Map 8). Cai came as a supplicant, in his words, "a humble refugee pleading for money and grain."[28] Yu offered Cai whatever he needed; Cai borrowed money and twenty piculs (almost twenty-seven hundred pounds) of rice—and returned to try to right the Yuyao county office. His first step, ironically, was to assist people in Cixi County. He decided to send extra monies to Cixi County people who had become separated during flight or who needed to bury their dead, also allotting five yuan to each man in the self-defense regiment and twenty yuan for those who had been wounded. At a time when funds were short, this generosity was an act most certainly undertaken out of guilt that he had not been aggressive enough in demanding Zhang Ju's evacuation.

Cai frequently mused about the realities of China at war.

> At this time defeated soldiers and fleeing civil officials were like a pair of wolves in tremendous difficulty, set on mutually devouring each other. What about me? I had best say that at this time everyone must continue to resist the enemy and restore the country. Though there have been defeats, there has also been glory. Enemy forces outnumbered us, and they clearly perpetrated war crimes. Now shifting to a guerrilla strategy will save us from both defeat and flight. After I wrote this, I thought it over: there was nothing wrong with what I said. I was rationalizing the situation and perhaps projecting future developments as overly rosy—I don't know when I had taken up [inadvertently?] Ah Q's approach.[29]

The Report of Wang Nairen

After Cai returned to Yuyao County itself, to the big garrison in the town of Heilongtan in the Siming Mountains, where the county government would once more be established, he read the latest intelligence report from the keeper of the county government chop, Wang Nairen. It reflected the same realities that Cai had been living since taking his post:

fear and uncertainty, fractured government, unpredictable Japanese actions, and tragedy for the Chinese people. It reads,

> Heilongtan is in the area actually controlled for the present by Shangyu County. It's a place that is easy to enter, but there is no good emergency exit from this very deep and remote valley; it's not on any transportation route. We are presuming that the enemy will not choose to enter this isolated valley. Yuyao County Secretary Jin Yinian, a Shangyu County native, brought a large number of Shangyu associates into the Yuyao government in Heilongtan; I am one of them. I carry the Yuyao county chop with me at all times; whoever holds it maintains authority. [It is perhaps an indication of Cai's relative lack of involvement in county affairs during his displacement that he was not in possession of the chop.] Yinian uses landlords and local leaders with status to help in handling problems; he is adept, quick, and busy—there's little dullness at Heilongtan.
>
> The county government is fractured. The radio-telephone and encoder office moved to Xujiata; between ten and twenty people remain in Heilongtan; and some colleagues have hidden in the mountains, not coming to the town even to eat. At night many government staffers go down the mountain to stay at homes of area residents. Any intelligence we garner comes via rumors. We constantly fear that the enemy will come to Heilongtan.
>
> At 3 A.M. I was startled awake by the sounds of machine-gun and cannon fire—aimed at Heilongtan. I did not flee; if I did so and ran into the enemy, their capture of the county chop would be a disaster. I stayed in bed.
>
> Not very much later, a county staffer entered my room and called to me. He said, "The enemy has not yet arrived. There's still time; we must quickly leave." Trembling with fear, I crawled out of bed. Shaking, I climbed Hou Mountain with the staffer. It was about dawn and the inky-black sky was beginning to turn shades of gray; another round of Japanese bombers also appeared in the sky. Looking down from the top of Hou Mountain, I also saw several thousand Japanese troops with over a hundred cavalrymen. They were not headed to Heilongtan. Later I learned that with the soldiers were ordinary Chinese whom the Japanese had commandeered to guide them to Heilongtan. But the Chinese civilians led them purposefully to Bailongtan instead in a show of resistance disguised temporarily as collaboration. But they paid a huge price. When the Japanese discovered that they had been led astray, they killed all the Chinese.

With the Japanese going past, I carried the county chop down the mountain. I met up with Secretary Jin and a group of the staff. On the road we passed straggling Japanese soldiers, whose visages took on the curious combination of being caught in a terrible plight yet at the same time exhibiting ferocity and malice. We kept our distance as we passed. The third day we went to Dagangshan, where I am protecting the official county chop.[30]

Resignation or Dismissal?

Wang made it clear: "Any intelligence we garner comes via rumor." False rumor or valid intelligence: this was the issue that continually dogged refugees, the military, and the civilian governments. In summer 1941, less than two months after Yuyao fell, Cai had a different object lesson in wartime truth and fiction. He accidentally saw in the *Dagongbao,* published in Chongqing, the headline "In Eastern Zhejiang Our Army Recovers Yuyao." Cai wrote,

> This was certainly news to me, the Yuyao magistrate—I didn't know whether to laugh or cry. There was absolutely no truth to the story. What actually happened was that one day a unit of Yuyao soldiers agreed with an outside unit to make an evening attack on the Yuyao county seat, to harass the enemy and the traitors. When the time came to meet, the outside unit failed to appear; the county unit proceeded as planned. When it neared the city wall, the soldiers fired their guns and set off firecrackers. The next day we found out that the people living in the county seat nearest the wall had been panicked and fled; most of the residents did not. But the troops, hearing about this reaction, described the episode as a victory; and a news agency sent out word of victory by telegram. After this happened there was a succession of copycat rumors: "The enemy army had fled all of the townships in Sheng County"; "A division of Japanese soldiers was beaten"; "Japanese soldiers were losing their will to fight"—all wishful thinking. And on our side: "We spread our resistance coolheadedly and calmly"; "our units bravely attacked"; "the enemy beat a precipitate retreat"; "we've seized victory." These kinds of claims in the face of contrary reality make people weary and wary.[31]

Cai's group of exiles in the mountains at the end of the day could only have a melancholy hope that eventually the national army would become involved. Then out of the blue, they received a telegram from the provincial government that they had reassessed the current military situation and had decided to send the Twenty-sixth Division to Yuyao and Shangyu within the month. The government ordered that the current refugee magistrates meet with the commander of that division in Sheng County to discuss the deployment. Cai went to Sheng immediately and met Commander Wang, a Sichuan man, who said he could send two full regiments to enter Yuyao from the north to link up with Cai's county government in the mountains. In addition, a regiment would be sent directly into the mountains to facilitate the joint effort. There were now finally the outlines of a strategy, though specific details of military and government cooperation still had to be worked out.

The next day Cai and Wang left Sheng County. On the way Commander Wang told Cai three important points that Cai had to guarantee for him: Wang would depend on Cai's county government for intelligence information (no small order); he would depend upon Cai's county government for dependable directions; and the county would establish and nurture a temporary county government behind enemy lines. The last was what Cai had not even mentioned at this point, let alone tried to do; and it was what an act that likely had gotten Magistrate Zhang killed. Cai answered that he also wanted three guarantees from the commander: that Wang guarantee that his troops would be strictly disciplined; that his troops would be willing to fight and not run away; and that Wang and his troops would absolutely take seriously and cooperate with the county government. The last point was crucial for Cai; and, when he thought Wang assented, Cai thanked the commander warmly.

Early the next morning Cai went to Commander Wang's office to take his leave to return to those at Heilongtan, to discuss the new situation with government colleagues and local elites. As they were finishing breakfast, an officer brought in a telegram for Wang. He said, "Ah, this is very good!" He handed it to Cai. It was from the regional commander's office, with news that troops were being transferred immediately: the Twenty-sixth Division would start at 9 A.M. to gather in Jinhua, to wait for specific orders. Wang said, "These several sentences should console you." Then Wang left quickly to command the soldiers.[32] He did not say one word about working cooperatively—or about any of the details about the military's linking up with the county government.

Cai went into a funk: he wrote,

So despite all the hopes I had felt so recently, I was downcast and in low
spirits. I returned to Dagangshan, but would have preferred to vanish into
thin air. Now, it appeared I would have little or no say about the site or the
goal of military actions. And in the Siming Mountain portion of Yuyao
county—the guerrilla base—the county government actually had no control. Various units made up the guerrilla armies, and each unit made policy
decisions and directed matters in the area that it occupied. While the guer-
rillas might, in the end, help win back occupied territory, for now the people
in the area had to put up with eating bitterness; they were being ground
down by a plague of taxes: everything imaginable was taxed to provide
money for the guerrilla armies. This was a great political illness. And my
power could not overcome it. I decided I had no choice but to resign.[33]

Cai's reaction is, on the one hand, quite mystifying, given the fact that
at last sufficient military help was in his grasp. But if he saw that essentially he would have no power, perhaps even less than he had had in the
government in exile, his defeatism is more understandable. He had never
had the courageous and determined streak that marked Zhang Ju's
career record.

When Cai broached his resignation with the gentry, they pleaded with
him to stay on. But Cai thought it best to say good-bye to the Siming
Mountains, Yuyao County, and his Yuyao gentry friends. To stay on, he
thought, would be painful and frustrating. He wrote, "I took my leave at
the Yuyao Native Place Association in Sheng County. Whatever will and
determination refugees had in order to flee, they still must be filled with
a great reluctance to leave and a strong feeling of regret whenever they
see and hear of the trial and tribulations of their friends who had already
fled. When I look back at my refugee guerrilla life for the past two years,
now concluded, I absolutely did not feel I was in that great a danger, and
it was not that my life had been dominated by the sighs of pain and suffering. But there is righteous indignation and grievance. When I took my
leave from this Yuyao refugee community, refugee students, who came to
hear my departing words, were just like myself—their faces and words
were heartbreaking."[34]

Cai wrote, "When I went to the Siming Mountains, I received my suc-
cessor as Yuyao magistrate, Jiang Xianqi, a man from Hunan who was in

the fifth graduating class from Whampoa Military Academy. He'd been serving on the staff of the Third Wartime Region commander. He was thus coming from a top level military position. At least he could respond to the mixed units of guerrilla warfare—in this regard, he was much better qualified than I. Further, on the field of battle, he could much better direct the action than I."[35]

In the end, we come back to Cai's seemingly rather sudden decision to resign. Given his rather hesitant leadership and one of the guarantees demanded by Commander Wang—that Cai establish and nurture a Yuyao county government behind enemy lines—there may have been some, even considerable, disgruntlement with his leadership. His replacement seemed to offer those military advantages and knowledge that would be needed for the immediate future in the county. Though there is no direct evidence, circumstantial evidence suggests it is at least possible that Cai was either asked to resign or was dismissed. In that case, Cai was simply spinning rationalizations about why he might have been compelled to resign. I have found no independent observer of the affair: the reason for his leaving the magistracy at such a crucial time remains an open question.

In April 1942, with the heat making it feel already like summer, Jiang and Cai went to Jinxi in Sheng County to manage the transfer of power. Cai congratulated himself on not "losing a single item" during his magistracy. When things were settled, he went to Jinhua. But in the next month, the Japanese launched their most extensive invasion into central Zhejiang. After months of flight, Cai had to flee again.

In late March 1941 a memorial service for Zhang Ju was held at the Officers' Club in Jinhua City.[36] Present were Governor Huang and key provincial government and party figures; newspaper reports indicated that over a thousand people attended and over four hundred written encomiums were displayed. Governor Huang delivered the eulogy. He noted that Zhang's accomplishments were many: "In wartime it is the local official who has the responsibility of protecting the locality [tu]. When a county has been lost, it must be retaken. Magistrate Zhang understood this deeply." Huang concluded by pointing to the virtue displayed when Zhang gave his life in his role as the father-mother official.

EIGHT

✦

Guerrilla Education

WITH THE JAPANESE INVASION into northern Zhejiang in November and December 1937, the apparently panic-stricken provincial Ministry of Education ordered each Zhexi school to close and faculty, staff, and students to evacuate. For faculty and staff this directive meant loss of livelihood; for students it meant that a semester near its end would, in the end, simply become a lost period of education. In some cases, schools abruptly stopped and students scattered; in others, cooler, if more adventuresome and risky, heads prevailed. Faculty, staff, and students became southern-bound refugees, carrying their institutions with them on the road. Most schools had to move at least four—and even up to eight times—to escape the war blasts of the enemy.

It is important to understand the socioeconomic status of many of the students who fled to the deep hinterland to continue their education. Robert Culp's study of tuition, fees, and room and board at state-mandated middle schools during the Nanjing decade indicates that these figures totaled between 52 and over 130 yuan per year—meaning that even those schools at the lower end of the fee scale would "have limited the student body in most secondary schools to children of families whose income was in roughly the top 10 to 15 percent of the urban national average."[1] These were then elites trekking among the masses into poverty-stricken areas.

This chapter looks at five important schools and their refugee experiences. Three were long-established institutions: the Shaoxing Middle School, which was the public Shaoxing prefectural middle school; the private Shaoxing Jishan Middle School; and the private Xiang Lake Normal School. Two were refugee schools that amalgamated into temporary institutions, pooling resources, teachers, and students: the Provincial Temporary United Middle School in Lishui and the Jiaxing Prefectural United Middle School near the Zhejiang-Anhui border. All were schools that moved roughly from a hundred to two hundred miles from their original sites.

Not all schools moved: certainly no schools in counties that were unoccupied or occupied a month or less moved. Other schools moved once or more within their county site, contributing to kaleidoscopic wartime structures. Thirteen schools made such intracounty moves:

Chun'an Lower Middle School—four moves
Dongyang Lower Middle School—seven moves
Huangyan Middle School—one move
Jiangshan Municipal Zhicheng Lower Middle School—one move
Jinyun Private Xiandu Lower Middle School—four moves
Linhai Private Huipu Middle School—two moves
Old Jinhua Women's Lower Middle School—one move
Shangyu Private Qunhui Middle School—two moves
Sheng County Middle School—one move
Wenling Lower Middle School—one move
Yin County Private Lower Normal School—three moves
Yongjia Private Baixide Upper Nursing School—one move
Yongkang Lower Middle School—two moves

The relatively large number of lower middle schools making shorter moves likely points in part to the lower ages of the students, though in all cases age was not necessarily the deciding factor.

The Shaoxing Middle School

Much of the fate of individual schools lay in the hands of their principals; that is underscored by what happened to the two Shaoxing middle schools. On hearing that the city of Ningbo was bombed in late April 1938, Principal Shen Jinxiang realized that the same could happen in Shaoxing (it did on May 3). Not one to mull over options interminably, Shen and the school board decided immediately to send the upper middle school *(gao zhong)* students—in their last three years of the six-year middle school—to Lanting, about eighteen kilometers south-southwest of the city (see Map 12). Shen decided that the lower middle school, perhaps because of the younger ages of the students, would not relocate permanently outside the city, but he put into effect an "open country" education: that is, early every day the teacher would lead the students out from Shaoxing to a site about three miles from the city.[2] The general age range of middle school students was twelve to twenty, though there were larger numbers of students in their late teens and early twenties than might be expected. At the Jiangsu Provincial Shanghai Middle School, in 1928, a good 63 percent of the students were eighteen or older; this dropped in the 1930s, although in 1933 it was still 31 percent and in 1936 still 29 percent.[3]

After the bombing, which destroyed a classroom and hit the corner of a dormitory at the school site in the city, Shen moved the school out of Shaoxing, with part of the upper middle school remaining at Lanting and part moving to Lizhe, about six kilometers away; the lower middle school and school office moved to the big village of Huamingquan in Zhuji County (see Map 12). One striking phenomenon in the history of "education refugees" was the way institutions, which had operated in one site and as one unit, seemed to casually split up. Such splits were obviously necessary, if only because small villages, even towns, could not subsume large numbers of outsiders at one time; in 1939 Shaoxing Middle School had 745 students, though we do not know the percentage in the lower and upper sections. It is not surprising that the lower middle school could operate at a different site from the upper, but to divide the upper middle seems more challenging. A ramification of these splits—since the principal could obviously not be in three places at once—was that teachers became more important administrative decision makers; that decision making crucially included determining the route to lead the students out of harm's way if the Japanese seized a nearby area. Another important result was the loss of any sort of central vision and direction for the school.

At Huamingquan, the school rented the large corridor of a silk factory to serve as a classroom. But when Xiaoshan County, contiguous to Shaoxing, fell in January 1940, Lanting, Lizhe, and Huamingquan were abandoned for Sheng County, to the southeast to the village of Ershiba du, near the town of Chongren (see Map 12). The school left some equipment at Huamingquan, hoping apparently to be able to return there; but that decision meant that two staff people had to remain in Huamingquan to protect the equipment. The Ershiba du area was noted for its large number of lineage halls; each class of the middle school was able to have its own lineage hall. One of the students, named Ruan, later noted the "spacious accommodations" there as a "good place to study in wartime."[4]

The frequent moves, disrupting any sort of educational continuity, and the splitting up of resources like books and laboratory equipment were burdens enough. But schools in Zhejiang were faced with a provincial education minister, Xu Shaodi, who strived mightily and jealously to build his own power and to wield it quite arbitrarily—at a time when schools were on the move and communication, if not impossible, was never certain. One concern shared by many was the future of former students in occupied Zhejiang, the three northern prefectures. To keep open their educational possibilities, the Education Ministry opened three temporary middle schools in the rear areas, one of which was to be located in Yuyao County, east of Shaoxing—a decision not too logical in the sense of compelling refugee students to trudge even farther through the Chinese countryside. Xu must have thought better of it and announced, without any consultation with Shen, that Shaoxing Middle School would now become the school that the northern Zhejiang students would enter. Principal Shen was livid; he replied to Xu that there was no place to house these additional students. Xu said that was an excuse to cover up Shen's inability to manage the situation. Xu's anger was so intense that when it was time for the current seniors to graduate, the minister refused to affix the ministry seal to the graduation certificates, without which the students would not be official graduates. Shen made do, using the school's seal on the certificates.[5]

When Shaoxing fell in April 1941, Shen and the school quickly headed south; in fact, they left so quickly that they did not carry much along. They traveled in at least two groups, one led by Shen and the other led by the teacher in charge at the Lizhe campus, a man named Li. At night, deep in the mountains of Dongyang County, they slept outdoors in the grass (see Map 5). Their supplies and provisions were insufficient. Each student got two hundred grams of rice per day. Local residents let the students use their cooking pots for making rice. Once during the month they were there, locals slaughtered and prepared for them a large hog. When Principal Shen and his contingent arrived, they rented a village temple to live in, and Shen organized upper middle males to participate in military training. The quality of this kind of stop-start-stop educational cycle cannot have been very effective.

Both groups went on farther south after a month, to Huzhen in Jinyun County, but we are not told the reason for that additional move (see Map 10). When they arrived in Huzhen, they found that the private Anding Middle School from Hangzhou, with 1,119 students, was already there. This reality made the move there seem like a ridiculous waste of time and energy. After talks, the Anding principal agreed that they would give up some of their rented houses so that Shaoxing Middle School could rent them; at that point, the latter numbered about 320 faculty and students. Several days later two more schools—Ningbo Middle School with 856 students and the Provincial Sericulture School with 179 students— poured into Huzhen. It is easy to see how such a population influx could heighten social pressures and tensions in a village or small town.[6]

Shaoxing Middle School did not have to suffer any long-term problems of overcrowding, because in August 1941—after spending three months on the road with short bursts of "education"—the school returned to Ershiba du in Sheng County, without Principal Shen. He later wrote that he was physically and emotionally exhausted by his leadership of the school; he resigned, to teach at a branch of Zhejiang University that had been set up in Longquan County. The middle school's move back to the favorable location for education came after the Japanese military pulled out of Shaoxing County back into Xiaoshan. It worked for the school year. Then, just as students were studying for their final examinations in May 1942, the Japanese army began their largest campaign in the province, driving through its heart along the Qiantang River to Jiangxi Province. The principal, whom student Ruan called "extremely irresponsible," simply left the school, telling students in effect that they were on their own. The school stopped functioning for fifteen months. It reopened in September 1943 in Tiantai County, where it would remain, with one internal move, until January 1946.

In the fifteen months' interim, Ruan and a group of about thirty-five students traveled to isolated Xuanping County, a journey marked by assorted unpleasant contacts with both the Chinese and Japanese armies—

some of his group were captured by the Japanese and conscripted to serve as porters; others were killed. Those survivors of this group reached a high mountain village and simply stayed; but life there was extraordinarily difficult. There were too many people and only a small pond of water—for drinking and washing clothes and bodies. The polluted water led to rampant dysentery; there were no doctors or medicine. The ill were isolated in a temple, given a door plank to lie on and a bucket to use as a latrine; seven or eight students died. The group were also beset by scabies, which was extremely contagious from bodily contact among people living in tight quarters. In the most severe cases, festering flesh meant not being able to walk or even to hold a writing brush.[7] This group never made it to Tiantai for the reopening of the school.

The Shaoxing Jishan Middle School

Shao Hongshu became principal of the private Jishan Middle School in August 1940. A specialist in agricultural economics, he had studied at Tokyo Imperial University and had served as teacher and professor before he became administrator.[8] Unlike Shen Jinxiang, Shao seemed more laid back about the danger from Japanese bombing. The Jishan school had two campuses: the upper middle school was at Pingshui, thirteen kilometers southeast of Shaoxing (see Map 12). On the evening of April 16, 1941, Shao and a teacher from the Pingshui campus took most of the students from Pingshui to the production in Shaoxing of Cao Yu's popular play, *Thunderstorm,* performed by the Guomindang's "86th Army Drama Troupe."[9] Since early afternoon there had been rumors that the Japanese army was on the march and not that far away. Military authorities refuted the rumor: the play would go on if only to prove that the whisperings were just a rumor. Before the play began, a few people had allegedly heard the sound of gunshots carried on a strong wind from outside a city gate. Half an hour into the play, there was a commotion on the stage. Slowly at first, but then, with some panic, people began to leave the theater. Shao and the students went to the main campus.

Thus, Principal Shao—unlike Principal Shen, who had planned well ahead to avoid any such crisis for his middle school—had to face the problem of getting his students safely out of the city in the midst of crisis. On April 17, Shao tried to send a small squad of students to the Pingshui campus; but they returned with the news that Japanese soldiers were guarding the city gates. Shao knew that the 369 students, faculty, and staff could not travel together; he quickly divided the total into thirty-five contingents—roughly ten each. One by one, they were to scatter toward the South Gate; between it and the Jishan Gate was a breach in the wall in its old foundation, through which people could pass. But that meant that the refugees had to cross two canals, one inside the city, the other, outside the city wall; neither had bridges in convenient places. Thus, students, faculty, and staff had to swim across. Physical education teacher He Zigao found a bamboo pole by which nonswimmers could be pulled along. Not all the Jishan refugees made it out; one detachment tried going over one of the canal's bridges but was gunned down by Japanese soldiers; in addition, several dozen were captured.

The fact that the vast majority made it out safely was due to several factors; the goal was to get to a large rape field nearby and slither and crawl along the ground until they got beyond gun range. The students' clothes provided some camouflage: the male students had yellow student uniforms that could merge into the bright-yellow rape flowers; the female students wore grass-green military uniforms. The main reason for their generally successful escape, however, was the relative paucity of Japanese soldiers; although they "surrounded" the city, there were many places they could not cover. In addition, the student escape came when the Japanese were changing sentinels. Students crawling through the rape field did have shots fired above their heads, but the soldiers did not pursue them.

Panic-stricken students passed on their panic to other upper middle students when those from Shaoxing reached Pingshui. Rumors flew that the Japanese on horseback were only a mile away. The small groups of students left quickly, carrying only simple clothing and sundries. That last-minute exodus precluded taking library books or any educational materials or equipment. All day and into the night, every tree and bush seemed to be enemy troops. Unlike the Shaoxing Middle School refugees, who traveled in large groups, the Jishan Middle School students traveled in small groups, which produced a continuing panic all its own. There was no way to communicate to let others know of a group's whereabouts. There was clearly an announced destination, but late into the evening almost two hundred had not yet arrived. Concerns and fears

were voiced: Had they been martyred? Taken captive? Met some completely unexpected trauma or tragedy? To many who had arrived at the
tea warehouse, where they were to sleep on the cement floor, it could
not matter for the moment; they collapsed in their exhaustion.

The next morning Shao announced that they still had a long way to
go before they reached their destination, the Minghuang and Hushan
temples in Wuyi County. Then, noting the school's slogan, he said, "Now
we are really sleeping on brushwood and tasting gall," referring to the
story of King Goujian (reigned 497–465 BCE), who, after defeat and humiliation at the hands of the king of Wu, was able after many years of
"sleeping on brushwood and tasting gall" to avenge his earlier defeat.[10]
Shao pointedly noted that the students would now be in the great rear-
area, where they could work to bring victory over the Japanese. He told
the students they were involved in "guerrilla education" (youji jiaoyu).[11]

When this large group reached Hushan Temple in Wuyi, they began to
make plans to reestablish the school. Hushan would serve as dormitory,
while the school itself would be located at Minghuang Temple, about
three miles away. Shao ordered some students to go scout out Minghuang
Temple to see how much work would have to be done to make it func-
tional. It is not known how Shao had settled on this temple ahead of
time. When the group found the temple, it was already late afternoon; the
temple was deep in the mountains, in a dense forest. It was a desolate,
abandoned building; the walls were broken and crumbled. Inside was
nothing but weeds run amok, spider webs, and dust. The group broke out
in incredulous laughter: could this place be possibly ready for class in a
month? Then Principal Shao himself walked up, joking and laughing,
handing them their rations. He said, "Let's get to work"—and within a
month classes were being held in a crudely constructed building. Students slept on the ground and sat on the ground for their classes. Teachers
lived in mud huts. On white paper attached to a stone tablet, Shao wrote
"Sleeping on brushwood, tasting gall." Also placed on the tablet was a
picture of Sun Yat-sen.[12] Shao later reported that in addition to Jishan
students, the school also enrolled students from Wuyi and nearby Jinhua
and Yongkang counties.

But the method of the move, while it may have made sense logically
and logistically, was messy and filled with unhappy contingencies for the
groups. The following details underscore the difficulties and, at times,

absurdities of student efforts to continue their educations at schools dispersed around the province. An example was student Tao Yongming, who
decided against fleeing with his classmates and returned to his home
Taoyan, fifteen kilometers from Shaoxing. But he had come to feel that
life under the control of the Japanese and their puppets was intolerable.
He decided to flee with fellow native placer Xu Cengshen, to join the
Jishan school. After they left on August 13, 1941, and traveled by foot,
boat, and train to Jinhua, Tao repeatedly bemoaned the loss of his native
place and his separation from it: "The minute we got off the train, there
were air-raid sirens. We immediately ran off and hid. There were only
three planes: they flew past and were gone. After . . . [lunch], we walked
around Jinhua. We ran into many of our fellow Jishan students—all talking about the situation when Shaoxing fell."[13] The fact that four months
after the original flight students had not yet made it to the school underscores the reality that there was really no way to know who would show
up, when, or by what route.

At Jinhua, Tao, Xu, and the other Jishan students heard that Jishan
had reopened classes at Wuyi's Minghuang Temple; they set out to rejoin their old school. They found the temple but then learned the bad
news. Shao told them that the finances of the school were in shambles,
so much so that in the current semester, the school could open only an
upper middle class for those who were going to be graduated. If students in the other classes wanted to continue, they had to go to Xiuxi
Township in Changshan County, 150 kilometers to the west. This was
one of three regional temporary middle schools set up by the Education Ministry; it was known as Zhedong Temporary Middle School.
The others were the Zhexi First and Second Temporary Normal School
in Yuqian and Tonglu counties. The third was the highly mobile Provincial Temporary Middle School, located for very brief periods of
time in seven different counties.[14] These three were to serve students of
the respective regions and educational needs of the students (in two
regional middle schools and one normal school).

Tao, Xu, and the others bound for the middle school in Changshan
trekked almost to the Jiangxi border, only to find that the school would
not open until November, still two months away. They waited for the
opening and then took classes for about a half year before the school
closed because of the Japanese Zhe-Gan campaign. One of the teachers at

the school, a Mr. Chen, offered to teach the third year for lower middle students: there were forty-three students that needed that class-year and ten others from other grades who were interested. To make a long story short, Chen and the fifty-plus students walked back to Longquan County, where Chen believed he could get financial assistance from the county Education Office. But then he found a letter waiting for him with the news that his mother was dangerously ill; in the end, after all the traveling and preparations for teaching, he left the students to go visit his mother. The students, having lost their teacher, had to decide what to do. Some prepared to return home to Japanese-occupied areas; others wanted to remain in the rear areas if they had friends or relatives there. There were thirteen students from Shaoxing. They decided to go to Yunhe County to see if Education Minister Xu Shaodi could help—at least to introduce them to another school. Since Xu had moved to Jingning County, the students plodded on. When at last they found his office, he refused to meet with them (his reputation was one of arrogant self-centeredness and self-absorption), and he made it clear that he would play no part in introducing them to another school. There is little doubt for understanding why Tao titled his memoirs "Wandering Around in a Desperate Plight." In the end, hearing that educational opportunities were better in Fujian Province, at the beginning of August 1942, Tao and Xu went to Chong'an in Fujian, where both graduated from middle school in July 1945.

Principal Shao's financial problems in the summer of 1941 (as he explained to Tao and Xu before they left for Changshan) must have been exaggerated, for, in spring 1942, he opened a new class for both the upper and lower middle school. Classrooms and dorms were still in mostly ruined buildings, but the level of students was supposedly high. That spring a former classmate of Shao's, Zheng Wenlin, a native of Wuyi and a teacher, came to join the school staff. When the Japanese invaded Wuyi County in May 1942, Shao led most of the teaching staff, workers, and the highest-level students to Yuzhang Village in Jingning County (see Map 10); that fall only eighty-six students enrolled. Shao and the Jingning branch remained there until war's end. Zheng Wenlin proposed to Shao that Zheng remain in Wuyi and open the Wuyi branch of the Jishan Middle School, with several friends who had experience in middle school teaching. As the Japanese took only the northern portion of the county, remaining in southern Wuyi was doable, even though the Japanese presence, for as long as it remained for that summer, was always threatening. Shao approved Zheng's idea; both upper middle and lower middle students were enrolled as the school branch moved to the town of Yuyuan (see Map 5).

In 1943, the upper middle and the business course joined Shao in Jingning; even after that departure. the Wuyi branch still had two hundred students. We actually have more information on that branch than on the one that Shao headed. The "campus" was much better physically than the Minghuang Temple; rather spacious temples both east and west of town were used. Conditions were still, however, quite primitive. At night when students did homework, two students had to share a tong-oil lamp; they had to use three or four rushes for the lamp wick, and even then it put out a very dim light. The burden of seeing was compounded by poor-quality paper, a gray-yellow, coarse paper that took ink very poorly.[15]

Outside of classes, students had active extracurricular lives. They had their own self-government association that organized student life and directed special activities and events. They put up a daily newspaper wall, held entertainment and exercise activities—drills, singing, mountain-climbing races, basketball games, and cross-country races. The 79th and 21st divisions of the Guomindang army were stationed at Yuyuan; there was considerable contact between the soldiers and the school. The school asked the commander of the 79th Division to lecture at the school; it asked the head of the 235th Regiment (an artillery company) to give military training to staff and students, focusing on drills and marksmanship. That regiment sponsored a basketball team that often came to school to play the upper middle students. In the fall of 1942, before most upper middles left for Jingning, the students performed a play for the soldiers, carrying scenery, costumes, and props over the mountains for the performance; as a special show of appreciation, the soldiers slaughtered several hogs to give the students a feast.[16]

Xiang Lake Normal School in Songyang County

Even before its flight to the south in late 1937, Xiang Lake Normal School had a history and record of progressive education. Established by famed educator Tao Xingzhi, a student of John Dewey at Columbia University from 1915 to 1917, the school had the goal of linking study to action; Tao worked with long-time principal Jin Haiguan to set up a school that would serve simultaneously as a training center for teachers and as a base for the reconstruction of local society. A graduation requirement was teaching at an elementary school in the area. The school also carried forward Tao's "little teacher" effort, in which school-aged children began to teach illiterate adults to read—with the hope that these adults would be so excited that they would enroll in school-sponsored night classes. The school emphasized manual labor as well as "book learning": each student was required to work on the thirty-five-acre school farm, and they participated in building dikes and roads, digging wells, opening streams, and constructing public buildings.[17]

That such policies would continue when the school moved, therefore, does not seem surprising. The difference, however, lay in the contexts. Xiaoshan County, where Xiang Lake was located, was in the relatively modernized core on Hangzhou Bay, connected by rail to Shanghai, Ningbo, and Jiangxi, and linked by water to the interior and the outside world as well. Modern changes began there in the early years of the century. Songyang, the new site for the relocated school, in contrast, was surrounded by mountains (see Maps 2 and 10 for location). There was only one road in Songyang that ran into Suichang County, making the town, in effect, a dead end. The Songyang River emptied into the Ou River; on the Songyang one could use rowboats or rafts. Transportation and communication, were, therefore, inconvenient in the extreme. Isolated from the outside world, the people had no spirit of the new or the modern; a newspaper reporter noted that "dress is like it was in ancient times" and that "the appearance of everything is old and shabby."[18] That was then; now the Xiang Lake Normal School brought change. On March 27, 1938, the school sponsored at Gushi, the town where it was relocated, an informational mass meeting of all the organized groups, schools, army units, and people male and female and of all generations; the gathering had the sociocultural impact of an earthquake.[19] The school organized thirty-six night classes through the county, each with its own board of directors; Jin's hope was that these boards would help fund the undertaking.[20] The project was given a boost by one Zhou Xihou of the county, who purchased the pedagogical materials and, perhaps as important, gas lamps to make night study possible. Students organized the Wake the People drama troupe and the Harmonious Sounds singing group.

There was the Wartime Painting Society, which sponsored a traveling exhibit of the paintings students produced. Students went out to different locations to lecture. On November 4–5, 1938, the school linked up with local leaders to stage a "console the troops and their families" dramatic production. Commemorating the Marco Polo Bridge incident on July 7, 1939, was a large ceremony on the school exercise ground, with over three thousand in attendance; the event was even covered in the Shanghai press.[21]

The reporter covering Songyang County wrote that one could see how much change was occurring by just looking at the people of Gushi; it seemed as though the students worked incessantly to encourage mass participation. Counties in the periphery were often the destinations for schools—generally farther away from the Japanese and in areas that the Japanese generally had no reason to pursue. When a school (or several) moved to such an area, each had a substantial impact—whether for good or ill. The first Gushi reaction to the move of this school from the outside was tension: there were 528 students at the school with their own needs for food and other essentials. But with the school's almost immediate organizing activities and contributing services for the local community, the tension quickly abated. In this way "guerrilla schools" had positive impacts on many sites to which they fled.

The Provincial Temporary United Middle School (Lian Zhong)

In terms of higher education during the war and the exodus of colleges from Japanese-occupied territory, the most famous institution was the Southwest Associated University in Kunming, a temporary union of the three famous universities of Beijing, Qinghua, and Nankai. But there were several such temporary institutional amalgams of lower-level schools within Zhejiang, the most famous being the Provincial Temporary United Middle School (hereafter, United Middle) at the town of Bihu in Lishui County (see Map 10). United Middle joined together seven schools: Hangzhou Upper and Lower Middle; Hangzhou Normal; Hangzhou Women's Middle; the Hangzhou Masses Experimental School; Jiaxing Middle; and Huzhou Middle.

When the Japanese occupied Zhexi, the education minister, Xu Shaodi, ordered the closure of all the schools in the occupied area. The politics and trajectory of the decision making that created United Middle are not entirely clear. Zhang Yintong, principal of Jiaxing Middle School, initiated talks with the Education Ministry; his goal was to receive provincial support to establish an institution with "Provincial" in its title. Though there is only circumstantial evidence, it seems likely that there may have been a quid pro quo arrangement. Education Minister Xu, ambitiously grasping, had been named by Governor Huang to head the Wartime Youth Training Unit in Bihu, a unit for young men who had fled to rear areas from occupied ones. It seems likely that Xu's needs to reinforce his position may have been part of the deal; otherwise, it becomes difficult to understand why all these schools chose to come to one place. The fact that all young males from these schools participated in the six-month training course before their schools were allowed to open also seems to corroborate such a scenario.[22]

The treks south for these schools differed substantially from those of Shaoxing Middle School and Jishan Middle School. Shaoxing Middle had moved as several units to the south; it then returned to Sheng County near Shaoxing, only to have to trek south once again. Jishan Middle fragmented, with small groups making their own way and finding their own routes, though some never did. In the case of United Middle, the schools traveled en masse. Zhang Yintong moved the Jiaxing Middle School, leaving Jiaxing on November 11 (that city itself fell on November 29). Huzhou Middle was the most spastic in its actions, starting out en masse but going only as far as Wukang County—about twenty-five miles—and then disbanding. How many of its students and faculty reached Bihu is unknown; three of its Lower Middle teachers taught at the Lower United Middle.

Hangzhou Lower Middle and Hangzhou Women's Middle traveled together, six hundred strong. When Nanjing fell on December 13, the two schools went west-southwest to Chun'an County, on the border with Anhui Province. The schools were serious about finishing the semester. The library at Chun'an Middle School was still open; students finished their classes and took the end-of-term examinations. Male teachers took a boat to Lanxi and then made it overland to Bihu. Women, both teachers and students, went by boat most of the way, but there had to have been some walking on the journey. The boats on which the women traveled also carried the schools' libraries, laboratory equipment (including microscopes), chemical reagents, medicines, and large-sized luggage belonging to teachers, so any walking required porters. Male students walked the whole way, about 120 miles.

After the six-month military training course (we are not told what the women students did during this time), specific planning for United Middle got under way. Initially, the administration was "principal by committee," composed of Zhang Yintong of the Jiaxing Middle; Tang Shifang, principal of Hangzhou Lower Middle; and Xu Xudong, principal of Hangzhou Normal. Though Hanghzou Upper Middle was apparently the foundational school in forming United Middle—Hangzhou Upper Middle had left the north earlier than the other component schools and provided the majority of the teaching staff—it was inexplicably not represented on the main administrative committee.

Concerns in preparatory meetings were staffing, student-admission procedures, and financial aid. Most teaching positions were generally already filled; vacant staff positions were taken by Bihu residents or by qualified personnel from nearby. Students who had been attending one of the seven component schools were automatically accepted; however, students from the local region (Bihu and Lishui and Songyang counties) had to take an entrance examination. Many took the exam, but the number of openings was very few; the total from nearby localities was then, in the end, minimal. Each student was ranked for purposes of financial aid; essentially, financial aid came from refugee relief funds. Students from occupied areas and military veterans, in top priority, had all expenses covered, including food and assorted fees. Those in the second category had half their food expenses covered but had to pay the assorted fees. Those in the third ranking were relieved only of paying their assorted fees. The background differentiation between rank two and three is not spelled out in available sources.[23] The shortage of money for the Education Ministry was notorious, and Xu Shaodi was infamously stingy with his funds; we do not know how much students in each rank actually received. Students at normal schools were subject to a completely different system, in which only a specified number could receive aid at all. We are told the 1938–1939 salaries of the faculty and staff: fifty yuan per year for principal and teachers, forty yuan for administrators, thirty yuan for secretaries, and 10 yuan for workers. (This was at the time when a modest home rented for three or four yuan per month.)[24]

United Middle was united only in the loosest sense. Each unit was in charge of its own affairs, including its own budget. In the fall of 1939, the three sections which until that point had operated with three separate managers—United Upper Middle, United Lower Middle, and United Normal--became three separate schools, but Principal Tang reported that there was essentially no change in how the schools continued to work and cooperate. United Middle constantly showed, in its planning and concern for making the student refugee experience truly an educational one, that it was a cut above most refugee schools. Its peak enrollment was over two thousand students. The three components of United Middle shared some classrooms and had its headquarters in the Son of the Dragon Temple. The United Lower Middle was based in two lineage halls. Female students and faculty lived in the Ye lineage hall. Males and some male faculty lived in the Shen lineage hall. All United Middle students came to the large Shen ritual hall for convocations and presentations. In an empty space behind the Shen hall, the school built a long and wide building with mud walls and a thatched roof; it housed twelve classrooms and four offices, a library, and a recreation room. The classrooms had windows on two walls; in the estimation of Principal Tang, there was sufficient light, and the cross ventilation kept the air inside fresh. To the northwest of the building was a big exercise field, and to its north, the hospital.

To the side of the classroom building was a cave, where the students ate their meals, where there were tables but no chairs: thus, students stood to eat their meals. Students managed the kitchen: all students were required to work in the kitchen on a rotational basis. Former student Wu Tianlin remembered, "The money we had for food was very little: it provided only for plain tea and simple food. Hungry and at the end of our rope, we could go out for two meals a week, when we could eat some small amount of meat." Another student, Zhang Boquan, noted, "Through 1940, our lives were very difficult; there was a dearth of rice. . . . Bihu is a rice-producing area, but too many people had moved here, and supply did not meet demand." Zhang himself volunteered to go to neighboring Songyang to try to purchase rice, though rumor had it that there were so many people struggling to purchase available rice that his effort might prove unsuccessful. He succeeded in purchasing two hundred piculs of rice (eleven tons), renting several boats to row it back to Bihu, where he was met by ready teachers and students. Whether Zhang indeed purchased that much rice in light of the pressing demand for it at that time is not known. He did say that the next problem was finding enough wood and kindling to cook the rice.[25]

Courses taught at United Middle included Chinese language and literature, civics, math, chemistry, biology, botany, physics, music, art, home economics, library management, physical education, and manual training. Four or five microscopes were brought along for the science classes; and reportedly, though this is hard to believe, there were no fewer than eight pianos for music classes and performances.[26] The library in the mud-walled, thatched-roof new construction was a large, square room; there is no count of the numbers of volumes, though important series of books were named as its holdings. The library's reading room reportedly had various dictionaries, atlases, journals, and a surprising array of current newspapers: *Dagongbao* from Guilin, *Qianxian ribao* from Shangrao, *Dongnan ribao* from Jinhua, *Zhejiang ribao* from Yongkang, and the *Yibao* and *Libao* from Shanghai. One wonders whether there were more than scattered copies of these, but dailies from Jinhua and Yongkang were surely possible, even if they were several days old. Nighttime reading was by oil lamps, which produced not only a dim light but an unfortunate thick layer of smoke.[27]

One of the hallmarks of the United Middle program was its strong emphasis on its Boy Scout training; it coalesced with the civics courses and the school's strong emphasis on the expression of nationalism. Former student Yang Jicheng from Ningbo recalled that three people led the male students; one, Hou Chongsan, was specifically in charge of the Boy Scouts and taught the class, and two were physical education teachers (one male and one female), who helped out in the drills: "Hou was our 'dawn' manager. He prepared us. We took delight in his direction. Each day at dawn a bugle sounded. He stood at the door of our room bellowing, 'Get up'!" The Boy Scouts rolled out of bed, dressed in their military uniforms, and ran to the exercise field. An obligatory three laps was followed by standing at attention at the reviewing stand and hearing Hou give a speech inspiring the boys to fight for the nation. Then it was time for breakfast. At 3 P.M., following classes, the scouts would hurry to run back to the exercise field for more activities. Women students at these times were involved in sewing or nursing classes.

There was time for extracurricular activities; indeed, the town of Bihu itself had become one of the more exciting places in the large provincial rear area. The war made it a bustling town, displacing its prewar somnambulant state. Refugees came in great number, as did military units and merchants from surrounding towns and counties, ready to cash in on new and expanding businesses. Then there were the schools. Not only the United Middle School but the provincial elementary schools, Children's and Five Peaks, moved there from Yongkang to join the Bihu Elementary School, which was already functioning. For a time the provincial Chuzhou Middle School also moved into the Bihu area.[28] One writer waxed "poetic," with far-fetched mixed similes: "The small town of Bihu had schools like forests and students like clouds."[29] Large numbers of patriotic intellectuals gathered in the town. Three bookshops in town sold politically progressive books; especially significant was the New Knowledge Bookstore (xinzhi shudian). Its books introduced many students to revolutionary thought. Under prompting by Chinese Communist Party operatives, the Chinese National Liberation Vanguard Unit was formed. Students, at least from United Normal and United Upper Middle schools, organized a reading club that focused on progressive books.[30] United Middle students established an educational extension office to foster and carry out mass education.[31]

The progressive students at United Middle got into hot political water in April and May 1939, when they attacked "character-development education," which included, they discovered, having their actions spied on and then reported. The hubbub was complicated by the pique of Education Minister Xu, his personal (strained) relationships with the United Lower Middle's Principal Tang, Xu's continually high-handed actions, and student unwillingness to back down—indeed to strike instead. The upshot was the expulsion of one of the seven students who had been involved.[32]

In extracurricular activities, students had their own journal, United Lower Middle School Friend (Lianchuxiao you). One of the art teachers formed a drama troupe that performed anti-Japanese plays at the school and at Bihu fairs. Students sponsored newspaper walls in the town. Some students even wanted to get in on the action of organizing a local production cooperative, seeking funds from cooperative assistance organizations to set up equipment to manufacture soap and glycerol. They were able to establish such a cooperative, but there is no record of its success or lack thereof. (It is a spirit like this that kept alive United Middle's name. In 1985, on the fortieth anniversary of the end of the war, between twenty and thirty alumni of the school returned to Bihu to see what might still be left of the school.)[33]

A doctor was assigned to each school unit; the government had built a small hospital, which was open to Bihu residents as well as students. Malaria was endemic to the area, and most student and faculty came down with the disease. In efforts to control malaria, the school purchased a new kind of mosquito netting; and the doctors ordered batches of quinine powder and glutinous rice paper. Students were enlisted to make "pills," filling the rolled paper with the powder. In the spring of 1939, a form of glandular fever reached epidemic proportions, primarily because the doctors did not insist on instituting a quarantine.[34]

The course of war ended United Middle in summer 1942, when in the Japanese Zhe-Gan campaign, half of Bihu was burned to the ground. The three component parts of the temporary school scattered in two directions, to escape the Japanese onslaught. We are not told how the parts divided the school's resources; we are told that Education Minister Xu categorically refused to provide any money for the moves. We know the most about the United Upper Middle School. Its students formed a "moving corps" that floated library books, lab equipment, classroom desks, and food on rafts down the Ou River, ending up at the village of Nantian in Qingtian County. Isolated and surrounded by mountains, Nantian made Bihu seem like Hangzhou; life at Nantian was one of untold hardships. The school rented a temple for the school office and several lineage halls for classrooms and dormitories, the pattern used by most schools in exile. The progressiveness of the days in Bihu did not follow the school to Nantian. New principal Cui Dongpo (Zhang Yintong had resigned) stressed democracy but forbade progressive publications. When students wanted to stage *Thunderstorm*, Cui refused to give his permission, saying that that drama was on Jiang Jieshi's forbidden list.[35]

United Lower Middle School moved south to Jingning County. There is no available record of its time spent there; the school did move three times within the county before its return to Hangzhou in October 1945. United Normal School also traveled to Jingning, but it yoyoed back and forth between Jingning sites and Bihu: it moved to Jingning in June 1942 and back to Bihu in September 1942, back to Jingning in spring 1943, back to Bihu (date uncertain), back to Jingning in late 1944, and back to Bihu in the summer of 1945. It returned to Hangzhou in January 1946. Such lack of stability cannot have resulted in a very productive education.[36]

Jiaxing Prefectural United Middle School

While the Provincial Temporary United Middle School was made up mostly of young people who were refugees from Japanese-occupied territory in the north of the province, there were many students in those occupied areas who were, for a range of reasons, unable or unwilling to travel between a hundred or two hundred miles to attend schools that might be ephemeral and poorly equipped.[37] Some counties in the occupied zone, Pinghu and Jiashan, for example, established lower middle schools; many students did not find attending schools that had to hew to Japanese and puppet guidelines very attractive: such education in Japanese-controlled areas was customarily referred to by Chinese as "enslaving" or "slavish." The counties of Chongde, Tongxiang, Wukang, and Deqing had jointly managed a school in the resort area of Moganshan (in Deqing County), yet this was an area of frequent Japanese action, and the constant moving of the school to escape the Japanese was not conducive to learning.

From the fall of 1939 to the fall of 1940, Jiaxing sent more than three groups of over seventy students each to link up first with Shaoxing Middle School (an initiative, as we have seen, that was vehemently opposed by Shao Principal Shen Jinxiang) and then with the Provincial Temporary Fourth Middle School in Yuyao County. But the distance involved (both to Shaoxing Middle, meeting at the time in Sheng County, and to Yuyao) was at least 125 miles; traveling over long distances through occupied and unoccupied territory posed many difficulties. Many educators in the occupied zone felt it essential to have some school operating in the rear area but quite near to the occupied territory.[38]

A leader of this effort was Lu Chujue, the head of the Zhexi Relief Committee, presided over by the Rear-Area Jiaxing Seven-County Prefectural Native Place Association, which operated in the widely dispersed counties of Yongkang, Yuyao, Yuqian, and Fenshui.[39] Each branch of the association in these counties set up Righteous People's Reception Offices, to help with refugees from Jiaxing counties and provide food without charge. The importance of these offices at times of spatial and physical displacement cannot be overestimated. They provided an important link between occupied territory and the great rear-area. Though far from Jiaxing, they also were small "Peach Blossom" villages far from Jiaxing where Jiaxing native place identity could nevertheless be affirmed and harrowing displacement could be temporarily ameliorated.[40]

In January 1939 Lu Chujue was elected to serve in the first session of the wartime Zhejiang Provisional Provincial Senate; he also assumed the title of manager of the Zhexi Office of the Provincial United Chamber of Commerce, moving to the rear area near the occupied zone in Tianmushan, the location of the West Zhejiang Administrative Office. He thought deeply about solving the educational issues for his native place; he knew that out of all the graduates of Jiaxing primary schools, only 20 percent had gone on for more study and that, more often than not, the 80 percent that had not pursued more education tended to be found among the unemployed. Thus, in early 1939, he requested that the West Zhejiang Administrative Office alter the bleak situation by establishing a four-county (Jiaxing, Jiashan, Haining, and Haiyan) united middle school; but the Administrative Office took no action.[41]

In the fall of 1940, Lu, then living in Yuqian County (see Map 2), invited men "of responsibility" from the seven counties that had made up the former Jiaxing prefecture to come to discuss the matter. In contrast to the Provincial Temporary United Middle School in Bihu, which had been established at the initiative of educators themselves, this initiative came from local elites, who would not stand to get jobs if the project were realized. The discussions led to decisions: a school would be set up, to be managed by the seven counties; its name would be the Jiaxing Prefectural United Middle School (*Jiashu qixian lianli linshi zhongxue*), literally "the united temporary middle school of the seven counties belonging to Jiaxing." It focused on short courses that emphasized the vocations of banking, business, and sericulture.[42]

In his capacity as member of the Board of Directors of the Rear-Area Jiaxing Seven-County Native Place Association, Lu consulted with a variety of men with educational expertise and negotiated with a deputy of the West Zhejiang Administrative Office.[43] The deputy, Shen Dazan, a Jiaxing native (perhaps a critical detail), was a Beida graduate in English literature who had taught many years and served as educational administrator as well. He was enthusiastic; indeed, he became the school's first principal. The school was to be funded by the seven counties, a tricky proposition, given the fact that these counties were controlled by the Japanese and their Chinese collaborators. But it should be remembered that the West Zhejiang Administrative Office existed to support Guomindang county governments in the occupied territory; supporting this school, indeed, could be seen as a way of fulfilling the political goals of the Administrative Office.

The school was established near the end of February 1942 at Jiakou, a small town in Changhua County on the road between Hangzhou and Huizhou in Anhui Province (see Map 11). Jiakou was chosen because of available former school buildings and temples that could house the new school; because of the town's ease of evacuation should the Japanese invade the area (it was near mountains and only a few miles from the Zhejiang-Anhui border); and because of Jiakou's convenience on the major road from Hangzhou. Lu was general manager; Shen Dazan became principal (though he died six months after the school opened); and the trustees included the seven magistrates of the Jiaxing counties and famous native sons now in the rear area, including Feng Zikai and Shen Jinxiang, principal of Shaoxing Middle School.

Finances, as in all refugee schools, posed the most continual problem, though at the beginning it looked as though money issues would not be serious. Lu received fifteen thousand yuan from the West Zhejiang Administrative Office for preparatory expenses, but the counties themselves had to come up with the lion's share—in the amount of one hundred thousand yuan per year, to be funneled to the Administrative Office, which would disperse the funds. Each county was assessed a sum (the basis for the assessment is not clear), ranging from twenty-eight thousand yuan for Jiaxing County at the high end to seventy-two hundred yuan for Haining County at the low end. The first two years of operation (1942 and 1943) saw steady expansion of the courses being offered. At the school's opening, only two class years met. In spring 1943, a complete upper middle school and a shortened normal class opened. In fall 1943, the school had upper and lower middle school classes and two classes of the shortened normal course—with close to four hundred students. The elasticity of courses and classes prevented students from planning their courses of study with any certainty.[44]

By late 1944, there were over five hundred students, only about one in eight of whom came from the area around Jiakou; so the composition of the student body seemed to be fulfilling the goals set out by the school's founders. Two aspects of the student body were noteworthy. Several small towns in Zhexi contributed many students: there were, for example, ten students at the school from the small town of Fengqiao in Jiaxing County; eight students hailed from the even smaller town of Xindai in Pinghu County. There were also multiple students from certain families: six from the Dai family of Ganyao in Jiashan County, three from the Han family in the Jiaxing Town of Wangdian, and three from the Yang family from Dingqiao in Haining County. There were, indeed, more than twenty other families who sent multiple students to the schools.[45]

Students were expected to be recommended by their counties; once they arrived in Jiakou, students filled out a school application and applied for a loan or relief aid from their counties. Relief aid came in three categories, the sum of relief differing as to whether it included money for tuition, food, clothing, and books. Despite the requirement that students be nominated by their counties, many came directly to Jiakou without county support. When students went home for summer and winter breaks, they passed word of the school all around and would often return with crowds. Student-aged travelers between Hangzhou and Tianmushan occasionally heard about the school while on the road and went on their own to Jiakou to seek admittance. The school seemed quite open to admitting even those without their county approval. Whether these students could receive relief aid is, however, unclear. In many cases, these students would not formally register; they simply audited classes; they could then leave anytime without having to cancel their registration. The student body was thus much more fluid than a refugee school located deep in the rear area.

Most of the school's thirty-eight teachers and eighteen staff personnel were from Jiashu, or Jiaxing Prefectural United Middle School. Many had worked in education offices in county government; some had studied abroad; some had gained fame in the Shanghai-Hangzhou corridor in the 1930s; and one had been an editor at Kaiming Shudian, an important Shanghai publishing company.[46]

The chronicler of the school noted four of its defining characteristics. The first stemmed from the school's relative poverty. The school did not employ outsiders for construction, maintenance, and upkeep. Students repaired roads and the wall around the school compound. They undertook repairs in school buildings. They traveled up into the nearby mountains for timber and other resources. It was said that there were no cloth shoes, only straw sandals; no rice, only assorted grains. A second characteristic of the school, which it shared with many other schools in exile was that daily life and activities were permeated with patriotic nationalism. Third, there was much emphasis on physical exercise, drills, and an austere lifestyle. Students did not use hot water because of the dearth of firewood. Finally, the school cultivated a student body, generally made up of fourteen- to eighteen-year-olds, that exercised some power over its own affairs. The Student Self-Government Association or, simply, the Student Association, planned activities, publicized them, and carried them out. The Student Food Management Committee, with each class having a representative on the committee, arranged and supervised the kitchen and set the time for verifying accounts. Each day, two students supervised in the kitchen, that duty rotating among classes. The other student organization was the Boy Scouts, which played a role in inviting outsiders to make scholarly presentations, in helping to organize an art exhibit, and in participating in an all-school program on the nature of fire and its control.[47]

In the school's history through the end of the war, there were periods of great stress. A meningitis epidemic during the school spring-break trip to southern Anhui in 1943 led to some deaths. Later that same year, the Japanese approached the Jiakou area in a mopping up action; the school withdrew up into the mountains for a period. Although the Japanese did not reach Jiakou, they were active in many counties of Zhexi, especially the seven counties of Jiaxing. The money that had been nourishing the school from the counties began to dry up. Faculty salaries were cut; the food budget was cut. In late 1944, the head of the West Zhejiang Administrative Office, He Yangling, asked the provincial government to make the school an official provincial school so that it might get monetary support from the province. The provincial government, while noting the successes of Jiaxing Prefectural United Middle School, declined and asked the Administrative Office to use a certain fund to assist the school.[48]

But the situation only grew more dire. The principal begged county governments to contribute; he sought to borrow more from the Administrative Office; he even approached other counties in the rear area to contribute. Faculty salaries were cut yet again; food quality plummeted; meals were cut from three to two per day. Each person received only a tiny spoon of table salt for the day. Students began to grow ill from lack of enough food. When war ended, this once-successful wartime educational experiment died after its lengthy financial illness.[49]

Schools that became like refugees, unlike individual and family refugees, had an agenda once they reached their destinations, an agenda that kept alive their prewar identities. That continuity of identity plus the experience of being uprooted as part of a larger group may have made being a refugee less terrifying than it was for private refugees, that is, individual and family refugees. However, while private refugees could take as few items along on their trek as they wanted, schools that became refugees were burdened with libraries, microscopes and chemicals, and other equipment. Without them, teachers and students could not have carried on once they reached their destinations.

The long treks and the determination to make schools work amid trying, often dangerous circumstances, even to put new schools together in ad hoc fashion so that learning could continue, were admirable. But one wonders how effective the education students received under such circumstances actually was. When a school on the move was in one location for three weeks, the unpacking and the packing back up to move again must have consumed huge amounts of the time that was theoretically available for studying. When schools moved four to eight times in four to eight years, what kind of educational successes were possible? The splitting of schools so that parts would be in one location and other parts in another thirty miles away meant also that school resources had to be divided.

Perhaps it was the trek itself that was significant—getting out of occupied territory and walking huge distances in a China not yet under Japan's heel, making a kind of "long march" to schools whose focus seemed to be on the nation, military drilling, and the Boy Scouts. The spirit of the school in exile perhaps was more important than the substance. Many of the refugee schools had been situated in modernized urban cores.[50] Of the counties to which schools fled, 62 percent were located in the poorer economic, little modernized peripheries; the number is actually higher, for those who first went to other core counties (a destination I included in the computation) were there only briefly before they headed toward peripheral areas. For many young Chinese, this was their first lengthy time in a China without electricity, in whole counties without roads, cut off from the outside world, mired in shocking poverty; indeed this experience may have been *the* educational value of schools-turned-refugees.

Consider the situation from the perspective of the locals. It was nothing less than an invasion: three outside schools coming and staying in a mountain village; Xiang Lake Normal School barging into Gushi, bringing their progressive ways, and organizing and educating people of town and county; the quiet town of Bihu turning into a bustling, colorful marketplace of ideas and commodities. The moves of schools into small, usually closed communities cannot help but have opened the eyes of the locals, even if some were repulsed by the outsiders and their ways. For some communities, the presence of extra mouths to feed when resources were already frighteningly scarce or of thirsty mouths to fill when there was precious little water added to tensions and misunderstandings. But it is safe to say about both sides (rather, all sides, since the situations between locals and outsiders were complex) that their lives could never be quite exactly the same.

⇥⇤

NINE

Wartime Business

IN HIS DESCRIPTION OF evacuating factories mostly from occupied territory into the interior, Governor Huang Shaohong subtitled the section "Defeat in Moving Factories."[1] While schools had their own difficulties in transporting libraries and laboratory equipment and supplies, industry faced problems that were much more daunting. Fearful of the likelihood of Hangzhou's occupation, Huang had ordered each factory to move inland; if factories fell into Japanese hands, they would likely strip them or, as in certain cases, like the Hangzhou electrical power plant, benefit from them. The prewar provincial pattern of industrialization had been expansion along the coast and in key riverine cities; except for small handicraft mills, there were essentially no industries in the interior. Wartime reality, however, made moving industries and businesses into the interior pragmatic and logical. If industries stayed in Hangzhou, Ningbo, and Wenzhou, they would likely be destroyed by Japanese aerial bombing or burned in that Japanese trademark of destruction, arson. If the great rear-area of the province was to have sufficient goods to survive and flourish sufficiently to meet the Japanese threat, there had to be some factories producing in the hinterland. This especially became a great problem after Pearl Harbor, when the foreign settlements in Shanghai fell into Japanese hands; items that had once come into Zhejiang through Wenzhou no longer could be sent from the settlements.

Huang recognized the problems as well as the advantages of moving the factories: one of the greatest difficulties was how to move the heavy machinery of many factories. The machines would be carried by truck and on boats on inland rivers and creeks: but the financial costs of the move itself would be too high for many factory owners to even give it a second thought. If a factory were moved, would there be sufficient fuel and materials to make the factory operational when it reached its destination? These resource needs in the interior differentiated the moving of factories from that of schools, which could bring their own libraries and equipment but not need to continually replenish them. The factory owner also had to be concerned with whether he could find sufficient skilled labor in the interior. These difficulties made it fairly clear that large factories could not really move, but some small factories "followed the war"; that is, they moved to unoccupied territory, escaping the Japanese onslaught.

The government had an obvious stake in heavy industry that could help fuel China's war machine—foundries that could cast weapons, chemical plants, oil refineries, and machine tool factories. But wartime needs could also give rise to light industries like textiles. In early 1938, for example, Governor Huang was apprised of the military need for gauze, absorbent cotton, and bandages; to meet the need, he sponsored the Zhejiang Weaving and Dyeing Mill established in the Confucian temple in the Yunhe county seat almost four years before Yunhe became the provincial capital in exile.[2]

The ten counties that made up the former Chuzhou prefecture, many of them ruggedly mountainous and starkly isolated from modern developments, became the focal point of interior industrialization—in part because the area was so isolated and physically foreboding that the Japanese were less likely to attempt to invade and occupy it. But industrialization there was hampered by lack of effective power sources to run machinery. The province in general lacked good coal reserves. At war's outbreak, there was no electricity at all in Chuzhou's counties. Some small rushing streams and rivers were potential sources for small hydroelectric projects; but establishing them was painfully slow. When they were developed, it was at sites where factories from occupied Zhejiang had been transplanted. Yunhe County had already served as provincial capital for two years when it got its first electricity in 1944; the Longquan county seat had a very small electrical generator for use by a factory, but the county seat and its market town of Anzhen did not get electricity fully until 1945. As a mark of the slowness of the spread of electricity to residents' homes, in 1938 some 68 households in the ten counties had electricity; by February 1941 the number was 2,524 households.[3]

The Zhejiang Provincial Iron Works

There were two main types of industries that were uprooted mostly from occupied territory: those contributing primarily to the military and those manufacturing articles for the daily needs of civilians.[4] Most significant was the displaced ironworks factories: their work contributed directly to the war effort, not only in Zhejiang, but in other provinces as well. Smaller industries focused on supplying goods for the population at large. Both types of industries moved primarily to the counties of Lishui and Longquan, with occasional sites in Yunhe and other counties in Chuzhou (see Map 10). The migrating industries and businesses were primarily from Hangzhou and the coastal port of Wenzhou. The provincial government encouraged Wenzhou industries to move inland to escape Japanese bombardment from the sea. In the end, substantial numbers of rather small industries from Wenzhou and its neighboring county to the south, Ruian, moved to Chuzhou: seventeen foundries, seven textile plants, thirty-three printing presses, and twenty-nine lumber mills.[5] Many workers followed their factories into Chuzhou. During the Zhe-Gan campaign in 1942, another, smaller wave of refugee industries from Jinhua and Lanxi counties also relocated in Chuzhou.

One of Huang Shaohong's first acts as governor after he arrived in Hangzhou was to call together the factory managers of each of the city's ten or so ironworks. He ordered them to dismantle and move their factories as quickly as possible and asserted that if they could not move themselves, engineers would be dispatched to bomb and destroy their current factories and facilities. Some managers argued that they wanted to wait and see; they realized the Japanese were coming but thought they could still continue to produce arms. They told Huang that there was no way they could dismantle and move their factories quickly. Five factory managers, however, did agree to dismantle and evacuate their ironworks.

Because this was a forced (and frantic) dismantling and evacuation, transportational logistics were very difficult. Although workers were mobilized to participate, the insurmountable problem was crossing the

Qiantang River: there were too few boats; panic-stricken masses fleeing Hangzhou crowded the boats to a degree that they became unsafe. Though movers worked late into the night of December 22, the machinery and equipment that had been ferried to the other side of the river was no more than 30 to 40 percent of the total. Much heavy equipment remained piled on the Hangzhou side of the river. On December 23, the skies were bright and clear—but time was running out. That day Huang Shaohong's car ride across the Qiantang River's auto and rail bridge was the last before the bridge was blown up to prevent the Japanese from using it. The Xiaoshan County riverbank was then sealed off. The next day the Japanese took Hangzhou. The machines and equipment piled on the wharves along the Hangzhou riverbank were all discarded, in effect thrown away. Furthermore, in the frantic "forced march" of evacuation, some of the equipment that had made it across the river was not immediately picked up and became lost.

These costly losses seem largely unnecessary: they show a government that was frankly derelict in its duties. All the leaders knew that Shanghai (120 miles from Hangzhou) had been attacked in August; even more, all the leaders knew that the Japanese had attacked northern Zhejiang on November 5, almost seven weeks before the actual stripping of the factories and partial evacuation. During these seven weeks, Hangzhou had watched as Japan moved toward the provincial capital. Some of this dillydallying may have stemmed from the lame-duck nature of the term of Governor Zhu Jiahua; Huang did not arrive in Hangzhou until December 18. Zhu should have made plans and started their execution. It is another example of the tendency among many decision makers, in the opening days of the attacks, to be flagrantly naive about the Japanese in the war, perhaps about war itself. The ironworks managers who thought they could continue to produce arms for the Chinese army while laboring in occupied territory is an excellent indicator of this naivete—as is the government's lack of preparation for boat transportation for critical, defense-oriented industries.

The machinery was carried to Jinhua, reportedly with many transportational difficulties en route. Since many of the foundries' staff, workers, and their families were unwilling to remain in an occupied Hangzhou, they had fled as refugees. When they arrived in Jinhua, food and lodging was an immediate problem; there was, of course, no work for them.

Making circumstances even worse were the almost-daily bombing raids that Jinhua experienced. The ironworks' already depleted machinery was piled in open air, where it could easily be destroyed in the bombing or damaged by rain or snow. The Reconstruction Ministry, which had been charged with the evacuation, requested instructions from Governor Huang. Recognizing both Jinhua's strategic vulnerability and the priority of protecting the machinery, Huang decided that the machinery be moved and that production begin at the small village of Dagangtou in Lishui County.

Dagangtou, poor and relatively isolated, was about fifteen miles from the county seat as the crow flies, but twenty-two miles on the upper waters of the Ou River, which was plied by small wooden boats and wooden and bamboo rafts. Located at the confluence of the Songyang and Ou rivers, the village in 1938 had a population of only six hundred to seven hundred. To say it was not ready to absorb the five thousand foundry workers or their families, who brought the total up to at least ten thousand—roughly a fifteenfold increase—is an understatement. Once production got under way, the Zhejiang Ironworks was divided into four units according to function, in newly built factories, with three of the units moving to neighboring villages. Dagangtou, therefore, did not have to provide permanent residency to all ten thousand, but the population pressure on the whole generally impoverished area can perhaps not be easily imagined—sources do not give any specifics about how problems between residents and newcomers were worked out.

In the beginning there were even questions about what the ironworks would produce. In the end, this was the division of function: The factory at Xiaoshun (about twelve miles from Dagangtou) produced rifles, and it was also the factory with the greatest scope in functions, including bench work, smithing, casting, thermal treatment, oxidizing, and carpentry; the factory also had a workshop for putting everything together. The Shitang factory (about nine miles from Dagangtou) produced machine guns; the factory at Yuxi produced hand grenades; and the main factory at Dagangtou produced machine tools and spare parts for the guns. None of the private firms that had joined to create the Zhejiang Ironworks were state-of-the-art companies. The quality of the first products underscored that problem. The machine guns would not repeat firing on their own mechanisms; the rifles, once a soldier took aim, were not accurate and the range of fire was not far. Governor

Huang, who had managed an arsenal in Guangxi Province, brought in experts, who raised the production standards for rifles and machine guns.

It was the production of hand grenades that pointed to the drawbacks of locating the ironworks in a peripheral region. Many hand grenades were duds and did not explode; Governor Huang sought out experts, who said the reason was the use of saltpeter instead of dynamite, which had been used in making grenades. Most of the dynamite before the war had been purchased from Germany, so that would have been a problem no matter what other circumstances existed. The experts advised stopping grenade production. Someone suggested digging up unexploded bombs that had fallen on Jinhua. Finding men to take on this dangerous task was not easy; but Huang's decision to give generous rewards attracted some men who became bomb extricators. The first group of unexploded bombs produced between ten and fifteen kilograms of dynamite. With this source, courtesy of the Japanese, hand-grenade production resumed. Because of the importance of these factories for the war effort, a police unit was attached to each factory; police guarded the doors around the clock, protecting the security of the ironworks, which also operated around the clock.[6] In the end, the four factories produced 9,918 rifles, 497 machine guns, 204,037 hand grenades, 2,703 dynamite charges, 172,476 rifle grenades, and 3,506 bayonets.[7]

The operation of the ironworks was a mix of official and private management. The firms had been privately owned; indeed, the machinery and equipment still belonged to the owners. But because what was produced was necessary for national defense, private management could not be permitted. The ironworks was managed by a board of directors, chaired by Governor Huang and including heads of provincial government ministries and some of the original private factory owners. The board appointed the ironworks' manager. The involvement of the government and the perceived importance of these defense factories led to positive policies toward laborers in the plants.

Some ironworks employees followed the plant to Dagangtou; others were recruited in Hangzhou, Wenzhou, and Ningbo; finally, there were many inexperienced youthful workers from the local area. A workers' club was established to sponsor Beijing and Shaoxing opera troupes and a modern stage-play group—and to provide costumes, props, and musical instruments for the amateur actors. How much the workers did themselves and how much was provided by management is not clear. Clearly management was responsible for purchases and the costs of constructing a theater in Dagangtou Village. Other recreation included organized choirs, basketball teams, soccer squads, and arranged entertainment every Saturday and Sunday. Management opened a factory library and arranged for the establishment of a factory hospital with a staff of ten. Finally a ten-room factory school was set up in a village near Dagangtou; the school had ten teachers and close to two hundred students.

The ironworks production was significant. Huang Shaohong noted that "the upper reaches of the Ou River were virtually transformed into a military industrial zone."[8] Adding to this sense of a "military industrial zone" was the decision of Zhejiang–Jiangxi Railroad vice president Wu Jingqing to dismantle no-longer-needed machines and even train cars and to take them to an ironworks factory in Longquan so that steel axles could be transformed into mortars, machine guns, and other weapons.[9]

Not only was the factories' production aimed at supplying the provincial self-defense regiment, but weapons were also sold to forces in Guangxi, Guangdong, Guizhou, Fujian, Anhui, and Gansu. Perhaps it was in part this wider pattern of distribution that in early 1942 prompted the national government in Chongqing to send inspectors to the four ironworks; they were reportedly amazed at the efficiency of production and at the energy and commitment of the workers, perhaps sustained at least in part by the range of their free-time activities. The inspection had ulterior motives: the national Guomindang government had decided that all arsenals and munitions making had to be centralized. In March 1942, the three weapons-producing factories were pulled out of Lishui, with some of their workers following. Many workers did not follow: they felt settled and comfortable there and were not willing to move. The Dagangtou plant remained, to make equipment for agriculture and industry; but, in the end, it was destroyed by Japanese aerial bombs.

Industries Move to the Periphery

Industrial enterprises moving to the rear area and new factories constructed there totaled about one hundred. They included seven paper mills (using bamboo as raw material); fourteen textile mills (making bolts of cotton and silk, underwear, towels, and socks); and thirteen printing presses.

The following tables detail the specific firms from northern Zhejiang that relocated in Chuzhou. The role of government in the moves and reestablishment of industries is noteworthy, whether these efforts were supported by the provincial government without reference to specific government ministries or specifically by the Reconstruction Ministry. It is also important to see, however, that private entrepreneurs were much involved. Those firms catalyzed by "government initiative"—by the Provincial Industrial Improvement Office *(sheng gongye gaijinsuo)*—were headed by individuals who undoubtedly had close connections to government figures. The industrial sites were primarily in three areas: the Lishui county seat (the villages of Yanquan and Shuinan were contiguous to the county seat), and Bihu and Dagangtou in the southern part of the county. Though the recorded number of workers is vague and nowhere near complete (only nine of the twenty-two factories have even an approximate number), the "total" here of about seven thousand (plus whatever family members joined the employees) points to a surge of population in the area, where resources were often insufficient for even its native population.

The available data from Longquan County on industries that moved there are sketchier than that from Lishui. We are not generally told about the initiative for the industry's establishment and in some cases about when the move came; nor are we told the number of workers in any factory.

Longquan County was even more removed from transportation and communication lines than Lishui was. Therefore, on the whole, the imprint of the government on Longquan's wartime industries was even greater than that on Lishui's. During the Zhe-Gan campaign, a number of Lishui industries resettled in the relatively safer Longquan.

Industrial development was very limited. For the region, it was the first step toward modern industrial development and could be seen to have provided a base of sorts for future development. However, this was an economically backward area with insufficient resources to sustain a large infusion of factories. Small-scale industries did, however, provide important supplies for the population. Items targeted in the interior for production by the Provincial Industrial Improvement Office included flour, soy sauce, cotton goods, towels, absorbent cotton, gauze, ethyl alcohol, wax paper, paper, chalk, ink, and sealing wax. In 1939, the money produced by the sale of these products totaled over 300,000 yuan.

Table 9.1 Lishui County Firms Relocating from Northern Zhejiang

Factory	Site	Date Begun	Employees	Sponsor
Zhejiang Provincial Ironworks	4 sites	1938	2000+	Prov. Gov't.
Zhejiang Chemical Factory	Lishui	1939	500+	RM
Zhedong Electric Company★	6 sites	1938		Prov. Gov't
Zhe Highway Dept. Auto Repair Plant★	Dagangtou	1937	700	Prov. Gov't.
Zhejiang Kerosene Refinery	Junxi	1941		Prov. Gov't
Zhejiang Paper Mill★	Lishui	1938	100+	RM†
Zhejiang Chemical Fertilizer	Bihu	1939		Prov. Gov't
Zhejiang Camphor Refinery	Shuinan	1941		RM
Zhejiang Printing Company	Lishui	1939	300+	Zhejiang Local Bank
Xinda Printing Company	Baiyunshan	1940	20+	Zhejiang Local Bank
Fumin Flour Mill	Bihu		20+	RM
Southeast Chemical Company	Lishui			Private
Bihu Chemical Factory	Bihu			Private
Model Sugar Cane Press	Lishui			Private
Provincial Transportation Equipment Factory	Lishui	1938	155	Prov. Gov't
Agricultural Products–Processing Factory	Bihu	1938		Prov. Gov't
Noodle Factory	Bihu	1938		Prov. Gov't
Cultural Implements Factory	Yanquan	1939		Prov. Gov't
Tool Factory	Shuinan	1939		Prov. Gov't
Plant Oil Lamp Factory	Shuinan	1940		Prov, Gov't
Lishui Textile Demonstration Institute	Bihu	1940		Prov. Gov't
Zhejiang Tannery	Bihu	1940		Zhejiang Local Bank
Zhe-Guang Travel Bureau	Lishui	1940		Zhejiang Local Bank

★Destroyed by Japanese bombing, 1942

†RM = Reconstruction Ministry

Sources: *Lishui quyu zhi* [A gazetteer of the Lishui region] (Hangzhou: Zhejiang renmin chubanshe, 1993), pp. 637–638; *Lishui wenshi ziliao*, v. 5, #1 (N. p.: N-p., 1988) pp. 156–159.

Table 9.2 Longquan County Firms Relocating from Northern Zhejixzn

Factory	Site	Date Begun	Sponsor
Zhejiang Paper Company	Longquan	1940	Prov. Gov't
Zhedong Electric Company	Longquan	1938	Prov. Gov't
Paper Industry Improvement Workshop	Yingtou	1938	Prov. Gov't
Zhenan Candle Company	Longquan		Third Wartime Regional Command
Jusheng Printing Company			
Tongji Rosin Company	Longquan		
Jicheng Printing Company			
China United Ironworks Company	Nandayang		
Cotton Textile Mill	Anren		RM*
Silk Weaving Mill			RM
Liufang Village Soap Factory	Liufang Village		RM
Chemical Factory	Huangyun Village		RM
Stationery Factory	Xiangbian Village		RM
Zhejiang Co-op Office Equipment and Supplies Printing Press			
Southeast Chemical Plant			
Shipowner Cigarette Company			
Provincial Protect the Peace Machine Repair Factory			Prov. Gov't

*RM = Reconstruction Ministry

Sources: *Lishui quyu zhi* [A gazetteer of the Lishui region] (Hangzhou: Zhejiang renmin chubanshe, 1993), pp. 637–638; *Longquan wenshi ziliao*, V. 3 (N.P.: N.p., n.d.) pp. 126–130.

The Wartime Role of the Zhejiang Local Provincial Bank

With the fall of Hang-Jia-Hu [Hangzhou-Jiaxing-Huzhou] in fall 1937, four national banks at least partially retreated to the rear areas—the Bank of Communications, China Bank, Central Bank, and Farmers Bank.[10] Bank managers and staff had to bring with them cash reserves, account ledgers and copies, and assorted materials. It was a risky and dangerous undertaking in time of war. A report from China Bank could speak for all the banks when it said, "Our employees at a time when the area is actively engaged in warfare, must devise plans to deal with any situation in order to brave the dangers of moving public things.... In the end [the manager noted], nothing at all was lost."[11] The Bank of Communications, China Bank, Central Bank, and Farmers Bank, given wartime realities and the predilections of their managers, cut back in scope and trimmed their financial profile: displaced banking institutions were often far removed from those with whom they did business; further, the moves the banks made to safer areas obviously required an increased outlay of expenses for the moves. In Zhejiang, only the Zhejiang Local Provincial Bank *(Zhejiang sheng difang yinhang)* went against the conventions of wartime banking and struck out on the road of expansion by sponsoring and financing the establishment of industries. What accounts for this expansion?

It was by no means a given. The early war created many problems for this provincial-based bank. When Jiaxing and Huzhou fell, its two branches there retreated to Hangzhou. The bank left for the rear area on December 18, moving respectively, over months, to Lanxi, Lishui, Yunhe, and then to Longquan, where it rode out most of the war with the four national banks. Cut from its financial moorings during these moves, the Local Provincial Bank came through a temporary crisis, helped by financial assistance from the Central Bank. Zhejiang Local Provincial Bank initially made its head office at Lishui, but when Yongkang became the capital in exile, the bank established an office of equal importance in Yongkang. During 1938 and 1939, the relationship of the Zhejiang Local Provincial Bank with the provincial government became closer. During the same time period, most of Hangzhou's big enterprises had gathered in Jinhua: indeed, the Local Provincial Bank expanded its Jinhua office into a full-fledged bank branch.

After northern Zhejiang fell and the rail link with Shanghai was cut off, the province's "trade throat" with the outside was Ningbo and Wenzhou. Direct remittances between Zhejiang and Shanghai were no longer possible. The central provincial interior trade focused on Jinhua; monies collected at Jinhua for payment of goods were remitted to Ningbo or Wenzhou. At least two of the three national banks, China Bank and the Bank of Communications, were reportedly very averse to risk-taking in their new localities and preferred to deposit their monies being dispatched to Ningbo and Wenzhou in the Local Provincial Bank. Because of this, the remittance business at this bank's branches in Jinhua, Ningbo, and Wenzhou was brisk; and the bank's reserves were bolstered.

At the time the government and other institutions had begun their retreat in late 1937 and early 1938, two of Governor Huang Shaohong's trumpeted boosterlike slogans were "Build Zhedong in order to win back Zhexi" and "Raise wartime production to struggle economically with the enemy and their puppets."[12] The head of the Zhejiang Local Provincial Bank, Xu Enming, was a wholehearted supporter of these views. Xu's analysis showed that many businesses and industries were using huge sums to move—money that had been made in years before the war: in other words, earlier economic profits were being exhausted by these moves—many to questionable venues. Further, leading to even greater economic contraction, businesses were hoarding to pay for living expenses once they reached their destinations, a certain recipe for economic deterioration and bankruptcy.

The Zhejiang Local Provincial Bank played two important roles in trying to change the scenario and to stimulate production. First, now headquartered in Chuzhou prefecture, it saw one of its key functions as trying to be a responsible participatory member of its new wartime community. It became instrumental in renovating and activating a program in farm loans. In fall 1938 the Lishui branch worked to clarify loan procedures and expand its loan system. The branch established three rural loan offices in townships to the east, south, and west of the county seat, in 1939 issuing over 3 million yuan in farm-production loans, most likely in seeds and equipment. After 1940, it expanded by setting up instruments for greater loan opportunities—supply and marketing loans and small rural industrial and irrigation loans.

Before the war, banks could not legally engage in business enterprises. However, at one or two meetings on banking at the Finance Ministry after the war had begun, the decision had been made that provincial banks could directly take charge of transportation processes for firms in financial trouble or for those enterprises wanting to move to the rear area—the purpose: to encourage production. Xu reasoned, "Ordinarily this bank supports [provides for] enterprises. From now on, we support enterprises in order to support the bank."

While the Zhejiang Local Provincial Bank had been joined by the China and Farmers banks in the farm loan programs, the Local Provincial Bank was the only one to engage in backing local enterprises. It first had to decide which firms it would support. We are not told of the process: how the firms were chosen or who made decisions or how it was decided how much would be invested in particular enterprises. Presumably, the government whose Reconstruction Ministry was at work with its own list of supported enterprises provided advice and assistance. The Local Provincial Bank constructed warehouses at Yongkang, Lishui, and Longquan; purchased and imported machines for selected factories; and then paid for the factories' moves into the rear area. We are not told the interest rate the bank charged each firm for warehousing, buying new machinery, or moving; nor are we told what portion of the profit went to the bank. Because the bank was essentially carrying out a policy supported by the government, it is possible that government funds subsidized the bank's actions, a strategy that would have not taken so much from an underwritten factory. In any event, preparations for establishing factories by the bank began in 1939, with many of the industries being reestablished in 1940.

All the factories underwritten by the bank were rather small in value. One goal of the bank was to fund factories that would produce materials for farmers to purchase, presumably at reasonable rates. In line with the traditional business model that was not displaced by the war, the factory was managed by merchants but had official government force to stand behind it. Reportedly the dispersal of capital and the organization of the factories in terms of management and workforce went without major problems. In the end, the bank funded (and profited) from thirteen enterprises, not all of them in Chuzhou. The list shows the range of undertakings underwritten by Zhejiang Local Provincial Bank.

1. Zhejiang Tannery—moved from Wenzhou to Longquan
2. Zhejiang Printing Company—moved to Lishui, then to Longquan; a branch was opened in Pucheng, Fujian.
3. Xinda Printing Company—located at Lishui
4. Zhe-Guang Gongchang—moved from Lishui to Longquan; car-repair facility
5. Zheng Da Cotton Mill—located in Sheng County; produced woven cotton products
6. Da Fang Cotton Mill—located in Linhai County; produced bolts of cotton cloth
7. Yuan Da Silk Mill—located in Sheng County; the mill was built but never opened.
8. Jianye Paper Mill—located in Qu County; produced strawboard and stationery
9. Tingda Tea Company—located in Pingshui Town, Shaoxing County
10. Xinye Paper Office—located in Wenzhou: local paper transport and sales
11. Zhe Guang Travel Agency—located at Lishui, with branches in Yongkang, Songyang, and Longquan
12. Bai Yun Agricultural Farm—located at Lishui to cultivate vegetables, fruit, and grain
13. Da Zhong Huazhuang—main office located at Ningbo; branches in two towns in Yuyao County and in one town in Cixi Country; it substituted for the official Provincial Trade Office *(shengying maoyichu)* to purchase Yuyao-produced cotton for the two cotton mills listed above: over 100,000 piculs of cotton purchased.

This last firm underscores the close relationship between the bank and the government, in that the bank essentially performed a role in place of the government Trade Office. The whole bank endeavor was dealt a serious blow when its founder and director, Xu Enming, was killed in the Japanese bombing of Lishui in April 1941.

The bank was, on the whole, very successful in its undertakings. Table 9.3 shows the business dealings and financial status of the bank from 1937 (before the move) through the end of 1940, that is, before inflation was ratcheted up to its fever pitch as the war progressed. Supporting business enterprises was obviously good business strategy for the bank.

Table 9.3 Business Dealings and Financial Status of the Zhejiang Local Provincial
Bank, 1937–1940

Year	Reserves	Loans	Remittances	Net Profit
1937	2,748	2,548	8,700	45.4
1938	3,550	2,559	8,299	43.4
1939	4,887	3,411	17,488	84.1
1940	6,900	5,770	33,000	No information

Source: Zhang Genfu, *Kangzhan shiqi Zhejiang sheng renkou qianyi yu shehui yingxiang*
[Population migration and its social impact on wartime Zhejiang] (Shanghai: Sanlian
shudian, 2001), p. 262.
Note: Units represent 10,000 yuan.

The Zhejiang Printing Company

An analysis of one of the Zhejiang Local Provincial Bank's projects reveals more fully aspects of the bank's undertakings and issues of a company's development during wartime in the rear areas.[13] When the bank
first moved from Hangzhou to Lishui, it was to a building at the foot of
White Cloud Mountain in the county seat. But there were several concerns about its location. Because Lishui was the county seat, prices were
higher there than elsewhere in the county; further, there was fear that
Lishui would be a bigger target for Japanese bombs—a definite threat to
the security of a new industrial enterprise. Staffers were dispatched to
find a site in Songyang County, but when the isolation of that county,
which was completely encircled by mountains, became starkly clear, they
returned to Lishui County and chose for the printing company the area
around the town of Bihu. This was a logical choice since, with the number of schools in Bihu, the town brought many students to the area. The
need for textbooks and other educational materials, stationery, newspapers, and magazines made it certain that the company would be serving
the needs of local society.

In the end, printing company executives decided on the village of
Shangzhao, where they were helped in several ways by the local head
of a *baojia* unit, Zhao Xiuming. Zhao helped the printing press get at a
low price about four thousand square meters of land (about an acre) to
use as an advantageous factory site; he also arranged for hiring about

two hundred workers from Dongyang County, three counties to the north of Lishui. We are not told why he went outside the county for these workers; presumably his connections of one sort or another facilitated the arrangement and prioritized using those outsiders rather than mostly needy locals. While the factory was being built, the printing company rented the He lineage hall to begin work. The rent, the money for the factory construction, and costs for printing machines and equipment (housed at White Cloud Mountain until the factory was completed) were all paid by the Local Provincial Bank. It was indeed the bank directors themselves who appointed the factory manager, Tu Tieshan. Through the bank, the printing company also used important connections that the bank and its leaders afforded them. In part, the press's access to electricity probably came from such connections. The only electricity-producing facility in the area was at Bihu. The Zhejiang Printing Company had access to electricity while other commercial establishments did not.

When the factory opened in 1939, the workforce was composed of about two hundred Dongyang laborers, a handful of workers who had worked at the company when it was in Hangzhou (they had followed their factory), and about a hundred local workers. Some of the last allegedly joined the printing-company workforce to evade the draft. How working for this company accomplished that end we are not told, unless it was that the connections gained from working at this rather privileged company protected a young man from the draft.

The company, for all the financial support it was being given by the bank (and again, we do not know the exact nature, amount, or terms of the bank's financial assistance), insisted that it could pay its employees only "national crisis salaries," in this case twelve yuan per month. Workers got one meal a day with two meat or fish dishes and two vegetable dishes: on its face, not a bad deal. But when one considers that the cost for a half kilogram of white rice on the market was forty-five yuan, it was apparent that twelve yuan per month for a family was hugely insufficient. The company had the workers over a barrel; administrators simply said, "Take it or leave it." Workers who had followed the company were from occupied territory and had no place to return if they lost the job. For local men who had joined the company's workforce actually to evade the draft, leaving that position would make the draft a more likely reality. So the workers did not protest the low wages, much less join together to strike.

Bombings began in the area in summer 1942. Workers and staff heard the warnings, scattered, and returned when the warnings silenced. But later the bombing became more intense. There was no thought given to moving the whole factory. Parts of some sections were moved to Ju Village in Yunhe County (about thirteen miles away) for temporary housing and protection. Two staff members had to stay to guard the equipment. But then came the Japanese invasion from Lishui to Bihu and Shangzhao Village; the Japanese burned down half the buildings on the main commercial street in what had been the bustling wartime town of Bihu. At Shangzhao Village, they burned the printing factory with its supplies of paper to the ground. The company had operated a little less than three years. It had provided employment and needed goods to the local community, thereby fulfilling what the bank had intended. Fortunately for the bank, not all its investment projects had such a tragic end.

Transportation Obstacles

While transportation is of crucial concern in any war—moving troops, moving supplies, moving refugees (individuals, families, and institutions)—the patterns of Japan's war in Zhejiang, where contiguous counties could be occupied or not and parts of the rear area saw some counties occupied for eight years and others for a few weeks or not at all, meant that straight line direct travel or long-distance travel of any kind was difficult. When that wartime reality is coupled with Zhejiang's relatively primitive transport technology, the seriousness of the absence of coherent and direct transportation is apparent.

For example, when the war broke out, Longquan County, the site of important government institutions, banks, and small-scale industries, had four sedan chair companies and two rickshaw companies, which had a total of eight rickshaws. In the whole county there were only fifteen cars. Small passenger buses and small trucks wended their way on expanded walking paths that were often impassable in bad weather. With the Zhe-Gan campaign of 1942, even many of these would-be roads were destroyed so that the Japanese could not use them; then, again, neither could the Chinese. We have seen in various war stories that human legs were the most common means of transport.

The most important wartime transportation in terms of volume and freight was the wheelbarrow. We have seen the importance of wheelbarrow brigades as work relief and their importance in the government move to Yongkang. It was a convenient vehicle, fairly easily manipulable on crowded walkways; but in Chuzhou prefecture, with its rugged mountains, a wheelbarrow was none too easy to push when it held a heavy load. Certain routes were almost gridlocked with wheelbarrow traffic. Between Jinhua and Lishui, for example, wheelbarrows shuttled back and forth in an unbroken stream, the road crowded to capacity. Between February and October 1938, organized wheelbarrow brigades carried 5,908,588 *jin* of oil (a *jin* is half a kilogram); 4,731,423 sheets of paper; 10,021,392 *jin* of tea; 726,405 *jin* of ham and of cowhide (a strange pairing of commodities); 217,935 *jin* of medicines; and 2,448,524 *jin* of "other," altogether 24,422,212 jin—or a little over 13,460 tons.[14]

The few available cars and trucks tended to be old and in bad shape. Even if there had been more vehicles and those in good condition, gasoline was hard to come by. Indeed, in the interior at least, cars came to be powered (as it were) by charcoal. "Charcoal cars" could only drive very slowly and could not travel over high hills; a common problem was that a car could not make it up a hill and then begin to roll back down. The rule of thumb was that each car had to have two "drivers," one of whom, should the car start rolling backward, jumped out with large stones or pieces of wood to place behind the wheels to stop the car from rolling. The charcoal alternative to gasoline was, in short, not a good one.

Another possibility was camphor oil.[15] Wu Tingfang, head of the Reconstruction Ministry, took the lead in experimenting with this source; indeed, the camphor oil refinery was managed by the Reconstruction Ministry. One of the transplanted industries underwritten by the provincial government, the camphor oil refinery pointed to Chinese creativity in trying to meet crises, to the crucial lack of technological development, yet to the pragmatic, make-do approach to issues on the part of some leaders during wartime. Refining camphor oil for use in place of gasoline was laborious and technologically difficult, and it required careful precision. Labor was intensive: workers had to climb steep mountains to cut down camphor trees, move them down the mountains, and saw them into wood strips. Iron cauldrons about six feet tall with openings 3.25 feet wide were used in the refining. Problems came because the refinery managers did not have advanced enough technology, equipment, machines, or even tools: problems like not completely evaporating water in the refining process produced a final (and unusable) product in which water was mixed with oil. Another problem was the necessity of stoking the fires constantly during the refining process: they had to be kept going eighteen straight hours. Equipment often failed. Extreme care had to be taken when mixing ingredients; certain items had to be added in a correct order to produce the highest-quality oil, which could be produced in four different quality grades. For such a laboriously taxing job, men were paid a little more than ten yuan per month; their overseers received thirty per month. One meal was provided per day, usually green vegetables.

When the oil was produced, it was fairly expensive. From the beginning of its refining in 1939 until the end of March 1942, some 45,522 catties (22,761 kilograms) of refined camphor oil was sold: the costs to the consumers were 199,421 yuan, or 8.76 yuan per kilogram. Very few private individuals could afford this—not that many had cars to begin with, of course. But camphor oil also had medicinal properties for the treatment of rashes and various types of wounds. The experiment was hardly largely successful, but it indicated the lengths to which state and society would go at times of crisis and dearth.

The best and most efficient means of transportation was the boat; its huge disadvantage was obvious: it was restricted to rivers and streams, which often did not flow where one needed to go. The war gave rise to many fast boat companies in Wenzhou, which competed to carry both passengers and freight on the Ou River upstream to the Chuzhou counties. Many such companies were begun in wartime to take advantage of the new importance of Wenzhou as a port of entry and of the political and military significance of the Chuzhou counties as the center of the great rear area. Many of these boat companies were started by refugees. We have seen, for example, how Zhang Dayan, who had fled Hangzhou, was instrumental in the 1940 formation of the Li-Qing-Wen Fast Boat Company. Two brothers from Suzhou, surnamed Jian, founded the Yong-Li Fast Boat Company and turned it into one of the most flourishing of the new boat lines. In 1939 six hundred vessels carrying grain and salt traveled upstream from the coast; they carried 25,000 piculs (1666.67 tons) of grain and salt each month.[16]

Wartime in many regions of the rear areas fostered a "get rich quick" mentality. Very quickly the Li-Qing-Wen boat company was joined by other fledgling boat firms. There were within months four additional companies sending boats downstream to Wenzhou, and four additional companies (eventually three when two merged) sending boats upstream to Longquan and Songyang. Some companies made little money in the beginning. Competition was intense; violence in the form of retaliatory beatings and robberies were common. There were simply too many boats for the number of passengers and the amount of cargo. At one point, several of the companies pushed the formation of a transport boat guild, hoping that it might be able to defuse the raw competition and foster less-bitter rivalry. A guild was formed, and Zhang Dayan was elected its manager, but it never functioned and was dead from the start.

"Like Spring Shoots after a Rain": Wartime Business in Chuzhou

It would be an understatement to say that, before the war, commerce was not flourishing in Chuzhou. Lishui was described as "an isolated place in the mountains where transportation is inconvenient and markets are bleak."[17] The war turned this reality on its head. Not only the county seat but smaller towns like Bihu and Dagangtou became busy, marked by increasingly fiercely competitive markets. In 1937, the whole county of Longquan had 287 merchant establishments, capitalized at about 4.5 million yuan; in 1943 it had 1,071 establishments, capitalized at over 33 million. It was said the streets of the county seat were so thronged with people that falling raindrops were not be able to reach the ground. A catalog of all these retail stores, restaurants, and taverns can be mind numbing, but simply reading the numbers of stores does not suggest the range of goods and services that were available to people who so recently could shop only in very bare-bones standard market towns. In 1945 the population of the Lishui County seat was 16,161. Moving into it during the war was

The Provincial Trading Company (which also had a branch in Longquan)
Provincial Wartime Matches Company Outlet

Da Cheng Department Store

Shanghai Chinese-American Drug Company

Hangzhou Tianxianglou Restaurant (This business and the next in the list
    were two of Hangzhou's most famous restaurants.)

Hangzhou Zhiweiguan Restaurant

Hangzhou Tianzhen Chinese-Western Restaurant

Hangzhou Fanzhuang Restaurant

Hangzhou Jinfeng Yuan Restaurant

Hangzhou Loutaixiang Restaurant

Hangzhou Xiangxuelou Restaurant

Hangzhou Cake and Pastry Shop

Hangzhou Gaoyitai Piece-Goods Shop

Hangzhou Chu Feng Yuan

Hangzhou Mao Yuanchang Eyeglasses

Hanghzou Watch Shop

Hangzhou Leather Suitcase Shop

Hangzhou Shoe Store

Zhe-Guang Travel Bureau

The Longquan county seat had even more stores coming to the hinterland from Shanghai and Hangzhou.

The Provincial Trading Company

The Chinese Tea Company, Zhejiang Branch

Jianzhong Enterprises

Zhejiang Cigarette Outlet

Southeast Sales Office

Shanghai Provisioning Shop

Shanghai Foodstuffs Store

Hangzhou Vegetables and Foodstuffs Store

Hangzhou Tianxianglou Restaurant

Hangzhou Zhiweiguan Restaurant

Hangzhou Qiantang Restaurant

Hangzhou New Asia Restaurant

Hangzhou Zhenyang Wineshop

Hangzhou Golden Dragon Teahouse

Hangzhou Zhenyang Teahouse

Hangzhou Guanshengyuan Teashop

Eastern Zhejiang Market
Wuzhou Market
Zhang Xiaoquan Hardware and Glass Store
Beikai Department Store
Dalu Silk Market
Youth Movie Theater
Hangzhou Mao Yuanchang Eyeglasses
Heng Dali Clocks and Watches Store
Guanlun Clocks and Watches Business
San Yang Cart Store
Bai Shou Advertising Agency
Xinyi Financial Services
Li wen Wireless
Big China Grocery
East Zhejiang Travel Bureau
Hangzhou Travel Agency[18]

It is worth noting that once the war ended, these businesses (and the industries as well) returned to the cities and towns from which they had come. During their wartime sojourns in the periphery a crucial question arose for these businesses and especially for the businessmen who had uprooted themselves to move to the rear areas: with the added commodity and service-offering businesses migrating to Chuzhou, how many people were well enough off to be able to take advantage of the first-time-ever wartime opportunities?

The Liyong Dyeing and Weaving Mill

At the end of the war, the manager of the Liyong Dyeing and Weaving Mill (unnamed in the account) gave a report on what had happened to the mill during the war.[19] This company was based in Lishui, which endured over 350 bombing attacks and two invasions: what happened to this company is a bitter example of the ordeal and tragedy that industries and businesses in the rear areas experienced, both at the hands of the Japanese and as the result of unforeseen contingencies.

The Japanese first bombed Lishui in early 1938; mill workers were panic-stricken; they all fled, obviously doing no work. On February 1, the manager convened a meeting of the mill's board of directors; it was tense.

Members of the board decided to maintain the situation temporarily; if a day came when there was no way to sustain mill work and remain in Lishui, the manager should decide on the basis of expedience how to handle the situation. The mill was able to operate two more years, withstanding sporadic bombing attacks. But on February 14, 1940, the magistrate ordered the mill to move; it complied, moving a short distance to Subu, where it rented the Nanming Tea Firing Factory. But that move was a disaster: seven months later, on September 22, 1940, that building was destroyed in an aerial bombing raid; the machines it contained and all the finished woven cloth was destroyed. Consequently, the manager, staff, and workers all returned to Lishui.

At that time boats from Shanghai could not reach Lishui on the Ou River. An alternative route for transporting finished goods to Wenzhou and then on to Shanghai was to use porters to carry the goods to the Ao River, which flowed into Pingyang County just south of Wenzhou. In March 1941, the mill had sent thirty cases of cotton yarn to the mouth of the Ao. The Inspection Office broke open the cases to inspect the goods. The inspectors were careless about getting the yarn back into the cases or just downright malicious: much yarn disappeared. The mill manager reported that he telephoned to have a company representative check things out. The representative reported in amazement that the inspectors would not do anything to rectify the situation. In the end, the company lost the equivalent of over sixty bales of yarn. Repeated company attempts to negotiate and be repaid for its losses brought no results.

On April 11, 1941, Japanese bombers were again over Lishui, dropping their bombs. Part of the factory building was blown up. The manager decided to take the raw materials, separate them into several batches and disperse them in several places. One batch of eight cases of cotton yarn were sent to the home of one Yu Wutao in Shuinan, several kilometers from the county seat. Who could have known, the manager said in his report to the stockholders, that on April 22 the Japanese would bomb both Lishui and Shuinan? Bombs hit the Yu household: it burned to the ground, and all eight cases of yarn went up in flames. On May 22 the factory was hit again: four rooms were obliterated; all the windows were blown out; the walls and the tile roof were badly damaged. The manager wrote, "Count it up: three disastrous attacks in forty days, bringing tragedy and loss."[20]

Then on June 22, 1942, the Japanese invaded Lishui. Their brutal invasion was worsened by floods: creek and stream waters had risen so high that they were flooding; furthermore, with the deep and rushing water people could not cross the streams. While people in the eastern and northern townships of Lishui could evacuate, people in the western and southern townships were blocked by water. There was physically no way to evacuate the factory; and the manager realized that if the Japanese occupied the area, it would be impossible then to evacuate the raw cotton, yarn, and dyestuff. The Japanese used the factory for their own purposes: one room was used as a horse stable; walls, windows, and machines were destroyed.

Once the Japanese retreated, the mill manager and others hurried back to check things out. What they had put in the storeroom—cotton yarn and dyestuff—had all been stolen by people who lived in that Lishui neighborhood. Like the inspectors at the Ao River port, these Chinese neighbors had become vulturelike, preying on their neighbors as the Japanese preyed on them. War and its upheaval eroded morality and civility. After the mill put out a detailed inventory of what had been stolen, some scattered goods were returned; but it was only one shipment—and another never came. And the Japanese were still making raids on Lishui and its surroundings. About twenty-five kilograms of dyestuff that had been hidden at the home of stockholder Ye Keyou were all lost.

In the aftermath of these experiences, the manager opened a board of directors meeting on November 20, 1942. They agreed that the occupation losses were uncommonly heavy. They decided to close temporarily in order to rehabilitate the factory, a process to be overseen by the manager. After a period of relative calm and quiet and the completed rehabilitation, the board called a shareholders meeting to discuss issuing more shares of stock and to move toward the reopening of the mill. The company did issue more stock and reopened the factory.

In March 1944, enemy planes pounded Lishui for three entire days. Over ten bombs fell on or just outside the factory; an incendiary bomb pierced the roof and landed inside, but fortunately it did not detonate. However, other bombs did, and over twenty rooms in the factory were destroyed. The tiles on the roof had been broken and scattered. The manager hired roofers to repair it in order to keep out precipitation and avoid mildew and rot. But he was uncertain about the feasibility of organizing and rebuilding the mill; he sent the board of directors a letter asking them to scrutinize the situation carefully.

In May 1944, the manager dispatched a mill worker to the Yunhe county seat to check on the status of large stores of colored yarn that the mill had stored there for a long time for protection from bombing. The manager was concerned that it may have been mildewed or rotted; he wanted it brought back to Lishui whatever its condition. When it reached Lishui, they decided to store it all at the home of one trustee, Chen Shaolin, in Huang Village in East Township. The manager queried, "Who could have known that at this exact time Japan's second invasion of Lishui would occur?" The goal of the mill was to take the yarn far away to Jinyun County; but before employees had a chance to do so, a small contingent of Japanese soldiers visited Huang Village— and burned the yarn.

After the Japanese abandoned Lishui, the Chuzhou area became a lair for Chinese bandits. During the war, large numbers of Lishui's temples and houses were destroyed. Now the numbers of soldiers billeted in the county seat were huge. The original mill and dye works were occupied by Chinese soldiers. The board of directors and manager agreed that a move to Lishui was not wise, that it would not be a peaceful place. What was left of the machines and raw materials were carted to Huzhen Town in Jinyun County (see Map 10); and it did not amount to much, since the manager in his report to stockholders noted that the company's wealth and machines had been completely ruined.

In the end, evaluating the movement of business and industry into the hinterland is a mixed bag. For most businesses, it was probably not an economically viable choice. The risks were too great: the huge costs of the move, the issue of where to go, the unpredictabilities of the Japanese bombings and military campaigns, the lack of a qualified and dependable labor force, the scarcity of resources, and chance itself. Some businesses moved, survived, and returned to Hangzhou and other cities after the war. Those with government and military ties had a better chance of making it than the private firms. But of all the refugee groupings, business and industry faced the most daunting tasks, the bitterest in the sea of refugeedom.

>‹

TEN

Scorched Earth

IN *A HISTORY OF WARFARE,* John Keegan argues that "war is always an expression of culture."[1] In what seems a suggestive, if still rather tenuous, generalization, he claims that Chinese war making—as opposed to Western war making—is distinguished by "evasion, delay, and indirectness," qualities that he attributes to the Confucian tradition.[2] Part of this war-making strategy, Keegan continues, may include "withdraw[ing] when confronted with determination and count[ing] upon wearing down an enemy to defeat rather than by overwhelming him in a single test of arms."[3] One bitter form of such resistance, which can be used by a withdrawing defender, is the self-directed aggression of scorched earth, a strategy used in many wars throughout history. The destruction of industrial plants, communication and transportation facilities, agricultural crops, and property of all sorts in order to deprive the enemy of their use may be undertaken after careful calculation or in the midst of desperation, perhaps even panic. While undertaken as acts of resistance against the enemy, after war they come to be seen for what they really are—self-inflicted wounds. This chapter looks at four case studies of scorched-earth actions in Zhejiang Province during the Sino-Japanese War: the blowing up of the Zhakou Power Plant, the demolition of the Qiantang River Bridge, the blocking of the Yong River entrances to Ningbo with sunken ships, and the destruction of the Quzhou air base. This chapter surveys the sources, extent, and judgment of Chinese officials and the long-term consequences of the actions. All scorched-earth policies grew from the Japanese war of terror and were at the time deemed necessary, and even advantageous, by the Chinese victims.

The Destruction of the Zhakou Power Plant

The first electric power plant in Hangzhou began operation in 1909 on the time-honored structural principle of a government-owned, merchant-managed industry.[4] Because of economic difficulties, in 1917 management responsibilities went to the Zhejiang Industrial Development Bank, which expanded the plant in its location in the New Market area near West Lake. In 1919 because of increased silk- and cotton-textile mill electricity needs, branch electric-power stations were started in various suburbs contiguous to the city. In 1929, the government once again emerged as key actor and began construction of a new power plant in the southern suburb of Jianggan at Zhakou.

In 1931, however, the office running the electric plant was abolished and replaced by private ownership—banks and wealthy entrepreneurs, who formed a business consortium *(qiye yintuan)* to be run by a board of directors. In November 1932, through contract the government gave up its sovereign rights for the production of electricity for thirty years, until November 1962. The Zhakou plant began to provide electricity in October 1932. Its manager was one Cai Jingping.

Power plants obviously became targets of Japanese aerial bombing attacks once the war began. The 812 plant workers, who worked three shifts, were constantly restive, though they had practiced air-raid drills for over a year before the war began. The power plant roofs were camouflaged; and the plant did have its own antiaircraft guns for protection. Manager Cai claimed that between August 14 and December 22, the city had over 180 bombing raids. While the power plant was never damaged and no worker ever injured or killed, it played its role to protect the city, putting in place a signal network with its own blackout system. Through this system, when there was an air-raid warning, the power plant automatically extinguished streetlights and all lights outside homes; in serious emergencies, all power inside and outside residences and businesses was shut off.

By December 21, after fighting had raged in the northern two prefectures of Jiaxing and Huzhou since November, two-thirds of Hangzhou's three hundred thousand residents had fled, leaving only those abject poor whose poverty prevented them from fleeing and those leaders and officials who had detailed plans about where to head when the absolutely specific time came. The chairman of the Chamber of Commerce had discussed the situation with a number of older merchant elites, who planned to stay and try to preserve some stability. Cai met with them and a group of foreign missionaries and representatives from Buddhist and Daoist temples, to set up over twenty refugee reception centers in the city. At dusk on December 21, Cai drove to the office of the Chamber of Commerce to find out the latest news, making it back to the power plant only after 10 P.M. When he was going to bed about midnight, he received a call from the head of the local police bureau with the news that between 2 and 3 A.M. the major wharf for the only ferry company that crossed the Qiantang River, the Jianggan Ferry located in Zhakou, would be blown up, making it impossible for more refugees to leave the area that way. Cai did not outwardly react.

He went to bed but slept only briefly before the guard on duty pounded on his door, saying that an unscheduled train had entered the grounds of the power plant on a small branch track from the main trunk line. Cai woke up Hong, the plant's chief engineer, to investigate this unexpected intrusion. Hong reported that the people on the train claimed they had been ordered to come to the plant to blow it up in order to prevent the enemy from seizing and using it. Cai, who had heard nothing about this, was incredulous. He talked to the man himself, General Liu Jianxu's bomb squad leader, a man named Zhang. General Liu and his troops had passed the power plant earlier in the evening in an evacuation south toward Fuyang and Tonglu counties. Zhang said his direct order came from a district commander, Ma Shaobing, who declared the order came from no less than the provincial governor, Huang Shaohong himself: the plant was to be destroyed at 6 A.M.

Cai emerges in the scorched-earth cases in this chapter as the only person to raise serious questions about the strategy and to try to abort the destruction. He said that to use "scorched earth" (jiaotu) at the time of a resistance war was perhaps an understandable reaction, but he wanted desperately to save the plant. He rapidly recorded a copy of the order, to get word to as many members of the board of directors as possible. His strong sense was that the plant was a private company and was the property of shareholders. At 2 A.M., he drove into Hangzhou, hoping to see Governor Huang and plead for saving the plant, but Huang had already left the city; indeed, the provincial reconstruction minister and

Hangzhou's mayor had also already fled. Cai went to the provincial Public Security Bureau head, who was in the very midst of preparations to flee; he told Cai that there was no way to save the electric plant. The head of the special Police Security Bureau said he had no power in the matter. Dejected, Cai left. Arriving at the plant, he heard loud explosions: obviously the blowing up of the Jianggan Ferry wharf. Momentarily, the Chamber of Commerce head arrived at the plant; Cai explained what was happening and that there was nothing he could do to stop it. However, Cai, out of his concern for the ramifications of the action, made one last trip into Hangzhou (since telephone service was dead), to warn the head of the city's Guangqi Hospital that it would soon be without electricity. It was 5 A.M. when Cai once again returned to the plant.

The army's bombs were detonated at 6 A.M. as planned. Cai and Chief Engineer Hong watched from considerable distance as windows and roof tiles soared in every direction, the walls blew out, and the roof collapsed, crushing the equipment and all else. Cai commented that Hong, who had built the plant, cursed: it was, Cai said, almost like killing one's son: "What great pain and distress! . . . Scorched earth—what a great sacrifice."[5]

Once the Japanese took the city, they conscripted Chinese for forced labor to rebuild some of the power plant quickly. Whereas the destroyed plant had produced fifteen thousand kilowatts of power per day, the rebuilt plant supplied only two thousand kilowatts. What this meant in actuality was that the Japanese supplied what they needed for themselves; it was the Chinese residents who suffered from Chinese scorched-earth policy. Running water was not restored until 1940.[6]

The Demolition of the Qiantang River Bridge

The Qiantang River, flowing from central Zhejiang into Hangzhou Bay, had been throughout history an important separation between eastern Zhejiang, on the one hand, and western and northern Zhejiang on the other (see Map 3). As the river enters Hangzhou Bay, the Qiantang is wide, and the currents are treacherous; because of the latter, silt is deposited in great abundance but in completely unpredictable and constantly changing patterns. From the mid-nineteenth century, a ferry provided passage across the river from the suburbs of Hangzhou to Xiaoshan

County. The Zhejiang Provincial Assembly at the beginning of the Republic adopted a resolution to construct a large bridge across the river, but the turmoil of the warlord period and the money for construction proved to be obstacles too large for carrying out the plan.[7] With the establishment of the Guomindang government in Nanjing in 1928, impetus for building the bridge came anew, in efforts to build a transportation and communications infrastructure. Financed by loans from the largest national and provincial banks, construction on the bridge began in January 1935. The nature of the river, especially the riverbed of heavy, shifting sediment, made the construction extraordinarily difficult and slow.

The outbreak of war in July 1937 added military urgency to completing the construction of the first dual-level railway-highway bridge in the country.[8] The lower railway bridge was finished in September 1937, and the highway bridge in November. Not only was the Qiantang River Bridge the biggest bridge in eastern China, but it was also China's longest railroad bridge. The highway bridge was over a mile long—at 5,590 English feet; it had sixteen arches, totaling 4,550 feet in width. Construction costs were 4 million yuan. From the beginning, the bridges were busy conduits, with heavy passenger and freight traffic. When the Japanese invasion spread into northern Zhejiang in November, the bridges became indispensable for troop transport, for army supplies, and for general commodity supplies. At the end of November, however, the Bridge Construction Office, which had overseen the bridge's erection, noted the increasingly precarious situation of Hangzhou as the Japanese continued to advance. In conjunction with military leaders, the office decided to make preparations to blow up the bridge. Follow-up meetings with men from the army demolition school put in place the specific plans for the destruction.

The outgoing provincial governor, Zhu Jiahua, had some reservations about the decision. He argued, "To build a bridge is not easy. When the war is over and we've won the victory, we must then demobilize. This bridge has not even been completed three months yet. If we destroy it completely, later there may be no strength [li] to repair and restore it." Thus, Zhu advocated bombing only one or two bridge piers, just enough to keep the enemy from using it effectively.[9] Certainly with the bridge intact, the Japanese could have much more easily and quickly transported larger quantities of materials in an invasion to the east of the river. The

Bridge Office and demolition specialists, however, made plans to destroy four piers. At the base of the fourteenth pier, they placed twenty-two chests of dynamite (each chest contained 220 kilograms); at two sides of the thirteenth pier, they placed fourteen chests; and at each end of the bridge, they prepared eight chests of the explosive.

As Japanese forces began to near the city, the flow of people and goods over the bridges to Xiaoshan County was incessant. Railroad company offices estimated that at least two hundred rail cars and over three thousand trucks and automobiles evacuated over the dual bridge on December 22 alone. After noon that day, military authorities sent a platoon to the north bank of the river to prepare for the demolition. Action was delayed until after 5 P.M. because of the panicked fleeing masses. But as darkness closed in and as concern spread that traitors (hanjian) also might be among those crossing the bridge, traffic was halted and the explosives detonated. One difficulty with scorched-earth policies is that it is difficult to control the amount of destruction, especially when using dynamite charges on a truss bridge built of steel and concrete. Whereas four piers had been targeted, five were immediately destroyed and a sixth damaged when one of those that collapsed cut two-meter-wide, six-meter-long gashes in the side of the next pier, knocking out considerable concrete and exposing the steel girders.

From September 1940, after having seized both banks of the river earlier in the year, the Japanese used what was left of the frame of the bridge and put down a makeshift wooden bridge for automobile traffic. They had to deal with many gaping holes and destroyed areas, and the wooden bridge tilted and sloped. Any traffic had to move very slowly and could not be very heavy. Clearly the Japanese could not depend on such a bridge to deploy large numbers of troops or quantities of materials. When they took the former prefectures of Shaoxing and Ningbo in the spring of 1941, the invasion force, significantly, did not use the bridge for crossing, but soldiers were landed on the southern coast of Hangzhou Bay. Despite the evident inefficiency of the bridge, the apparent "logic" of scorched earth drove Chinese guerrilla forces to continue to focus on the bridge and target even more piers for destruction. Bringing explosives at night by boat, the guerillas attached charges to two more piers (the fifth and sixth); both sustained great damage in the explosion, though they still remained standing. At most this damage was a minor irritant to the Japanese, but it cost the Chinese time and effort.

At the end of 1943, the Japanese established the Qiantang River Bridge Restoration Bureau to begin to restore the piers and bridge. To counter this threat, Chinese guerrilla forces completely blew up the fifth pier on March 28, 1944. This act did nothing to stop the Japanese construction; the railroad bridge was reopened on October 7. Another response from the Chinese came on February 4, 1945, when they completely demolished the sixth pier. By May the Japanese had repaired enough of the destruction to be able to use the bridge again. But at the end of the war, only the railroad bridge was usable. The highway bridge was not rebuilt and reopened until March 1, 1947, almost ten years after it had first been opened and used for about a month; to help pay for its reconstruction, it became a toll bridge.

The Qiantang River Bridge was clearly one of the major accomplishments in the Nanjing decade's effort to "reconstruct" China, yet the strategy of scorched earth to prevent use of the bridge by the Japanese required that it be destroyed only one month after the completion of the highway bridge. As one writer described the situation, the bridge was planned by the Chinese, built by the Chinese, and destroyed by the Chinese.[10] While Governor Zhu called for a calculated policy of just enough destruction to incapacitate the bridge, military men doubled the number of targeted piers Zhu suggested; and the actual bombings themselves increased the level of destruction even more. Whereas initially scorched earth was a strategy in regard to the bridge, as the war wore on and the Japanese made halting attempts to use the bridge, scorched-earth guerrilla actions had little more impact on the Japanese than hassling them and slowing them down slightly. Yet Chinese men and materials continued to be used for this purpose. Time and energy expended in further demolition efforts seems questionable, especially in light of the fact that the Japanese undertook no major military action in the province after the summer of 1942. One can also wonder why Chinese were bombing the bridge as late as early 1945 when, with the war winding down, the likelihood of Chinese having to rebuild the bridge soon was looming. Certainly scorched earth can be often attributed to fear; but the bombings in 1944 and 1945 cannot have had that strong impetus. Ultimately these bombings raise questions about the degree of rationality in the choice of military policy and action, about decision making and control over guerrilla forces, and about whether the Chinese making these decisions were blinded by the war itself from imagining China after the war.

Decommercializing Ningbo

From the case of a seemingly uncritical application of scorched-earth policy that necessitated more reconstruction and thus more money after the war, we now go to a case in which the particular scorched-earth policy made the fighting of the war itself considerably more difficult. With the Japanese seizure of non–Settlement Shanghai in November 1937 and the conquest of Hangzhou and northern Zhejiang by December 24, the transport of commodities between Shanghai and the interior of China was seemingly cut off. The Japanese blockade of the coast, announced in late August, prevented Chinese-registered ships from trading. Further, as Yangzi River ports fell quickly into Japanese hands, the Japanese closed the Yangzi to third-party shipping. Because railroads from Shanghai into Zhejiang and Jiangsu were occupied by the Japanese military and truck traffic was curtailed by a paucity of vehicles, gasoline, and usable highways, large-volume overland transport was not a feasible option.

Historically Ningbo had the more flourishing ocean traffic with Shanghai in terms of people and commodities. As nontrade evidence of this relationship shows, in 1941, some 2,230 Shanghai industrial and business firms were controlled by Ningboese, and at the end of the war there were 36,490 members of the Ningbo native place organization [*tongxianghui*] in Shanghai.[11] From early 1938 to mid–1939, Ningbo continued to enjoy a flourishing trade with Shanghai, yet the shape of Ningbo's development also points out the constraints that war, resistance, and individual decisions placed on commerce. In this period, commodities imported daily from Shanghai in general averaged over ten thousand tons, while exports were generally about half that figure. The chief exports to Shanghai were tea, cotton, tinfoil, paper products, grass hats, and silk items. The main imports were cotton cloth and yarn, cigarettes, sugar, gasoline, kerosene, auto parts, electrical equipment, and medicines. Most important, these commodities were then transshipped through various routes into China's interior, where many of the commodities were desperately needed in the Chinese war effort.[12]

Following the general orders of the Chinese government, the Ningbo defense commissioner—in the name of defense and resistance—in late 1938 took actions that began to hinder the progress of trade and make more difficult the crucial shipment of commodities into central China. As the first line of defense, he ordered the placement of stakes at the bottom of the entrance to Zhenhai Harbor, to block the Yong River, which led to Ningbo (see Map 7). Within a short time, because the stakes had prevented the entrance of large vessels, a passageway was made for ships of under 1,000 tons. But in 1939 the creation of a second line of defense made the use of the Yong River impossible: eight steamships, three landing crafts, and eight large junks were filled with heavy stones and sunk in the mouth of the river. In July 1940, two more steamers were sunk. The steamships, ranging from 200 to 3,640 tons, were requisitioned from Shanghai and Zhejiang shipping companies. They created a "palisade" at the bottom of the harbor opening. In all of China to the end of 1939, eighty-seven steamships were sunk in harbor openings; the fact that 9.2 percent were sunk in the mouth of this relatively small river suggests that authorities had likely overreacted to the supposed threat.[13]

In efforts to deny Japanese access to the ports, this scorched-earth policy denied any ships, including Chinese vessels, access to those ports. By their actions, the Chinese had displaced trade and trade routes. When one notes the importance of this particular port to the reception of needed commodities and war matériel in the interior, irrationality in decision making emerges as a significant issue. Were Chinese decision makers unable to project possible consequences of their actions? Or is it the case that the crises and terror of this war generally constricted combatants' views, giving rise to shortsightedness and rash action? Had the Japanese so terrorized Chinese and the Chinese military that Chinese decision makers were willing to cut off their nose to spite their face?

Whatever the reasoning behind such extensive sinkings in Zhenhai Harbor, the result was that any ships coming to the port of Ningbo had to be anchored outside Zhenhai Harbor and unloaded onto small boats or barges. To profit from the situation, the head of Ningbo's dockworkers' union conspired with the defense commissioner and Ningbo's chief of police to have the Ning-Shao Steamship Company lease them barges to form the Ningbo Barge Company, which had exclusive rights to carry cargo from ships outside Zhenhai Harbor. But more than one group could become a war profiteer from the situation: the Ning-Shao Company made available only small barges in poor condition, compelling slow travel. As a result, there were often ten ships at the mouth of the harbor and sometime as many as twenty waiting to unload their cargo—a wait that could last up to half a month. To further compound trade difficulties, the barge company, in the name of anti-Japanese defense, charged extortionate fees on imports and exports and a per capita tax on traveling merchants from Shanghai; the company later added a water portage-charge, a barge-transport charge, and an "emergency" fee, which added 10 percent to the passenger fare.[14] The blockage, the extortion that it spun off, and the resulting inordinate time delays were huge obstacles to trading and to using Ningbo at all as a port of entry for the rear areas.

Ningbo's disastrous self-imposed commercial displacement became a boon for other, smaller ports. The commercial scene in Ningbo after a flourishingly prosperous 1938 became a disaster. Adjusted for inflation, the rough value of direct foreign trade and of transshipped Chinese commodities as recorded by Chinese customs officials dropped from 62.03 million yuan in 1938 to 409,200 yuan in 1939 to 325,400 yuan in 1940.[15] By any consideration, Shanghai trade with Ningbo did not develop into what one would have ordinarily expected, given the longtime relationship that existed between the two cities and the relative proximity of the two ports (just about one hundred nautical miles). When the Japanese seized Ningbo outright in April 1941, trade slowed to a trickle. Ocean-going commercial vessels rarely visited the port; then in early 1945, the Allied bombing campaign provided the coup de grâce to any Shanghai-Ningbo trade.

Destroying Roads and Railroads

The Japanese launched their Zhe-Gan campaign in May 1942, leaving a path of destruction to the southwest into Jiangxi. The campaign posed an acute emergency for the provincial government in Yongkang County. On May 17, Governor Huang ordered that the whole government be moved beginning that very day. He also ordered that after all ministries and their bureaucrats were out of the area, the highway from Yongkang to Jinyun to Lishui was to be destroyed: after that, there would be no roads and no use of cars, an example of the Chinese "cutting off your nose to spite your face" scorched-earth policy. In the same vein, in July

1939 the commander of the Third Wartime Regional District, Gu Zhutong, ordered that the whole public highway connecting Longquan, in the province's far southwest, to the temporary capital of Yongkang be completely destroyed to prevent its use by the Japanese.[16]

Though much of the southwestern part of the province had no roads, much less highways, Lishui was connected by highway to Wenzhou (in Yongjia County) to the southeast and to Longquan and Songyang counties to the west and southwest. But in the winter of 1938, after the first months of war, the Chinese government, desperate to stop the Japanese onslaught, ordered all the highways leading to Lishui to be destroyed. This resort to scorched-earth policy was, it turns out, completely self-defeating. As a result, moving goods and commodities to and from Lishui became totally dependent on the Ou River, in many places shallow, rocky, and difficult to navigate.

In central Zhejiang during the 1942 Zhe-Gan campaign, sixty-two thousand workers were requisitioned to destroy railroad tracks, highways, and even small mountain and village roads in a frantic and futile effort to stop the Japanese.[17] As with all the "logic" of such scorched-earth efforts, this strategy seems almost obscenely self-defeating. The Japanese had already made the Zhe-Gan railroad inoperable when they blew up its railroad bridges; what was the logic that called for using forced labor to add to the destruction by literally ripping the tracks out of the earth? The destruction of the highways, like the destruction of the Qiantang Bridge, obliterated the most successful provincial government reconstruction efforts of the 1930s. Governor Huang seemed to treat the highway destruction incredibly nonchalantly, noting that of the 3,717 kilometers of highways constructed in the province before the war, only 759 kilometers were destroyed under Chinese government order.[18] Yet that figure represents over 20 percent of the total purposefully destroyed. Such questionable self-destruction seems to suggest not only panic but, more importantly, a tragic loss of perspective and sense of reality on the part of both the military and civil authorities.

The Quzhou Air Base

If the previous scorched-earth strategies have touched on the absurd, the story of the Quzhou air base is one of scorched-earth policy carried to the extreme. If this episode were comedy, it would be seen as unbelievable farce; but since it was tragedy, it must be seen as almost incredible disaster.

Chinese national authorities knew from the outbreak of war that the airfield at the suburb of Guanqiao outside Hangzhou would be a target for attack. It was one of China's most important air bases; it was also, in the words of Governor Huang Shaohong, the cradle *(yaolan)* of the air force, being the site of both the Central Aviation School and the Defense Air School. On the afternoon of August 14, 1937, thirteen Japanese planes flying from Taibei bombed the air base; another raid followed the next day. When it was plainly evident that the air force central command could not remain at Guanqiao, it moved to Quzhou in November (see Map 9).[19] The Quzhou air base, about three miles southeast of the city, thus replaced Guanqiao as the main provincial air base. The tragic story of this base reveals some possible reasons for disaffection with the Guomindang regime. Though this time the focus of the scorched-earth policy was on the military, the historical record of the base and the war at Qu City evidences patterns of mobilizing the populace—forerunners of the great mobilizations of the People's Republic—that showed a leadership callous to the needs of its people and all too ready to destroy its own infrastructure, almost in automatic reflex in the name of stopping the Japanese.

The Quzhou air base was planned beginning in 1933 with the advice of Colonel Zhang Guodong, a teacher at the Central Aviation School. The site of the base was on a broad plain of fertile cropland that had originated in silt from the Xin'an and Dongji rivers, on either side of the site. To construct the base meant dislocating all resident farmers out of this productive agricultural area, seizing their land, and destroying their dwellings. The initial step for construction was digging drainage ditches to prevent water collection on the level plain.[20] In 1934, the decision was made to enlarge the original field by 75 percent. From the beginning of the project, workers in the thousands were commandeered. The base was not completed until 1936.

Even before the decision that Quzhou would become a substitute for Guanqiao, the Quzhou base had become a crucial center for the war effort in China's southeast. Its location at the gateway to four provinces meant continual comings and goings of officers and troops. The ordnance corps took the area as a base for storing ammunition, supplies, aviation equipment, gasoline, and vehicles. But much work had to be done to firm up the runways and make the field usable for large numbers of planes. Using requisitioned labor, the construction entailed digging to a depth of five feet, filling the space with three layers of stone (the top layer of the three being crushed stone), and then covering the stone layers with sandy soil. In January 1938, the command ordered additional extensions of the southwest and northeast corners of the field (two hundred meters long and seventy meters wide) to allow for more taxiing room; the expansion was completed in July 1938. It was during this work that the first Japanese bombing of the airfield occurred, resulting in more than fifty worker casualties.[21] This expansion itself necessitated moving the Quzhou–Lanxi highway five hundred meters north of its previous route. Also, because the military wanted space around the airfield cleared for purposes of defense and safety from sabotage, all villages for a little over two miles east and west had to be destroyed, and farmers were forced to contribute their land, some of the most fertile in the county. The most recent gazetteer likely does not reveal the considerable upset and perhaps resistance that military demands stimulated; it not very compellingly rationalizes with a patriotic spin: "The residents in the vicinity of the airfield destroyed their homes and contributed the land; their action illustrates the determination of all the people to resist."[22] (It's not likely such a charitable reaction came from those who thus lost their source of livelihood.) A month after the completion of the expanded field, Quzhou became the Thirteenth Air Force Headquarters (zhan), directing air force actions in Zhejiang, Jiangxi, and Anhui.[23]

In February 1940, after seizing Xiaoshan County, the Japanese momentarily pressed toward the market town of Linpu on the Zhe–Gan railroad. There is no evidence that the Chinese military leadership had any credible intelligence about Japanese intentions; but on the possibility that the Japanese might be readying a drive to the south, those in command took what must be seen as precipitous action by ordering the destruction of the Quzhou air base, to preclude its being used by the Japanese. Over seven thousand workers were requisitioned to dig crisscrossing ditches of several thousand meters across the airfield in the dead of night and to destroy adjacent bridges and buildings. Oil reserves were also removed and hidden to preclude their being blown up by the enemy.[24] When, after a few days, the Japanese stopped their move to the south, destruction of the base was halted. As did the destruction of the Qiantang Bridge, this incapacitation of the air base by the Chinese inflicted considerable damage on themselves and what had been the beginnings of an increasingly modernized economic infrastructure. It also nullified the man-hours of forced labor already spent on the project.

What workers destroyed they then had to reconstruct, for the Chinese use of the airfield was imperative. All ditches had to be filled, bridges and buildings rebuilt, and access roads for about three miles around the field reconstructed to be used as escape routes during air raids; along these routes the workers built large thatched structures—simulated dwellings—to camouflage parked airplanes. At the time of the reconstruction of the base, electric lines were hung to the north and south of the field and surveillance towers erected. Fifteen thousand workers were requisitioned for the task.

In mid-1941, following the fall of Shaoxing and Ningbo, the Military Affair Bureau decided that it was crucial for Zhedong's future that the Quzhou airfield be further expanded. Not long after Pearl Harbor the commander of the Third Wartime Region, Gu Zhutong, and the vice-commander and provincial chair, Huang Shaohong, called a meeting of the fifth adminstrative inspector and the magistrates of counties in that inspectorate (the old Quzhou prefecture).[25] The meeting's central objective was to discuss the expansion of the air base: the goal was for the facility to be capable of accommodating fifty American bombers. Gu announced that he wanted it completed within six months. To go beyond that time limit, he argued, would be damaging to military operations; to put force behind his orders, he promised that punishment would be meted out to leaders who fell behind. There was general consternation among the magistrates, who feared that the time was too short even to allow for gathering and transporting of the construction materials themselves, much less for constructing the base itself. Gu made it clear that the military plans had been made and that they were not going to be changed. Governor Huang tried to put the task in military perspective: "We bear local responsibility; naturally it's difficult. But compared to the role of the soldiers, our role is much less dangerous. When military officers order anything, we must do it—even if it becomes our bloody sacrifice. This is our solemn responsibility."[26] The onerous and bloody sacrifice would not, of course, become that of the decision makers but of those who were compelled to complete what, in effect, became a forced march.

The officials decided on the amount of materials needed for this large construction job, which, like the labor, would be requisitioned from the populace: the people were ordered to cut down 3.6 million fir trees, which each had to be at least twenty centimeters in diameter (a total of about 500,000 square meters of wood) and 900,000 bamboo timbers.[27] The populace was then required to transport them to the Quzhou air base. The huge amount of these materials (the exact purposes for which are not described in sources) could not, obviously, be supplied by Qu County alone but had to be gathered in surrounding counties: Suian, Chun'an, Jiande, and Tonglu counties to the north; Wuyi, Yongkang, and Jinyun counties to the east; Suichang and Songyang counties to the south; and Jiangshan, Changshan, and Kaihua counties to the west (see Map 2). It was to determine an allotment per county (the final method of allotment is not given). But perhaps the most difficult problem was transporting the timbers to the area of Qu City and the air base. Some contiguous counties could use waterways, but other counties were over two hundred kilometers away so that logs and timbers had to be carried some distance overland.

Wang Guangsheng of Suian County provides details on the specifics of what was referred to as this "wood tax." All males, 18 to 60, were ordered to participate, each required to move at least thirty kilograms of wood, most on their own backs. If men in this age range were incapacitated, they were required to hire someone else to do the job. Suian County used township and baojia units to organize the effort, which involved eighty thousand men. Different areas of the county, grouped according to townships, were routed differently to Quzhou, one transporting the wood completely overland and three others on rivers. Transportation was thus dissimilar, depending on the embarkation point. In this area, where there were really no roads and no vehicles, the men had to depend on their own legs and backs. The transport had to be completed in one month.[28]

The requisition came at the Lunar New Year, when that year snow blocked many of the mountain roads. It fell to each county to mobilize all its able-bodied men to go to the mountains to cut and transport the wood—a total of up to a million or more men braved wind, mountain heights, and mountain snow. Some magistrates and Guomindang leaders participated in the treks through deep snow and treacherous mud; believing that the masses must be aroused by those in charge, the magistrate of Shouchang County, for example, actively participated; but he fell while carrying timber and was seriously injured. Casualties of the cold, of falling, even of drowning were reported daily. The Suian County narrator commenting on this "wood tax" reported that men in at least his "detachment" carried cornmeal with them, drank unboiled water, and slept out in the open in "grass nests." How this bedding worked in areas of deep snow, one can hardly imagine. He wrote that carrying the timbers had rubbed raw or broken open skin so that the men had to bear heavy injuries. Clothes were torn, with no way to mend or replace them—in order to provide cover from more injury or offer warmth in the frigid winter weather. Some men's straw sandals broke, so having to go without shoes left their feet bloody and swollen.[29] The demands of the state at this time of war amounted in many cases to personal torture.

But within a month, the total had almost miraculously arrived in the vicinity of the county seat. At that point, inspectors were punctilious about the timbers' having the required diameter; smaller trees had to be joined together to form a unit; thus, in the end, the total numbers of separate timbers even had to exceed what was requisitioned. It is no surprise that the years 1940 to 1943 saw a substantial deforestation of the area.[30] We are not told of the requisitioning of other materials, especially stone, that would have been needed for the construction effort and that would only have been more onerous to transport.

About thirty engineers (at least some of them with experience in highway construction) from the Qu district Engineering Office directed the construction. In addition, about three hundred Southwest University students were brought in to become work supervisors. Work was organized in military-style units, with each county's magistrate serving as battalion commander, township and town heads serving as regiment commanders, and village heads taking the title of detachment commanders. Workers in these units were drafted per county on the basis of the county's number of able-bodied men; the construction force generally totaled twenty to forty thousand; but at peak times there were over forty thousand. There were no provisions for living quarters or sanitary conditions. The conscripted workers were completely on their own.

They had to carry their own provisions and cooking utensils and cook their own food. They worked around the clock, at night by the light of torches and lanterns. There was no heavy equipment to press the crushed stone to tamp down the runways. The workers had to maneuver heavy lead pipes weighing tons to do the job.[31] The construction tasks extended to the construction around the air base as well: various structures—command posts, offices, weather and communications towers, dormitories, bathhouses, and infirmaries, air-raid shelters, trenches, and moats—were built from the area around the field to a distance of over eight miles in all directions for the army's Sixty-seventh Division, whose task it was to guard the base. Governor Huang Shaohong years later noted how this construction work under government direction caused untold suffering for the Qu County and City residents and how the small pittance that they received for their backbreaking and, for some, life-sacrificing work should have been at minimum twenty times more.[32]

Almost from the beginning of the construction, the Japanese knew of the expansion and began bombing. Out in the open and with little protection nearby, many workers were killed and wounded. They ran pell-mell whenever the Japanese planes appeared, workers scattering into ditches and, if possible, under trees on the edges of the field. In one raid over forty of fifty workers seeking shelter in a ditch were killed in a direct hit. Then the Japanese began night bombing. The raids were always disruptive of the work, and the resulting bomb craters only created new work. Thus, although there were many workers, the construction went painfully slowly.

The Zhe-Gan Campaign

The Doolittle Raid enraged the Japanese. Even before it, they were aware of the potential that air bases in eastern China had for strikes against the Japanese islands. Now the Japanese felt compelled to act. The drama of the Quzhou air base was beginning its denouement. The forced construction had continued in the wake of Doolittle's raid, despite Japanese bombing attacks. Qian Nanxin, engineer with the Base Construction Office, had the specific task of ascertaining damage to the runways within fifteen minutes after bombing raids and reporting the information to Chongqing. He noted that everyone involved in the construction went on a war footing, adding a new effort of fighting the fires ignited by incendiary bombs. The first massive raid had seen wave after wave of Japanese planes, the first a low-flying reconnaissance of runways and access roads, followed by planes spraying machine-gun fire and firebombing buildings in the nearby woods and around the airfield's base. In Qian's description, the area was a sea of fire from which people ran helter-skelter into likely death from the machine-gun fire of continuing waves of bombers. Quzhou and the air base were, of course, not the only target: the Japanese successfully bombed key bridges on the Zhe–Gan Railroad line and sites in Zhuji, Jinhua, and Jiangshan counties.

The commander of the air force's Thirteenth Headquarters, Chen Youzhao, called an officers' meeting after the middle of May to discuss options. The officers decided that the army would continue to protect the air base and that the air force command would continue takeoffs and landings. If the time came, however, when there was no way to protect the base, then Chen would fly to Lishui, important aviation equipment would be rushed away lest it fall into Japanese hands, and a scorched-earth policy would be instituted on the base and its perimeter.

On May 27, the commander of the Third Wartime Region, Gu Zhutong, who had less than six months earlier given the ultimatum to complete the base's construction in six months, in a gut-wrenching déjà-vu of early 1940, ordered its destruction. In the morning twenty thousand workers were repairing and expanding the runways, filling in bomb craters; in the afternoon came the orders to destroy the base within three days. Almost a thousand more workers, including old men and women, were commandeered to help in the destruction, once more digging crisscrossing ditches across the runways. A corps of military engineers then dotted the runways with land mines.[33] Within three days and nights, it was all destroyed—all the labor of the mammoth mobilization for tree and bamboo cutting and transporting, for the laying and smoothing of the runways, for the collateral construction to establish the support for the Sixty-seventh Division, whose central role was to defend the airfield at all cost, now all destroyed by the Chinese to keep it out of possible Japanese use. Nullified also were the many lives that had been given to build and protect the base. The panic of this scorched-earth approach seems somewhat irrational: the Japanese themselves were destroying the

base. The Japanese had other air bases that they could use more effectively than the Quzhou field, on which they had already inflicted so
much damage. What was the logic that necessitated forced labor, with
many being killed in the process, to help the Japanese destroy the base?

It became Engineer Qian's task to prepare the equipment and materials for evacuation. Those in the air force and the military police had
already fled with weapons and ammunition. Qian was inexplicably left
without military or government support (yet another indication of the
panic of the military leadership)—left, in other words, to his own devices. Qian had known of an old man whose extended family had eight
ferry and fishing boats and who knew well the lay of the river and was
willing to take public goods upstream to the Jiangshan river port of
Xiakou. There were three other households living on the water who
were also willing to shoulder the responsibility. Eighteen boats lined
end to end made the journey upstream, during the day motionless
along the riverbank and camouflaged by trees to avoid Japanese bombers and at night towed forward from along the bank. Because of the
shallowness of the water and the shoals, the advance was very slow.
Once they reached Xiakou, the goods were taken by timber carts to the
Jian'ou Air Base in Fujian.[34]

The Chinese military had touted the battle for Qu County as the decisive battle of the campaign. But when the time came, the problems
brutally evident in the construction, destruction, reconstruction, destruction, and abandonment of the air base seem magnified: poor judgment,
lack of vision and perspective, disregard for human life, and lack of reso-
luteness. The collapse of Qu City was a study not only in Japanese airpower (including the use of poison gas) and its withering artillery attacks
but also in the panic and callousness of the Chinese military leadership.

On June 1, the Sixteenth Division of the Eighty-sixth Corps, defending
Qu City to the north, was attacked; officers and soldiers fled to the city.
The division commander, Mo Yushuo, fled from the battle on his own—
followed by much of his army in chaos—toward Jiangshan County. Attacking on five routes, Japanese forces—using five divisions and three
mixed brigades (about fifty thousand soldiers)—soon had Qu City half-
surrounded. On June 3, the Third Wartime Region commander decided
to prevent Qu County from becoming a battleground: two weeks and
two days after naming the county "the site" of the decisive battle, Chinese

military forces were ordered to withdraw, allegedly luring the enemy even deeper into the hinterland in hopes of dealing with different Japanese units separately. It was an admission that staking all on a defense to the death in Qu County was a mistake, that the Japanese forces were simply too powerful to have all their military forces concentrated on one target.

On the morning of June 7, the Japanese began their eighty-four day occupation of Qu City. One of their first actions was to send seven thousand captured Chinese soldiers to the air base to clear it of land mines and to fill in the ditches. Thousands of others were sent to repair roads and bridges damaged or destroyed by both Chinese and Japanese. The air base was repaired within several days for Japanese use. At the end of August, when the Japanese began their retreat, as might be expected, they gathered about ten thousand workers to destroy the air base yet another time, enemies aping the same scorched-earth game previously played by the Chinese. The workers labored under whip and threat of bayonet, later describing this last forced destruction of the airfield as especially bloody: Japanese military supervisors, aware that they were retreating, wantonly attacked Chinese workers and soldiers with bayonets and hoes. It was mercifully the death of the air base; although there was reportedly discussion in 1944 of repairing it, those in authority dared not initiate more forced labor for the ill-fated field.[35] Its reconstruction would wait until the early 1950s.

All varieties of scorched earth are self-inflicted wounds. One of the most infamous scorched-earth episodes in modern history, the burning of Moscow during Napoleon's 1812 Russian campaign, not only deprived Napoleon of the campaign's prize but left several hundred thousand Moscow residents homeless in a bitterly freezing winter.[36]

The human costs of the scorched-earth episodes described in this chapter were highest in the air base tragedy, but for the nation and the people directly affected, all such episodes were costly. As indirect resistance strategies, scorched-earth actions were put into operation in calculated, controlled ways. In the case of the blowing up of the Zhakou Power Plant, we have the only example in these accounts of a Chinese man trying to keep the bigger picture in mind, asking how long the destruction would actually derail Japanese plans or hold them back and who would, in the end, be hurt. In the case of the Qiantang River Bridge, even of the destruction of the ferry wharf, civilian leadership recognized the likely difficulty of postwar reconstruction and cautioned limiting the destruction; even though the military doubled the recommended number of piers destroyed, it still limited the bombing. But Chinese military units, apparently following the "logic" of their military superiors, continued the destruction of the bridge, striking well into 1945.

Using tactics that had traditionally been followed in wartime, the Ningbo blockade was a following of orders to defend against Japanese incursions. But the willful destruction of highways, roads, and railroad track and the horrific tragedy of the Quzhou air base in early 1940 seem to be scorched-earth policies that were irrational from the start. The air base's destruction before the 1942 Japanese campaign, in contrast, seems based in rational concern about how Japanese would use the base should they seize it. But in all these cases, the supposed calculated restraint of scorched earth gave way to destruction greater than had been envisioned or that may have been rationally necessary. No only were more bridge piers destroyed than were called for, but the entrance to Zhenhai Harbor was blocked with far more ships than necessary; and the degree of destruction of air base, railroad track, and highways seems wildly excessive. And in the end, the strategy did not dissuade the Japanese; it only slowed down their conquest, impeded their actions, and perhaps increased the ferocity of their terrorism.

Part of the reason for the excessive destruction in the case of the air base, railroad, and highways in 1942 may well have been the great fear through which the Japanese were perceived. By this time, the Japanese had used poison gas and biological warfare against Zhejiangese. What seems such excessive overreaction may stem in part from the irrationality of war and decision making—when the immediate danger overwhelmed the Chinese with a panicked fear that demanded the destruction of anything that the Japanese might use—and that further demanded destruction to the greatest extent possible.

In the cases of the bridge, air base, railroad, and highways, the self-inflicted wounds meant the destruction of many of the Nanjing decade's infrastructural accomplishments relating to the modernization of transportation and communications; these wounds also meant the consequent necessary costs of rebuilding this infrastructure in the postwar world. Perhaps an even more significant wound was the self-inflicted damage that Guomindang scorched-earth decisions likely made on its reputation for decision making and for the treatment of its citizens. While in the war's aftermath Governor Huang Shaohong could note how policies regarding the air base caused immense suffering for the people in the Quzhou area, the story of decision making and the use of the population for forced labor in the air base tragedy showed the Guomindang government to be seemingly unmindful of the lives and interests of the population, whose support it would need after the war.

><

ELEVEN

Trading and Smuggling

LIKE THE WARTIME DISPLACEMENT of business and industry into the poverty-ridden periphery, the wartime economic trading system was itself turned on its head. With the Japanese seizure of non–Settlement Shanghai in November 1937 and the conquest of Hangzhou and northern Zhejiang by December 24, the transport of commodities between Zhejiang (and indeed the interior of China) and Shanghai was seemingly cut off. The ensuing Japanese coastal blockade, the Japanese closure of the Yangzi to third-country shipping, Japanese control of railroads leading out from Shanghai, and the general decline in overland transport—all suggest that one analyst's judgment was, on its face, on target: "To speak of trade in the war years is really like trying to find snow in midsummer."[1]

When the termini of the Hankou–Guangzhou Railroad fell into Japanese hands in August 1938, the east coast of Zhejiang, not yet seized by Japan, emerged as the main passageway into and out of the networks of rivers and streams of the interior provinces. And until the Ningbo defense commissioner shot Ningbo in both commercial feet, and perhaps its head as well, beginning in 1938 with his scorched-earth blocking of the Yong River, that city and Wenzhou initially emerged as the most important entrepôts linking Shanghai to inner China. The years 1937 and 1938 were good ones for both ports.

In many ways the Japanese blockade was fairly easy to circumvent. In order to participate in the coastal trade, Chinese shipping lines sought reregistry for their ships at consular offices in Shanghai. It was a strategy to keep in place the prewar system. Able then to fly a foreign flag, the ships would have some presumed immunity from seizure and detention by the Japanese navy. Foreign companies drove hard bargains to make the reregistry as lucrative as possible. Though a fee of 20 percent in tonnage may have been a general standard, reportedly if a Chinese owner was "in a poor bargaining position," he sometimes had to agree to a 65 to 70 percent share.[2] Reregistry had to be negotiated ship by ship; it did not cover all the ships of the firm. For example, the Lian'an Shipping Company, based in the port of Haimen in Huangyan County, had four steamships involved in the Shanghai trade. Two flew German flags; one, Portuguese; and the last, Greek.[3]

In 1939 the thirty reregistered Chinese ships plying the waters between Shanghai and Ningbo flew the flags of England, the United States, Germany, Italy, and Norway; the Wenzhou route, in addition, included ships with the flags of Portugal, Belgium, Hungary, and Greece. Reregistered Chinese ships, both passenger and freight steamers, were from Shanghai and Zhejiang firms.[4] One of the ships that sailed to both ports serves as an example. In 1939 two powerful figures in Shanghai's Ningbo clique *(bang)*, Yu Xiaqing and Yuan Ludeng, made a deal with the German firm Carlowitz and Company to reregister with the German consulate the *New Ning-Shao*, a ship belonging to the Chinese Ning-Shao Shipping Company. We do not know the specific tonnage share demanded by Carlowitz, but in its German incarnation, the 1,538-ton freight and passenger ship was known as the *Mohlenhoff* (in Chinese, *Moufu*).[5] How many trips the *Mohlenhoff* made during the six years of its German identity is not known; but if that identity gave the *New Ning-Shao* continued life as a participant in the lucrative trade, it eventually destroyed it: flying its German flags, it was bombed by Allied planes shortly before the Japanese surrender, the ship's casualties numbering between six and seven hundred.

Control of shipping at ports in Zhejiang and Fujian lay in the hands of the Customs Office and the Shipping Administration and Management Office *(chuanzheng banshiqu)*, both of which had been administratively subordinate to the respective offices in Shanghai before the war began.[6] During the war's first year, a customs clearance was sufficient for Chinese and foreign ships to leave ports; but after October 1938, ships also had to have a shipping certificate from the Administration and Management Office. The military, responsible for each port's defense and security, frequently inserted itself into the administration of the port's shipping, in effect placing itself over the two government offices. According to regulations in the fall of 1938, if the Military Affairs Office deemed a situation "a military emergency," the office could prohibit shipping. It could also order various techniques to block river and harbor channels in order to forestall Japanese entrance—and in the process that of trading vessels as well. After Ningbo fell to the Japanese in April 1941, military authorities at Wenzhou tightened control further: ships could not obtain the shipping certificate until they had received military clearance. This extra bureaucratic hurdle was often an occasion for military extortion. In January 1941, for example, the steamer *Minhe,* flying a Portuguese flag, had cleared customs; but its Chinese owner was unable to come up with the cash demanded by the Wen-Tai (Wenzhou-Taizhou) Defense Command. He was arrested without other cause. The Portuguese consul in Shanghai telegraphed the Ouhai customs commissioner at Wenzhou for assistance, but he was powerless in the situation. The ship was detained for seventeen months, after which time it was sunk in a Japanese bombing attack.[7] It is clear indeed that the military context for trade was, on its face, not conducive to a thriving commerce, even if a trader could manipulate the system.

The difficulties of trade and indeed the rigors of any intercourse between the ports is best shown by the procedures required to get permission from the Japanese military to leave one port and enter the other. Generally, those seeking to go to Shanghai or to leave Shanghai for Ningbo and Wenzhou or smaller ports were small traders, the so-called traveling merchant *(danbangke).* One needed approval from one's *baojia* head; a validated card with a photograph; evidence of a guarantee from a merchant company; evidence of smallpox vaccination and an epidemic prevention form; and a certificate for travel, forthcoming only after payment of an "action" fee. Similar regulations were in effect for land travel. Customs and tax collectors, set up at various points on the major roads, extorted whatever they could; a common technique was for the collectors to collude with peddlers who would seek bribes (called a "convenience fee") from the merchant to lower customs and other taxes; payment would entitle the merchant to go smoothly through each toll post. Having to face these hurdles paled in the face of other possibilities—having one's goods confiscated or perhaps being beaten by the Japanese military.[8]

By any consideration, then, the Shanghai trade with Zhejiang ports did not develop into what one would have ordinarily expected, especially given the longtime relationship that existed between Shanghai and Ningbo and the relative proximity of the two ports (just about one hundred nautical miles). After the blocking of the Yong River and the inordinate delays in off-loading ships, alternative—though much slower—trade routes were developed to get goods to Ningbo. The most important, a Shanghai-to-Shipu (Xiangshan County) route began to be used around September 1940 (see Map 7). Foreign ships and over twenty Chinese ships flying German, Italian, and United States flags participated in the trade, their most important cargo being bolts of cotton cloth and medicines for the Guomindang military; the ships also carried two to three hundred passengers per trip. Bamboo was a common cargo for the return trip to Shanghai. Shipu had a history as a significant entrepôt, and it is no doubt because of this new route and the consequent flurry of commercial activity that the Zhejiang provincial government established there in 1940 a customs station, tax office, ship and transport management office, and ship inspection office. During the year and a half before its capture by the Japanese navy, at least seven ships a day were inspected by customs agents in the harbor.[9] After unloading, the ship's cargo would be reloaded on steam launches and sailboats to be transported to Sizhoutou, carried by porter to Xizhou, reloaded on boats to cross Xiangshan Bay, and then carted via overland routes to Ningbo—a time-consuming and laborious process, one that simply underscores the frustrating and costly situation at Ningbo.

The other alternate routes were less used for large volumes of cargo but were important for passenger traffic. Three embarked from Shanghai for points in the Zhoushan Archipelago, and two other routes crossed Hangzhou Bay, with passengers and goods coming to Ningbo from the west. This development of alternate trade routes, all stemming from the Ningbo fiasco, points most obviously to the initiative, determination, and ingenuity of merchants involved in the Shanghai-to-Ningbo trade. The alternate routes brought in considerable numbers of passengers and some vital cargo that might otherwise not have reached Ningbo. The routes were ad hoc, with some being used sporadically and with segments of routes often changing or being abandoned for others. The routes entailed many risks: sea travel on small boats, overland travel in occupied areas, commodities that might be stolen or commandeered in commodity-poor regions, and the ever-present threat of the Japanese.

While trade with Ningbo was reduced to smuggling after mid-1939 on alternative trade routes spawned by the river-blockage debacle, when the Japanese seized Ningbo in April 1941, trade generally ground to a halt. The Japanese took over the management of the China Merchants Steamship Navigation Company and the British China Steamship Navigation Company by establishing the East Asian Maritime Joint-Stock Company *(Toa kaiun kabushiki kaisha)*. Together with the Nanjing government-controlled China Steamship Company, the ships of the new company plied the waters between Shanghai and Ningbo after August 1941. But the company's main cargo was war hardware. In the beginning of the Ningbo occupation, those ships originally flying foreign flags briefly revived their business; but when the Pacific War began, the Japanese commandeered most ships for military use. Ningbo shippers did organize their own East Zhejiang Steamship Company after the Pacific War began, the company buying two ships to participate in the little trade that was possible with Shanghai and to offer passenger service. After December 1941, ocean-going commercial vessels rarely visited Ningbo Harbor; in early 1945 the Allied bombing campaign provided the coup de grâce to the wartime Shanghai-Ningbo trade.

Wenzhou and the New Passageway to China's Interior

Wenzhou enjoyed marked economic prosperity in the fifteen months beginning in January 1938, a prosperity that stemmed in large part from its trade with Shanghai. Indeed, in 1938 Wenzhou experienced its greatest volume of trade before 1949; the total value in 1938 of imports and exports was 56,203,653 yuan, over four and a half times the 12,373,045 yuan in 1937.[10] A number of factors favored Wenzhou over Ningbo, despite the fact that Wenzhou was 320 nautical miles from Shanghai, over three times Ningbo's distance. Because of Wenzhou's relatively backward commercial and economic situation and its undeveloped transportation routes into the interior, the Japanese did not pay Wenzhou the attention it showed Ningbo and failed to maintain a very tight blockade of the area. In addition, from the Japanese perspective, the mountainous backdrop of Wenzhou and the large number of shifting sandbars in its vicinity made it a daunting potential landing or invasion site.[11]

Its geographical location far in the south of the province meant that Wenzhou was more oriented to Fuzhou and Xiamen in Fujian Province, Shantou in Guangdong Province, and Hong Kong than to Shanghai. Nevertheless, Shanghai was Wenzhou's most important trading partner during the war years. Seventy foreign-registered Chinese ships sailed between Shanghai and Wenzhou, as compared with the thirty participating in the Ningbo trade. Most of Wenzhou's 9,887 arriving ship passengers in 1939 came from Shanghai. Wenzhou exports to Shanghai included tong oil, tea, fresh shrimp, charcoal, wool, paper parasols, and lard. Among the city's imports were cotton yarn, woolen goods, cigarettes, rubber shoes, glass, and medicines, items all needed in China's interior.[12]

The realities of war impinged on Wenzhou's commercial traffic in April 1939, when Japan bombed the strategic point in the city's import-export trade, the East Gate docks, also the site of important warehouses. Japanese decision makers had obviously become concerned about Wenzhou's increasingly important role as the chief supply channel to Zhejiang and the interior provinces. As a result of the bombing, the number of foreign or foreign-registered ships entering the harbor fell significantly. In June the Japanese announced that Wenzhou would be treated as a military target and that they would tightly blockade the Ou River, Wenzhou's main artery into the interior. Specifically, they ordered that all boats leave the harbor by a certain date, after which they (apparently taking a note from the page of the Ningbo defense commissioner) would sink about thirty large and small boats at the mouth of the harbor, to block entry. They did so.

For several months no ships came to the port, but beginning in September 1939, the Chinese established another shipping channel, in currents on the far north side of the river's mouth. As a result, thirty-four ships came to the port in the last third of the year. On the whole, the tonnage of steamships from Hong Kong and Chinese ports was 37.5 percent less in 1939 than a year earlier, but Wenzhou's trade was gradually restored. During the first half of 1940, when the Japanese relaxed their blockade, thirty to forty ships visited the port each month. But the vagaries of war again slowed the trade. Continuing its on-again, off-again blockade pattern, the Japanese retightened the blockade in mid-July and applied pressure on the Shanghai Customs Office to refuse clearance to ships bound for ports along Zhejiang's east coast. After this, only a few large steamships came to Wenzhou; and the number of small steamers ranged only between one and eight per month. Tonnage of steamships from Hong Kong and Chinese ports was dramatically less in 1940 than in 1939.[13] Japan's first seizure of Wenzhou lasted from April 19 to May 1, 1941; though short-lived, the seizure seemed to inflict more damage on the shipping trade; from that point, at most a ship a month came to the port. Tonnage from Hong Kong and Chinese ports in 1941 was only 3.5 percent of what it had been in 1938. With the coming of the Pacific War, steamship traffic stopped completely.

Smuggling

And yet, despite the official figures, Wenzhou remained the crucial passageway into the interior until its most lengthy period of Japanese occupation began much later in September 1944. The commodities that passed through Wenzhou and enabled it to remain such an important wartime entrepôt were smuggled in, in well-developed maritime, coastal, and interior networks. Smuggling had been an activity endemic to this area well before the bombing of 1939, even though the Ouhai Customs Office had a reputation for its strict control.[14] As soon as the Guomindang government raised the tariff after regaining tariff autonomy in 1929, serious smuggling began. Smugglers based on islands off the coast near Wenzhou sailed up the coast to deal in such items as sugar, kerosene, cigarettes, and matches. In 1931 the Guomindang government added shipping regulations for small steamers and junks, to deter smuggling, and yet it is clear that the military and police connived in and participated directly in prewar smuggling. In June 1932, for instance, Ouhai customs agents seized a white-sugar-laden Taiwan junk that was being escorted by four customs agents and six maritime police officers.[15]

Smuggling often bred social violence. In the early 1930s, a local strongman, who headed a smuggling gang disguised as a local militia unit, directed his gang to seize his own detained smuggling boat from customs agents. In the ensuing fracas, two maritime police officers were killed, but the smugglers regained control of the contraband. The

Shanghai Customs Office, which dispatched agents to handle the case, did not bring about any satisfactory settlement. Following the episode, the Ouhai Customs Office assigned antismuggling surveillance boats and recruited customs police to support antismuggling efforts. On the eve of the war, there was one naval vessel patrolling the mouth of the Ou River and another patrolling the river itself. In the winter of 1937, these two ships steamed to Shanghai for inspection and repairs; but they never returned. Instead, several small steamers, ineffectual in dealing with the rapid smuggling sailboats, took their place.[16]

With the coming of war, avoidance of customs was not the only stimulus for smuggling. Commodity controls and regulations instituted by both Chinese authorities and the Japanese military were legion and confusing; they were almost a smuggling invitation to a commodity-starved or profit-seeking populace. The Guomindang placed gradations of restrictions on commodities, prohibiting some while only limiting others, in a complicated system that led to misunderstandings and actually facilitated smuggling. For example, officials prohibited the transport and sale of Japanese goods and liquor, precious metals, currency, grain, and linen cloth but only placed limits on the sale of livestock, table salt, cigarettes, cosmetics, and sundry luxuries. Other regulations stipulated that certain commodities could be traded only through import and export companies; those exports included tong oil, tea, lumber and wood products, charcoal, tobacco, cotton, and silk, while specified imports were grain, kerosene, metals, electrical equipment, and medicines. Hampering the possibilities for individual merchants, regulations specified that merchants could not, on the basis of their own individual identifications, request import and export permits. From the Japanese side, there were also many regulations and commodity-regulating structures. There were, for example, "commodity transport permits" that were necessary for eighteen specific commodities to enter the Shanghai district. No more than two items (*ma*) of silk or woolen goods could be transported from one area to another, and no more than two ounces of cotton or woolen yarn and no more than a half a kilogram of salt or sugar. Japanese regulations also specified that tong oil, cotton, raw silk, and hog bristles or intestines could not be transported without a special dispensation.[17]

Because of such controls and prohibitions on both sides, commodity flows were impeded and supplies invariably short. Prices in Guomindang-controlled areas and those in occupied areas often were separated by a wide gap. Established merchants and new seekers of wealth seized opportunities to supply cheaper but scarce commodities in one area and make a huge profit. An increasing number of people became involved in smuggling as the numbers of commodity controls only continued to increase while the war continued. Some went to the point of organizing smuggling blocs; one historian estimates that by 1941 there were over seven hundred smuggling bases *(judian)*.[18] There is ample evidence that some smugglers, as before the war, colluded with the military, the police, government and party bureaucrats, deserted soldiers, and roving braves. It was known that military units stationed at Huanghua near the mouth of the Ou River were colluding with smugglers (see Map 7). Despite the night curfew, the military did nothing to stop the smuggled goods being loaded and unloaded at the docks.

The scope of smuggling along the Zhejiang coast became extraordinarily large. Even an official Guomindang newspaper recognized it: "For a while smuggling was rampant along the Zhejiang coast; there were not only public officials protecting it, but important people in authority were in the background."[19] Not only could smuggling return a great profit; but with the Japanese coastal blockade, it became the only way to provide interior China with some of the basic commodities that were in short supply. In addition to a market for the military materials needed by interior forces, there was the increased demand for commodities, a demand stimulated by the large number of refugees who had fled Japanese-controlled areas. Certainly some official protection of smuggling, and people of authority hovering "in the background" for this reason, came to be a matter of considered public policy—even as it flew in the face of official customs laws.

In the smuggling enterprise, wooden sailboats that had traditionally been important in Wenzhou's regional trade were the crucial vessels.[20] In 1938 the tonnage of wooden sailboats entering and leaving Wenzhou Harbor was 303,466, a figure only suggestive, since we do not have the tonnage of other years. The Japanese navy had forbidden the use of Chinese wooden sailboats, because they were small, quick, and difficult for the Japanese to patrol. Originally used mainly in rivers and streams, these boats began to emerge in coastal travel after the first bombing of the port in April 1939. Short hauls soon stretched to Shanghai and points in between. After the stricter application of the blockade in July 1940, these small sailboats became even more important.

Smugglers sought small fishing villages in harbors far from customs stations. There were four main smuggling routes in the coastal waters of such villages; two of these routes duplicated ones that had sprung up to supply Ningbo as early as 1939: the Shanghai–Zhapu–Andong route and the Shanghai–Shipu–Ningbo route. The end points of a third smuggling route were the Lu River towns of Chaiqiao and Chuanshan, about thirty kilometers from Ningbo; the route did not directly affect Ningbo but could be linked to some of the routes that branched off into the interior from it (see Map 6). Goods were smuggled by boat from these two towns to Dinghai's Cen Harbor and Xiushan Island or for transshipment to Shanghai. Until the fall of Xiaoshan County in January 1940, goods smuggled from Shanghai on this route were taken west from these towns through counties in former Ningbo and Shaoxing prefectures to the Zhejiang–Jiangxi Railroad.

Smuggling routes to Wenzhou were most significant for the commodity transport to central China. Amid the wooden sailboats that dominated the smuggling, a few foreign-registered ships participated. The British-registered *Yulin* plied the Shanghai–Wenzhou route from January to April 1940, carrying goods from various towns in Yuhuan County to Shanghai. U.S.- and Italian-registered steamers sailing from Wenzhou to Shanghai in the last half of 1940 dropped anchor off Lingkun Island in the mouth of the Ou River and, from waiting sailboats, loaded tong oil and hog bristles to deliver to Shanghai.

The most important smuggling route to Wenzhou went from Shanghai to the town of Shenjiamen on the southeastern part of Zhoushan Island and then on to Wenzhou. Originally a fishing town, Shenjiamen gradually became the commodity collection and dispersal center for both occupied and Guomindang-controlled areas. It was seized by Japan in June 1939; the island's Japanese garrison battalion of 1,200 men and an infantry regiment of 160 were based in the town, headquartered at a local temple until May 1944.[21] During those five years, the town continued to prosper as the main maritime entrepôt in the coastal smuggling trade. The seeming anomaly of a Japanese military colluding with smugglers who were carrying valuable commodities to the enemy can only be explained by the reality that the Japanese were receiving commodities that they needed as well. As an indication of the town's importance and close connection to occupied Shanghai, in February 1940 Shenjiamen's postal bureau was placed into the Shanghai postal district; it did not revert back to Zhejiang postal control until the end of the war.[22] The commercial role of Shenjiamen only increased in importance after December 1941. Sailboats carried smuggled goods from Guomindang-controlled areas to Shanghai and other occupied areas: tallow, tong and rapeseed oils, grains, metals, timber, tea, ramie, alum, leather, and hog bristles. The inclusion of grains in this trade points to the further collusion of Chinese with Japan, for Guomindang commodity regulations strictly prohibited the transport and sale of grains except by import and export companies. The return trip from Shanghai brought cotton and synthetic cloth goods, dyestuffs, Western medicine, ginseng, cigarette paper, tobacco, lubricating oil, and other items needed in the interior or by the Japanese.

Goods unloaded at Shenjiamen were placed into smaller boats, which sailed generally to small fishing villages on or near the coast: to Lingkun Island in the mouth of the Ou River, to Dongtou and Sanpan islands off the coast of Wenzhou, and to the towns of Kanmen on the southern coast of Yuhuan County and Chumen on the west coast of Yuhuan on Yueqing Bay (see Map 7). From these points the goods were again shipped, to subsidiary dispersal points on the mainland, from which, in a network of water routes, they were carried inland. These subsidiary sites were towns like Zhu'ao and Shuanglou in present day Sanmen County; Zhu'ao lies on the main road connecting Ningbo and Linhai, the old prefectural capital of Taizhou prefecture, while Shuanglou, farther in the interior, is on a stream.[23] Another important transshipment point, Qingshuibu in Yongjia County, was situated on a sizable stream, Nan Creek, a tributary of the Ou.[24] The villages of Qili and Huanghua were on the north bank of the Ou River, downstream from Wenzhou (see Map 7).[25]

In an effort to stem the tide of smuggling, Guomindang customs announced in July 1942 that, under threat of punishment, merchants on wooden sailboats trading with occupied areas first had to make connections with a customs office in the rear areas; the merchants would report to that office, which would arrange procedures by which they could sail. But the law was not enforced. Despite earlier prohibitions against the use of sailboats, the Japanese navy eventually relaxed restrictions on wooden sailboats and permitted them to sail if they went through Japanese regulatory procedures and flew a Japanese flag; however, the boats had to sail in routes that the Japanese set forth in the regulations. If they did not, they risked being burned and sunk by the Japanese navy. In addition, sailboats of shipping companies along the coast had to pay off the pirate chief who controlled the region along the coast of Taizhou. Payment of a sum of money would entitle the payer to the pirate chief's name card and free passage. An account of the town of Kanmen notes that piracy was rampant in the early 1940s, making even fishing, much less carrying valuable commodities, dangerous.[26] One source notes that, unhampered by the Japanese navy and coastal pirates, smuggling became even more rampant.[27]

Patterns of Trade in the Interior

The networks of smuggling routes that branched out from the original four routes into a multitude of land and water routes converged on the Ou River before it reached Lishui, the capital of the former Chuzhou prefecture and one of the important hubs of the water transport routes. The trade generally followed prerailroad water and land routes. From Lishui, goods were shipped on makeshift roads through Jinyun and Yongkang counties to Jinhua, on the Wu River, a major tributary of the Qiantang. Before it fell to the Japanese in May 1942, Jinhua had been the economic center of Guomindang Zhejiang. Jinhua was linked to Ningbo by mostly water routes. Goods, whether originating from Wenzhou and its network of smuggling bases or Ningbo and its network, were floated down the Wu to the Qiantang, where the city of Lanxi served as another dispersal point to eastern Jiangxi, western Fujian, southern Anhui, Hunan, Hubei, Sichuan, and counties under Japanese control in northern Zhejiang. Goods from southern Anhui and northern Zhejiang could travel down the Xin'an River, a branch of the Qiantang, or the Fuchun River, the northernmost portion of the Qiantang, to Lanxi, where—since the trade routes went both directions—they could either be dispersed to other provinces or to Wenzhou or Ningbo, and on to Shanghai.

To develop foreign trade from Shanghai, Zhejiang Province established sixteen Transport and Sales offices to export some of the commodities brought from the interior on water routes. The most important were tong oil and tea, though also targeted were silkworm cocoons, cotton, timber, charcoal, paper, oranges, chicken eggs, parasols, and grass hats. Tong oil and tea were transshipped to international markets from Shanghai. The course of the war made tong oil Wenzhou's most important export. After the Yangzi River and the Hankou–Guangzhou Railroad transport routes shut down, tong oil from Hunan and Sichuan was exported from Wenzhou. Tong oil was also produced in central Zhejiang counties. Those who purchased the unrefined oil transported it to Lanxi or Lishui. After it was refined and barreled, the Transport and Sales Office consigned it to a transport company to take the oil via inner water routes to Wenzhou, where the control of the freight was transferred to the China Plant Oil Products Factory, which managed the export. The oil was generally transported to either Shanghai or Hong Kong for shipment abroad. In 1938 Wenzhou exported almost three times its previous high amount of oil. Tea, in contrast, was first gathered from many transport routes in three collection sites based upon former prefectural groupings. The Yuyao county seat served as collection center for all sites in Ningbo, Shaoxing, and Taizhou prefectures. Early in the war, the tea collected there was sent to Ningbo for transshipment to Shanghai. Later, it had to be taken to Wenzhou for export. The intermediate collection point for tea from the prefectures of Jinhua, Quzhou, and Yanzhou was Jinhua; tea collected there was sent on to Wenzhou, which was also the collection point for Wenzhou and Chuzhou, and the transshipment site for Shanghai.

The interior trade routes were extraordinarily busy. From May to December 1939, for example, when these areas were still under Guomindang control, 349,533 boats were recorded as having entered and left the Fuchun, Cao-e, and Ou rivers—again, it is a difficult figure to evaluate, given the lack of other years' data and information on boat size, but on its face impressive. By 1944 the province had 288 transport companies, most having developed after the war began; all of Jinhua's 42 firms and all but one of Lishui's 42 companies had been established after 1938.[28] After the fall of Ningbo and Shaoxing in April 1941, all major maritime smuggling routes except the Shanghai–Shenjiamen–Wenzhou route were cut off. Wenzhou's importance loomed ever larger. But, like a worm growing back segments that had been cut off, new internal routes sprang up. With the rapid development of new internal trade routes, the Ouhai Customs Office established eighteen customs stations in interior counties, all but three at county seats. This system lasted little more than a year. In the summer of 1942 with Japan's seizure, if only temporary, of many counties along the trade routes, eleven customs stations fell into Japanese hands, while four reverted to Shangrao (Jiangxi) Customs. Only three customs stations in the interior—at Tonglu and Qu, along the Qiantang, and Chun'an, along the Xin'an River—remained. The fact that so many interior customs stations had been established to be controlled by the Ouhai Customs Office points again to the stunning significance of Wenzhou in internal trade.[29]

The maintenance of the Chun'an customs station reveals the two approaches of the Guomindang government to the issues of trade and smuggling (see Map 2). Dai Li , the head of the Guomindang secret services, used his various positions—head of the Smuggling Prevention Bureau and head of the Commodity Transport Control Office—as cover for his deep involvement in smuggling between Guomindang and occupied areas. In 1943 he joined Du Yuesheng in forming the Tongqi Company as one structure for smuggling, buying, and selling; they established a branch of this company at Chun'an, to make the county the transshipment center for smuggled goods.[30] The continued presence of the customs station at the smuggling center points to the Janus-faced Guomindang government, which was, in Lloyd Eastman's word, "ambivalent" about its policies with Japan.[31]

An Economic Boom

Sites along trade and smuggling routes—the beginning/end points (for all such routes, the beginning was also an end) and transshipment points in between—tended to become prosperous. For many localities that had been mired in poverty, the war years built economies, spurred commerce and even industrialization, and brought considerable wealth to those able to seize the opportunity. This economic development is apparent in Ningbo and Wenzhou, where often Shanghai merchants were involved, but also at many sites along the coast and in the interior, where local elites and people with ties to Ningbo and Wenzhou played key roles.

The booming commercial activity that Ningbo experienced in 1938 into early 1939 through open trade and that activity which continued to a degree through smuggling until 1941 had a tremendous impact on the economy. On the eve of war, Ningbo—in part because of general international economic deterioration—had many businesses contract and its cotton market largely collapse. With the coming of war, every aspect of trade flourished, with new jobs becoming available for dockworkers, ship hands, and warehouse workers. The city was invaded by merchants coming from inside and outside the province, from large, established merchant houses to military provisioners to private individuals wanting to get in on the action.[32]

Especially significant during the smuggling years were the latter—small retailers or peddlers *(danbangke)* without ties to commercial firms.[33] Their tack was to make use of the price differentials between localities and make a profit on goods smuggled in from elsewhere. The Shanghai-Ningbo connnection was strong here, with many Shanghainese—men and women—coming to Ningbo to sell items they had bought in Shanghai, the most common of which were cotton cloth, general merchandise, metals, Western medicines, and cigarettes. Small items that were easy to carry, like medicines and dyestuffs, were also highly valued and brought high prices. Some of the goods sold in Ningbo by Shanghai merchants were Japanese products to which the merchants had given Chinese brand names and "made in China" attributes. In any case, the overall business was so lucrative for these independent traders that many who had worked in established firms or others who had never been involved in trade joined in the action.

Often colluding with the traveling independent merchant were informal brokers who drummed up business between the goods owner and the customer. Working on commission, brokers established connections both with the *danbang* merchant and with merchants from the interior who had come to purchase the goods that Shanghai and Shanghai-based trade routes had to offer. Brokers reportedly swarmed around hotels and brothels, inquiring about the situation of merchants newly arrived from the interior, introducing them to merchant-sellers and promoting their own role. In an atmosphere where interior merchants were commodity hungry, wholesalers also flourished. An estimated three to four hundred wholesale stores operated in Ningbo at this time, capitalized both individually and in partnerships. Most of the stores' storage facilities were reportedly lit up each night so that shopkeepers and apprentices could pack up commodities for retailers.

The people who struck it rich were legion. There was Shen, a former clerk at a southern-goods store, who left his job to become a *danbang* and then a broker. After making his cash, he opened three Western medicine shops. Another small retailer, named Dai, had made wooden spindles; for-saking that occupation, he became a *danbang* and soon opened the con-spicuously imposing Empress Department Store, specializing in Jiangxi products. And there was Zhou, a *danbang* whose extensive networks with customs agents, the military police, boat workers, and dock bosses allowed him to smuggle cash and goods with impunity.[34]

The service industry—transport firms, restaurants, hotels, taverns, and brothels—prospered. Four new hotels were built along the trade routes in the first year of the war, and their names reflect the presence of mer-chants from all over Guomindang China. There was the Lu Cheng (the name of an island in the Zhoushan Archipelago), the Xiang Nan (South Hunan), the Zhe–Gan (for Zhejiang–Jiangxi, the abbreviation designat-ing the railroad that ran from Hangzhou to Nanchang and that brought many merchants from the interior into the area), and the Rong Cheng (Rong is another name for the city of Fuzhou). The brothel business was especially active, with associated taverns being sites where business deals were frequently struck. The city's Tongfuchang Department Store, for example, came into being in a brothel-tavern discussion and agreement between Hunan and Jiangxi traveling merchants.[35]

If individual entrepreneurs were undercutting established commercial firms, they were also beginning to weaken local financial firms, espe-cially native banks. The accumulation of capital allowed for the opening of many small-scale native banks. Some did not even formally establish a business but simply relied on connections and past dealings with people; profits were reportedly immense.[36] It was tricky business to deal with non–Settlement Shanghai because the Guomindang government strictly forbade currency from flowing to occupied areas; therefore, re-mittances were not legally possible. Ships sailing from Ningbo to Shang-hai were treated suspiciously by customs inspectors checking especially for cash and bank notes. When smugglers went to Shanghai to arrange for the purchase of goods, they needed cash. To avoid detection, they hid it on their persons or among miscellaneous packed items, or they bribed a worker on the ship to hide it. When many factories and stores needed to take large sums of cash to Shanghai, often the only method was to bribe a sailor or ship worker. One Ningbo native bank, the Yuanhe, spe-cialized in dealing in cash for the smuggling business. It sent cash gained in business dealings with the Shaoxing wine and tinfoil industries by wrapping it in parcels, packing it in chests hidden among other items, and smuggling it on vessels to Shanghai. The bank's Shanghai branch would then make this money available to traveling merchants at higher rates than the going rate in Shaoxing. Shanghai traveling merchants in the cotton cloth and tobacco trade were especially active in receiving financing from the Yuanhe native bank.[37] Many merchant houses and merchants traveling from and to the interior engaged this native bank to send illegal remittances.

Because the financial relationship between Shanghai and Ningbo institutions had been very close before 1941, a few speculative businessmen and native banks in Ningbo had secret channels of communication with counterparts in Shanghai. In addition to long-distance telephone and telegraph, the merchants made use of shipping companies' transmitters-receivers. Linked directly to Shanghai, the use of these devices made the spilling of secret information less likely. There were some speculative merchants who even collaborated with radio stations, agreeing on time and wavelength to transmit secret communications. Thus, on the air waves there were frequent messages notifying Ningbo merchants about certain aspects of a particular financial situation.[38]

Finally, it was not only in the expected worlds of commerce and finance that economic changes came, but perhaps more significantly also in the realm of industry. The Hefeng Spinning Company, for example, expanded during the war to twenty-six thousand spindles, the largest number that ever operated in that factory. The Wuxing Cigarette Factory, which had earlier closed, reopened and did a flourishing business. When the Hengfeng Weaving Mill moved to Shanghai, over fifty smaller mills were capitalized and began operation. The Taifeng Flour Mill, established in 1931, expanded its facilities at the same time as it was handing out bonuses in the first quarter of 1941 to stockholders, directors, managers, and workers. The mill was also able to escape the Japanese bombing by signing a trade agreement with the German firm Carlowitz and Company and painting swastikas on its factory and storage-facility roofs.[39]

The economic and social changes in Wenzhou, moreover, far surpassed those in Ningbo. Partly that more rapid and dramatic change came because of the lower economic baseline from which Wenzhou began to change and partly from the much longer time that Wenzhou remained free from mishandled defense decisions and from Japanese attack and occupation. Mostly the extent of change stemmed from Wenzhou's closer linkage over a longer period to trade with the great interior of the country. Wenzhou experienced the same kind of commercial bustle that Ningbo did, what with the *danbang,* brokers, wholesalers, and especially merchants flooding in from Jiangxi, Anhui, Fujian, Hunan, and Sichuan—and with the service industry supplying their needs.

The commercial prosperity necessitated the construction of an additional dock in the harbor. On the eve of war, the city had had seven boat transport companies; between 1941 and 1944, six more were established. Three new steamship lines were opened, and four tugboats were added to the harbor's fleet.[40] The number of regional passenger lines increased dramatically, reportedly from one to seven, knitting Wenzhou as never before to significant towns in the region and thereby contributing to greater regional cohesion.[41] Before the war the city had about 2,200 transport workers. In 1938 and 1939, large numbers of men from rural villages in the region flocked into the thriving city for work; by the end of 1939, there were no fewer than 5,335 transport workers. Dockworkers and porters had begun to organize in the 1920s into unions based on role and sometimes commodity—for example, porters, barge workers, passenger boat workers, timber transporters. With the numbers of transport workers growing by 143 percent in two years, the number of workers' unions and other associations increased as well, to over forty.[42] Because the transport workers were contentious, in 1939 the county government appointed an official charged with maintaining control and collecting taxes. Despite his presence, there was frequent fighting among workers' organizations. In 1943 workers from a native place–based organization and the pine wood transporters fought at close quarters over dock space, leading to two deaths and dozens of injured workers; that same year the East Gate (dock) sugar workers clashed with a group of Shandong workers, also leading to a death.[43]

In commercial development, stores retailing almost every commodity grew in number: silk stores from around seventy before the war to over one hundred; the northern- and southern-goods business added over twenty stores. Many merchants were involved in both wholesale and retail operations. The numbers of wholesale stores dealing in dyestuffs, metals, kerosene, and both Chinese and Western medicine increased dramatically. Coming from Shanghai were not only the continuing tides of smuggling *danbang* but also a wave of cotton wholesalers. By the spring of 1938, as Wenzhou became increasingly central in the interior trade, Shanghai cotton wholesalers bringing finished cotton goods flocked to that southeastern port. Before the war Wenzhou had had only retail cotton shops; but during the war the numbers of Shanghai whole-sale stores shot up from an initial dozen to almost one hundred. By way of comparison, Shanghai cotton wholesale stores in Guangzhou, where the Shanghainese were also active, grew in number from over twenty to between only thirty and forty.[44]

Because of trade and business expansion and the accumulation of capital, Wenzhou's wartime experience led to rapid industrial expan-sion. Consumer demands from the interior spurred on not only the Shanghai wholesalers but local Wenzhou enterpreneurs. The nine cot-ton mills before the war rapidly increased to thirty-three; numbers of weaving looms catapulted from five hundred before the war to over seventeen hundred by early 1939; numbers of workers rose from about one thousand to over three thousand. The leather-goods industry ex-panded from just over ten tanneries before the war to over forty; the number of soap factories grew from five to thirteen. In 1939 wealthy businessman Wu Baiheng funded the establishment of the Western Hills Porcelain Factory, manufacturing especially for the interior areas vari-ous kinds of tiles and porcelain items for electrical needs. Industrial and commercial expansion was also a stimulus to Wenzhou's financial insti-tutions: during the war two new Western-style banks, seven branch banks, and at least seventeen native banks were established.[45] Indeed, the changes at Wenzhou were significant enough that in the area it was called "little Shanghai."[46]

If both Ningbo and Wenzhou experienced great change, so also did all the coastal and interior towns and villages that served as transshipment sites in trade and smuggling. Shenjiamen, the crucial entrepôt on the Shanghai–Wenzhou route, saw substantial growth, with many new stores and boisterous market activity; Shenjiamen also became known, in fact, as "little Shanghai" in its area.[47] Shipu, a pivot of one of the Shanghai–Ningbo routes, experienced rapid economic development. Established at the port during the war years were three steamboat lines; a transport, sales, and marketing firm; a food-trading company; and a yarn and paper mill. In 1940 the impetus of Shipu's involvement in the Shanghai trade brought about the organization of commodity associations *(tongyehui)* for such local products as fresh and dried fish, bamboo, and livestock. In 1940 the town had 139 business firms. The impact of the war on the town is shown by the startling report that in 1946 there were over 400 businesses, not including those involved in the fishing industry.[48] The population of the town of Andong on the southern coast of Hangzhou Bay, the transshipment point on the Shanghai–Zhapu–Andong–Ningbo route, swelled to 15,000 with its large number of traveling merchants and its large service industry (in 1988, in contrast, its reported population was 13,741). Known also in its region as "little Shanghai," it fell to the Japanese in 1941 and went into economic depression when the Japanese in February 1943 placed it inside a bamboo palisade as part of Japan's rural pacification efforts.[49]

Small interior villages realized similar changes. Two villages between Ningbo and Wenzhou, Zhu'ao and Shuanglou, in present-day Sanmen County, became important transport centers. The former (which in 1988 had a population of 1,714) built over thirty hotels and inns during the war; restaurant construction also flourished. Other villages in the area became known as particular markets for sale of commodities like salt, which had been made scarce by the blockade. Thriving periodic market Tingbangcheng, for example, had to add additional market days for interior provincial merchants who flocked to the town.[50] In the interior trade, Yangkou in Fuyang County, as another example, became an important center overnight because it was not regulated by the Chinese or the Japanese, neither country having forces stationed there; so many throngs of merchants came to Yangkou that the local residents called them the "ant brigades."[51]

Perhaps the clearest examples of the impact of Shanghai-to-Wenzhou trade and smuggling were a number of small Yueqing County towns in a stretch along the north bank of the Ou River as it neared the ocean. The two most significant were Qili and Huanghua. Because the Guomindang laid mines in the southernmost entrances to the river and the Japanese sank ships there, Wenzhou's import and export trade had to pass by these towns, where shippers would unload cargo onto smaller boats and use rivers and streams to reach Wenzhou. The towns had five large wooden sailboats to participate in the trade and to export local products—wood products, tong oil, and paper—and to import commodities brought from Shanghai, such as cotton, cosmetics, dyestuffs, medicines. Because of the increased trade, a new tax office was opened in 1942, and townspeople were able to accumulate substantial capital to start new businesses and industry. By 1943, they had established fifty-five firms; their number and the extent of their capitalization reflects the flood of capital that the smuggling trade had brought. Seventeen of the firms were capitalized at between five hundred thousand and two million yuan; only nine firms were capitalized at under one hundred thousand yuan.[52] Because of the increased trade in these Yueqing towns, a new tax office was opened in 1942.[53] The smuggling-based prosperity also led to some industrialization: the Yandang textile mill, capitalized at five hundred thousand yuan by Yueqing merchants residing in Wenzhou, operated from the fall of 1942 until its destruction by the Japanese in September 1944; and a cigarette factory was established in 1941.[54] Huangyan County to the north of Yueqing also experienced commercial expansion during the war, constructing three new wharves, one of which ceased operating in the late 1940s, when trade declined.[55]

Economic Displacement and Replacement

Despite the Japanese coastal blockade, the disruptions and catastrophes of war, the plethora of commodity prohibitions, regulations, and restrictions, and human errors of judgment (the Chinese military's incapacitation of the port of Ningbo), trade between Shanghai and Zhejiang's eastern coast flourished during the war. We cannot document that reality with statistics, because much of the trade was smuggled; but the circumstantial evidence of the thriving economies of coastal, and interior entrepôts underscores that reality. The war transformed the prewar Zhejiang-Shanghai trading system, changing its nature by forcing much of it undercover and its orientation by forcing the establishment of new routes with new destinations. War displaced and transformed the prewar trading system's space, making proximate areas in reality "hinterland" and distant areas "near." War destroyed the regional urban hierarchy, making small fishing villages more essential to the continuation of the system than cities and county seats, making Wenzhou closer and more essential to Shanghai than Ningbo, Shanghai's longtime commercial partner. War thus allowed the regional trading system to penetrate to much lower levels in the regional landscape than it had before the war and to work capitalistic power there.

Shanghai was the central entrepôt in a hierarchical network of entrepôts. At the higher levels—Shanghai to Shenjiamen, Shanghai to Shipu—the routes of the network were single-stranded, traveled mostly by steamers. But once goods reached the steamers' destinations, network routes branched out in a web to smaller destinations—Shenjiamen to Kanmen, Chumen, Qili, Huanghua, Dongtou, Lingkun, and Sanpan islands—visited by small wooden sailboats carrying commodities, sometimes to Wenzhou for further transshipment. Other times the boats went to points inland—Qingshuibu, Zhu'ao, Shuanglou—all names of heretofore very insignificant places, which were now made, by the wartime magician of displacement, central in this crucial trade. The multistranded networks of waterways converged at Lishui, where smuggling again became single-routed until the dispersal into interior networks at Lanxi. Contingencies and exigencies of war could make strands on the multiroute phases of the smuggling process ephemeral; new routes developed overnight to replace older ones.

It is striking that three urban "centers" along these routes—Wenzhou, Shenjiamen, and Andong—all came to be called "little Shanghai" by local and regional residents. Such a nickname suggests not only their perception of Shanghai as the model for commercial prosperity but also the role that metropolitan Shanghai was playing in each locality. In a very real way, Shanghai penetrated these areas more than it had ever done in prewar days, personified by its traveling individual merchants, brokers, wholesalers, and ad hoc native bankers who all moved to these three centers to stimulate and participate in commercial activity. This penetration of Shanghai into trading system localities was not only through steamer-sailboat commodities. Other Shanghainese also came along these routes, indicating their importance beyond commerce. A reporter for Shanghai's *Resistance War (Kangzhan)* noted refugees in the streets of Lishui who were "newly arrived from Shanghai" in June 1938.[56] In that same year, seven hundred able-bodied Shanghai refugees were taken to Wenzhou and, on the interior routes, to Jiangxi Province to join the New Fourth Army.[57]

The commerce-stimulated economic development of cities, towns, and villages in Zhejiang and the regional trading system is noteworthy. There, war was a positive catalyst—so long as it was kept at a distance. For most towns and villages, the economic development was short lived, disappearing by the late 1940s. In Wenzhou, however, the changes were longer lasting, tying the city more integrally into its regional base and establishing industry and businesses that lasted at least into the 1950s. The extent of individual entrepreneurship shown not only by Shanghainese but also by local residents at this time of considerable risk and danger is striking.

Studying Zhejiang's coastal wartime trade underscores the reality that, amid the contingencies of war, "place" and displacement seemed to become more significant as explanatory variables. On the one hand, the towns of Qili and Huanghua on the north bank of the Ou River owed their wartime prosperity principally to their location (and to their ability to take advantage of the smuggling situation). On the other hand, the town of Kanmen, also an important entrepôt in the Shanghai trade in the first years of the war, was attacked by Japan; and its fishing fleet was largely destroyed in 1940.[58] The Ningbo situation, however—its presumed importance because of proximity to Shanghai being destroyed by human action—cautions that place, while significant, is never determinative.

If the role of place may be heightened in importance during war, wartime identity and actions were made more ambiguous by the always changing situation. What "trade" with Settlement Shanghai was for the Guomindang Chinese before 1941 would always have been smuggling to the Japanese, who were trying to maintain the coastal blockade they had declared. But the Japanese takeover of Settlement Shanghai in late 1941 turned the trade into "smuggling." Especially problematic in the fluid realm of wartime ambiguity, as seen in the nature of the Shanghai trade, are the meanings of aggression, collaboration, and resistance. The Japanese controlled the important smuggling port of Shenjiamen from 1939 to 1944. During these years, there were several battles by different groups: in March and November 1940, Guomindang units attacked the port; in spring 1941 Nanjing puppet troops engaged in mopping-up operations in and around Shenjiamen; and Japanese troops executed over forty Shenjiamen residents in 1942.[59] And yet, Shenjiamen's commercial importance as an entrepôt only grew. On the whole, Japanese actions in Shenjiamen seemed an un-likely combination of both aggression and collaboration. Or on the Chinese side, Guomindang military units at the coastal town of Huanghua and at an official branch organ at the important interior entrepôt of Chun'an col-luded in smuggling goods from Guomindang-controlled areas to Japanese-occupied areas and vice versa. Chinese actions seemed to join collaboration and resistance in an ambiguous policy toward the aggressors. The ambiguity grew from the necessity of seeing action as relative to survival and eventual victory, not to some nationalistically politically correct or policy ideal.

In the war-produced trading system, it is clear that both Chinese and Japanese received commodities through smuggling that were vitally im-portant in carrying on the military struggle. Analyzing the trading system, ironically, underscores in many ways the pragmatism (not the patriotism or nationalism) that frequently motivated, amid the military depredations and brutalities of war, the actions of both combatants and noncombatants—actions that included reregistering ships; developing new trade and smug-gling routes; venturing, on the part of the Shanghainese, to distant entrepôts as risk-taking capitalists; smuggling cash into Shanghai; and even trading with the enemy.

TWELVE

✦

Bubonic Bombs

WHETHER THE REFUGEE MOVEMENTS of governments, schools, or business and industry during the Sino-Japanese War, such travel generally left more modernized locales for a less modernized hinterland. In a sense, for these refugees there was not only a spatial displacement but also a temporal displacement—in terms of settling in a place where the level of modernization was one that they had already passed by, some many years ago, in the homes from which they fled. The refugees were, in effect, returning to the past, at least in physical context; in many ways this temporal displacement created more social and psychological problems than the spatial displacement did. Refugees were introduced, in the words of one scholar, into "a different kind of time."[1] In this chapter, I survey the spatial, social, and psychological displacements brought by Japanese biological warfare at three places situated in what might be called three kinds of "modernization time." Leaders in each place reacted to bubonic plague in acutely different ways.

Single Japanese planes flew over the city-centers of Quzhou in west-central Zhejiang Province on October 4, 1940 (see Map 9) and the port of Ningbo on October 27, 1940 (see Map 7). The planes' payloads in Quzhou and Ningbo were not bombs but parcels of rice, wheat, and wheat chaff, parcels designed to break open in midair, with their fourth ingredient—bubonic-plague-infected fleas—falling to the earth. In Quzhou, within eight weeks twenty-one of twenty-two infected people died; in 1941, some 275 of 281 infected people died. Japanese bombing drove infected residents to the countryside, displacing tens of thousands and tragically further spreading plague. Merchant and laboring sojourners (that is, outsiders living and working in this river port) were displaced from their jobs (the plague bomb targeted the central business and commercial district) and returned to their home counties, many people thus infecting family and friends. In this area, plague killed over 2,000 people. In Ningbo, rain washed plague-infected material from roofs into jars collecting drinking water. The first deaths occurred three days later. By the end of the year 106 were dead, with twelve whole families totaling 45 people wiped out. The successful quarantine area in this city displaced hundreds—and permanently: the entire area was burned to the ground. In contrast to Ningbo and Quzhou, the epidemic of plague in Yiwu County was brought by infected travelers; out of 682 infected, 630 died, a death-rate of 91.7 percent.

Different Political Cultures

The reactions of leaders in Ningbo, Quzhou, and Yiwu to the plague crisis reveal the import of starkly different political cultures—the constellation of social and political assumptions, frameworks, and patterns that helped shape leaders' responses. Ningbo was an important seaport on the East China Sea and an early treaty port, which had, as we have seen, close relationships to Shanghai. Visiting Ningbo in 1916, Sun Yat-sen noted that its openness to the outside world and its residents' enterprising nature had produced its prosperity, which in turn gave rise to a local political elite that was confident and assertive in its dealings with officials. City political elites during these years were primarily businessmen, journalists, and teachers, most of whom had traveled extensively and many of whom had close ties to Shanghai.

In contrast, a reporter from Zhejiang's most important newspaper wrote in 1940 that the spirit of the city of Quzhou was marked by simplicity and slowness to change and that the spirit of the community had been "shaped by its circumstances."[2] The reporter was not more explicit about these "circumstances," but analysis of the city's political culture reveals what they were. Quzhou (meaning "thoroughfare") was an important port on the Qu River near the juncture of rivers linking Quzhou to three neighboring provinces. Perhaps in part because it was a transshipment center, its leaders in commerce and business—from merchants to bankers, from stevedores to freight brokers—were outsider, sojourning merchants, not local residents.

To a large extent, this outsider leadership was the city residents' own doing. It was said that working the docks was such an exhausting life of poverty and hard labor that locals did whatever they could to avoid it. The 1992 county history noted, "County people for the most part are not very good at merchant life; [therefore] city and county stores and shops are all in the hands of merchants from Fujian, Jiangxi, Anhui, Ningbo, and Shaoxing."[3] Even though locals may have allowed such control, they resented it and what they saw as their subordination to the outsiders. Listen to the resentful words of Zheng Yongxi, a city leader for over thirty years, in the 1929 official county history: "The monetary situation and whether prices rise or fall are completely in the hands of the 'guest gang.' Traders from other provinces and cities raise pennants to oppose others in the home of locals who have very little role in this business and who have to beg for part of the profits."[4] The enmity between residents and sojourning merchants sometimes flared into social unrest in commodity crises, such as in a famine at the end of the war, when merchants were storing grain on Quzhou's docks for transshipment and doing nothing for Quzhou, itself suffering a severe rice shortage. About the generally tense relations between outsider merchants and local elites, a 1994 county history noted that "sometimes there was communication between them, sometimes not; sometimes relations were fair, sometimes bad; sometimes there was much struggle, sometimes less."[5] The bottom line: there was never a time when relations were good or when there was no struggle.

In contrast to Quzhou, where local residents were intimidated by though resentful of outsiders, Yiwu was a county where many men were sojourning merchants; it was a rough-and-tumble place, where gambling, bullfighting, and social violence became the norm in the early twentieth century. It was also famous as a commodity center and served as a base for the province's itinerant peddlers, who were known for selling various kinds of candy products made from the green-skinned sugarcane that grew in the county.[6] Before the Taiping Rebellion in the mid-nineteenth century, these peddlers had traveled as far as Xuzhou in the north to Changsha in the west. They, in the intepretation of one scholar, had developed an elaborate distribution system with their own trading routes, special hostels, remittance mechanisms, and collective security arrangements—all of which enabled tens of thousands of Yiwu villagers to leave home in the company of a few veterans of the trade, carrying no more than a change of underclothing and their candy pole, prepared to journey hundreds of miles on foot for a whole year.[7] Through such outside involvement, many Yiwu natives had a much different outlook and approach to issues than Quzhou residents did. Further, the passage of the Zhejiang–Jiangxi Railroad through the county in the early Republic provided a rapid way to transport Yiwu products to Hangzhou and beyond. Water transportation was also convenient; its important streams and rivers fed into tributaries of the Fuchun and Qiantang rivers. Mobility, in short, was a county trademark.

Ningbo Battles the Plague

Though plague was endemic in some counties on the border between Zhejiang and Fujian provinces, Ningbo, Quzhou, and Yiwu had not previously experienced the disease. In Ningbo, the first plague deaths occurred on October 30, only three days after the attack. Initially threatening delay in handling the epidemic efficiently was the competition between hospitals to be the first to accurately diagnose the symptoms— high fever, headache, confusion, unsteady gait, and swollen lymph glands, especially in the groin—a situation complicated by the fact that one hospital was in the process of moving to a different location. Tests on lymphatic fluid and blood led to the diagnosis on November 8, nine days after the first death.

Fortunately, authorities had already moved to act, assuming that the illness was plague. Four days after the first death, the county magistrate convened a meeting of medical personnel, who decided to quarantine the plague area and to publicize news of the crisis. On November 3, it issued a bulletin in Ningbo's most important newspaper: "This illness is very easy to transmit. People who live in the plague area and carry out items will have those items burned; . . . friends and relatives must refuse to receive those who are ill. If they do not know the extent of their illness and nevertheless secretly receive them, then a neighbor should report this by telephone to the government office." The newspaper played a crucial role during the plague episode, informing the public of developments and of procedures to follow.[8] On November 5, it published instructions about where to go if people had symptoms, where families of the infected should go, and tips on catching and killing rats. These tips ran from the expected—trapping or poisoning rats or getting a cat—to a rather over-the-top fumigation method: "Close off a small room (to prevent rats and the fumigated air from escaping). Take sulfur (for every ten square meters use two kilograms of sulfur placed in a crock or tub). Sprinkle with a little alcohol or kerosene; ignite a fire. After about twenty minutes, tear out the ceiling and the floorboards to kill the rats and fleas [hiding there]."

It is noteworthy that local elites took the lead in managing the crisis. Initiatives sponsored by township heads included a "clean-up campaign" to rid the area of refuse and garbage, and the offer of money to the Health Department to pay a dime for each captured rat, dead or alive. The Health Department worked to promote public-spiritedness in a culture often noted for paying little attention to people with whom they had no connections: "We must absolutely have the immediate cooperation of the average people. . . . If people in the plague area do not understand the government's urgency in the situation and do not heed the instructions of the epidemic-defense workers; if people look on others' problems with indifference and don't become involved, then the plague area will grow."

Fighting plague in Ningbo was efficient, systematic, and strict. Early on, the county magistrate set up the Epidemic Defense Office (EDO). As a measure of its commitment to winning the plague war, the EDO staff and committees met twenty-one times from November 6 until November 30, that is, everyday but three. The EDO formed committees to oversee constructing a wall around the quarantine area, searching for evaders from the quarantine area, organizing burials, and setting up a vaccination program. There were three separate hospital sites: the first tended the most acutely ill; the second, those suspected of having plague; and the third, families of the infected or those exposed in the plague area. The last two groups were to be held for ten days and then released if there were no sign of infection. The disease thus meant displacing, at least temporarily, those suspected of having plague or their family members.

The quarantine area itself was about 5,000 square meters (1.2 acres).
Inside, officials closed businesses, theaters, and an elementary school. On
the night of November 7, they constructed a twelve-foot-high brick wall
around the area. Since it was completed by the next morning, many
people must have been mobilized. To prevent rats from getting out, a
curved sheet of galvanized iron was pressed down on the top of the wall.
The workers dug a ditch 1 meter wide and 1. 3 meters deep outside the
wall, to impede transport into or out of the area. Sixty-nine residences of
the infected were fumigated and disinfected with steamed sulfur. Anything removed from these houses was registered and disinfected. Plague
workers were disinfected before they left the area. Another strategy for
preventing spread of the disease was inoculation. Eventually, 23,343 people
living near the plague zone were vaccinated. A search committee began
house-to-house searches in adjacent areas for anyone who had left the
zone before it was quarantined or who had simply disregarded the quarantine. In the end, seventy-six such people were found, thirty-two of
them already dead. The places where the evaders were found were disinfected twice and then isolated in miniquarantines for ten days.

In the early days of the crisis, the county government had notified the
national and provincial health departments, who dispatched doctors,
technicians, and bureaucrats. But by the time they arrived, the situation
was well in hand under local leadership. By November 30, the Ningbo
plague had been quelled. One last issue was the fate of buildings in the
plague zone. In the end, in a significantly telling revelation about political
decision making and the landscape of political power in the city, the
EDO conducted extensive talks with the Ningbo sojourners' association
in Shanghai and reached a decision to burn the whole plague area.
Though living in Shanghai, these mostly wealthy businessmen continued
to play decisive roles in their native city. On the evening of November 30, some 137 houses were burned to the ground, along with an undisclosed number of shops and businesses. Thus, there were many people
and businesses permanently displaced by the Japanese dropping of plague-
infused material and by the Chinese response. Overall, the city's battle
with plague, ending with the dropping of the quarantine on December 1,
thirty-one days after the first plague case, was successful—a success attributed to the health specialists, local organizations, and city residents of
all classes and occupations.[9]

The Struggle over the Plague in Quzhou

The story of the handling of the plague in Quzhou was as different from that of Ningbo as day from night. It was a tragedy of errors, inefficiency, lack of local initiative, and much more severe physical and psychological displacement. After the lone plane attack on October 4, one Xu Jingshan gathered some of what had rained down and sent it to the county's civil defense corps to forward to the provincial Public Health Department lab the next day. After culturing the germs, the head of the department, Chen Wanli, who had held this position only since September 1940, announced that there were absolutely no bacilli that could cause illness.[10] Ironically, the aftermath of the plague attack initially seemed to corroborate Chen's (ultimately) fraudulent finding. Not until November 12, thirty-eight days later, did a young girl became ill and die. She had gone to a private doctor who, not suspecting plague, did not report it to local authorities. Several other doctors treated patients but also failed to report the cases; one doctor treated a man for plague and then incredibly sent him home, without getting his address. The infected man was found, but the inattentiveness of the local doctors is notable. Within the next three weeks, twenty-one people were infected, with all but one dying.

It was not until two months later that Chen admitted what had actually happened. The county's civil defense corps collected the fleas but wrongly sent them to the provincial air defense command, which sent them to the provincial government office, which, in turn, finally forwarded them to the Health Department. They did not reach Chen's office until November 30, eight weeks to the day after they were sent. So his first report was a lie. When the fleas were examined at the end of November, only miscellaneous bacteria were present. At that point, the collected fleas were all dead and shriveled. An Austrian plague specialist with the League of Nations in China was called on; he claimed that the plague bacillus could continue to exist up to several months in dead fleas. But the Health Department lab had thrown away all but one, and that was one they had already studied. In the Chinese bureaucracy, delay and obstacles were notorious and legendary. One observer in the late 1930s noted that "a document arriving at a provincial government office was transmitted through 37 steps, each of which consumed from a few hours to a few days. A reply after a half year's time was a surprise to no one. Not a few documents perished in their long and dreary journey, buried alive in someone's desk drawer."

Not until a week after the first death (on November 11) was a report on seven deaths in the city center sent to the county police and health departments. Two days later health department leaders decided to proceed as if the disease were plague, though it was not yet verified in lab tests. On November 21, the administrative inspector *(xingcheng ducha zhuanyuan),* a government executive overseeing all the counties in Quzhou prefecture, reported the situation to the provincial government. The county police chief warned the magistrate to take immediate preparations to preclude an epidemic.[11] The next day, the administrative inspector called an emergency meeting of the magistrate, representatives of the Public Security Bureau, and members of civic organizations and established the Plague Prevention Committee (PPC), made up of several task-related teams to deal with investigation, treatment, quarantine, disinfection, and burial.[12] On November 25, two weeks after the first death, a quarantine office was set up to isolate the infected area.[13] Even before the quarantine took effect, two patterns that would dog the Qu City effort were apparent: first was a dilatory response (after the gone-awry sending of the fleas to the provincial Health Department). Second, and probably more important, the local populace was not served by local elites, who seemed to take no part, not even by the magistrate (who had to be prompted by the police chief), but by the administrative inspector, whose orientation—despite his being headquartered in the city—was mostly to issues beyond the city.

Even worse, the dilatory response at Quzhou seemed to invite recriminations among those in authority. In light of the provincial Health Department lab's initial lie and then inability to find the plague bacillus, many had lost confidence in the professional ability of its head, Mr. Chen. Had the bacillus been found, precautions could have been taken to control the spread of the disease more promptly and effectively. That lack of trust prompted Commander Gu Zhutong of the Third Wartime Region in early December to ask the central government to send someone from the national Public Health Office.[14] When Rong Qirong, the head of the national Public Health Office, came to Quzhou, he alleged that Chen's laboratory had not found the plague bacillus because of slipshod laboratory procedures.[15] Chen lashed back, charging that the lab had not detected the bacillus because local officials had forwarded insufficient infected material. Accused by the administrative inspector for failing to act properly, the county magistrate defensively dismissed that argument.[16] Mr. Rong's self-justifying 1941 report on the plague episode claimed that Rong was holding meetings in Chongqing on Quzhou's situation by mid-November and planning a visit at that time.[17] This was a ridiculous claim, given the fact that at that time there had been only one death, the diagnosis was not certain until November 30, and the military commander did not even request help from Chongqing until December 6. Rong's delegation did not come for over a month—on January 12. In other words, like Chen, who lied about and gave alibis for the botched lab examination, Rong was lying and trying to make himself look as good as possible to mask the slow reaction of the central government to the crisis.

Part of the problem leading to this confusion was that the typical plague incubation period after a flea bite was at least three to seven days, possibly as many as fourteen. In Quzhou, it was thirty-eight days between the attack and the first case. Health professionals debated whether it was possible that the Japanese plane drop had even begun the plague epidemic. Eventually, decision makers deduced that it had, for the fleas involved were not native to the area; they were Indian red fleas, which the Japanese had used in biological warfare elsewhere. Experts from the central government seemed obsessed with the disease's etiology rather than with the practical problems of controlling the epidemic.

A host of regulations and procedures were announced on wooden placards erected around the city, not in newspapers as in Ningbo. But regulations and their enforcement were inconsistent. While the city's train station was ordered temporarily closed, boats could continue to dock on the east riverbank contiguous to the plague zone—a policy that was clearly an effort to cater to merchant interests. Enforcing the quarantine was difficult. Most fundamentally, the people did not understand what caused the disease and what steps were necessary to prevent its spread—the very thing on which the specialists and experts descending on the city should have focused. Rats ran freely in the city. A one-day effort to capture as many as possible to test for the plague bacillus netted 1,588 rats of which 133 (8.4 percent) were carrying plague. Until people understood the relationship between rats and the illness, they could not be mobilized to act rationally. Not until the summer of 1941 did the city PPC hit upon the tactic of paying people for turning over captured rats, one yuan for big rats and five jiao for small ones.[18] The Ningbo elites had used this tactic within the first week after the initial plague death. It is difficult to understand why the provincial Health Office, which obviously knew of Ningbo's experience, did not advise Quzhou officials to adopt the same tactic earlier.

He Caifu, the head of the PPC, recounts an episode that underscored the residents' lack of understanding about disease. The highest hill in the city was known as Turtle Peak Mountain; located at its foot was the prefectural government offices. Many residents saw the turtle as linked closely to the city's identity. Near one of the city gates in the plague area, there was a building that housed a rice-milling device driven by waterpower. It used five stones that pounded with great thuds. As the plague spread, some of the city's residents became angry at the rice mill, saying that the shape of the city was like that of a turtle and that people were becoming ill and dying because the five stones were being pounded all day on the turtle's head. In the end, several hundred stormed the mill and destroyed the "guilty" machine.[19] The episode is interesting for several reasons. Perhaps it is not surprising that Quzhou residents would believe their explanation for plague: local gazetteers noted that the people of the city also believed that illness might be caused by seeing ghosts with horns or hearing the quacks of malevolent duck spirits. The turtle explanation for the plague obviously pointed to their complete medical ignorance. But there is more. The mill was located in the city center, where outsider sojourners dominated and the owner of the mill was a sojourning merchant from Ningbo.[20] Given the mob's destruction and its specific linking of the mill to the identity of the city, it is likely that the act had wider political and psychological significance—an effort of anxious locals to strike against the sojourners who so dominated lives of native people and who had displaced them from what they believed were their rightful roles.

As for the quarantine area, people simply could not understand why they had to leave, why they were being displaced. The national plague office noted that in Quzhou there was simply no way to maintain the quarantine.[21] It is hard to understand why not, given the supposed enforcement of the quarantine by military police, though we are never told specifics about the numbers of police or how seriously they tried to enforce it. In one case, at least, the regulations seemed unnecessarily harsh and arbitrary. If a family reported an illness, those who were not sick were forced to spend a month isolated (essentially imprisoned) on a boat in the middle of the river, with no contact with their ill family member; their necessities were to be sent via a gangplank that could be used only by a guard. The prospect for such bitter displacement undercut the policy. When people became ill, families did not report it. When the unreported victims died, their deaths also were not reported. When Public Security forces broke down the doors of several families who had not been seen for a number of days, they found whole families dead. Noninfected families whose homes were in the quarantined area had to move to the Fujian *huiguan* [native place association].[22]

Burial of the dead became a significant issue. Infected plague lymph glands could break open after victims died and leak infected fluid onto clothes or even into the wood of coffins. In Ningbo, a committee of the EDO managed burials, directing that the dead be taken outside the city to an out-of-the-way site and buried deep in the ground. In Quzhou, authorities ordered that corpses be buried in the plague area itself. Family members were not allowed to buy coffins without a permit. Even with a permit, only special teams could perform burials, to prevent family members from becoming contaminated by the corpse. But people refused to cooperate. Some families maneuvered to buy coffins and carried the corpses out of the quarantine area. One problem was that quarantine regulations did not consider the funerary customs in the city, where certain rites, like the family's washing the body and selecting the best place for burial, were considered essential. Quarantine rules displaced and contravened traditional customs. In March 1941 regulations on coffins and burials were reissued, a clear indication that they were not being carried out. Another reading of this flagrant local disregard of the quarantine was that local ignorance might have been a willful ignorance. James Scott notes that the "systematic use of ignorance . . . [is a way] to thwart elite power."[23]

In early June the provincial government sent yet another deputy, with more money, to deal with the outbreak, but reports in late June showed that another wave of plague had spread through the city, well beyond the city-center.[24] In August 1941, new regulations were announced by the

PPC, revealing ongoing problems.[25] With various public units continuing to issue orders, the fundamental question of who held ultimate decision-making and management authority continued even as the plague did.

The national Health Office in April 1941 contended that the main difficulty was that city elites simply did not mobilize themselves for the war against plague and that the PPC essentially abdicated its control to the provincial Health Department. In Quzhou, local elites seemed to see themselves as victims of the disease, much as they saw themselves as victims of outsiders; in both senses of victimization, they seemed unable to take the initiative. Once the local leadership vacuum allowed outsiders to become crisis managers, the issue became who among the outsiders held the ultimate authority for decision making. There were simply too many outsiders, each with a slightly different agenda. In contrast to Ningbo, where only a few outside consultants arrived after major decisions had already been made, Quzhou was visited by representatives of no fewer than seven provincial and national plague prevention units, and this before many of the crucial steps were taken.[26]

In 1941, Quzhou authorities inoculated 114,312 people against the plague. But there is evidence that there was no systematic approach to administering the shots or even an understanding among health-care givers about the nature of inoculations. A man named Chun reported that as he was walking on a Quzhou street, a white-clothed medical worker approached him and grabbed his arm. Chun asked him what he was doing. The inoculator asked, "Have you been inoculated?" Before Chun had a chance to reply, the medical worker pulled him closer and inoculated him. The man then gave Chun a form on which to fill out name, address, and the number of times he had been inoculated.[27] Based on this account, we do not know how many of the 114,312 inoculated people may have been counted more than once, but the very asking of the question about times inoculated reveals a lack of understanding of the procedure and the presumed salutary effect of a single inoculation.

A Secondary Epidemic in Yiwu

Although Yiwu was the only one of the three counties not to suffer a direct hit from a bubonic bomb, more people died of plague there than in Ningbo. At the end of August 1941, Li Guanming, a ticket

seller at the Yiwu county seat station of the Zhe–Gan Railroad,
journeyed to Quzhou. While there, he contracted plague on September 2.[28] He returned to his home on the north side of the Yiwu county
seat by train on September 5. He died the next day. Over the next few
days, some thirty people, his family and neighbors, became ill with
plague. Eventually eighty-three people in his neighborhood got plague;
seventy-one died.

There were two main culprits in the spread of plague in Yiwu. The
most important was people's fleeing from the plague. As in Quzhou,
residents of Yiwu did not understand what caused plague. Their tendency
when a person in their village or neighborhood became ill was to flee in
panic. Often among those fleeing were some already in the beginning
stages of the illness; their flight simply spread the disease to previously
plague-free areas. The other culprit was the Zhe–Gan Railroad itself. It
was not only Li Guanming who carried the plague by train. Eventually
over 350 households in thirty-two villages were affected by this epidemic.
All the affected villages except for two were near train stations on the
Zhe–Gan line; those two villages were considerably far from the train
line but on a stream that passed through a town near the line. One of
the prime steps taken by the Zhejiang provincial government as the epidemic spread was to order the Zhe–Gan Railroad not to stop at stations
where plague was already in the community.[29]

One difference of the Yiwu plague experience from that of Quzhou—
which was occurring at about the same "modernization time" as Yiwu,
though with a completely different political culture—was the interest
that the provincial government showed in the situation in Yiwu. The
county was contiguous both to Jinhua, where Governor Huang Shaohong lived and where the military headquarters for the province was
located, and to Yongkang, where most of the provincial government was
established. The *Southeast Daily* reported on October 18, 1941, "The big
outbreak of plague in the Yiwu county seat has the central and provincial
governments very concerned."[30] The Zhe–Gan Railroad ran directly
from Yiwu into Jinhua. Governor Huang earmarked fifteen thousand
yuan in a special fund for use as defense against the plague. Though, initially, an official from the provincial Public Health Office was dispatched
to direct the fight against plague, eventually no less a figure than the head
of the Public Health Office, Chen Wanli (who had not distinguished

himself a year earlier in Quzhou), joined by the administrative inspector of the Fourth Wartime Region, came briefly to the county to manage the campaign. The fear of plague spreading to Jinhua launched a large antiplague campaign in that county, with massive cleanup campaigns and huge campaignlike informational meetings, also intended to mobilize the populace in the fight.

The antiplague effort in Yiwu included the usual repertoire of policies and tactics. Quarantined areas were clearly laid out; though lacking the elaborate wall that Ningbo erected, Yiwu built a small earthen wall around the area, demarking the area as Quzhou had not done. In hopes of limiting the spread of the disease, officials forbade people to leave or to enter the quarantined area. As another indication of the seriousness with which the government viewed the situation, army troops were brought into the county in an effort to facilitate a massive cleanup to deny rats places to flourish. The chief goal of the provincial and county Public Health offices was to kill rats and try to exterminate fleas.[31] Students organized propaganda brigades to stir up people's energy and determination. The payment for a live or dead rat was one jiao (a dime). Inoculations were made available for people in villages where plague existed.

The tragedy of the Yiwu story was the village of Chongshan, on a highway slightly east of the Zhe–Gan line and equidistant from the county seat and the Yiwu-Jinhua border. It was a large village of some nine hundred households (about three thousand people). In the fall of 1941, Dr. Wang Daosheng was called to a nearby village to treat a desperately ill middle-aged man; not until the doctor made a visit to the man did he recognize plague. Dr. Wang himself was infected and died quite quickly. In Chongshan, the epidemic spread: it was the hardest hit of any of the Yiwu villages—133 people died. The greater tragedy came when Chinese collaborators with the Japanese, who were controlling this portion of the county, learned of the epidemic. Fearful that it would spread, the collaborators torched the village, destroying some five hundred homes, turning many people into refugees. Rumor had it, although the sources are not completely clear, that some plague victims were burned alive in their homes.[32] Purification by fire seemed to be the accepted way of dealing with plague.

These case studies reveal sharply different political cultures, approaches, and actors in the cities of Ningbo and Quzhou, and the rural county of

Yiwu, The differences helped shape the management of the bubonic plague crisis in each place. While Ningbo elites exhibited initiative and determination in combating the epidemic, Quzhou elites seemed saddled by inertia or perplexity after many years of sojourner domination. Outside government elites took the lead in Yiwu primarily because of their fear of plague spreading to counties with important provincial political functions. In Ningbo, stanching the epidemic went relatively smoothly without intervention from province or Chongqing. It is revealing about the Ningbo decision-making realities that local officials made the difficult decision to burn the plague area only after consulting with the Ningbo sojourners' association in Shanghai.

In Quzhou, nothing went smoothly: the whole episode was dogged by bad luck, ignorance, and incompetence. Among the local people, there was little understanding of the cause of the plague; the same could be said of the people in Yiwu. Quzhou's brazen local disregard of the quarantine can also be interpreted as a willful ignorance, that is, as a way "to thwart elite power."[33] On the part of the authorities, there was little enforcement of the quarantine, no attempt to round up quarantine breakers, and an inexplicably poor choice to displace and isolate exposed family members in a repugnant location, a policy that deterred cooperation. The inoculation program was haphazard, and its effects seemed to be misunderstood even by those executing it. Most crucial in Quzhou was that local official and nonofficial elites never mobilized to deal with the crisis, leaving instead upper-level officials serving in the area (the administrative inspector and the military head of the Third Military Region), provincial officials, and national officials to step into the decision-making vacuum. Further, on the ground in Quzhou, bureaucratic accusations and one-upmanship, plus days spent trying to pin down the cause of the epidemic, took precious time and concentration away from actually combating the plague.

One further comparison of the three that underscores the difference in the communities' political, cultural, and material culture: what I call "the rat reward index." All areas gave rewards to encourage people to turn in rats, both dead and alive. Ningbo and Yiwu gave out ten cents per rat; Quzhou gave out one dollar for large rats and fifty cents for small rats. I would surmise that Ningbo and Yiwu gave the smallest reward because its people were easier to mobilize in the effort; Ningbo's many schools, fairly large newspaper readership, and close ties to relatively cosmopolitan Shanghai made it almost certain that many in the city had at least a modicum of scientific medical understanding. Because government leaders and officials played such an important role in Yiwu's plague fight and because Governor Huang came up with a special fund for the fight, the reward in Yiwu also could have been expected to be small. Quzhou offered its residents five to ten times what Ningbo and Yiwu gave out, to stimulate more participation in the antirat campaign; no newspapers were used in the effort in Quzhou; and a scientific health and medical understanding were clearly absent there.

In his study of the plague in seventeenth-century England, Paul Slack asks why "crises of government" occurred in some towns and not others; in a similar way, we see the obvious crisis in Quzhou, not in Ningbo. In Exeter and Salisbury of the 1620s, where the plague was handled in exemplary fashion, the magistrates, as Slack points out, were "not simply accepting the need for direct action against the plague; they were taking the lead in providing it." Even more, he notes that the motivation of local leaders often included desiring to maintain the coherence and authority of the ruling group. The extraordinary frequency of the meeting of Ningbo's EDO staff and committees during November 1940 may well have been motivated by a desire to keep outsiders out of the decision-making group. Finally, Slack calls attention to the unremitting and grueling nature of the "day-to-day administration demanded by plague regulations." That necessity of constancy suggests even more why the management of the plague in Quzhou foundered; when decision makers were not always "on the ground" to react to changing situations or were not fully engaged in fighting the plague or were not all on the same page in terms of what should be done or what the priorities were, policies could not likely have been effective.[34]

In 1997, a group of 180 Chinese citizens, including many from Quzhou and Ningbo, launched a suit against the Japanese government, demanding that Tokyo admit that it had used biological weapons, apologize, and pay each of them 10 million yen. In a ruling in August 2002, the Tokyo District Court acknowledged that Japanese military activities had caused immense suffering and were clearly inhumane. But the court turned down the plaintiffs' other demands, saying that all compensation issues had been settled when Japan and China normalized diplomatic ties in the 1970s. In February 2005 the Tokyo High Court turned down an appeal of those Chinese citizens, again rejecting demands for compensation. The leader of the Chinese plaintiffs immediately took their case to the Japanese Supreme Court.[35]

It should be said that in the 1990s and the first decade of the twenty-first century, Japanese lawyers, historians, and citizen activists vigorously supported the more than two dozen lawsuits filed by Chinese victims of Japanese biological warfare, abandoned chemical weapons, the Nanjing massacre, indiscriminate aerial bombing, military sexual slavery, and forced labor. Despite the fact that all suits failed, many Japanese judges engaged in historical "fact finding" instead of rejecting claims without comment. This produced an incontrovertible record of Japan's war conduct where little or nothing existed before. For example, whereas the Japanese government still insisted it knew nothing about the activities of the notorious Manchurian Unit 731—which produced the plague bacillus that was used in the biowar against Ningbo and Quzhou, and spun off into Yiwu—a Tokyo court concluded that the unit killed many Chinese through biological warfare and human experimentation. Japanese judges occasionally even suggested that the government should proactively settle claims from Chinese war victims via national legislation and a compensation fund, the approach by which Germany and Austria came to terms with Nazi-era forced labor.[36]

But in April and May 2007, the Supreme Court of Japan issued decisions that Chinese individuals had absolutely no judicial right to demand compensation or war reparations—using the rationale of the Tokyo District Court in 2002: that right was abandoned when diplomatic relations were established in the early 1970s. The Supreme Court's decisions related not only to germ warfare but to forced labor and military sexual slavery, as well.

➤◄

Remaking Homes

ONE OF THE MOST DESPERATE DECISIONS that people in any culture must make in the wake of war, ethnic cleansing, epidemic, or famine is to flee their homes and become refugees. Yet hundreds of thousands of people choose that option (or are forced to) almost every year, as has been evident in recent years in Sudan, Lebanon, and Iraq. The Office of the United Nations High Commissioner on Refugees noted in June 2006 that the numbers of uprooted peoples living in refugee-like situations in their home countries totaled 20.8 million, an increase of 1.3 million over 2005.[1] The refugee crisis is an ongoing tragedy that is not abating. Anthropologist Anthony Oliver Smith calls forced migration and re-settlement *totalizing phenomena* that are always painful and almost inevitably produce a sense of powerlessness and alienation.[2] Refugees have lost their world and their social identity—a sentence that spins off the laptop easily but which can only adumbrate the cataclysmic trauma of human displacement.

In recent times, most NGOs and related organizations have used Western models to manage refugee populations who experience this "sea of bitterness." Into the 1990s, the general modus operandi in dealing with refugees had been to offer culturally Western diagnoses to refugee ills and to utilize culturally Western approaches as solutions. Many Westerners assumed the universal applicability of these ideologically imperialistic diagnoses and solutions, based, as they were, on a model that tended to see the causes and burdens of social responsibility within the individual. Yet anthropologists have long warned about the

intellectual and practical inappropriateness of taking the Western con-
cept of the individual and applying that sense of selfhood to individuals
in other cultures. Experiences in one culture must be seen in that culture's framework.[3]

Increasing numbers of medical and psychological specialists have argued in recent decades that it is a fallacy to assume that becoming a refugee is a universal experience without regard to culture. The claim, for
example, that up to one-third of all refugees experience post-traumatic
stress disorder might be appropriate for Western refugees but might
perhaps not be relevant for communities in the non-Western world.[4]
Medical anthropologists have shown from work in Uganda, Nicaragua,
Mozambique, Cambodia, and El Salvador that focusing on the individual
and his or her treatment may be inappropriate in cultures where the
group precedes the individual, where the individual finds his primary
meaning in the group.

While culture is never determinative (people can choose to act or not
to act within certain cultural parameters), the values of traditional Chinese
culture remained generally pervasive into the 1930s and 1940s. In traditional China the group preceded and therefore had precedence over its
individuals; maintaining the group and its harmony was of primary concern. The group constrained the individual, much as if he or she were
linked by invisible threads to a group net. Psychiatrist and medical anthropologist Arthur Kleinman has argued that Chinese cultural beliefs stress
"intimate relationships with more affective significance than one's own
thoughts, fantasies, desires, and emotions. Family and other close interpersonal relations become a person's paramount interests; coping with them
becomes a sign of adult competence, and problems with them are more
important to him than other personal problems."[5]

In another view of traditional Chinese culture, anthropologist Edward
Hall posited in various works, including *Beyond Culture,* that cultures dif-
fer according to how human activity is related to context.[6] In low-context
cultures, like most western European nations and the United States,
people tend to pay attention to facts, communication screens out surroundings, and decision making tends to be relatively rapid. In contrast, in
high-context cultures close attention is paid to all surroundings and complete contexts—social settings, history, class, age, gender, education, appearance, social status, gestures, and tone—with the result that judgments,

decision making, even communication itself, tend to take more time. Hall names Japan and China the two highest-context cultures. Though Hall's paradigm must be handled with care (there is obviously a huge range of personality types related to contextual issues within cultures), it is at least suggestive of what cultures prioritize.

In addition to Chinese high consciousness of context and of the group—whether family, social network, political faction, school, business, industry, or organizations like the Red Swastika or Boy Scouts—two other Chinese cultural elements crucial in the refugee experience were the perceived cultural centrality of native place and the essentiality of social connections for living a meaningful and productive life. A family's base and chief source of identity was traditionally the ancestral home, where a person, like generations before him, would live, die, and be buried. In the words of Anthony Giddens, "time and space remained essentially linked through place."[7] Identity was strongly territorialized. Becoming a refugee was thus having to deal with a lost way of life and a change in one's own identity. In such a situation, place became, in Giddens's summation, "phantasmogoric."[8]

Feng Zikai mourned the loss of Yuanyuan Hall and its way of life during his long plight as refugee; the hall was such an integral part of his life—identified with family and his own work—that it was clearly a piece of his identity. Feng's attachment to Yuanyuan Hall underscores the reality that *place* is actually a product of social activity, not simply an arena for it.[9] During his years as refugee, the idea of place, specifically Yuanyuan Hall, could remain unscathed, unsullied, and unchanged in his mind. But when Feng returned there in 1946, his beloved sanctuary had been truly lost forever, totally destroyed early in the war. In a similar way, student Tao Yongming of the Shaoxing Jishan Middle School continually bemoaned his absence from his native place, as he wandered all around the province in search of a school.

Basic social identity came not only from family and native place but from various all-important social connections and the networks that developed from family and place. As Giddens has pointed out, "Trust relations were localised and formed through personal ties."[10] One Western commentator noted the distinct Chinese social mental universe: "Chinese ... instinctively divide people into those with whom they already have a fixed relationship, a connection, *guanxi,* and those that they don't. *Guanxi* have created a social magnetic field in which all Chinese move, keenly aware of those people with whom they have connections and those they don't."[11] For refugees, those from other places and with whom one had no social connections were perceived as the Other, strangers, often threatening and dangerous. The decision to become a refugee, in effect, to leave one's localized and "ontologically secure" identity behind and travel to a world without connections—a domain of strangers and potential antagonists—was, if anything, likely riskier than the decision might have been in some other cultures.

In the world of refugees, one scholar observes, "an indefinite range of possibilities present themselves, not just in respect of options for behaviour but in respect also of the 'openness of the world' for the individual." The intimidating, even frightening reality for the refugee is that "'the world' . . . is not a seamless order of time and space stretching away from the [individual's native place]"; rather, the world "intrudes into a [refugee's] presence via an array of varying channels and sources."[12] Individual refugees like Feng Zikai, war diarists Feng Zongmeng and Jin Xihui, and labor conscripts Zhang Dayan and Wu Yingcai faced the Other directly, the latter two facing two different Others (the Japanese and unknown Chinese). Zhang and Wu were obviously on their own. Many refugees—perhaps most—like Feng Zikai, Feng Zongmeng, and Jin Xihui, traveled with their families. At times of crisis the family was the core default unit, as its integral value in Chinese society was reasserted. While families often remained together, the safety of the family weighed on heads of households as a heavy responsibility.

Institutional refugees—governments, provincial and county; schools; businesses; and industries—in a sense took with them their "home" and many of those people with whom they had connections. People who traveled as part of institutions were much less individually open to threats from the Other, and they had institutional bases, retaining personal connections that predated the coming of war and the decision to flee to the rear area. Yet there were other kinds of problems with the lives of institutional refugees, among them, disruptions in the institutional work that were caused by the moves. Schools and governments moved repeatedly; governments were dispersed and fragmented; businesses and industries had resource, supply, and labor difficulties. And the moves were to areas that were years behind the institutions' home bases in terms of "modernization time." The move of the provincial government from Hangzhou to Fangyan to Yunhe was a move in time from 1937 back into the nineteenth century. Thus, refugees traveling both as individuals and as members of institutions faced psychological shocks and challenges as they tried to make a new life. As Peter Loizos of the London School of Economics put it, "From the moment of displacement on, experiential, maturational, and sociological time clocks are all ticking, registering changes of different kinds."[13]

This study has focused on the narratives of individual, group, and institutional refugees. That refugees, who had chosen to wrench themselves from their homes or been forced to do so by institutional or other constraints, would write narratives of their experiences is not surprising: narratives were vehicles to create and give meaning to their lives and create their own wartime identity, to bring order out of their troubled, totally novel, and disjointed experiences. Uprooted from their heretofore lived lives, the comfortable muddling through each day, the known social connections and friendships, and the daily routines, they were forced to face the realities of displacement, the disjuncture of space and time. As one scholar has noted, refugee studies have often used "cultural bereavement" as an analogy: "Loss of home, of social relations, of the meanings which the regularities of life impose on existence, is most like the loss through death of parent, spouse, child."[14] The narrative, a self-conscious reconstruction, lifts the constrictive bars encompassing Before and After, making a coherent, if certainly not planned and not always satisfying, whole—and giving fuller meaning and a greater sense of order to the experience.[15] Narrative also embedded the narrators in contexts of national importance.

If the refugees had, of necessity, to change, in David Turton's words, "the way [they] collectively imagine[d] the world and their place in it," then "displacement is not just about the loss of place, but also about the struggle to *make* [emphasis in the original] a place in the world, where meaningful action and shared understanding is possible."[16] Although all the refugee institutions had to struggle to make a new place in the world, probably the best example in Zhejiang of such a place was Lu Gongwang's refugee textile mill, first set up in Yongkang County, where it thrived, and then partially moved to Jiangshan, but mostly reestablished in Yunhe in 1942. During the four years the mill was in Yongkang, there was a spirit of living and working with a new family or, perhaps more accurately, living in a new neighborhood—providing a thoroughly new identity. Another new place made by a refugee institution was the Provincial Temporary United Middle School in Bihu in Lishui County, an amalgam of seven schools; although the unity was loose, there was a spirit among students and teachers that generated a sense of community, which anthropologist Turton has defined as "substantive social forms in which *locality* [emphasis added] is realized."[17] In both the textile mill and the middle school, the workers and the students, respectively, found new identities. In looking in general at the refugee experience in Zhejiang, the reality is that not many struggled mightily to make a new place. Short-term refugees had no need to do so; long-term refugees, both individual and institutional, longed for the end of the war and the opportunity to return to their home bases or their native places. The reality was that the *real place* for most wartime refugees was limbo.

What of the larger issues that war so clearly limns? Repeatedly, individuals and institutions revealed a lack of preparedness or readiness for war or for the Japanese onslaught. Was this simply a result of naivete? Was it perhaps a wrongheaded use of native place security to "filter out" threatening, heightened anxiety? Was there a widespread disbelief (exhibited, for example, by Feng Zikai and martyred magistrate Zhang Ju) that, even with Japanese forces in the vicinity, one wouldn't (couldn't?) be touched? Perhaps the possibility was so far away from Chinese realms of experience, from their own personal histories, that enemy actions could not even have been imagined. Feng Zongmeng noted that in November 1937, while enemy planes flew over the Pinghu county seat for days and Japanese ships massed in Hangzhou Bay just offshore, the townspeople made no contingency plans to deal with a possible invasion. Many times this "it can't happen to me" syndrome had serious, even deadly consequences. The lack of preparedness for the Japanese attacks in Shaoxing and Ningbo was stunningly unconscionable, given the common knowledge of the proximity of Japanese army divisions. The number of Chinese villages occupied by Japanese soldiers and their Chinese labor conscripts where it was obvious the Chinese villagers had gotten out just in the nick of time—right before the enemy entered—also illustrates the same phenomenon. Certainly many refugees, especially as word spread of the kind of brutal and terroristic enemies the Japanese were, took the threat seriously. And yet, merchant Wang Mengsong in Qu County still had trouble believing that the actions of Japanese soldiers could be even more brutal than propaganda had led him to believe.

The decade before the war had been a period of state building for the Guomindang, which was focusing on institutions and infrastructure. Some have seen the war experience as providing the base for postwar and even post–civil war institutions and governmental approaches.[18] In the handling of the displaced and displacement in general in Zhejiang, the state had a record that was clearly more negative than positive, creating situations that undercut the likelihood that the postwar state could continue. There was some initial success in dealing with the refugees—until the refugee tide became a tidal wave within a matter of months. The spatial dispersal of provincial government bodies and the consequent lack of communication between key ministries and bureaus led to governmental impotence. When the government did take forceful action, it appeared the ogre. The forced labor of hundreds of thousands of civilians in the widespread deforestation of central Zhejiang to construct the Quzhou air base and the almost Sisyphean quality of the forced civilian labor in multiple construction, destructions, and reconstructions of the base cannot have raised the image of the state in the eyes of the people. Scorched-earth policies destroyed much of the infrastructural gains of the 1930s and made life increasingly difficult for Chinese citizens while doing, in the long run, nothing to block the Japanese war machine. The failure of the provincial Health Department to correctly analyze the bubonic plague bacillus in Quzhou and the subsequent tragedy simply underscored governmental incompetence, the episode standing in stark contrast to the outbreak in Ningbo, which was successfully handled by local elites and officials without the involvement of the provincial or national governments. One could even posit that war experiences showed the state in the worst possible light and that, in Zhejiang at least, instead of state building or, at the least, state maintenance, there was state erosion.

Historians have long debated the extent and depth of national feelings at various periods among the Chinese populace. Over four decades ago, Mary Wright saw nationalism as the "moving force" in a "rising tide of change" in the first decade of the twentieth century.[19] But her focus was primarily on cities in core zones. Bryna Goodman found the ingredients for nationalism among native place organizations of sojourning merchants in Shanghai; she calls her period of investigation from 1853 to 1937 an "era of developing nationalism."[20] Again, the focus is on metropolitan Shanghai. Certainly there have been many studies showing nationalism among the 1911 revolutionaries, in the ideology of Sun Yat-sen and other political leaders in the 1910s into the 1930s, among May Fourth reformers and May Thirtieth demonstrators. In terms of the countryside, Chalmers Johnson posited that nationalism was born among the Chinese peasants as part of the Resistance War against Japan; he focused on north China, where the Communist Eighth Route Army was at work mobilizing peasants.[21]

What of the masses during the Sino-Japanese War? Though collaboration has not figured into this study, the large numbers of Chinese who collaborated with the Japanese—admittedly for many diverse reasons—raise questions about the depth of national feeling. Among the Zhejiang refugees in this study, I found precious little evidence of overt nationalism or patriotic fervor. Instead, the reality seemed to me more like the peasants in the "shut" cycle of G. William Skinner's "open and shut case."[22] That is, as war came, individuals and families desperately strove to spread a protective mantle over themselves—saving themselves, their families, and their native places: the local, not the nation, became the focus. The war was a "localizing" phenomenon; it was hard to get a bigger picture when one's native place was occupied or when one was isolated in a poverty-marked, undeveloped rear area. This, of course, does not mean that localism and nationalism could not coexist; I have argued elsewhere that provincialism and nationalism were not mutually exclusive. And, in the end, "localizing" is not necessarily a bad strategy; the Communist revolution, when it came, was built on the reality of localities: indeed, that was the secret of the Communist success.

But the absence of patriotic thoughts and expression in these refugee accounts (even in that of an intellectual like Feng Zikai) is rather remarkable. Since many of these memoirs were written well after the fact, the inclusion of nationalistic or patriotic rhetoric would almost have been expected in order to elevate the "patriotic stature" of the narrator. Though I have already spoken here about native place, it is worth reiterating the words of diarist Jin Xihui. He did not say about the Japanese, "The devils brutally occupied China or my country." Rather, he said, "The devils brutally occupied our native place." And again: "I had tears in my eyes looking at my own native place about which ... I felt so ardent."

Indeed, many Chinese tended to see the Chinese army as a threat equal to that of the Japanese army. The expectation of middle school students like Wu Yingcai was that Chinese and Japanese troops would act basically the same way. When the Feng family of Tongxiang were returning home after a period as refugees, it was Chinese soldiers who stopped their boat and robbed them. Feng Zikai distrusted and feared what Chinese soldiers might do, rather naively dismissing what Japanese might do. Chinese civilians commonly took advantage of refugees, charging outrageous prices and cheating them in countless ways. Fear of labor and military conscription by Chinese forces was widespread—actions which indeed amounted, in effect, to kidnapping and military imprisonment. Refugees feared having their escape boats commandeered by Chinese soldiers. Bitterness flared about Chinese troops barging into civilians' homes to make their meals. There was not, in short, much praise, if any, for the troops of the fatherland.

It was only in the schools in exile where a specific appeal to patriotic nationalism and a sense of wider national purpose was mounted. In contrast, there was the stance of business and especially industry; though a small number of companies moved, Huang was bitterly rebuffed by most industries when he tried to get them to retreat into the interior in order to contribute to the national cause. Most industrialists and businesspeople chose to live under Japanese control in the major modern cities of the province. The spatial dispersion of the provincial government, as I have noted, cannot have helped create a sense of a unified polity, either as province or nation. The bitter factional feuding and rampant political personal ambitions and animosities, while perhaps par for the course, especially during crisis periods, did not reveal or express "national" ideals or, indeed, much commitment beyond self, faction, and locality.

But perhaps in any war the chief goal is self-protection, protection of family, protection of home—at time of extreme and intense fear and emotion, the nation might just not be in the picture. Among refugees and those who stayed to live under Japanese control, who were muddling by to survive, any sense of "nation" was incipient at best. Among the masses, nationalism in China was still incubating and would not emerge generally as a key in Chinese life until much later, in the People's Republic in the 1980s and 1990s, when national pride could finally overcome the humiliations, foreign and domestic, that had been suffered for decades.

Paul Fussell notes that even in World War II, when nationalism, democracy, and the defeat of totalitarianism's horror should, we would think, have been motivating and prioritizing factors, that was not the case—even among fighting soldiers. Fussell reports that soldiers were motivated not by nation or patriotism but by the comradeship of their units and a desire, in the words of John Hersey, "to get the goddam [*sic*] thing over and get home."[23]

Home: it was, after all, the beacon, the real Peach Blossom Spring—what the refugees dreamed of and sought, the memory that sustained many of them through some of the unspeakable horrors they experienced. When the war was over, institutions—governments, schools, businesses, and industries—did return home, if to a changed, largely unrecognizable world, to continue nevertheless as institutions. For individuals, homecoming was a mixed bag. For some, it may have been good, but all their worlds had been thoroughly changed. Others, like Feng Zikai, found that there was no longer any home to which to return. For them, spatial and social displacement was permanent; perhaps, indeed, for all refugees psychological displacement was a natural product of their wartime experiences. All were faced with remaking their "homes"—spatial, social, and psychological—in a China that was beginning to remake itself.

Notes

Book epigraph: David Gascoyne, "An Autumn Park," October 1939, from Selected Poems (London: Enitharmon Press, 1994).

Introduction

1. Lu Xun, *Selected Stories of Lu Hsun,* trans. Yang Hsien-yi and Gladys Yang (New York: W. W. Norton, 2003), p. 143.

2. *Yuhang xianzhi* [A gazetteer of Yuhang County] (Hangzhou: Zhejiang renmin chubanshe, 1990), p. 25. See also "Guzhen xuelei" [The ancient town's tears of blood], in *Tiaoshang nuhuo: Yuhang xian kangRi douzheng jishi* [Flames of fury among the local residents: Accounts of the anti-Japanese struggle in Yuhang County] (N.p., 1991), pp. 80–84.

3. Feng Xinfa, "Qiaosi datusha mujiji" [An eyewitness account of the Qiaosi massacre], in *Tie Zheng* [Irrefutable evidence] (Hangzhou: n.p., 1995), pp. 20–23.

4. Derek Summerfield, "Discussion Guide 1: The Nature of Conflict and the Implications for Appropriate Psychosocial Responses," pp. 32–33, http://earlybird .qeh.ox.ac.uk/regexp/pdfs/1_3pdf.

5. David Turton, "The Meaning of Place in a World of Movement: Lessons from Long-Term Research in Southern Ethiopia," *Journal of Refugee Studies* 18, no. 3 (2005): 258.

6. Fujiwara Akira, "The Nanking Atrocity: An Interpretive Overview," in Bob Tadashi Wakabayashi, ed., *The Nanking Atrocity, 1937–38: Complicating the Picture* (New York: Berghahn Books, 2007), p. 33.

7. Peter Loizos, "'Generations' in Forced Migration: Towards Greater Clarity," *Journal of Refugee Studies* 20, no. 2 (2007): 193.

8. This description is by Anthony Giddens, whose wider canvas is modernity and the self, but whose descriptions fit the disjunctive crisis faced by the displaced perfectly. See his *Modernity and Self-Identity Self and Society in the Late Modern Age* (Stanford, Calif.: Stanford University Press, 1991), pp. 36–37.

9. Pierre Nora, *Realms of Memory,* vol. 1: *Conflicts and Divisions,* trans. Arthur Goldhammer (New York: Columbia University Press, 1996), p. 3.

10. Giddens, p. 72.

1. A World Where Ghosts Wailed

1. "Wei zai Zhedongde nanminmen hechu" [Why are there cries coming from the refugees in Zhedong], *Dongnan ribao,* January 13, 1939, p. 4.

2. Zhang Genfu, *Kangzhan shiqi Zhejiang sheng renkou qianyi yu shehui yingxiang* [Population movement and its social impact in Zhejiang Province during the Resistance War] (Shanghai: Sanlian shudian, 2001), pp. 43–44.

3. Feng Zikai, "Tonglu fuxuan" [Bearing the tumult (of war) in Tonglu (County)], in *Feng Zikai wenji* [The collected writings of Feng Zikai], (Hangzhou: Zhejiang wenyi chubanshe, 1990-1992), vol. 6, p. 3.

4. Zhao Zhangtai, "Kangzhan shiqi wo zai Lishui diandi" [Bits of my experience during the Resistance War in Lishui], in *Lishui wenshi ziliao* [Historical materials from Lishui], vol. 2 (N.p., 1985), p. 103.

5. See Zhao Pochu, "Kangzhan chuqi Shanghaide nanmin gongzuo" [Refugee work in Shanghai at the beginning of the Resistance War], in *Shanghai wenshi ziliao* [Historical materials on Shanghai], vol. 32 (Shanghai, 1980), p. 31.

6. See Marcia R. Ristaino, *The Jacquinot Safe Zone* (Stanford, Calif.: Stanford University Press, 2008), pp. 51–52.

7. Percy Finch, *Shanghai and Beyond* (New York: Scribner, 1953), p. 362, cited in Ristaino, *Jacquinot Safe Zone,* p. 52.

8. "Nanmin fangwen" [A visit to refugees], *Dongnan ribao,* "Nanmin fangwen" [A visit to refugees], November 23, 1937.

9. Zhao, "Kangzhan chuqi Shanghaide," p. 103.

10. Lou Shiyi, "Lunxian shengya" [My career in occupied land], in *Yuyao wenshi ziliao* [Historical materials on Yuyao], vol. 8 (N.p., 1990), p. 2.

11. Feng Zikai, "Ci Yuanyuan Tang" [Taking leave of Yuanyuan Tang], in *Feng Zikai wenji* [The collected writings of Feng Zikai], vol. 5 (Hangzhou: Zhejiang wenyi chubanshe, 1992), p. 130.

12. Joshua Fogel, "The Nanking Atrocity and Chinese Historical Memory," in Bob Tadashi Wakabayashi, ed., *The Nanking Atrocity, 1937–38: Complicating the Picture* (New York: Berghahn Books, 2007), p. 279.

13. "Jiashan kangRi zhanzheng shiqi dashiji" [Important events in Jiashan's Resistance War against Japan], in *Jiashan wenshi ziliao* [Historical materials on Jiashan], vol. 1 (N.p., 1986), p. 4.

14. The information on the Hangzhou Bay landing comes from *Pinghu xianzhi* [A gazetteer of Pinghu County] (Shanghai: Shanghai renmin chubanshe, 1993), pp. 719–720 and 722, and from *Pinghu wenshi ziliao* [Historical materials on Pinghu County], vol. 1 (N.p., 1988), pp. 1–2.

15. Zhang, *Kangzhan shiqi,* p. 46.

16. Sun Zuoliang, "Tanghui kangRi nanwang shi" [A hard-to-forget account about the Resistance War in Tanghui Town], *Jiaxing shi wenshi ziliao tongxun* [Journal of Jiaxing City's historical materials] 16 (July 1995): 6–7.

17. Li Yuchang, "Wode kunan he jianwen" [Information about my bitter life as a refugee], in *Tongxiang shi kangRi zhanzheng shiliao* [Historical materials on the Resistance War in Tongxiang City] (N.p., 1995), pp. 52–57.

18. All the information on Li Genpan's experiences comes from his "Binan jian-wen" [Experience on taking refuge], in *Jiashan wenshi ziliao* [Historical materials on Jiashan], vol. 1 (N.p., 1986), pp. 60-61.

19. Li Genpan, p. 60.

20. Li asserts that the "refuge" was about a month; but he also claims that they did not return to Jiashan until the second month of 1938. Since the other dates he includes accord with the lunar calendar, I assume this "second month" does also; the first day of the second lunar month in 1938 was March 13 in the solar calendar.

21. All the information about the Feng family experiences comes from Fang Zhen-hua, "Tongniande monan" [The hardships of childhood] in *Tongxiang wenshi ziliao* [Historical materials on Tongxiang], vol. 14 (N.p.: N.p., 1995), pp. 59-63.

22. Fei Xiaotong, *From the Soil: The Foundations of Chinese Society,* trans. Gary G. Hamilton and Wang Zheng (Berkeley: University of California Press, 1992), p. 92.

23. *Haining kangzhan banian dashiji* [Important events in the eight-year Resistance War in Haining County] (N.p., 1987), p. 5.

24. See R. Keith Schoppa, *Xiang Lake: Nine Centuries of Chinese Life* (New Haven, Conn.:Yale University Press 1989), pp. 220–222.

25. The quotation is from Chen Jican, "Gucheng lijie ji" [A record of the historical disaster in the old city], in *Shaoxing wenshi ziliao xuanji* [A collection of historical materials on Shaoxing], vol. 3 (N.p., 1985), pp. 228–229. Also see Li Shenkeng, "Shaoxing jiaotong yinhang lunxianshi zaojie shimo" [The complete story of the calamities that befell Shaoxing's Communications Bank], in *Shaoxing wenshi ziliao* [Historical materials on Shaoxing], vol. 4 (N.p., 1988), pp. 73–74; and Bawu laoren, "Shaoxing lunxian shiqi jianwenlu" [An account of experiences in Shaoxing during the occupation period], in *Shaoxing wenshi ziliao xuanji,* vol. 1 (N.p., 1983), p. 198.

26. Bawu laoren, "Shaoxing lunxian," p. 198.

27. *Zhoushan shizhi* [A gazetteer of Zhoushan City] (Hangzhou: Zhejiang renmin chubanshe, 1992), p. 16.

28. Ibid., p. 17.

29. *Zhenhai xianzhi* [A gazetter of Zhenhai County] (Shanghai: Zhongguo dabaike quanshu chubanshe, 1994), pp. 17–18 and 279–280.

30. Zhang, *Kangzhan shiqi,* p. 63.

31. See, for example, the case of Shaoxing, "Shaoxingjiao jizhan" [Pitched battles in Shaoxing and its vicinity], *Dongnan ribao,* April 18, 1941, p. 2; and of Ningbo, "Zhedong zhanju" [The war situation in Eastern Zhejiang], *Dongnan ribao,* April 20, 1941, p.2.

32. Zi Xi, "Zai zainan zhongzhong rizili" [Days of serious calamity], in *Xinchang wenshi ziliao* [Historical materials from Xinchang County], vol. 6 (N.p., 1995), p. 19.

33. Ibid.

34. Ibid.

35. Ibid.

36. Lu Zuoyang, "Wo yijia zaoyu" [What my family encountered], in *Xinchang wenshi ziliao* [Historical materials from Xinchang County], vol. 6 (N.p., 1995), pp. 16–17.

37. Cited in Duane Schultz, *The Doolittle Raid* (New York: St. Martin's Press, 1988), p. 178.

38. *Quzhou shizhi* [A gazetteer of Quzhou municipality] (Hanghou: Zhejiang renmin chubanshe, 1994), p. 949.

39. Ibid., pp. 949–950.

40. *Qu xianzhi* [A gazetteer of Qu County] (Hangzhou: Zheijang Zhejiang renmin chubanshe, 1992), p. 387.

41. See the discussion of Zhang, *Kangzhan shiqi,* pp. 58–61.

42. Ibid., p. 61.

43. Ibid., p. 65.

44. Wang Weiying, "Kangzhan yinian lai Zhejiang sheng jiuji nanmin gaikuang" [A survey of refugee relief during the last year of the resistance war], *Zhanshi banyuekan* [Wartime bimonthly], 1945, no. 6, p. 5.

45. Zhang, *Kangzhan shiqi,* p. 63.

46. These figures are from Zhang, *Kangzhan shiqi,* pp. 72–74.

47. Zhang, *Kangzhan shiqi,* p. 81.

2. Confronting the Refugee Crisis

1. *Dongnan ribao,* January 5, 1938.

2. *Dongnan ribao,* November 19, 1937.

3. Huang Shaohong, *Huang Shaohong huiyilu* [Memoirs of Huang Shaohong] (Nanning: Guangxi renmin chubanshe, 1991).

4. Huang Shaohong, *Huang Shaohong huiyilu,* pp. 459–460.

5. *Dongnan ribao,* April 21, 1938.

6. Zhang Genfu, *Kangzhan shiqi Zhejiang sheng renkou qianyi yu shehui yingxiang* [Population movement and its social influence in Zhejiang Province during the Resistance War] (Shanghai: Sanlian shudian, 2001), p. 101.

7. Ibid., p. 95.

8. Feng Zikai, "Tonglu fuxuan" [Bearing the tumult (of war) in Tonglu (County], in *Feng Zikai wenji* [The collected writings of Feng Zikai] (Hangzhou: Zhejiang wenyi chubanshe, 1992), p. 22.

9. Lu Gongwang, "Zhejiang sheng zhenjihui nanmin ranzhi gongchang shimo ji" [The whole record of the refugee relief textile mill in Zhejiang], in *Yongkang xianzhi* [A gazetteer of Yongkang County], (Hangzhou, 1991), p. 780.

10. *Dongnan ribao*, May 18 and May 23, 1938.

11. Feng Zongmeng, "Danghu mengnan lu" [A record of being confronted by danger in Pinghu] ,in *Jiaxing shizhi* (A gazetteer of the Jiaxing metropolitan area], vol. 2 (Beijing: Zhongguo shuji chubanshe, 1997), p. 2319.

12. *Dongnan ribao*, March 4, 1938.

13. *Dongnan ribao*, September 5, 1938.

14. *Dongnan ribao*, January 13, 1939.

15. *Dongnan ribao*, February 16, 1938.

16. Huang, *Huang Shaohong huiyilu*, p. 462.

17. Zhang, *Kangzhan shiqi*, p. 87. All quotations within the discussion of this list are taken from Zhang.

18. *Dongnan ribao*, March 5–7, 1938.

19. *Dongnan ribao*, April 7 and 21, 1938.

20. *Dongnan ribao*, April 16 and 21, 1938.

21. *Dongnan ribao*, May 18, 1938.

22. *Dongnan ribao*, June 1, 1938.

23. *Dongnan ribao*, June 25, 1938.

24. *Dongnan ribao*, October 16 and December 16, 1938; February 2, 1939.

25. *Dongnan ribao*, August 2, 1938.

26. *Dongnan ribao*, March 2 and December 21, 1939.

27. *Dongnan ribao*, July 18, 1941.

28. *Dongnan ribao*, July 21, 1941.

29. *Dongnan ribao*, August 5, August 19, and September 12, 1941.

30. *Dongnan ribao*, January 13, 1939.

31. *Dongnan ribao*, November 26, 1937.

32. *Dongnan ribao*, April 14 and 20 and May 6, 1938.

33. *Dongnan ribao*, December 1, 1939.

34. Ying Baorong and Lu Shilian, "Lu Gongwang jingli 'nanmin gongchang' zhi shimo" [The whole story of the "refugee factory" under manager Lu Gongwang], in *Jinhua wenshi ziliao*, vol. 2 (N.p., n.d.), pp. 151–162.

35. Lu Gongwang, "Zhejiang sheng zhenjihui nanmin ranzhi gongchang shimoji" [The full story of the Refugee Dyeing and Weaving Mill sponsored by the Relief Society in Zhejiang Province], *Yongkang xianzhi* [A gazetteer of Yongkang County], vol. 2 (Hangzhou: Zhejiang renmin chubanshe, 1991), p. 780.

36. Ibid.

37. See Li Xugen, "Lu Gongwang jiangjun zai Chishi" [General Lu Gongwang in Chishi], in *Yunhe xian wenshi ziliao* [Historical materials in Yunhe County], vol. 2 (N.p., 1985), pp. 12–15.

38. *Dongnan ribao,* August 26, 1943.

39. *Dongnan ribao,* April 1 and June 19, 1939.

40. Zhang, *Kangzhan shiqi,* p. 91.

41. Ibid., p. 92.

42. *Dongnan ribao,* March 3 and April 27, 1938.

43. Unless otherwise indicated, this discussion on work relief is based upon Zhang, *Kangzhan shiqi,* pp. 93–95.

44. Ying Baorong, "Yiqie weile kang zhang" [Everything for the Resistance War], in *KangRi zhanzheng zai Yongkang* [The Resistance War in Yongkang] (Yongkang: n.p., 1995), p. 185.

45. On the city wall, see *Dongnan ribao,* January 26, 1939.

46. *Dongnan ribao,* July 26, 1939.

47. Unless otherwise indicated, this discussion of other forms of government aid comes from Zhang, *Kangzhan shiqi,* pp. 95–97.

48. Huang, *Huang Shaohong huiyilu,* p. 460.

49. See, for example, *Dongnan ribao,* October 13, 1942, and February 8, 1945.

50. *Dongnan ribao,* January 13, 1939 and March 2, 1939.

51. Zhang, *Kangzhan shiqi,* p. 89.

52. Ibid., p. 95.

53. *Dongnan ribao,* March 2, 1939.

54. *Dongnan ribao,* April 12, 1938.

55. *Baojia* was a traditional community system for mutual security-surveillance, in which all Chinese households were to be assigned. A group of one thousand households comprised a *bao;* and these were divided into ten *jia.* The *baojia* head was traditionally chosen by *baojia* members and served on a rotating basis.

56. Zhang, *Kangzhan shiqi,* p. 96.

57. *Dongnan ribao,* December 20, 1937.

58. *Dongnan ribao,* September 18, 22, and October 16, 1938.

59. Zhang, *Kangzhan shiqi,* p. 96.

60. Ibid.

61. *Dongnan ribao,* December 20, 1937.

62. Zhang, *Kangzhan shiqi,* p. 97.

63. Wu Yisun, "Zhanshi Zhejiang linshi shenghui—Yunhe" [Yunhe, Zhejiang's wartime capital], in *Yunhe wenshi ziliao,* vol. 4 (N.p., n.d.), pp. 41–42.

64. This discussion on native place associations is based, unless otherwise noted, on Zhang, *Kangzhan shiqi,* pp. 98–100.

65. *Dongnan ribao,* March 21, 1938.

66. Zhang, *Kangzhan shiqi,* p. 100.

67. Zhou Feng, ed., *Minguo shiqi Hangzhou* [Hangzhou during the Republic] (Hangzhou: N.p., 1997), p. 145.

68. Zhang, *Kangzhan shiqi*, pp. 102–103.

69. *Dongnan ribao,* January 14, 1941.

70. Prasenjit Duara, "Of Authenticity and Woman: Personal Narratives of Middle-Class Women in Modern China," in Yeh Wen-hsin, *Becoming Chinese: Passages to Modernity and Beyond,* ed. Yeh Wen-hsin (Berkeley: University of California Press, 2000), pp. 342–343.

71. Bob Tadashi Wakabayashi, ed. *The Nanking Atrocity, 1937–38: Complicating the Picture* (New York: Berghahn Books, 2007), p. 202. For the "elite" designation, see Prasenjit Duara, *Sovereignty and Authenticity: Manchukuo and the East Asian Modern* (Lanham, Md.: Rowman and Littlefield Publishers, 2003), p. 118.

72. Timothy Brook, *Collaboration: Japanese Agents and Local Elites in Wartime China* (Cambridge, Mass.: Harvard University Press, 2005), pp. 136–137.

73. Unless otherwise noted, the following information on the actions of the Red Swastika Society come from Zhang, *Kangzhan shiqi,* pp. 104–109.

74. *Dongnan ribao,* February 23, 1938.

75. Zhang, *Kangzhan shiqi,* p. 106.

76. See the chart in Zhang, *Kangzhan shiqi,* p. 110.

77. William T. Rowe, *Hankow: Conflict and Community in a Chinese City, 1796–1895* (Stanford, Calif.: Stanford University Press, 1989), p. 228.

78. Rowe, *Hankow,* p. 228.

79. Rowe, *Hankow,* p. 131.

80. Fei Xiaotong, *From the Soil: The Foundations of Chinese Society,* trans. Gary G. Hamilton and Wang Zheng (Berkeley: University of California Press, 1992), pp. 60–61.

3. Veering into the Ravine

1. Geremie Barmé, *An Artistic Exile: A Life of Feng Zikai (1898–1975)* (Berkeley: University of California Press, 2002), pp. 216–217.

2. The material in this section is based on Feng Zikai, "Ci Yuanyuantang" [Leaving Yuanyuan Hall], in *Feng Zikai wenji* [The collected writings of Feng Zikai], vol. 5 (Hangzhou: Zhejiang wenyi chubanshe, 1992), pp. 117–141.

3. Feng Zikai, "Tonglu fuxuan" [Bearing the tumult (of war) in Tonglu (County)], in *Feng Zikai wenji* [The collected writings of Feng Zikai], vol. 6, p. 3.

4. As translated in Barmé, *An Artistic Exile,* p. 237.

5. Barmeé claims that the total number of refugees was sixteen: Feng and his wife, his mother-in-law, his older sister, four children, an eleven-year-old boy, a ten-year old girl, collateral relatives, and servants. See his *An Artistic Exile,* p. 238.

6. Barmé, *An Artistic Exile,* p. 13. He is quoting Feng Zikai's description from "Tonglu fuxuan," p. 1.

7. Feng, "Tonglu fuxuan," p. 3.

8. Ibid., p. 4.

9. Ibid., pp. 6–7.

10. Wei Qiao, ed., *Zhejiang sheng mingzhen zhi* [A gazetteer of the famous towns in Zhejiang Province] (Shanghai: Shanghai shudian chubanshe, 1991), p. 95.

11. Feng, "Tonglu fuxuan," p. 7.

12. Ibid., p. 9.

13. Ibid., p. 10.

14. Ibid., p. 11.

15. Ibid.

16. Ibid., p. 15.

17. Ibid., p. 16.

18. Wang Ziliang, *Zhexi kangzhan jilue* [A record of the Resistance War in western and northern Zhejiang] (Taibei: Wenhai chubanshe, 1973), p. 112.

19. This episode is from Feng, "Tonglu fuxuan," pp. 17–18.

20. Ibid., p. 22.

21. Feng, "Juexin" [Determination], in *Feng Zikai wenji* [The collected writings of Feng Zikai], (Hangzhou: Zhejiang wenyi chubanshe, 1992), vol. 5, p. 649.

22. Feng, "Ci Yuanyuantang" [Leaving Yuanyuan Hall], vol. 6, p. 52.

23. Quoted in Barmé, *An Artistic Exile*, p. 273.

24. Ibid., p. 272.

4. Days of Suffering

1. Jin Xihui, "Ten Days of Being Confronted by Danger in My Native Place" [Guxiang mengnan shiri ji], in *Dongyang wenshi ziliao xuanji* [A collection of historical materials on Dongyang County), vol. 5 (Dongyang: N.p., 1987), p. 73.

2. The following excerpts are taken from Feng Zongmeng, "Danghu mengnan lu" [A record of being confronted by danger in Pinghu], in *Jiaxing shizhi* (A gazetteer of the Jiaxing metropolitan area], vol. 2 (Beijing: Zhongguo shuji chubanshe, 1997), pp. 2318–2328.

3. The following excerpts are taken from Wang Mengsong, "KangRi qijian Riben qinluezhe zuixing jianwen lu" [A record of what I saw and heard about the crimes during the Japanese invasion during the Resistance War], in *Quzhou kangRi zhanzheng shiliao* [Materials on Quzhou's Anti-Japanese War] (N.p., 1985), pp. 59–74.

4. For Jin's diary see "Ten Days," pp. 72-83.

5. Quoted from Geremie Barmé, *An Artistic Exile: A Life of Feng Zikai (1898–1975)* (Berkeley: University of California Press, 2002), pp. 272.

6. Paul Fussell, *Understanding and Behavior in the Second World War* (New York: Oxford University Press, 1989), p. 36.

7. Tao Yuanming, "Peach Blossom Spring" in Cyril Black, ed., *Anthology of Chinese Literature, Volume I: From Early Times to the Fourteenth Century* (New York: Grove Press, 1965), pp. 167-168.

8. The description is by Barmé, *An Artistic Exile,* p. 13.

5. The Kidnapping of Chinese Civilians

1. For systematic abuse of conscripted labor, see Ju Zhifen, "Labor Conscription in North China, 1941–1945," in *China at War: Regions of China, 1937–1945,* ed. Stephen R. MacKinnon, Diana Lary, and Ezra F. Vogel (Stanford, Calif.: Stanford University Press, 2007), pp. 207–226.

2. The material in this chapter on Zhang comes from Zhang Dayan, "Rikou tietixiade kuli shengya" [My career as coolie under the oppression of the Japanese bandits], in *Lishui wenshi ziliao,* vol. 8 (N.p., 1991), pp. 57–68; "KangRi shede Oujiang jiaotong chuan" [Ou River boat transportation during the war against Japan], in *Lishui wenshi ziliao,* vol. 5 (N.p., 1988), pp. 98–109; "KangRishi Oujiang huoyun dadui" [The Ou River transport group during the war against Japan], in *Lishui wenshi ziliao,* vol. 5 (N.p., 1988), p. 110; and "Lishui huayuan fandian" [The Flower Garden Restaurant and Hotel in Lishui], in *Lishui wenshi ziliao,* vol. 5 (N.p., 1988), pp. 111–113.

3. Zhang Dayan, p. 63.

4. The account in this section is based on Wu Yingcai, "Quehou yusheng yi dang nian" [Memories of my life that year I was taken], in *Jinhua wenshi ziliao,* vol. 5 (N.p., n.d.), pp. 83–92.

5. Qian Nanxin, "Tulide jiangjun guo Quzhou zhenxiang" [The truth about General Doolittle passing through Quzhou], *Zhejiang yuekan* [Zhejiang monthly] 20, no. 3 (March 1988): 23.

6. Ibid., p. 93.

7. Zhou Baohe, Ding Xianghe, and Ding Weilu, "Rikou lafumu ji" [An account of the Japanese bandits pressing us into service], in *Sheng wenshi ziliao,* vol. 10 (N.p., n.d.), p. 132.

8. Yuan Yichang, "Wo qu Ningbo zhongxue dushushide tici quenan" [The time I left Ningbo Middle School and retreated into hardship], in *Sheng wenshi ziliao,* vol. 3 (N.p., 1986), p. 175.

6. Government on the Move

1. Huang Shaohong, *Huang Shaohong huiyilu* [Memoirs of Huang Shaohong] (Nanning: Guangxi renmin chubanshe, 1991), pp. 367–368.

2. *Dongnan ribao,* September 27, 1938. This article goes on to show the changes from late 1937 to the early fall of 1938.

3. Ruan Yicheng, "Fangyan yu Yunhe," in *Ruan Yicheng zixuanji* [Ruan Yicheng's autobiography] (Taipei: n.p., 1978), p. 84.

4. These points reflect my arguments in "The Capital Comes to the Periphery:Views of the Sino-Japanese War Era in Central Zhejiang," in *Constructing China: The Interaction of Culture and Economics,* ed. Kenneth G. Lieberthal, Shuen-fu Lin, and Ernest P. Young (Ann Arbor, Mich.: Center for Chinese Studies, 1997), p. 125.

5. The wheelbarrow data is taken from Ying Baorong, "Yiqie weile kang zhang" [Everything for the Resistance War], in *KangRi zhanzheng zai Yongkang* [The Resistance War in Yongkang County] (Yongkang: n.p., 1995), pp. 184–186.

6. See Ruan Yicheng, *Yicheng zizhuan nianpu ji zishu* [An autochronology of Yicheng's life], vol. 3 (N.p., 1976), p. 12.

7. Ru Guanting, "Guomindang tongzhi shiqi Zhejiang sheng minzhengting jianwen" [Information about the Ministry of Civil Affairs in Zhejiang under Guomindang rule], in *Zhejiang wenshi ziliao xuanji* [Collection of historical materials on Zhejiang] (Hangzhou: Zhejiang renmin chubanshe, 1982), p. 125.

8. Zheng Qinyin, "Huiyi 'Liyuzuo tanhui'" [Remembering discussions at the "Liyu Study Society"], in *Hangzhou wenshi ziliao* [Historical materials on Hangzhou], vol. 4 (Hangzhou: Zhejiang renmin chubanshe, 1984), p. 91.

9. Ruan Yicheng, "Kangzhan chuqi Zhejiang sheng zhengfu zai Yongkang Fangyan bangongji" [A record of handling business at the beginning of the Resistance War for the Zhejiang provincial government at Yongkang and Fangyan], in *KangRi zhanzheng zai Yongkang* [The Resistance War in Yongkang County] (Yongkang: n.p., 1995), p. 230.

10. Ibid.

11. Ru, "Guomindang tongzhi," p. 125.

12. Huang, *Huang Shaohong huiyilu,* p. 369.

13. Ying, "Yiqie weile kang zhang," p. 174.

14. Huang, *Huang Shaohong huiyilu,* p. 369.

15. Ying, "Yiqie weile kang zhang," p. 177.

16. Unless otherwise noted, Huang's discussion of these problems is taken from *Huang Shaohong huiyilu,* pp. 468–470.

17. Ruan, *Ruan Yicheng zixuanji,* pp. 9 and 12.

18. Unless noted, the information on these administrative offices comes from Lin Ze, who served as head of political affairs in both administrative offices. See his "Kangzhan shiqi Zhexi Zhedong liang xingshude mianmao" [Features of the

administrative offices of Zhexi and Zhedong during the Resistance War], in *Zhejiang wenshi ziliao,* vol. 47 (Hangzhou: Zhejiang renminchubanshe, 1992), pp. 230–248.

19. For an evaluation of He's leadership, see Wang Fei, "KangRi zhanzheng shiqide Zhexi xingshu" [West Zhejiang Administrative Office in the war against Japan], in *Hangzhou wenshi ziliao* [Hangzhou historical materials], vol. 10 (Hangzhou: Zhejiang renmin chubanshe, 1988), pp. 69–70.

20. Tu Wei and Yu Long, "Zhejiang C. C. de paixi fen zheng" [The factional rivalry of the Zhejiang C. C. Clique], in *Zhejiang wenshi ziliao xuanji* [A collection of Zhejiang historical materials], vol. 3 (Hangzhou: n.p., 1962), p. 32.

21. Ibid., p. 30.

22. See Ying Zhanxian, "Huang Shaohong yu CC zhengduo Zhejiang zhanshi qingnian shunlian tuande jingguo" [Huang Shaohong and struggles with the CC Clique over the wartime youth-training bodies], in *Zhejiang wenshi ziliao xuanji* [A collection of Zhejiang historical materials], vol. 5 (Hangzhou: n.p., 1963), pp. 91–96.

23. Tu and Yu, "Zhejiang C. C.," p. 38. See also Ruan's account in *Ruan Yicheng zixuanji,* pp. 27–29.

24. For Huang's side of the story, see his *Huang Shaohong huiyilu,* p. 429; for Ruan's, see *Ruan Yicheng zixuanji,* p. 29.

25. Huang, *Huang Shaohong huiyilu,* p. 432.

26. Xu Dequn, "Linshi shenghui zai Fangyan" [Provisional provincial assembly at Fangyan], in *Hangzhou wenshi ziliao* [Historical materials on Hangzhou], vol. 10 (Hangzhou: n.p., 1988), pp. 29–30.

27. Ruan, *Ruan Yicheng zixuanji,* p. 154.

28. Huang, *Huang Shaohong huiyilu,* p. 433.

29. All the material in this account is based on Ruan, *Ruan Yicheng zixuanji,* pp. 166–175 and 209–210.

30. The information in this section comes from "KangRi zhanzheng shiqi Zhejiang sheng zhengfu qian Lishui diqu jishi" [An account of the moves to the Lishui district of the wartime Zhejiang provincial government], in *Lishui diqu zhi* [A gazetteer of the Lishui region] (Hangzhou: Zhejiang renmin chubanshe, 1993), pp. 629–633; Wu Nanlian and Zhang Shaowen, "Kangzhan liuwang zai Longquan danwei zonglan [A general view of the units of refugees in Longquan during the Resistance War], in *Longquan wenshi ziliao* [Historical materials on Longquan], vol. 3 (N.p., 1985), pp. 126–130; and Wang Zunyi, "Shenghui zai Yunhe" [The provincial capital at Yunhe], in *Yunhe wenshi ziliao* [Historical materials on Yunhe], vol. 2 (N.p., 1986), pp. 1–5.

31. Ruan, *Ruan Yicheng zixuanji,* p. 175.

32. Ruan Yicheng, "Kangzhanshi zai Lishui" [Wartime in Lishui], in *Lishui wenshi ziliao* [Historical materials on Lishui], vol. 8 (N.p., 1991), p. 46.

33. Li Jiaji, "Yunhe suoyi" [Trivial recollections from Yunhe], in *Yunhe wenshi ziliao,* vol. 4 (N.p, n.d.), p. 112.

34. *Dongnan ribao,* October 25, 1943.

35. Ruan, *Ruan Yicheng zixuanji,* pp. 215–216.

36. The following account and all quotations are taken from Shen Songlin, "Yunhe jiushi" [Old tales from Yunhe], in *Yunhe wenshi ziliao,* vol. 4 (N.p., n.d.), p. 57.

37. Wang Cunyi, "Zhongzhu Zhezheng, zhubi Yunhe" [Ruling again over the Zhejiang government, garrisoned in Yunhe], in *Yunhe wenshi ziliao,* vol. 4 (N.p., n.d.), p. 9.

38. Zhong Sheng, "Linshi shenghui shiling" [Tidbits from the temporary provincial assembly], in *Yunhe wenshi ziliao,* vol. 4 (N.p., n.d.), p. 51.

39. Zhong, "Linshi shenghui shiling," p. 51.

40. Wang Cunyi, "Zhongzhu Zhezheng," p. 9.

41. Zhong, "Linshi shenghui shiling," pp. 52 and 53, and Wu Yisun, "Zhanshi Zhejiang linshi shenghui yiyi yunhe" [Items taken up one after another at the temporary provincial assembly at Yunhe during the war], in *Yunhe wenshi ziliao,* vol. 4 (N.p., n.d.), p. 42.

42. *Dongnan ribao,* October 25, 1943.

43. Ibid.

44. Li Xugen, "Lu Gongwang jiangjun zai Chishi" [General Lu Gongwang at Chishi], in *Yunhe xian wenshi ziliao* [Historical materials in Yunhe County], vol. 2 (N.p., 1985), pp. 12–15.

45. Ruan, *Ruan Yicheng zixuanji,* pp. 213–214.

46. This account and quotation is taken from Ruan, "Kangzhanshi zai Lishui," p. 49.

47. Lan Rongqing, "Ruan Yicheng zhanshi xingjue" [Ruan Yicheng's wartime wanderings], in *Yunhe xian wenshi ziliao* [Historical materials in Yunhe County], vol. 4 (N.p., 1985), pp. 35–36.

48. Ibid, pp. 36–37.

49. This account is based upon Wang Cunyi, "Woju shancheng xiu shengzhi—shishu huali ji haoqing: Yu Shaosong xiansheng zai Yunhe" [Revising the provincial gazetteer from mountain fastenesses—and poet and artist entrusted with great responsibility: Memories of Mr. Yu Shaosong in Yunhe] in *Yunhe xian wenshi ziliao* [Historical materials in Yunhe County], vol. 4 (N.p., 1985), pp. 22–30.

7. Playing Hide-and-Seek with the Enemy

1. The two primary sources for this chapter are Cai Zhuping, "Liuwang zai Simingshan" [In exile in the Siming Mountains], in *Ningbo wenshi ziliao* [Historical sources on Ningbo], vol. 12 (Ningbo: Zhejiang sheng Ningbo xinhua yinshuaguang, 1992), pp. 186–221, and in the same volume, Fang Zichang, "Wei kangRi

xunnande Cixi xianzhang Zhang Ju" [The martyrdom of Magistrate Zhang Ju of Cixi County during the Resistance War], pp. 222–227. Note also "Cixi xianzhang Zhang Ju kangRi xunguo qianqianhouhou" [Memories of Zhang by his sons Zhang Guolin and Zhang Guoping and his friend Zhou Zhanbing], in *Cixi wenshi ziliao*, vol. 10 (N.p., 1995), pp. 107–108.

2. Cai, pp. 206-207.

3. Cai, p. 207.

4. Ibid., p. 186.

5. Ibid., pp. 186–187.

6. Ibid., p. 188.

7. Ibid., p. 189.

8. Ibid., p. 190.

9. Ibid.

10. Ibid., pp. 191–192.

11. Ibid., pp. 196-198.

12. Ibid., p. 197.

13. Biographical data on Zhang comes in part from *Cixi xianzhi* [A gazetteer of Cixi County], (Hangzhou: Zhejiang renmin chubanshe, 1992), pp. 988–989.

14. Fang, "Wei kangRi xunnande," p. 224.

15. Ibid., p. 225.

16. Ibid., p. 226.

17. The account of his first trip to occupied Cixi County is in Zhang Ju, "Xuncha Cixi xianzheng" [Inspecting Cixi county government], *Dongnan ribao*, September 30, 1941.

18. Ibid.

19. Ibid.

20. The account of his second trip to occupied Cixi County is in Zhang Ju, "Xuncha Cixi xianzheng" [Inspecting Cixi county government], *Dongnan ribao*, October 10, 1941.

21. *Dongnan ribao*, September 30, 1941.

22. Cai, "Liuwang zai Simingshan," p. 201.

23. Ibid., pp. 207–208.

24. The following account is from Fang, "Wei kangRi xunnande," p. 228.

25. Cai, "Liuwang zai Simingshan," p. 210.

26. Ibid.

27. Ibid., p. 211.

28. Ibid., p. 213.

29. Ibid., p. 214. Ah Q was the chief character in one of Lu Xun's most famous short stories, "The True Story of Ah Q." Ah Q was a notorious rationalizer who made the worst character traits sterling qualities and rotten situations into best-case scenarios.

30. This account comes from Cai, "Liuwang zai Simingshan," pp. 214–216.

31. Ibid., pp. 216–217.

32. Ibid., p. 219.

33. Ibid.

34. Ibid., pp. 219–220.

35. Ibid., p. 220.

36. "Cixi Zhang xianchang xunzhi Zhe gejie kaihui zhuidiao" [A memorial meeting of all Zhejiang circles for the Cixi County Magistrate Zhang who died at his post], *Dongnan ribao,* March 30, 1941.

8. Guerrilla Education

1. Robert Culp, *Articulating Citizenship: Civic Education and Student Politics in Southeastern China, 1912–1940* (Cambridge, Mass.: Harvard University Asia Center, 2007), p. 27.

2. Unless otherwise noted the information on Shaoxing Middle School comes from Shen Jinxiang, "Shao Zhong shinian" [Ten years leading Shao Middle School], in *Shaoxing wenshi ziliao* [Historical materials on Shaoxing], vol. 2 (N.p., n.d.), p. 146.

3. Culp, *Articulating Citizenship,* p. 26, n27.

4. Ruan Maoxiao, "Shaoxing lunxian qianhou zai shengli Shao Zhongde dushu shenghuo" [Student life at Shaoxing Middle School both before and after Shaoxing was occupied], in *Shaoxing wenshi ziliao xuanji,* vol. 3 (N.p., n.d.], p. 254.

5. Shen Jinxiang, p. 147.

6. Shen Jinxiang, p. 148; Zhang Genfu, *Kangzhan shiqi Zhejiang sheng: Renkou qiani yu shehui yingxiang* [Population movement and its social impact on wartime Zhejiang] (Shanghai: Sanlian shudian, 2001), p. 165.

7. Ruan, "Shaoxing lunxian," pp. 257–258.

8. Jin Jixian, "Fenghuo shushing" [The sound of books amid beacon fires], in *Shaoxing wenshi ziliao xuanji,* vol. 12 (N.p., 1996), p. 133.

9. The following account is based on Shao's own account; see Shao Hongshu, "'Siyiqi' Jishan zhongxue tuwei jishi" [April 17—Jishan Middle School breaks out of an encirclement], in *Shaoxing wenshi ziliao xuanji,* vol. 1 (N.p., 1983), pp. 164–169.

10. See the important work by Paul A. Cohen, *Speaking to History: The Story of King Goujian in Twentieth-century China* (Berkeley: University of California Press, 2009).

11. Shao Hongshu, "'Siyiqi' Jishan zhongxue," p. 168.

12. Jin, "Fenghuo shushing," p. 135.

13. Tao Yongming, "Ji Shaoxing lunxianhou wode dianpei liuwang shenghuo" [My record of wandering around in a desperate plight after Shaoxing's occupation], in *Shaoxing wenshi ziliao xuanji,* vol. 3 (N.p., 1996), pp. 245–246.

14. The counties were Dongyang, Jinyun, Tiantai, Lishui, Xinchang, Sheng, and Changshan.

15. Xu Doulun and Zhang Ruinian, "Zhanhuo zhongde xiange—Ji Jishan zhong-xue Wuyifenbude xuexi shenghuo [Amid the chaos of war life goes on—remembering the life of study at the partial unit of the Jishan Middle School in Wuyi], in *Wuyi wenshi ziliao,* vol. 1 (N.p., 1986), p. 90.

16. Shi Zude, "Shaoxing Jishan zhongxue binan yu Wuyi" [The Shaoxing Jishan Middle School takes refuge in Wuyi], in *Wuyi wenshi ziliao,* vol. 1 (N.p., 1986), p. 87.

17. See the discussion of Xiang Lake Normal School in R. Keith Schoppa, *Xiang Lake: Nine Centuries of Chinese Life* (New Haven, Conn.: Yale University Press, 1989), pp. 205–210.

18. *Dongnan ribao* [Southeast Daily], November 14, 1938.

19. Ibid.

20. Ye Fang, "Jinian Xiang shi Jin Haiguan xiao chang" [Remembering Xiang Lake Normal School's Jin Haiguan], in *Songyang wenshi ziliao,* vol. 2 (N.p., 1986), p. 84,

21. Ibid.

22. Zhang Genfu (in *Kangzhan shiqi Zhejiang sheng,* p. 176) claims that United Middle came together after Education Minister Xu gathered responsible people from each school to plan it, as late as the summer of 1938. This strains credulity.

23. Tang Shifang, "KangRi zhanzheng chuqi zai Bihude shengli Lian Chu" [The Provincial Lower Middle United Middle School at Bihu during the Anti-Japanese War], in *Lishui wenshi ziliao,* vol. 9 (N.p., 1992), p. 138.

24. Ibid., p. 143.

25. Wu's and Zhang's memories are recorded as testimonials to United Middle's history; see ibid., p. 152.

26. Lin Huachun, "Lianzhong zai Bihu" [United Middle School at Bihu], in *Lishui wenshi ziliao,* vol. 2 (N.p., n.d.), p. 115.

27. Gao Bingsheng and Lou Xueli, "Kangzhan shiqide shengli Lian Gao" [The Provincial United Upper Middle School during the Resistance War], in *Lishui wenshi ziliao,* vol. 7 (N.p., 1990), p. 103.

28. Zhang Rongming, "Kangzhanzhong Chuzhou Zhongxuede jidu banqian" [How many times Chuzhou Middle School moved during the Resistance War], in *Lishui wenshi ziliao,* vol. 7 (N.p., 1990), p. 145.

29. Wang Junmu and Ye Fang, "Zai kangRi fengyin zhongbanxue yucai" [Amid the beacon fires of the war against Japan, running schools with educational talent], in *Lishui wenshi ziliao,* vol. 2 (N.p., n.d.), p. 87.

30. Lu Feiqiong, "Shengli Hangzhou shifan xuexiao" [Provincial Hangzhou Normal School], in *Minguo shiqi Hangzhou* [Republican-period Hangzhou], ed. Zhou Feng (Hangzhou: Zhejiang renmin chubanshe, 1997), pp. 559–560.

31. See the description in the Bihu-published periodical *Zhejiang qingnian* [Zhejiang youth] 11 (July 1943): 32–33.

32. Tang Shifang, pp. 142-143.

33. Gao and Lou, pp. 104 and 107.

34. Tang Shifang, p. 139.

35. Wang Minghong, "Lian Gao—Hang Gao xuesheng yundong jianshi" [Lian Gao—A brief history of the student movement], in *Zhejiang wenshi ziliao xuanji*, vol. 4 (N.p., n.d.), pp. 112–113.

36. Lu Feiqiong,, p. 560 and Ni Liande, "Shengli Hangzhou chuji zhongxuez" [Hangzhou provinicial Lower Middle School] in *Minguo shiqi Hangzhou* [Republican-period Hangzhou], ed. Zhou Feng (Hangzhou: Zhejiang renmin chubanshe, 1997), p. 562.

37. Unless otherwise noted, this discussion is based upon Xue Jiugao and Gu Weiren, "Kangzhan shiqide Jiashu Lian Zhong" [The Jiaxing Prefectural United Middle School in the period of the Resistance War], *Jiaxing wenshi ziliao tongxun* 14 (April 1995): 12–28.

38. Shen Jinxiang, p. 147.

39. Although Yuqian and Fenshui are contiguous, they represent two of the former prefectures—Hangzhou and Yanzhou, respectively. Yuyao was in Ningbo prefecture, while Yongkang was part of Jinhua prefecture.

40. Xue and Gu, pp. 12-13.

41. Ibid., p. 13.

42. Ibid., pp. 13-14.

43. Chu Fucheng, the head of the board of directors, and Shen Junru, the longest-serving member of the organization's standing committee, were in Chongqing.

44. Ibid., pp. 16-19.

45. Ibid., p. 18.

46. Ibid., pp. 18-19.

47. Ibid., pp. 19-23.

48. Ibid., pp 24-26.

49. Ibid., p. 27.

50. See my analysis of cores and peripheries in R. Keith Schoppa, *Chinese Elites and Political Change* (Cambridge, Mass.: Harvard University Press, 1982).

9. Wartime Business

1. This discussion is based on Huang Shaohong, *Huang Shaohong huiyilu* [Remembrances of Huang Shaohong] (Nanning: Guangxi renmin chubanshe, 1991), pp. 515–517 and is the source of the first three paragraphs.

2. Liu Mei, "'Zhejiang sheng ranzhi chang' he chuangshiren Chen Qingtang xiansheng" [The "Zhejiang Dyeing and Weaving Mill" and its originator, Mr. Cheng

Qingtang], in *Yunhe wenshi ziliao* [Historical sources from Yunhe County], vol. 4 (N.p., n.d.), pp. 45–47.

3. Zhang Genfu, *Kangzhan shiqi Zhejiang sheng renkou qianyi yu shehui yingxiang* [Population migration and its social impact on wartime Zhejiang] (Shanghai: Sanlian shudian, 2001), p. 253.

4. Unless otherwise noted, the source for much of the discussion of the iron-works is Hu Sixing and Ma Yingcai, "Ji Dagangtou 'Zhejiang sheng tiegong chang'" [Remembering the Zhejiang Provincial Ironworks at Dagangtou], in *Zhejiang wenshi ziliao,* vol. 21 (Hangzhou: Zhejiang renmin chubanshe, 1982), pp. 153–160.

5. Zhang, *Kangzhan shiqi Zhejiang,* pp. 218–219.

6. Lan Zhougen, "Dagangtou binggongchangde zuzhi shezhi" [Setting up the organization of the Dagangtou military arsenal] in *Lishui wenshi ziliao,* vol. 5, part 1 *(shang)* (N.p., n.d.), pp. 161–162.

7. Zhang, *Kangzhan shiqi Zhejiang,* p. 250.

8. Huang, *Huang Shaohong huiyilu,* p. 398.

9. Zhang, *Kangzhan shiqi Zhejiang,* p. 251.

10. Unless otherwise noted, the source for this section's account of the activities of the Zhejiang Local Provincial Bank is based on Hong Pincheng, "Zhejiang di-fang yinhang shimo" [The Zhejiang Local Provincial Bank from beginning to end], in *Zhejiang wenshi ziliao xuanji* [Collection of Zhejiang historical materi-als], vol. 46: *Zhejiang jindai jinrongye he jinrongjia* [Modern Zhejiang banks and bankers] (Hangzhou: Zhejiang renmin chubanshe, 1992), pp. 111–134. For basic information on the banks, also see Zhang Genfu, pp. 233-234.

11. Quoted in Zhang, *Kangzhan shiqi Zhejiang,* p. 261.

12. Huang Shaohong, p. 515.

13. The account of the Zhejiang Printing Company in this section is based largely on Hong Shengsan, "Zai Shangzhaocun yingyede Zhejiang yinshuating" [The Zhejiang Printing Press doing business at Shangzhao Village], in *Lishui wenshi ziliao,* vol. 5, part 1 *(shang)* (N.p., n.d.), pp. 167–174.

14. Ying Yurong, pp. 185-186.

15. See the account by Wang Peiru, who began work at the camphor refinery as trainee in 1940 and rose to become manager of a branch of the refinery: Hong Shengsan, recorder, "Wang Peiru tongzhi tan kangRi shide Zhejiang zhang nao you chang" [Wang Peiru talks about the camphor oil refinery during the Anti-Japanese war], in *Lishui wenshi ziliao,* vol. 5, part 1 *(shang)* (N.p., n.d.), pp. 171–174. All information in the discussion on camphor oil comes from this source.

16. Zhang, *Kangzhan shiqi Zhejiang,* p. 266.

17. Ibid., p. 223.

18. "KangRi zhanzheng shiqi Zhejiang sheng zhengfu qian Lishui diqu jishi" [An

account of the provincial government move into the Lishui region during the anti-Japanese war] in *Lishui diqu zhi* [A gazetteer of the Lishui region] (Hangzhou: Zhejiang renmin chubanshe, 1993), pp. 637-638.

19. All the information on this mill comes from the following source. "Liyong ranzhi gufen youxian gongsi kangzhan shiqi banian jingguo baogao" [A report on the experiences during the eight-year Resistance War of the Liyong Dyeing and Weaving Mill Limited], in *Lishui wenshi ziliao,* vol. 5, part 1 *(shang)* (N.p., n.d.), pp. 125–127.

20. "Liyong ranzhi," p. 127.

10. Scorched Earth

1. John Keegan, *A History of Warfare* (New York: Vintage, 1993), p. 12.

2. Ibid, pp. 387–388.

3. Ibid., p. 388.

4. Unless otherwise noted, the source for the complete account of the destruction of the Zhakou Power Plant is Cai Jingping, *Hangzhou lunxian zhi qianhou* [Before and after the fall of Hangzhou] (N.p., n.d), pp. 2–38.

5. Ibid..

6. Zhou Feng, ed., "Quangban diandeng zilaishui chengshi jianshede fazhan," [The development of the reconstruction of the city: creating the city waterworks] in *Minguo shiqi Hangzhou* [Hangzhou during the Republican period] (Hangzhou: Zhejiang renmin chubanshe, 1997), p. 367.

7. Ruan Yicheng, *Sanju buli ben "Hang"* [Three periods of not leaving my home in Hangzhou] (Taipei: n.p., 1974), p. 207.

8. This account, unless otherwise noted, is based on Li Wenji, "Baopo Qianjiang daqiao" [The demolition of the Qiantang River Bridge], in *Zhejiang wenshi ziliao xuanji,* vol. 29 (Hangzhou: Zhejiang renmin chubanshe, 1985), pp. 37–40.

9. Ruan, *Sanju buli ben "Hang,"* p. 208.

10. Li Wenji, "Baopo Qianjiang daqiao," p. 38.

11. Dong Qijun, "Ningbo luHu tongxianghui" [The Ningbo native place association at Shanghai] in *Ningbo wenshi ziliao,* vol. 5 (Ningbo: Ningbo ribao she, 1987), pp. 9 and 11.

12. *Zhejiang hangyun shi* [A history of Zhejiang shipping] (Beijing: Renmin jiaotong chubanshe, 1993), pp. 435–436.

13. Chen Deyi, "'Wuko tongshang' houde jiu Ningbo gang" [The old port of Ningbo after the opening of the treaty ports], in *Ningbo wenshi ziliao,* vol. 2 (Ningbo: Ningbo ribao she, 1984), pp. 21–22.

14. Ibid., p. 22.

15. The figures come from Chen, "'Wuko tongshang,'" p. 20. Since the statistics rise

in face value from 6,203 (in ten thousands) in 1938 to 9,044 in 1939 and to 20,861 in 1940, Chen claims that the Ningbo commercial scene was flourishing until the eve of the Japanese seizure of the city in April 1941. He does not adjust the figures for inflation. The adjustment for inflation is based on figures taken of wholesale prices recorded by Chongqing from June to December of each year. Taking 1938 as 100, the value of the yuan had dropped to 53.1 in 1939 and to 26.7 in 1940. See *Wenshi gangshi* [A history of the port of Wenzhou] (Beijing, 1990), p. 132.

16. "Longquan xian minguo shiqi dashiji" [Major events in Longquan County during the Republican era], in *Longquan wenshi ziliao,* vol. 10 (N.p., 1990), p. 63.

17. Huang, p. 402, and *Qu xianzhi,* p. 403.

18. Huang, p. 402.

19. Qian Nanxin, "Tulide jiangjun guo Quzhou zhenxiang" [The true story of General Doolittle passing through Quzhou], *Zhejiang yuekan* 20, no. 3 (March 1988): 21.

20. Sun Xiongfei, "Quzhou feijichang dui kangRi zhanzhengde gongxian" [The contributions of the Quzhou air base to the Resistance War against Japan], *Zhejiang yuekan* 7, no. 12 (December 1975): 21.

21. Wang Chenguo, "Quzhou feijichang qiangxiu yu pohuai" [The construction and destruction of the Quzhou air base], in *Quzhou wenshi ziliao,* vol. 5 (Quzhou: n.p., 1988), p. 174

22. *Qu xianzhi* [A gazetteer of Qu County] (Hangzhou: Zhejiang renmin chubanshe, 1992), p. 403.

23. Qian, "Tulide jiangjun," p. 21.

24. Sun Xiongfei, in "Quzhou feijichang," says this action came in October 1938, but the Japanese did not cross the Qiantang until their capture of Xiaoshan in January 1940. In this case, Wang Chenguo, magistrate of Kaihua County at the time is more accurate; see Wang Chenguo, "Quzhou feijichang." Sun was an elementary school student in Qu City at the time.

25. This report is based on Wang Chenguo and Huang Shaohong.

26. Wang Chenguo, "Quzhou feijichang," p. 175.

27. *Qu xianzhi,* p. 403. This source lists half the number of bamboo timbers requisitioned as all other sources.

28. Wang Guangsheng, "Juan mu zao jichang" [The wood tax to build the Quzhou airfield], in *Chun'an xian wenshi ziliao,* vol. 2 (N.p., n.d.), p. 35.

29. Ibid., p. 36.

30. *Qu xianzhi,* p. 142.

31. See the video depiction of this work in Errol Morris's film, *The Fog of War,* concerning the role of Robert S. McNamara in his roles in China, India, and Japan during the Pacific War. Sony Classics, 2004.

32. Huang, pp. 401–402.

33. See Qian, "Tulide jiangjun," p. 23, and Wang, pp. 176–177.

34. Qian, "Tulide jiangjun," pp. 23 and 33.

35. Wang Chenguo, "Quzhou feijichang," p. 177.

36. Keegan, *History of Warfare,* pp. 6–8.

11. Trading and Smuggling

1. Pan Yin'ge, *Zhanshi Shanghai jingji* [Wartime Shanghai's economy] (Shanghai: Shanghai jingji yanjiusuo, 1945), p. 81.

2. Eugene E. Barnett, *Economic Shanghai: Hostage to Politics, 1937–1941* (New York: Institute of Pacific Relations, 1941), p. 169.

3. Bao Zhonglin, "Lao chuangong huiyi *Taizhou* lun" [An old ship hand's remembrances of the steamer *Taizhou*], in *Huangyan wenshi ziliao* [Historical materials from Huangyan County], vol. 10 (Huangyan: n.p., 1988), p. 137.

4. *Zhejiang hangyun shi* [Zhejiang shipping history] (Beijing: Renmin jiaotong chubanshe, 1993), pp. 434–438.

5. Ibid., and Zhou Houcai, *Wenzhou gangshi* [A history of Wenzhou Bay] (Beiing: Renmin jiaotong chubanshem 1990), pp. 123 and 125.

6. *Zhejiang hangyun shi,* pp. 467–470.

7. Ibid., pp. 468–469.

8. Ibid., p. 442.

9. "Xiangshan jinbainian shishi cuolu" [Brief entries about matters in the last hundred years of Xiangshan's history], in *Xiangshan wenshi ziliao,* vol. 3 (N.p., 1988), pp. 71–72; *Xiangshan xianzhi* [A gazetteer of Xiangshan County] (Hangzhou: Zhejiang renmin chubanshe, 1988), pp. 186 and 305; and *Zhejiang sheng mingzhen zhi* [A gazetteer of famous Zhejiang towns] (Shanghai: Shanghai shudian chuban, 1991), p. 353.

10. Zhang Jian, "Wenzhou haiguan jianshi" [A short history of the Wenzhou customs service], in *Wenzhou wenshi ziliao* [Historical materials from Wenzhou], vol. 4 (N.p., 1988), p. 241.

11. Shen Tingzhi, "Zhejiang shengde jingdi" [Zhejiang's setting], *Kangzhan* [Resistance War], June 26, 1938, p. 8.

12. *Zhejiang hangyun shi,* pp. 439–440.

13. Zhou Houcai, pp. 131–132.

14. Huang Boyun, "Wenzhoude jianguan yu jianbu" [The construction of Wenzhou's customs service and port], in *Zhejiang wenshi ziliao xuanji* [A collection of historical materials on Zhejiang], vol. 1 (Hangzhou: n.p., 1961), p. 143.

15. Zhou Houcai, pp. 107–108.

16. Ibid., pp. 131–132. Li Peiguang, "Jiefang qiande Ouhaiguan" [The Ouhai customs service before Liberation], in *Wenzhou wenshi ziliao* [Historical materials on Wenzhou], vol. 4 (Wenzhou: n.p., 1988), pp. 226–227.

17. *Zhejiang hangyun shi,* p. 464.

18. Ibid., pp. 463–467, and Zhou Houcai, pp. 133–136.

19. *Zhejiang hangyun shi,* pp. 465.

20. Wu Yan, ed., *Wenzhou shi jiaotong zhi* [A gazetteer of transportation for the Wenzhou municipality] (Beijing: Haiyang chubanshe, 1994), pp. 55–56.

21. *Putuo xianzhi* [A gazetteer of Putuo County] (Hangzhou: Zhejiang renmin chubanshe, 1991), pp. 853–854.

22. Ibid., p. 553.

23. *Sanmen xianzhi* [A gazetteer of Sanmen County] (Hangzhou: Zhejiang renmin chubanshe, 1992), p. 458, and Chen Qiaoyi, *Zhonghua renmin gongheguo diming cidian: Zhejiang sheng* [A dictionary of place names in Zhejiang Province] (Beijing: n.p., 1988), pp. 308 and 332.

24. Chen Qiaoyi, *Zhonghua renmin,* p. 113; for Qingshuibu, see *Wenzhou shi jiaotong zhi,* p. 51.

25. Yuan Liang'an, "Huanghua, Qili—yidai shanghangde xingqi" [From Huanghua to Qili—a zone of rising commercial firms], in *Yueqing wenshi ziliao* [Historical materials from Yueqing], vol. 7 (N.p., 1989), pp. 127–132; and Chen Qiaoyi, *Zhonghua renmin,* p. 109.

26. Wei Qiao, *Zhejiang sheng mingzhen zhi* [A gazetteer of famous towns in Zhejiang] (Shanghai: Shanghai shudian, 1991), p. 743.

27. Zhou Houcai, p. 135.

28. *Zhejiang hangyun shi,* pp. 456.

29. Li Peiguang, "Jiefang qiande Ouhaiguan," pp. 227–228.

30. *Zhejiang hangyun shi,* pp. 464.

31. Lloyd E. Eastman, "Facets of an Ambivalent Relationship: Smuggling, Puppets, and Atrocities during the War, 1937–1945," in *The Chinese and the Japanese,* ed. Akira Iriye (Princeton, N.J.: Princeton University Press, 1980).

32. *Zhejiang hangyun shi,* pp. 436–437.

33. Li Zheng, "Jiefang qian Ningbo shi shangye gaikuang" [A survey of Ningbo's business and industry before liberation], in *Ningbo wenshi ziliao* [Historical materials from Ningbo], vol. 2 (N.p., 1984), pp. 49–50 and 53.

34. Ibid., pp. 50–51.

35. Ibid., p. 51.

36. Wang Gongmin, "Zhejiang qianzhuangyede xingshuai" [The rise and fall of the Zhejiang native bank industry], in *Zhejiang wenshi ziliao* [Historical materials on Zhejiang], vol. 46 (Hangzhou: Zhejiang renmin chubanshe, 1992), p. 160.

37. Mao Puting, "Jiushi Ningbode jingji dongmai—qianzhuang" [The economic artery for old Ningbo—the native bank], in *Ningbo wenshi ziliao* [Historical materials on Ningbo], vol. 4 (Ningbo: Ningbo ribao she, 1986), pp. 52–53.

38. Ibid., and Li Zheng, "Jiefang qian Ningbo," pp. 52–53.

39. Zhou Zhiyao, "Taifeng mianfen chang" [The Taifeng Flour Mill] in *Ningbo wenshi ziliao* [Historical materials on Ningbo], vol. 6 (Ningbo: Ningbo ribao she, 1987), p. 24; and *Zhejiang hangyun shi,* p. 437.

40. *Zhejiang hangyun shi,* p. 456.

41. Zhou Houcai, pp. 129–130.

42. *Zhejiang hangyun shi,* p. 456.

43. *Wenzhou shi jiaotong zhi,* p. 211. Workers organizations were differentiated by type of commodity (and sometimes subdifferentiated, e.g., wood transporters were divided by types of wood and length of timber), by boat-type involvement (i.e., riverboat, barge, steamship), by native place, and by particular docks. The port of Wenzhou in the early twentieth century attracted large numbers of Shandong laborers.

44. *Shanghai shi mianbu shangye* [Shanghai's cotton cloth industry] (Beijing: Xinhua shudian, 1979), pp. 268–269.

45. Zhou Houcai, pp. 129–130.

46. Ibid., p. 128.

47. *Zhejiang hangyun shi,* p. 465.

48. *Xiangshan xianzhi* [A gazetteer of Xiangshan County] (Hangzhou: Zhejiang renmin chubanshe, 1988), pp. 144, 181, 305.

49. Wei, *Zhejiang sheng mingzhen zhi,* p. 392; Chen Qiaoyi, *Zhonghua renmin,* pp. 74–75.

50. *Sanmen xianzhi, p. 458;* Chen Qiaoyi, *Zhonghua renmin,* p. 332.

51. Tao Juyin, *Gudao jianwen* [The experiences of the Solitary Island] (Shanghai: Shanghai renmin chubanshe, 1979), p. 264.

52. Yuan, "Huanghua, Qili," pp. 127–132.

53. Li Qun, "Yi Yueqing zhijie shui gongzuo" [Remembering the work regarding the Yueqing direct tax], in *Yueqing wenshi ziliao* [Historical materials on Yueqing], vol. 7 (Yueqing: n.p., 1989), pp. 53–56.

54. Zheng Jiefeng, "Yueqing Yandang fangzhi chang" [The Yandang textile mill at Yueqing], in *Yueqing wenshi ziliao* [Historical materials on Yueqing County], vol. 7 (Yueqing: n.p., 1989), pp. 86–87; and Xu Shanyu, "Da jing Taishan yanchang shimo" [The complete story of the Dajing Taishan cigarette factory] in the same volume, pp. 90–92.

55. *Huangyan xianzhi* [A gazetteer or Huangyan County] (Hangzhou: Renmin chubanshe, 1993), p. 335.

56. Shen, "Zhejiang shengde jingdi," p. 8.

57. Zhao Piaochu, "Kangzhan chuqi Shanghaide nanmin gongzuo" [Work with Shanghai refugees at the beginning of the Resistance War], in *KangRi fengyun lu* [Annals of the stormy resistance against Japan], vol. 2 (Shanghai; n.p., 1985), pp. 160–161; also in *Shanghai wenshi ziliao,* vol. 51.

58. Wei, *Zhejiang sheng mingzhen zhi,* pp. 742–743.

59. *Putuo xianzhi,* pp. 857–859, 1057–1059.

12. Bubonic Bombs

1. Peter Loizos, "'Generations' in Forced Migration: Towards Greater Clarity," *Journal of Refugee Studies* 20, no. 2 (2007): 193.

2. *Dongnan ribao,* January 19, 1939 and June 7, 1940.

3. *Qu xianzhi* [A gazetteer of Qu County] (Hangzhou: Zhejiang renmin chubanshe, 1992), p. 516.

4. *Qu xianzhi,* (1929), p. 36a. Zheng (1866–1931) had a traditional civil service degree as well as a modern school education. He had served as local education leader, was elected to the late Qing Provincial Assembly, and was elected to the county board *(canshihui)* in the first years of the Republic. After serving briefly in Hebei Province, he returned to Quzhou, where he remained but for a stint as provincial assembly secretary in Hangzhou. See *Qu xianzhi* (1992), pp. 557–558.

5. *Quzhou shizhi* [A gazetteer of the Quzhou municipality] (Hangzhou: Zhejiang renmin chubanshe, 1994), p. 3.

6. This description of Yiwu is based on Wen-hsin Yeh's *Provincial Passages: Culture, Space, and the Origins of Chinese Communism* (Berkeley: University of California Press, 1996), pp. 64–65.

7. Ibid., p. 64.

8. Wang Zutong, "KangRi zhanzheng shiqi Ningbo shuyi jishi" [An account of the plague in Ningbo during the Resistance War], in *Ningbo wenshi ziliao,* vol. 2 (Ningbo, 1984), pp. 181–185. For the newspaper report, see Zheng Fanghua, comp., "Ningbo baokan lu" [A record of the press in Ningbo], in *Ningbo wenshi ziliao,* vol. 3 (Ningbo, 1985), and Wu Weinong, "Jin Zhenxiang yu *Shishi gongbao* [Jin Zhenxiang and the Shishi gongbao], in *Ningbo wenshi ziliao,* vol. 3, (Ningbo, 1985), pp. 182–192.

9. Wu Zutong, pp. 191 and 193.

10. Rong Qirong, "Zhejiang shuyi diaocha baogao shu" [A report on bubonic plague in Zhejiang], reprinted in *Rijun qinlue Zhejiang shilu* [A record of the Japanese army's invasion of Zhejiang] (Beijing: Zhonggong dangshi chubanshe, 1995), p. 784. On Chen Wanli, see Tao Yi, "Kangzhan shiqi Zhejiangsheng weishengchu ren shi gaikuang" [A survey of personnel in the Public Health Office during the War of Resistance], *Zhejiang yuekan* [Zhejiang monthly] 19, no. 4 (1987): 5.

11. The administrative inspector's report is in *Quzhou shizhi,* p. 1156; the police chief's warning is reprinted in *Rijun qinlue Zhejiang shilu,* p. 773. The administrative inspector was the postimperial embodiment of the imperial circuit intendant; that is, he oversaw the administration of several former prefectures. This system was adopted in 1930.

12. Ye Bingnan, *Tiezheng* [Irrefutable evidence] (Hangzhou, 1995), p. 244.

13. See the slightly varying accounts in *Quzhou shizhi,* p. 1156, and He Caifu, "Ji Qu-

zhou shuyi" [Remembering the plague in Quzhou], in *Quzhou KangRi zhan-zheng shiliao* [Historical materials on the Resistance War in Quzhou] (Quzhou, 1985), p. 45.

14. A telegram of December 6, 1940, is reprinted in *Rijun qinlue Zhejiang shilu,* p. 775.

15. *Rijun qinlue Zhejiang shilu,* p. 784.

16. Ibid., p. 777.

17. Ibid., p. 780.

18. *Quzhou shizhi,* p. 1156.

19. He, p. 47.

20. *Quzhou shizhi,* p. 435.

21. *Rijun qinlue Zhejiang shilu,* p. 791.

22. *Quzhou shizhi,* p. 1156.

23. James C. Scott, *Domination and the Arts of Resistance* (New Haven, Conn.: Yale University Press, 1990), p. 133.

24. *Dongnan ribao,* June 3, 1941, and June 26, 1941.

25. *Dongnan ribao,* August 21, 1941, and August 28, 1941.

26. Quzhou was visited by representatives of the Provincial Plague Prevention Of-fice, the Provincial Public Health Plague Prevention Office, the Central Public Health Medical Prevention Unit, the Chinese Red Cross, the Military District's Plague Prevention Unit, the Military Political Bureau's Fourth Plague Preven-tion Unit, and the Fujian Public Health Office.

27. This episode is described in *Dongnan ribao,* April 6, 1943.

28. Unless noted, the following discussion is based upon Liu Shuchen, "Yiwu xian shuyi liuxing shimo" [The whole story of the plague epidemic in Yiwu County], in *Yiwu wenshi ziliao,* vol. 1 (N.p., 1984), pp. 30–38.

29. *Dongnan ribao,* October 17, 1941.

30. *Dongnan ribao,* October 18, 1941.

31. *Dongnan ribao,* October 19, 1941.

32. Liu Shuchen, "Yiwu xian shuyi liuxing shimo," pp. 33–34.

33. Scott, *Domination and the Arts of Resistance,* p. 133.

34. See the discussion by Paul Slack in *The Impact of Plague in Tudor and Stuart Eng-land* (London: Routledge and Kegan Paul 1985), pp. 385–400.

35. See http://www.taipeitimes.com/News/World/archives/2005/07/26/2003264263

36. See http://www.chinadaily.com.cn/china/2007-04/28/content_862644.htm

Conclusion

1. "Report of the United Nations High Commissioner for Refugees," General Assembly, Official Records, Sixty-first Sesssion, Supplement # 12 (A/61/12), pp. 2 and 10.

2. Quoted in Elizabeth Colson, "Forced Migration and the Anthropological Response," *Journal of Refugee Studies* 16, no. 1 (2003): 6. {Emphasis in the original].

3. See, for example, the arguments of Clifford Geertz, "From the Natives' Point: On the Nature of Anthropological Understanding," in *Meaning in Anthropology*, ed. K. Basso and H. Selby (Albuquerque: University of New Mexico Press, 1976), pp. 221–238, quoted in Roger D. Abrahams, "Ordinary and Extraordinary Experience," in *The Anthropology of Experience*, ed. Victor W. Turner and Edward M. Bruner (Urbana: University of Illinois Press, 1986), pp. 56–57.

4. See Patrick J. Bracken, Joan E. Giller, and Derek Summerfield, "Psychological Responses to War and Atrocity: The Limitations of Current Concepts," *Social Science Medicine* 40, no. 8 (1995).

5. Arthur Kleinman, *Patients and Healers in the Context of Culture* (Berkeley: University of California Press, 1980), quoted in Bracken, Giller, and Summerfield, "Psychological Responses," p. 1074.

6. See Edward Hall, *Beyond Culture* (Garden City, N.Y.: Anchor/Doubleday, 1976), especially pp. 74–147.

7. Anthony Giddens, *Modernity and Self-Identity: Self and Society in the Late Modern Age* (Stanford, Calif.: Stanford University Press, 1991), p. 16.

8. Ibid., p. 146.

9. David Turton, "The Meaning of Place in a World of Movement: Lessons from Long-Term Field Research in Southern Ethiopia," *Journal of Refugee Studies*, 18, no. 3 (2005): 258.

10. Giddens, *Modernity and Self-Identity*, p. 189.

11. Fox Butterfield, *China: Alive in a Bitter Sea* (London: Coronet Books, 1983), pp. 74–75, as quoted in Ambrose Yeo-chi King, "Kuan-hsi [Guanxi] and Network Building: A Sociological Interpretation," *Daedalus* 120, no. 2 (Spring 1991): 64.

12. Giddens, *Modernity and Self-Identity*, p. 189.

13. Peter Loizos, "'Generations' in Forced Migration: Towards Greater Clarity," *Journal of Refugee Studies* 20, no. 2 (2007): 194.

14. J. Davis, "The Anthropology of Suffering." *Journal of Refugee Studies* 5, no. 2 (1992): 157.

15. Edward Bruner, "Ethnography as Narrative," in *The Anthropology of Experience*, ed. Victor W. Turner and Edward M. Bruner (Urbana: University of Illinois Press, 1986). p. 143.

16. Turton, "Meaning of Place," pp. 258–259.

17. Ibid., p. 267.

18. See, for example, Stephen R. MacKinnon, *Wuhan, 1938: War, Refugees, and the Making of Modern China* (Berkeley: University of California Press, 2008), p. 54.

19. Mary Clabaugh Wright, *China in Revolution: The First Phase, 1900–1913* (New Haven, Conn.: Yale University Press, 1968), pp. 1 and 3.

20. Bryna Goodman, *Native Place, City, and Nation* (Berkeley: University of California Press, 1995), p. 312.

21. Chalmers Johnson, *Peasant Nationalism and Communist Power: The Emergence of Revolutionary China* (Stanford, Calif.: Stanford University Press, 1962).

22. G. William Skinner, "Chinese Peasants and the Closed Community: An Open and Shut Case," *Comparative Studies in Society and History* 13, no. 3 (July 1971): 270–281.

23. Paul Fussell, *Wartime: Understanding and Behavior in the Second World War* (New York: Oxford University Press, 1989), pp. 140–141. This is the site of the Hersey quotation.

Acknowledgments

In completing this study of spatial, social, and psychological displacement brought by total war between Japan and China, I owe debts to many people and institutions. In using the rich resources at Hangzhou's provincial archives and library and Zhejiang University History Department's extensive collection of historical materials *(wenshi ziliao)*, I especially want to thank Professor Que Weimin, now professor at the College of Urban and Environment Sciences, World Heritage Research Centre at Peking University. He was of immense help in countless ways. I also especially offer warm thanks to Professor Feng Xiaocai, now at Fudan University in Shanghai, a friend who expedited my research in various ways, including microfilming sections of an important newspaper, the *Southeast Daily (Dongnan ribao)*.

I owe deep thanks to Loyola University Maryland for bestowing on me the Edward and Catherine Doehler Endowed Chair in Asian History and for the generous sabbatical that allowed me to pursue this project. I am especially thankful to my Loyola colleagues for their collegiality, questions, and general support. As for monetary support, I have been generously endowed with grants from the John Simon Guggenheim Memorial Foundation, the American Council for Learned Society, Chiang Ching-kuo Foundation, and a National Endowment for the Humanities Fellowship for College Teachers.

I owe special and immense debts to those in the field who gave me platforms from which to spin off my ideas, especially Joseph Esherick and Paul Pickowicz at the Chinese Studies Center at the University of California San Diego and to William Rowe and Tobie Meyer-Fong at the Johns Hopkins History Department Seminar. The international conference, "Wartime Shanghai (1937-1945)" in Lyon, France, Ocober 15-17, 1997 provided me an opportunity to see the war in Zhejiang in a fresh new way; for that invitation, I give great thanks to Christian Henriot and the late Frederic Wakeman Jr. The Historical Society for Twentieth-Century China conferences offered especially important venues in Venice (1999), Vienna (2004), Singapore (2006), Honolulu (2008), and Philadelphia (2010), all presenting questions that provided new ways of my seeing the material.

Last, but undoubtedly most important, are my colleagues in the field who provided continual support, advice, criticism, laughs, and camaraderie (and I list you alphabetically—you each know what you have given to me): Timothy Brook, James Carter, Parks Coble, Brooks Jessup, William Kirby, Kevin Landdeck, Sophia Lee, Danke Li, Steve Phillips, Mary Rankin (my Zhejiang partner), Douglas Stiffler, and Wang Kewen. And though we have never met, I want to thank Geremie Barmé for his wonderful book on Feng Zikai, which led me to Feng's refugee accounts, which Barmé in his longer study could not include but which, as perhaps no other work has done, opened up for me the horrific, often mundane, but also often tragic details of refugee challenges and losses.

I also want to offer my most sincere thanks to the editors at Harvard University Press. Kathleen McDermott has been an absolutely brilliant, creative editor, providing me with cogent suggestions that will enhance, I believe, the power of the book. James Furbush has been consistently helpful and conscientious. Cartographer Philip Schwartzberg was interested, engaging, and always thoroughly professional. Since the substance of the book so relates to context, his excellent maps are indispensable.

Finally last, but really first, I want to thank my family, who has given me so much support at the times I needed it most. Beth has been (and still is) my rock through the vicissitudes of life. Our children, Kara, Derek, and Heather, have provided considerable challenges but great joys as well—and have always been there as sources of support. I cannot be more thankful to anyone else.

Index